# Abnormal Psychology

# Abnormal Psychology

**S.K. Mangal**
Formerly Principal, Professor and Head
Department of Post Graduate Studies & Research
C.R. College of Education, Rohtak

**STERLING PUBLISHERS (P) LTD.**
Regd. Office: A1/256 Safdarjung Enclave, New Delhi-110029.
CIN: U22110DL1964PTC211907
Phone: +91 82877 98380/+91 120-6251823
E-mail: mail@sterlingpublishers.in
www.sterlingpublishers.in

*Abnormal Psychology*

ISBN 978-93-86245-65-6
First Edition: 1988
Second Revised and Enlarged Edition: 2019, 2021



*Printed and Published in India by*

---

**Sterling Publishers Pvt. Ltd.,**
Plot No. 13, Ecotech-III, Greater Noida - 201306, U. P. India

# Preface to the Second Edition

The first edition of the text "Abnormal Psychology" was brought out in the year 1984. Although, there have been regular imprints of the text during all these years in the past with the good wishes and favour showered on the part of the readers of this text, yet it has suffered with a need of bringing a revised edition of the work in the previous years.

During this long period of more than three decades, a lot of changes have taken place in the areas related to the disciplines of Abnormal Psychology and Applied Medicines particularly with the emergence of a number of revised publications of DSM (Diagnostic and Statistical Manual) and ICD (International Classification of Diseases) brought out respectively by American Psychiatric Association (APA) and World Health Organization (WHO). Today at present we have DSM-5 (brought out in the year 2013) and ICD-10 (brought out in the year 2010) with us and the proposed draft of ICD-11(the official one coming out soon in the year 2020) for the classification, diagnosis, understanding and treatment of abnormal behaviours, mental disorders and diseases. These developments have provided sufficient grounds for bringing needed changes and modifications in syllabi of the courses related to the subjects Abnormal and Clinical Psychology in degree classes of the universities and higher institutions of our country. Consequently, in the present edition of the text all necessary attempts have been made to consolidate the subject matter of the text by adding a number of new topics and enriching the contents of the previous ones for enabling it to meet the requirements of the subject "Abnormal Psychology" syllabi of the Indian Universities. The mentionable attempts in this direction are as below:

- Since the entire scheme and theme of the revision of the text has been woven around the developments resulted through the evolution in Diagnostic Statistical Manuals (DSM's)and International Classification of Diseases (ICD's) during the past years, therefore a well- intended initiative in the form of the enriching the existing chapter 10 entitled as "Classification of Mental Disorders" has been taken by providing due place to the discussion of DSM IV-TR(2000), DSM-5 (2013), ICD-10 (2010), and a brief commentary on the coming ICD-11 in the revised text.
- Four entirely new chapters have been added in the revised text naming as (i) Attention Deficit/Hyperactivity Disorder (ADHD) and Autism, (ii) Elimination and Eating Disorder (providing essentials about the elimination disorders like Enuresis and Encopresis and eating disorders like Anorexia nervosa, Bulimia nervosa and Binge eating disorder), (iii) Sleep Disorders (discussing about Primary insomnia, Primary Hypersomnia, Narcolepsy, Breathing -related sleep disorders, Circadian Rhythm sleep disorder, nightmares, night sleep terrors, and Somnambulism-night walking), and (iv) Old Age or Degenerative

Disorders (throwing light on the conditions like Delirium, Dementia, Vascular dementia, Alzheimer's disease, Pick's disease, Parkinson's disease, and Huntington's disease).

- The existing chapter 4 of the text named as "Motivation and Adjustment" have been bifurcated into two chapters 5 and 6 named as "Psychology of Motivation" and "Psychology of Adjustment" in order to do more justice to these topics in the light of the changes required in the syllabi. Mentionable in this connection is the useful addition of the topic like Areas and Spheres of Adjustment, Maladjustment, Detection of Maladjustment, Methods of Adjustment in the newly created chapter 5 of the text.
- A number of useful topics have been added at various places in the existing chapters of the text such as (i) Conflict resolution, Stressors, Types of Stressors , Stress cycle, Effects or Outcomes of Stress, Adaptation to Stress and Coping with Stress; (ii) New varieties of Obsessive-compulsive behaviour disorders such as Hoarding disorder, Trichotillomania (hair-pulling disorder), Excoriation (skin picking disorder), and Body dysmorphic disorder; (iii) Cognitive-behavioural therapy for the treatment of abnormal behaviour etc.
- Besides this, due attempts have been made for providing necessary revision, modification and enrichment to the subject matter belonging to all chapters of the text. For serving this objective, some chapters have been re-written, re-organized, and updated with latest information and the necessary figures as well as tables have been added for providing more clarity to the subject matter.

With such enhancement, enrichment and modifications carried out in the text, it is hoped that the text will be serving more useful purposes in meeting the requirements of the syllabi of the subject "Abnormal Psychology" belonging to the degree courses of the Indian universities. Besides, this it will also be proving helpful to the students of the related disciplines such as Clinical Psychology, Guidance and Counselling, and also for those who opt "Psychology" as an optional paper for their Indian or Provincial civil services and other competitive examinations.

With all good wishes for the brilliant future to its readers,

**S.K. Mangal**
skmangal@gmail.com

Independence Day
August 15, 2019

# Preface

This book has been written for use as a basic text-book in an introductory course in Abnormal Psychology or as a book of general and clinical interest for those who are interested in the care of their own mental health or of others. It covers almost all the basic concepts and information regarding human abnormal behaviour through the following mainstreams:

1. Concept of abnormal behaviour and its science.
2. Etiology of abnormal behaviour.
3. Classification and description of abnormal behaviour.
4. Treatment of abnormal behaviour.

In the treatment of the subject, due care has been taken to make the book less ponderous and formidable for students, more interesting and meaningful, and more teachable and to bring it up to date with new developments. As far as possible a reasonable quality of thought and depth of treatment has been retained. In doing so, I have drawn upon three sources: theory, research and practical experience of various authors and writers, the work of whom, I gratefully acknowledge. I am also grateful to my colleagues, students and all those who have shared their experiences with me during the past several decades and, in doing so, have helped me learn and grow.

I hope that the book will be read by a lot of readers for whom it was not specifically designed and they will be benefited by it. They should feel free to write to me or the publishers with suggestions for the improvement of the book.

Rohtak
Independence Day 1984 **S.K. Mangal**

# Contents

## List of Figures



## List of Tables

# 1

# ABNORMAL PSYCHOLOGY-MEANING AND SCOPE

Man has always strived to know himself and his environment. Subjects such as philosophy, psychology and other basic and applied sciences have been instrumental in this task. Psychology, especially, has helped in the study of human behaviour in relation to the environment resulting in a better adjustment and adequate development of the individual for happy and contended life. The task is gigantic. Psychology for its wider application and usefulness has, therefore, been divided into different branches covering specific areas and fields of human behaviour and activities, for example, child psychology, adolescent psychology, adult psychology, individual psychology, development psychology, general psychology, experimental psychology, physiological psychology, educational psychology, industrial psychology, para-psychology, abnormal psychology, etc.

## Defining Abnormal Psychology

Abnormal psychology has been variously defined.

*Page*: Abnormal psychology is a sub-division (of the subject psychology) that is limited to the study of the mental processes and behaviour of abnormal people. (1976:16)

*Coleman*: Abnormal psychology is the field of psychology which specializes in the development and integration of psychological principles for the understanding of abnormal behaviour. (1970:21)

*Kisker*: Abnormal psychology is a specialized field of psychology dealing with personality disturbances and behaviour disorders. (1964:21)

*Rosen, Fox and Gregory*: Abnormal psychology is an attempt to understand and explain the abnormal within the framework of the normal and general. (1972:1)

*Mahoney:* By abnormal psychology we mean the study of deviation or variance from a so-called normal pattern. (1980:14)

The above definitions have a common understanding in realizing that abnormal psychology is a specialized branch or field of a discipline which deals with the behaviour and experiences of the abnormal people. But some questions remain unanswered:

1. Does abnormal psychology study the behaviour of the normal also along with the abnormal or does it limit itself to the study of the disorganised personality

and behaviour of the abnormal people as explained by both Page and Kisker in their respective definitions?

2. Does it limit itself to the formulation of broad principles, theories or techniques for the study of the abnormal behaviour or go further for the prevention and treatment of the abnormality or behavioural disorders?
3. Does it also care for the environmental set-up of the abnormal in the study of their experiences and behaviour?

The answers to these questions will help us to demarcate a boundary for the subject-matter or scope of abnormal psychology.

## Scope of Abnormal Psychology

The scope of this discipline can be discussed as below.

1. The study of the abnormal cannot be undertaken until we decide about the normal and the abnormal, or what behaviour and activities make an individual normal or abnormal. Abnormal psychology should essentially throw light on the concept of normality and abnormality in relation to varying situations and environmental conditions. The parameter is the normal population. Hence the study of abnormal psychology, to some extent, should include the study of the normal along with the abnormal, for the abnormal should themselves know how to behave and adjust in order to be labelled as normal
2. All human behaviour has its roots in motives and basic needs. The denial of basic needs and blocking of motives leads to frustrations, conflicts and stresses ending in maladaptive behaviour or maladjustment which, in turn, results in behavioural disorders. The subject-matter of abnormal psychology should, therefore, include the study of motives, basic needs, adjustment, frustration, conflicts and stresses.
3. In order to contribute to preventive purposes, abnormal psychology should be able to describe and explain the causes of abnormal behaviour—the conditions or factors generating maladaptive behaviour, the symptoms and syndromes of the various behavioural disorders. Since there is need for knowledge of common behavioural disorders, abnormal psychology should essentially include the study of abnormalities or disorders such as mental
4. Abnormal psychology, like its main stream psychology, has both pure and applied aspects. In its pure aspect it formulates broad principles, generates theories and suggests techniques for the study of the behaviour of the abnormal people which finds practical shape in its applied aspect where it helps us in taking preventive and curative measures.

### *Preventive Measures*

(i) Abnormal psychology helps us in protecting ourselves or others from situations or conditions that lead to maladjustment and behavioural disorders.

(ii) It may lead us to the modifications and restructuring of the uncongenial environment and prevailing circumstances for the growth of adjusted and balanced behaviour leading to a normal and happy life.

### *Curative Measures*

In its extended stage, abnormal psychology applies its knowledge and skills for the treatment of various behavioural disorders by suggesting practicable therapies and measures. Moreover, in its applied form, it tries to nourish related fields like clinical psychology, psychiatry, psychiatric social work, and legal psychology. The subject-matter of abnormal psychology should, therefore, include all practical aspects leading to the treatment of behaviour disorders and regaining normal behaviour and good mental health.

The subject matter of abnormal psychology may be considered to revolve round the following main pivots:

1. Concept of normality and abnormality.
2. Factors that lead to maladaptive behaviour and behavioural disorders.
3. Symptoms and syndromes of the abnormal behaviour.
4. Description of the main behavioural disorders.
5. The treatment of behavioural disorders.

## Importance of Abnormal Psychology

The significance and purpose of this subject can be summarized as under:

1. *Prevention and treatment of behavioural disorders or abnormality:* Abnormal psychology (i) helps in developing essential knowledge, skills, attitudes and interests in its students for the prevention and treatment of behavioural disorders or abnormality, and (ii) encourages or stimulates them towards behaving as normal and becoming better adjusted, and mentally healthy individuals.
2. *Differentiating abnormal from the normal:* Abnormal psychology provides insight into abnormal behaviour while differentiating it from the normal and thus protecting us or others from adopting or learning abnormal behaviour.
3. *Knowledge of the causes of abnormal behaviour: The* causes of abnormality studied in abnormal psychology will show that abnormality is generally a biological or socio-psychological problem. The affected persons can, therefore, be sympathetically considered and helped in getting rid of their abnormalities.
4. *Correct notions about abnormality:* The superstitions or misconceptions about abnormality or behavioural disorders may be removed through the study of abnormal psychology, for it tells us that there is a difference of degree in normality and abnormality. A normal can turn into an abnormal under stress and an abnormal can be made normal if helped in his adjustment.
5. *Environmental modifications for the growth of normality:* The knowledge of abnormal psychology helps in modifying and restructuring the environment and situations for the children the youth, and adults so that they may not fall victim to maladjustment and maladaptive behaviour.

6. *Knowledge of the symptoms and syndromes of abnormal behaviour:* The study of the various behaviour disorders leads us to gain knowledge of the symptoms and syndromes leading to the early diagnosis of specific disorders.
7. *Adopting proper measures for mentally retarded:* The study of mental disorders like retardation may help teachers and educators in planning schemes for the welfare of such children.
8. *Adopting proper measures for antisocial behaviours* The study of abnormal psychology reveals that antisocial behaviour is a sign of caution for the society. It is a social disease that calls for socio-psychological treatment instead of being dealt with by the law. The prevention and treatment of such behaviour may be carried out through tie study of abnormal psychology.
9. *Helpful in the related fields:* The related applied fields like clinical psychology, psychiatry, psychiatric social work, neurology may directly benefit from abnormal psychology. Lawyers and judges also need knowledge of abnormal behaviour and disorders for dealing with the cases of anti-social behaviour.
10. *Useful in everyday life:* The principles of abnormal psychology have far reaching implications with regard to many problems of our everyday life. Education, business and industry, politics, law and law enforcement, counselling are some of the areas where knowledge, skill and learning in abnormal psychology exercise direct application.

In this way, abnormal psychology has useful purposes to serve the cause of individuals and the society. By its specific nature and utility it may be defined as the specialized field, pure and applied, of psychology which differentiates and explains the behaviour and experiences of the abnormal people, within the frame-work of the normal, in relation to their environment and suggests ways and techniques for the prevention and treatment of abnormality and behavioural disorders.

## Summary

- Abnormal psychology is a specialized branch or field of psychology which helps in studying the behaviour of abnormal people in relation to their own environment for helping them in their adequate adjustment and better development.
- The scope or subject matter of abnormal psychology may centre round the focal points like
  (i) Concepts of normality and abnormality
  (ii) Causes of abnormal behaviour
  (iii)Symptoms and syndromes of abnormal behaviour
  (iv)Description of the main behavioural disorders and
  (v) The treatment of behavioural disorders.
- The study of abnormal psychology helps in
  (i) Understanding the true meaning of abnormality
  (ii) Differentiating the abnormal from the normal
  (iii)Studying the causes of abnormal behaviour

(iv) Modifying environment for the growth of normality
(v) Studying symptoms and syndromes of abnormal behaviour
(vi) Undertaking the prevention and treatment of behavioural disorders
(vii) Understanding its applicability in many related fields or branches and
(ix) Understanding its use in everyday life.

## REFERENCES


Coleman, James C. (1970), *Abnormal Psychology and Modern Life*, Bombay: D.B. Taraporewala & Sons.

Kisker, George W. (1964), ***The Disorganised Personality,*** (3rd International Students Edition), New York: McGraw-Hill.

Mahoney, Michael J. (1980), ***Abnormal Psychology,*** San Francisco: Harper & Row.

Page, James D. (1976), ***Abnormal Psychology,*** New Delhi: Tata McGraw-Hill.

Rosen, E., Fox and Gregory (1972), ***Abnormal Psychology,*** (2nd, International Student Edition), Philadelphia: Saunders

2

# CONCEPT OF NORMALITY AND ABNORMALITY

Abnormal psychology lays emphasis on the study of the behaviour and experiences of the abnormal people. In its practical aspect, it tries to describe some preventive and curative measures for the treatment of abnormal behaviour or disorders. It implies that advances in abnormal psychology can only be made if we are aware of or have clear concepts about the terms normality and abnormality.

The term 'normal' seems to be derived from the word 'norma' which means a carpenter's square or rule. A norm, therefore, became a rule, pattern or standard, and it was in this sense that the term 'normal' was introduced into the English lexicon. The term 'abnormal' with its prefix *ab* (away from) thus came to signify the deviance or variation from the normal. Anything not normal must, therefore, be abnormal. But there is some difficulty in deciding what is normal. In the basic or medical sciences, it is easy to decide what is normal. In examining the temperature of the body, blood pressure, the amount of sugar in the blood, pulse rate, beating of the heart, etc., are standard universal norms. On a psychological front, however, we can't have an ideal model of man or ideal behaviour to be used as standard norm.

As a result, the problem of deciding what behaviour is or is not normal has proved to be a difficult one. However, several attempts have been made for describing what is normal or abnormal.

## Normality and Abnormality Criteria

The criterion used for defining normality and abnormality can be grouped into the following two broad categories named as (A)Descriptive criteria and (B)Explanatory criteria. Let us know about them. They indicate the types of behaviour in which abnormal behaviour differs from normal behaviour or they tell us why the behaviour is abnormal.

The descriptive criteria may be further sub-divided into two groups—statistical or non-statistical. Under the non-statistical criteria we may place methods or approaches like ethical or moral view point, social conformity, ideal or perfectionism and legal view point, whereas under explanatory criteria, falls criterion like pathological or medical explanation,-psychological explanation and the explanation in terms of adjustment. This classification can be represented diagrammatically as below:

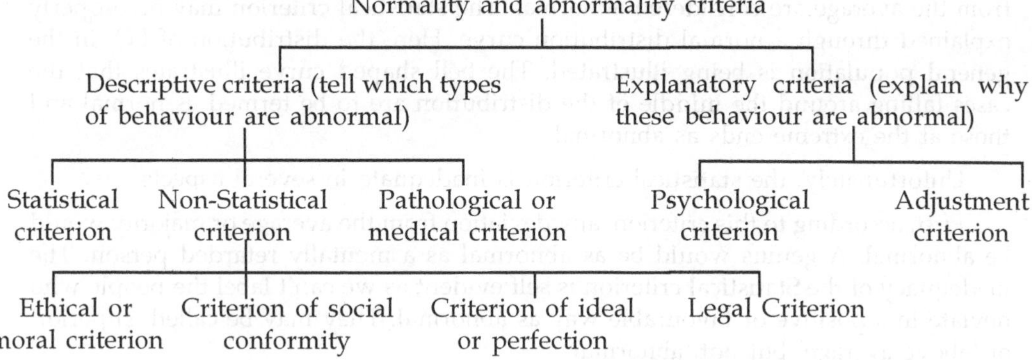


Fig: 2.1: Diagrammatic representation of the criteria defining normality and abnormality

## A. Descriptive Criteria

### (a) Statistical Criterion:

According to this criterion, 'average' is normal. A person is abnormal when he or she deviates from the 'average'. For example, there is an average height and an average weight for normal human being and those who come close to this average are considered normal while those who deviate from the average are considered abnormal. The statistical criterion may be properly explained through a normal distribution curve. Here the distribution of I.Q. in the general population is being illustrated. The bell shaped curve illustrates that the cases falling around the middle of the distribution are to be termed as normal and those at the extreme ends as abnormal.

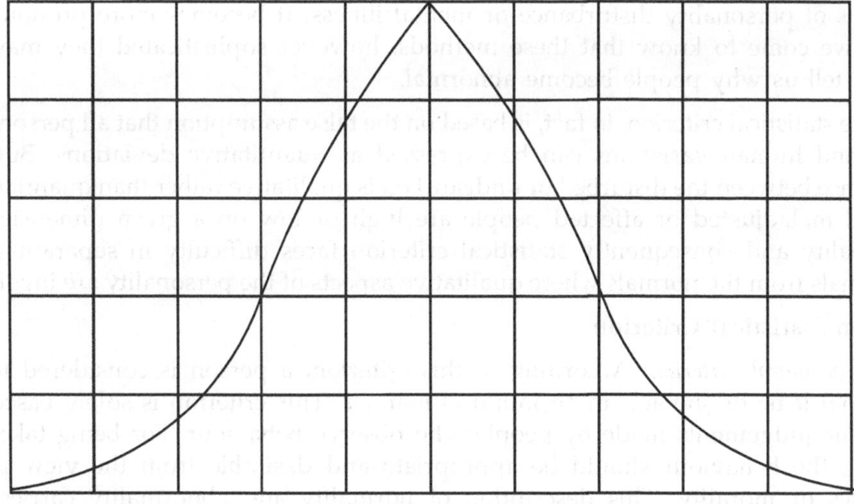

Fig: 2.2. The distribution of I.Q. in the general population
(I.Q. below 75 termed subnormal and those above 115 as abnormal)

there is an average height and an average weight for normal human beings and those who come close to this average are considered normal while those who deviate from the average are considered abnormal. The statistical criterion may be properly explained through a normal distribution curve. Here the distribution of I.Q. in the general population is being illustrated. The bell shaped curve illustrates that the cases falling around the middle of the distribution are to be termed as normal and those at the extreme ends as abnormal.

Unfortunately, the statistical criterion is inadequate in several aspects.

*First,* according to this criterion, any deviation from the average or majority would be abnormal. A genius would be as abnormal as a mentally retarded person. The inadequacy of the Statistical criterion is self evident as we can't label the people who deviate in a positive or favourable way as abnormal. They may be called 'superior' or 'above average' but not 'abnormal'.

*Second,* we are all deviant (or different) from one another in some dimensions. No two individuals are alike in interests, abilities or physical appearance. These are all potential dimensions of difference and an individual may sometimes deviate seriously from the norms or average set by us. If we take deviation from the average as the only criterion of abnormality then, perhaps, Gandhi, Vivekanand, Christ, Prem Chand, Newton, and Pythagoras would surely be listed as abnormal.

*Third,* to label as abnormal we compare the deviance of the people from the average which may change from time to time or from group to group. Behaviours which are considered normal in a particular society or culture may be labelled abnormal in a different society or culture. What was considered abnormal in the nineteenth century may fit well in the prevalent time, (for example, widow remarriage, use of modem birth control measures, etc.). Therefore, abnormality is not simply a deviation from some average as advocated by the statistical criterion.

*Fourth,* the inadequacy of statistical criterion also lies in its variability for the analysis of personality disturbance or mental illness. It becomes more pronounced when we come to know that these methods, however sophisticated they may be, hardly tell us why people become abnormal.

The statistical criterion, in fact, is based on the false assumption that all personality traits and human variations can be expressed as quantitative deviations. But the difference between the disturbed or undisturbed is qualitative rather than quantitative. Not all maladjusted or affected people are high or low on a given dimension of personality and consequently statistical criterion faces difficulty in separating the abnormals from the normals where qualitative aspects of the personality are involved.

**(b) Non-Statistical Criterion**

*Ethical or moral criterion*: According to this criterion, a person is considered to be abnormal if lie or she acts in an immoral manner. This criterion is solely based on the value judgements made by people who observe behaviour. For being taken as normal, the behaviour should be appropriate and desirable from the view point of ethics or morality. This description of normality and abnormality carries the following defects:

(i) The major problem with this perspective is that morality is not an absolute concept. What is 'moral' or 'immoral' may change from place to place and from time to time.

(ii) A person who is known to have high morality may show signs of known behavioural disorders, while many people who are labelled as psychologically deviant may not exhibit any immoral behaviour. To be affected with anxiety or depression cannot be labelled as immoral. Therefore, in any way, morality can't be made a criterion for deciding a behaviour as normal or abnormal.

2. *Criterion of social conformity:* According to this criterion, those who conform to societal norms are considered normal and those who do not care for them are labelled abnormal. This view is based on the assumption that normality is what the majority of the people approves of or follows. For example, if wearing short hair, tight jeans, or a sleeveless blouse gets social approval, it may be taken as normal or else it would be labelled abnormal. Hence, if we adopt social conformity as the sole criterion of deciding the behaviour as normal or abnormal, we will have to change our decision from place to place or culture to culture and in the same culture or place from time to time as we can't resist changes in attitude towards what is socially acceptable and normal.

3. *Criterion of ideal or perfection:* According to this criterion, normal behaviour is equated with perfect or ideal behaviour. A few persons attain a level of perfection difficult to be attained by the masses. They become ideals and serve a model for labelling as normal. A major flaw in this criterion lies in the fact that there exists nothing like absolute ideal or perfection. The judgement is purely subjective, for example, one may think the life and behaviour of Gandhi as ideal but for the activists and revolutionaries not he but Subhash Chandra Bose or Bhagat Singh may be the ideals. Besides, this approach is based on what ideal behaviour ought to be and not what it is. The model of ideal varies from situation to situation and, in a situation, from time to time. The behaviour which is considered ideal for a particular age in a particular situation may altogether be labelled abnormal in a different age or in a different situation.

4. *Legal criterion:* According to this criterion a law abiding citizen is normal but the one who violates the law is labelled abnormal. Behaviours like murder, rape, burglary or prostitution come from this legal definition arid are definitely labelled antisocial or abnormal. But what is legal or illegal is again a matter of controversy. In a dynamic society, laws change fast. Hence they are not absolute but change from society to society, place to place and even from time to lime. Moreover, the mere absence or presence of a few evidences may declare an act or behaviour legal or illegal. Therefore, the legal criterion cannot be made a reliable or valid criterion for the judgement of normality or abnormality.

## B. Explanatory Criterion

### (a) Pathological or medical criterion

According to this criterion, the normality or abnormality of the behaviour depends upon the functioning of the nervous system. In this way all abnormal people are affected with some mental illness or disease. Consequently, they should be sent to the mental hospitals as patients for treatment by persons who are trained to cure them. This view has a wide appeal and has been responsible for arousing a mass feeling that abnormal behaviour is somehow an indication of an illness or disease.

However, the inadequacy of this criterion has now also been proved. Most people who are found to be mentally disturbed do not suffer from the 'diseases' or 'illnesses' in the usual sense of these terms. They show no signs of structural damage or dysfunction in their nervous systems. Therefore, it may be seen clearly that the pathological or medical criterion does not make a reliable and valid criterion for the definition of normality or abnormality.

**(b) Psychological criterion**

According to this criterion, psychological functioning— whether defective or normal— is the deciding factor of the abnormal or normal behaviour. Eysenck (1960) writes, *"Abnormality then is not in terms of people suffering from mental diseases produced by definite causes; it is rather in terms of defective functioning of certain psychological systems."*

On analysing this criterion, it is seen that abnormality, whatever kind or form it may have, is linked with some malfunctioning of certain psychological systems. Abnormal people are definitely psychologically handicapped individuals, but their behaviour is not the exclusive product of psychological or sociological causes. In any case biological or physiological factors may not be ruled out in the explanation of the behaviour of abnormal people.

**(c) Adjustment criterion**

According to this criterion, a person is said to be normal or abnormal to the extent he feels adjusted or maladjusted with his self and his environment. Normal people get along well with themselves and their environment while the abnormal ones are on the warpath with their self as well as with human or physical environment surrounding them. The normal people always integrate or adjust their needs, motives, emotions, interests, aspirations and other cognitive aspects with those of other members of the society and thus exercise a proper balance between their own self-actualization and their contribution towards social welfare and progress, the abnormal people on the other hand, are neither able their needs, motives, emotions, interests, aspirations and other cognitive aspects with those of other members of the society and thus exercise a proper balance between their own self-actualization and their contribution towards social welfare and progress, the abnormal people on the other hand, are neither able to achieve proper self-actualization nor do they care to contribute towards the wellbeing and progress of the society. In many cases either their intentions or actions threaten their own self (by causing injury to their self), or the society (by breaking social norms).

## Conclusion Regarding Different Criteria

The different criteria discussed above represent the many ways and approaches for understanding the 'normal' and 'abnormal'. No criterion may be termed absolute criterion for the complete description or explanation of the normal or abnormal behaviour. One section of these views only describes and the other only explains which behaviour is not normal or normal. As far as the criteria of morality, social conformity, perfection or legality related are concerned, they are purely subjective, and hence, no reliability or validity may be placed in their utility for the judgement of normal or abnormal behaviour. Statistical criterion, which takes deviation from some average as the deciding factor for abnormality, also suffers from serious defects. Human behaviour which cannot be expressed as quantitative deviation cannot be adjudged as normal or abnormal through this criterion. Moreover, deviation on any scale does not necessarily imply abnormality. On account of the theory of deviation, the abnormal people have received social disapproval. The modern approach advocating the need for the healthy environment as the preventive and curative measure for the abnormal disregards the theory of deviation and replaces it with the concept of the variance. According to Mahoney (1980:8), such modern views in this respect may be summarised as below.

1. There are no thoughts, behaviours or feelings which are inherently crazy or abnormal. Normality of any act or pattern is 'relative' to many other factors, and it does not depend solely on the event itself.
2. All organisms vary in their thoughts, behaviours and feelings. Presumed differences between normal and abnormal persons (or actions) have to do with degree (and not of categories) of variance.

Empirical studies have now established that there are no 'normal' people on one end of the scale and 'abnormal' people on the other as suggested by statistical criterion. Behaviour, even in normal individuals, may fluctuate between normal and abnormal at times of stress. For example, a normal person may start drinking after an unhappy love affair, death of spouse or loss in business.

Therefore, statistical criterion does not give an adequate picture or line of distinction between abnormals and normals. However, its relative usefulness over the other subjective criteria for describing normality or abnormality cannot be questioned and for this reason the authors like Eysenck, Cattell and Guilford have demonstrated the effectiveness of the statistical criterion as compared to other criteria.

We will now evaluate the effectiveness of other criteria such as pathological or medical criterion, psychological criterion and adjustment criterion, in explaining normal or abnormal behaviour. It may be easily concluded that we can't depend upon any of these criteria in determining an individual as normal or abnormal. In some cases, pathological or medical approach helps in the diagnosis of abnormality, while in the other, the abnormality, in the absence of any organic cause, may be detected through the malfunctioning of certain psychological systems.

The pathological and psychological criteria lead us to the adjustment criterion which appears to be the only practicable criterion known so far for describing as well as explaining the normal or abnormal behaviour. The causes of maladjustment may be psychological, sociological or pathological in character but the fact remains that the maladjustment creates abnormality, behaviour disorders or mental illness. While adjustment to one's self and one's environment leads to the proper self-actualization and contribution towards social welfare and progress, the lack of adjustment either harms the self of an individual or compels him to rebel against his environment and social systems making in both cases his behaviour anti-social or self-damaging. In order to determine the extent to which one's behaviour may be termed normal or abnormal, the degree of his total adjustment or maladjustment (involving his self and his environment) in view of his self actualization and contribution towards the welfare and progress of the society must be identified. Devices like adjustment inventories, projective techniques for the assessment of the various personality characteristics may help us in this direction. With the help of such techniques we may not only come to know the extent to which one's behaviour may be termed normal or abnormal but also the special areas or aspects of one's personality or behaviour where one faces difficulty in adjustment or malfunctioning. The intensive diagnostic approach may then lead us to the root causes of the behavioural disorder and from there to a suitable remedy or treatment which may be planned with the help of experts.

Finally, we may say that normality or abnormality is a relative concept. To some extent, deviation from the average known through statistical criterion may help in identifying which behaviour is normal or which is not normal. But for the explanation as well as description of the normal or abnormal behaviour the criterion of adjustment has been found to be the most effective and practicable criterion. Malfunctioning of the nervous system or the psychological system in turn, ultimately leads to abnormality, behaviour disorders or mental illness

## Summary

- *In its simple meaning,* the term 'normal' stands for a set rule, pattern or standard while 'abnormal' for the deviance-or variation from the normal.
- Normality or abnormality is a relative concept. For deciding what is normal and abnormal the different criteria may be grouped as descriptive and explanatory. While descriptive criteria try to describe which behaviour is normal or abnormal, the explanatory criteria tell us why the behaviour is abnormal.
- Descriptive criteria may be further divided into statistical and non-statistical criterion.
- According to *statistical criterion,* average is normal and any deviation from the average would be abnormal. This criterion may be explained through a normal distribution (a bell shaped) curve. The main limitation of this criterion lies in separating abnormal from normal where qualitative aspects of the personality are involved.
- Under *non-statistical criterion* we may have criteria related with morality, social conformity, perfection and legality. They are more or less subjective criteria and hence much reliability or validity cannot be placed in them.
- Explanatory criteria may be divided into pathological or medical criterion, psychological criterion and adjustment criterion.
- According to *pathological criterion,* the normality or abnormality of the behaviour depends upon the functioning of the nervous system. Abnormal people are those who suffer from some specific mental illness or disease. This assertion is ruled out by the *psychological criterion* which links abnormality with the malfunctioning of certain psychological systems.

- According to *adjustment criterion,* a person is said to be normal or abnormal to the extent he feels adjusted or maladjusted with his self and his environment. By all means, it may be adjudged as the most satisfactory and practicable criterion for describing and explaining the normal or abnormal behaviour.

## REFERENCES

Eysenck, H.J. (1960), *Handbook of Abnormal Psychology,* Oxford: Isaac Pitman & Sons Ltd.,

Shanmugam, T. E. (1981), *Abnormal Psychology,* New Delhi: Tata McGraw Hill.

Mahoney, Michael J. (1980), *Abnormal Psychology,* San Francisco: Harper & Row.

# 3

# THE HISTORICAL BACKGROUND OF ABNORMAL PSYCHOLOGY

The historical perspective of a subject presents a fascinating Story of its development. Abnormal psychology, the science of the behaviour of the abnormal people, has reached its present stage through a long developmental process. Its historical perspective would not only give an insight into its past but also provides a base for understanding its present and equip us for setting the direction and trend for evaluating, preventing and curing abnormal behaviour. The history of abnormal psychology can be divided into the following sections.

A. The early age- Era of superstition
B. The bright period of the Middle age- Era of naturalism
C. The dark period of the Middle age- A return to superstition
D. Reappearance of the scientific approach- Era of reason
E. Emergence of modern thought- Era of modern science

## A. The Early Age — Era of Superstition

The attitude of the people towards abnormal behaviour, centuries ago was completely dominated by superstition. They believed devils, evil spirit and other supernatural beings to be responsible for abnormal behaviour. Archaeological discoveries have led to many ancient skulls with small holes which support the probability that these were made to allow the evil spirits to escape. Surgical operations consisting of chipping away a circular area of the skull by the available crude instruments, stone or iron, were performed for the treatment of the so-called abnormal or the mentally ills.

The early writings of the Egyptians, Chinese, Hebrews, Greeks, and Indians indicate that in the era of superstitions all mental disorders were attributed to demons and evil spirits. The treatment was usually given by priests and *tantriks* and consisted of the various techniques to make the evil spirits leave the body of the sufferer. Some were treated by prayer, charms and sacrifice in order to appease the Gods who had taken possession of them. Some were treated through *mantras* and magic and in the case of others measures like noise making, flogging, starving, burning, forcing to take wine, dung, or urine were used in an attempt to make the body of the sufferer so unholy or unpleasant a place that good or bad spirits would be driven out.

## B. The Bright Period of Middle Age — Era of Naturalism

The Greek and Roman civilization during their golden era gave a considerable thought to the problem of mentally disturbed individuals and developed a humane outlook and naturalistic medical approach for their treatment. Hippocrates (460-357 BC) the Greek physician who is called the "father of the modern medicine", along with his followers developed 'naturalism'. According to this doctrine, demons, spirits and heavenly bodies had nothing to do with the mental disorders. Mental illness or disorders were the results of natural causes requiring treatment like any other physical diseases. Hippocrates initiated pathological or medical approach by explaining abnormality in terms of the disease of the brain. He also emphasized that hereditary predisposition, environmental and emotional stress can damage both body and mind. He classified all mental disorders into three general categories-mania, melancholia, and phrenia. For the treatment, he advocated regular clinical observation with proper record. In this way, Hippocrates brought about a revolution in the history of abnormality by introducing a more humane approach involving pathology. However, he was handicapped by the restricted knowledge of anatomy and physiology of the time for adequate pathological definition of abnormality.

The doctrine and views propagated by Hippocrates were later supported by the Greek figures like Plato (427-437 BC), Aristotle (384-332 BC), and Galen (130-200 AD) They, in turn, extended and carried it to the Romans who adopted the pathological approach for the understanding and treatment of mental disorders. Notable among the Roman physicians who followed the Hippocratic tradition were Asclepiad (124 BC) and Aretaeus (second century AD)

Asclepiad was the first to discriminate between acute and chronic mental illness and to distinguish between illusions, delusions, and hallucinations. He was opposed to the undesirable measures like bleeding, purging, and mechanical restraints and strongly advocated and practiced the need for making the patients more comfortable. He favoured humanism and recommended the use of music as a therapy.

Aretaeus is known for the insight he gained in the importance of emotional factors and in the pre-psychotic personality of the patient. He was the first to describe the various phases of mania and melancholia and to consider these two pathological states, nothing, but an expression of the same illness.

Thus the bright period of the Middle Age contributed much to abnormal psychology through Hippocrates, his followers and other Greek and Romans physicians. Many of our modern concepts of mental illness and its treatment have unique resemblance with the views advocated during this period.

## C. The Dark Period of the Middle Age — A Return to Superstitions

The dark ages in the history of abnormal psychology begin with the death of Galen in 200 AD and collapse of Greek and Roman civilisation in the fifth century AD. The contributions and landmarks of the bright period of the Middle Age, known for its early scientific approach towards abnormality were soon lost in superstitions. The treatment of mental disorders reverted to the same practices prevalent in the early age of superstitions and demonology. The advent of Christianity and the dominance of religious heads paved the way for utter ignorance and blind superstition. Some of the so-called religious heads or saints declared themselves to have special powers in getting rid of the evil spirits or demons possessing the people. They established sacred shrines where the poor victims were taken for cure. Here the curative measures were varied. Somewhere holy water, ashes, lying on hands, sanctified ointments, relics, visit to holy places were thought to have a magic effect for curing mental illness. At other times, inhumane tortures like burning, starving, flogging, painful immersion in hot or cold water were resorted to enforcing the evil spirits to leave the body and mind of the mentally disturbed people.

The later part of this period (fifteenth to seventeenth century) witnessed a peculiar trend in mental illness involving 'mass madness' in which groups of people were found to be the cases of hysteria. In Italy it was known as Tarantism in which the whole group suffered from dance manias. The dancing mania later spread to Germany and the rest of the Europe where it was known as St. Virtus' dance. Other manias like biting and acting as wolf were also reported in some parts of Europe.

During this period beliefs concerning the excessive dominance of religion, evil spirits and demons took a turn for the worse. The old belief that the disturbed people were unwillingly seized by the evil spirits as a punishment by God for their sin was replaced by the belief that the individual, willingly, had a pact or friendship with Satan, the devil. The mentally ill came to be considered as heretics and witches responsible for storms, floods, ruination of crops, injuries to their enemies, sexual impotence or death and diseases. Consequently, measures were taken for the detection and punishment of the witches and witchcraft. The unfortunate mentally ill were thus subjected to unimaginable tortures like the cutting of the tongue, twisting delicate parts of the body, burning alive, beheading, strangling or mutilating.

The concept and horror of the witchcraft considering mental illness as a deliberate association with the devil dominated almost all civilizations of the world up to the end of the eighteenth century. However, the Arabs, during this period of darkness, followed a more enlightened approach towards mental illness. Their treatment was comparatively more humane than it was in Europe or America. The notable personality in Arabian medicine named as the "Prince of Physicians" was Avicenna (1080-1037 AD).

## D. Reappearance of the Scientific Approach — Era of Reason

This period in the history of abnormal psychology witnessed a struggle, even at the risk of the life, launched by the great men of their time for challenging and proving the hollowness of the concepts of witchcraft and demonology in explaining the behaviour of the mentally ill. With their continuous struggle, they eventually succeeded in establishing the era of scientific thinking and reasoning, and thus paved the way for the development and emergence of modern thought in this field.

Paracelsus (1490-1541), a Swiss chemist, was one of the first to point out that the dancing mania was not a creation of good or bad spirits but a form of disease. He also put forth the idea of psychic causes for mental illness and advocated "bodily magnetism" which later became hypnosis, in its treatment. However, his views, like the supernatural influence of the moon on the brain, show how religious or theological notions at that time exercised an overwhelming influence over the reasoning of intellectuals. He paid dearly for his unconventional views with his life under continuous persecution.

In the same period, the other voice of reasoning was raised by physician and writer Johann Weyer (1515-1588). He published a book on witchcraft and pointed out that a considerable number of those imprisoned, tortured and burned as witches were really sick, mentally or physically. He was one of the first specialists in mental disorders. For his progressive views on mental illness, he is regarded as the real founder of modern psychiatry. Being ahead of his time, he also met with vehement protest and condemnation and his works were banned by the Church and remained so until the twentieth century.

Reginald Scot (1538-1599), published *Discovery of witchcraft* in which he wrote that the mental disorders had no connection with demons or evil spirits while the witches were nothing but the diseased, unfortunate women suffering from mental illness like melancholy. His views were also attacked and King James I of England personally refuted and ordered the burning of his book.

Another person who at the risk of his life condemned demonology and witch horror was St. Vincent de Paul (1576-1660). He boldly declared that mental diseases were no different from bodily diseases and advocated the medical and humane treatment of the mentally ill.

Thus, the fifteenth and sixteenth centuries witnessed the struggle for the introduction of reason, in place of superstition and ignorance which paved the way for the return of naturalistic, non-theological physical treatment of mental disorders and also helped in diminishing the influence of religious heads in dealing with the mentally disturbed. As a result, for the first time in the history, Henry VIII, the king of England, was inspired to convert the monastery of St. Mary of Bethlehem in London, into a mental hospital in 1547. Such hospitals called asylums were also established later in other parts of Europe and in America. But the early asylums were run like prisons and the patients were treated more like wild animals than sick human beings. They were placed in dark cells and chained to posts, walls and beds in such a way that they could eat from bowls food fit only for animals. Severe measures like starvation, solitary confinement, cold baths and other methods of torture were often resorted to exercise control over the inmates. These asylums became places where the unfortunate inmates lived and died amidst the most inhuman conditions.

The first to raise voice against these asylums was a French physician Philippe Pinel (1745-1826). As in-charge of the La Bicêtre mental hospital in Paris, he started treating the inmates of this asylum as sick human beings and insisted on their chains being removed. The authorities, who were very reluctant to approve the daring plan, were astonished to see the success of the humanitarian approach. In England William Tuke (1732-1822) established the "York Retreat", an asylum for treating the mentally ill with kindness and consideration.

The success of the experiments of Pinel and Tuke prepared the ground for revolutionizing the treatment of the mentally ill throughout the civilized world. As a result, America witnessed a genuine humanistic approach for dealing with the mentally ill through Benjamin Rush (1745-1813), the father of American psychiatry. The views and methods advocated by him paved the way for scientific theories and therapies for the understanding and treatment of the mentally ill people which, in turn, led to the mental hygiene movement for prevention and cure of mental disorders and preservation as well as promotion of mental health.

## E. Emergence of Modern Thought — Era of Modern Science

The age of ignorance and superstition followed by the age of reasoning finally gave way to scientific thinking which gradually ushered in the era of modern thought consisting of advanced theories and techniques based on sound scientific reasoning. These thoughts represented two viewpoints—the organic and the psychological or socio-psychological.

The first systematic presentation of the organic view point was made by the German physician Wilhelm Griesinger (1817- 1868) who asserted that every mental illness or abnormality could be explained on the basis of brain pathology. Griesinger was followed by Emil Kraepelin (1856-1926) who furnished a classification of mental diseases and disorders in terms of organic basis. He regarded mental diseases or disorders to be characterized by a group of symptoms called syndrome. He also emphasized that each mental illness was distinct from others with causes of its own, and symptoms, course and outcome in much the same way as of measles, small pox and similar other physical ailments. His assertion, that schizophrenia was caused by the chemical imbalance in the body and the manic depressive psychoses due to irregularity in metabolism, is evidence of his organic or pathological view point for the explanation of mental disorders, The organic view point advanced by Kraepelin firmly established itself with the discovery of the nature and origin of syphilis and its relationship with general paresis. The germ theory of disease initiated by Louis Pasteur, a French scientist, further strengthened organic or physiological base for the interpretation of mental illness.

The second view point involving psychological and socio-psychological approach was the result of the failure of revealing a satisfactory organic cause in a number of cases. This new approach explained that mental illness was caused by psychological rather than organic factors. Historically, this view point first came from Anton Mesmer (1734-1815), an Austrian physician practicing "Mesmerism' a form of hypnosis, to cure hysteria. The method that he followed to induce mesmerism was so crude that he was branded a charlatan by his medical colleagues and was forced to flee the country. However, Mesmer's contribution, during the later part of the nineteenth century, aroused the interest of the medical practitioners in hypnosis. French physicians like Ambroise-Auguste *Liébeault* (1823-1904) and Hippolyte *Bernheim* (1840-1919) were able to demonstrate the success of the hypnosis (suggestion technique). Another personality who became interested in the research on hysteria during this period was Jean Charcot (1825-1893), a French neurologist. He subsequently did much to promote an understanding of the role of psychological factors in different mental disorders. Pierre Janet (1859-1947) was another Frenchman whose findings on hysteria further served to popularize the psychological view point.

The use of psychological approach got further support from Joseph Breuer (1842-1925), a physician in Vienna. He introduced a new method, known as catharsis, for curing hysteria. In this method the patient is made to discharge emotional tension associated with the repressed traumatic material by taking it out freely. Sigmund Freud (1856-1939), a Viennese physician got interested in hypnosis and catharsis as a method of curing mental disorders. He joined Joseph Breuer in the practice of treating hysteria using catharsis and with his collaboration published *Studies in Hysteria,* an important landmark in the history of abnormal psychology. This book advocated the doctrine of non-organic interpretation of mental disorders. Going further, Freud put forward the doctrine of psychoanalysis in which he replaced catharsis with a new technique known as free association. It consisted of (i) encouraging the patient to say freely whatever came into his mind without regard to logic or decency, (ii) analysing and interpreting what the patient said and did, and (iii) helping him to gain insight and achieve a more adequate adjustment. In this way Freud tried to advocate successfully the psychological view point in relation to mental illness

Freud was followed by his students Alfred Adler (1870-1937) and C.F. Jung (1875-1961). While agreeing with the psychological approach to the problems of mental disorders, they differed with the views of their teacher and ultimately developed their own systematic approaches known as the 'individual psychology' and 'analytical psychology'. The viewpoints emphasized by these two eminent medical men, coupled, with the unique contribution of Freud, tried to establish sufficient ground for understanding and curing mental illness or abnormality on the basis of psychological and socio-psychological causes.

Proceeding differently, the psychologists such as Ivan Pavlov (1849-1936), a Russian, and J.B. Watson and B F. Skinners, Americans, forwarded a view point that normal or abnormal behaviour is a learned act and many of the mental disorders are the product of some or the other learning. These ideas have contributed significantly to our understanding of abnormal behaviour and established the role of psychological or socio-psychological factors in relation to behavioural disorders.

Finally, it would be well to mention the role of the great American psychiatrist Adolf Meyer (1966-1850) who tirelessly advocated an eclectic approach through which he emphasized a fusion of organic, psychological or socio-psychological view points for the diagnosis, understanding and treatment of a mentally ill patient's behaviour. The abnormal psychology and psychiatry today, accept and apply this eclectic approach in the study of abnormal behaviour and mental diseases.

## Abnormal Psychology — Current Trends

This brief description of the historical background of abnormal psychology reveals how our understanding, diagnosis, prevention and treatment of mental illness or mental disorders have changed from barbarism and superstition to naturalism, humanism and empiricism, developing finally into an eclectic approach or tendency incorporating organic as well as socio-psychological points of view. Abnormal psychology, as we find today, is the result of the continuous struggle, experimentation and innovations of the great men of the time. Some of the major features and trends of the present day abnormal psychology may be summarised as under:

1. *Emphasis on empiricism:* In the current abnormal psychology, there is a trend towards empiricism, the view that knowledge must be based on experiences and evidences rather than speculation. Experimentation and observations leased on scientific method are becoming the major tools for the empirical research on the causes of abnormal behaviour.
2. *Emphasis on eclectic approach:* There has been a fusion of organic and socio-psychological viewpoints to mental illness or disorders into an eclectic approach emphasizing the following:
   a. **Integrating behaviour and personality** — For the understanding of a behaviour – normal or abnormal – an eclectic approach is essential, that is, the total personality of an individual should be studied.
   b. **Integrating internal and external factors** — Both internal and external factors (within the individual and outside him) are needed for diagnosis, understanding, treatment and prevention of mental illness or abnormal behaviour.
   c. **Integrating related areas of knowledge** — Eclectic tendency of the present day abnormal psychology is also evident from the fact that there is a tendency of taking help from all areas of knowledge like genetics, anatomy, bio-chemistry, physiology, neurology, psychology, sociology, anthropology, medicine and other related disciplines for the development and understanding of abnormal psychology.
   d. **Integrating various therapies** — For the treatment of abnormality or mental illness, no single therapy or general approach is recommended. There has been a trend for the combination of hypnotic and non-hypnotic techniques. The various forms of therapies, like psycho-analysis, client centred approach and behaviour therapy, are now used separately or in combination with the aim of helping the troubled.
3. *Emphasis on humanitarianism:* It has been realized that normal and abnormal behaviour are indivisible in categories but the difference is of degree only. Mental illness is not merely a biological or pathological problem but has a socio-psychological base also. The mentally ill or disturbed people now are dealt with ail essential sympathy involving humanitarian attitude.
4. *Emphasis on dynamics of behaviour or personality:* Maladjustment brings abnormality in behaviour. Understanding of this maladaptive process in its totality is, therefore, essential for the prevention and treatment of mental illness. A mere knowledge of the symptoms for this purpose is not sufficient. Hence, current abnormal psychology pays attention towards the underlying nature and etiology of the illness rather than emphasizing the knowledge of symptoms only.
5. *Emphasis on the team-approach:* The use of team approach for diagnosis, understanding, prevention and treatment of abnormal behaviour is another major trend in the present-day abnormal psychology. This approach involves an integrated team-work among the psychiatrists, clinical psychologists, psychiatric social workers and other specialized personnel.

6. *Emphasis on public education:* Today, abnormal psychology takes care of the fact that the solution of the problem of mental illness or behaviour disorders lies in the proper awareness and positive attitude of the general public. It makes people realise that a mental patient or disturbed person is not a special kind of organism, but a victim of maladjustment caused by internal or external factors and hence should be helped in his proper adjustment
7. *Emphasis on mental health services:* Prevention is better than cure. For this purpose present abnormal psychology emphasizes the provision of proper facilities and programmes for the development of good mental health of the individuals as well as community. The services of mental health experts are now made available where and when they are needed in the local community or organisations like schools, colleges, religious places, clubs, industrial concerns and military organisations. There is also a shift in emphasis from the custodial mental hospital to mental health services in the community in the form of community mental health centres or other related facilities. The maintenance of individual or community mental health is now considered as important as the maintenance of physical health or liquidation of general diseases.

## Summary

The period related to the history of abnormal psychology may be divided into five sections.

- *The period of early age*: The earliest period was completely dominated by superstitions. All mental disorders were attributed to super powers—good or bad—and were cured through *mantras,* magic and severe inhuman treatment by some priests and *tantriks.*
- *The bright period of Middle Age:* This period witnesses a somewhat humane outlook and naturalistic as well as pathological approach for understanding and treatment of mental disorders through the notable contributions of some Greek and Roman physicians like Hippocrates, Asclepiades and Aretaeous.
- *The dark period of the Middle Age:* This period from fifth century to seventeenth century witnesses a return to the age of superstitions. The later part of this period (fifteenth to seventeenth century) was dominated with the horror of witchcraft considering mental illness as a deliberate association with the devil.
- *Reappearance of the scientific approach:* The earlier part of this period witnesses a daring struggle made by Great men like Paracelsus, Johann Wayer, Reginald Scot, St, Vincent de Paul, who challenged the concept of witchcraft and demonology and paved the way for the return of naturalistic pathological treatment of mental disorders. It resulted in the establishment of mental hospitals called asylums. The prevailing inhumane conditions in the early asylums were later improved giving rise to the mental hygiene movement in the eighteenth century through the attempts made by Pinel (France), Tuke (England) and Rush (U.S.A.).
- *Emergence of modern thought:* The era belonging to the nineteenth and the earlier part of the twentieth century witnessed the application of modern science in

the understanding and treatment of mental disorders. In this era, while men like Griesinger and Kraepelin, advocated organic or physiological base, others like Mesmer, Charcot, Janet, Breuer, Freud, Adler, Jung, Pavlov, Watson and Skinner established the role of psychological or socio-psychological factors for understanding and treatment of mental disorders. The latest trend consists of an eclectic approach (a fusion of organic, psychological or socio-psychological view points) advocated by Meyer, an American psychiatrist.

- *Present day features and trends:* The present day current abnormal psychology witnesses some notable features and trends in relation to the diagnosis, understanding, treatment and prevention of mental disorders by emphasising empiricism, eclectic approach, humanitarianism, dynamics of behaviour, team approach, public education and mental health services.

## Suggested Readings

Alloy, Lauren B., Riskind, John. H., & Manos, Margaret J. (2004), *Abnormal Psychology: Current Perspectives* (9th Ed.) New York: McGraw Hill

Foucault, M. (1967), *Madness and Civilization: A History of Insanity*, London: Tavistock.

Shorter, E. (1997), *A History of Psychiatry from the Era of the Asylum to the Age of Prozac*, New York: Wiley.

Still, A. (2010) A History of Psychology. London: Sage.

Wallace, E.R. IV and Gach, J. (eds) (2008) *History of Psychiatry and Medical Psychology*, New York: Springer.

# 4

# PSYCHOLOGY OF MOTIVATION

A small bird collects the material to build its nest in the corner of the roof in our drawing room. We try to remove it, but the bird brings more straw and leaves, and engages itself in building its nest. Similarly, an athlete may be seen trying hard to improve his performance by continuous practice. A writer may be engaged in the task of writing a book. A student may be found in the class room, sketching the poses and figure of the teacher.

## Motivation

What makes the bird, the athlete, the writer or the student behave in such a manner? The answer to such questions, related to 'why of behaviour' lies in the key word 'motivation.' Their acts are the results of motivated behaviour. They act in order to satisfy their basic needs and to attain the desired goals. Moreover, interest is the central factor in any type of behaviour and motivation is closely related to this factor.

*Motivation may be defined as a mechanism and process of inculcating and stimulating the interest of an individual in a goal seeking behaviour growing out of some activating forces like needs, drives or motives.*

## Basic needs

Needs are general wants or desires. Every human being has to strive for the satisfaction of his basic needs if he is to maintain and actualize or enhance himself in this world. Ordinarily, the needs of an individual can be studied under two major heads:

A. Physiological or biological needs, also known as primary needs.

B. Socio-psychological needs also known as secondary needs.

## A. Physiological or Biological Needs

All our bodily or organic needs may be put under this head, and classified as follows:

1. In the first category of the organic needs may be included the need for oxygen, water and food. As far as our survival or existence is concerned, these needs are most basic needs and the satisfaction of which is essential. Nobody can think of his survival beyond a limited period if he is deprived of the sources for the satisfaction of these needs.

2. The second category of the organic needs, essential for survival, involves the following:
   (i) Need for rest when tired.
   (ii) Need for being active when rested.
   (iii) Need for sleep when deprived of it for long.
   (iv) Need for regular elimination of waste products from the body.
   (v) Need for having an even internal body temperature.
   (vi) Need for protection from the threats of physical environment like hazards of weather, natural calamities, wild animals etc.
3. The third category of the organic needs involves sex need and maternal need for the perpetuation of the species and satisfaction of the strong basic urges. Although one can physically survive and live without these needs being satisfied, yet they are essential for the well-being of the individual and society.

## B. Socio-Psychological Needs

Under this head can be included the following needs:

1. *The need for freedom or gaining independence:* An individual possesses a craving for independence. Nature has created us free and independent as individuals and requires us to remain so. Therefore, all human beings have an urge to remain free and independent.
2. *The need for security*: Every human being needs to feel secure. Not only does he need security of life in the physical and physiological sense, but he also needs to feel secure in economic as well as social sense.
3. *The need to achieve:* Each person manifests the need for achievement not only for standing well in the eyes of others but also for the satisfaction he will derive from his accomplishment. The particular mode of achievement sought by an individual depends a little upon his talents and the environment in which he lives. Some people seek achievement in athletic activities others in intellectual or academic field while still others in spiritual world. Thus, whatever be the form of achievement, the need for it is clearly shown by all human beings.
4. *The need for affection:* It is essentially a desire to love and be loved that leads to maintaining a pleasant relationship with others. Everybody, irrespective of his age, needs love and affection. He possesses an emotional craving for the satisfaction of this need. An environment which is healthy and affectionate provides a strong motivating force to the individuals.
5. *The need for recognition or social approval:* Another important need is that of feeling important and attaining recognition, appreciation and esteem among others. Each one of us wants to gain appreciation and recognition from our fellowmen and possesses an inherent desire to excel in order to gain social status, prestige or approval.
6. *The need for companionship*: Man is referred to as a social animal in the sense that he has an inherent desire to be with one's own kind and maintain social relationships with them. The strength of this need can be well estimated by the fact that one of the most severe punishment possible to all normal individuals consists of solitary confinement or social rejection.

7. *The need for self-assertion:* This is a powerful need that manifests in a desire to dominate people and things, it leads to 'power motive' and is a strong determinant of one's behaviour.
8. *The need for self-actualization:* This is also known as the need for self-expression and self-realisation. We all have inherent craving for the expression of one's self and actualization of one's potentialities. This need makes an individual think that there is something for which he is best suited and consequently he does not feel happy until he gets opportunities to do what he strives for.

In the above description an attempt has been made for the classification of basic human needs. This classification is quite arbitrary. Psychologists, from time to time, have tried to classify these needs according to their view points and criteria. Murray has given a list of thirty-seven needs for this purpose. The other theorists, as we will find in the discussion of the theories regarding motivation, have reduced this list to one or two.

## Drives

A need gives rise to a drive which may be defined as an aroused reaction tendency or a state of heightened tension that sets up activities in an individual and sustains them for increasing his general activity level. Drives of any nature are essentially the creation of basic needs and are divided into two categories – biological or primary drives and socio-psychological or secondary drives. The existence of a need moves or drives the individual from within and directs its activities to a goal that may bring about the satisfaction of the need. The strength of a drive depends upon the strength of the stimuli involving the related need.

## Motives

Motives are the dynamic forces which energize all behaviour. What we do, and the manner in which we do it, is governed by the motives behind it. Our acts are the results of our attempts to satisfy our motives. Motive has been variously defined.

*Fisher:* A motive is an inclination or impulsion to action plus some degree of orientation or direction. (Singh & Tiwari, 1971, p.72)

*Shaffer:* A motive may be defined as a tendency to activity indicated by a drive and concluded by an adjustment. (Singh & Tiwari, 1971, p.72)

*Rosen, Fox & Gregory (1972:41)*: A motive may be defined as a readiness or disposition to respond in some ways and not others to a variety of situations.

*Carroll (1969:21): A* need gives rise to one or more motives. A motive is a rather specific process which has been learned. It is directed towards a goal.

All these definitions lead us to generalize that:

1. Motive is an inner state of mind or an aroused feeling.
2. It is generated through basic needs or drives.
3. It compels an individual to respond by creating a kind of tension or urge to act,

4. It is a preparation for responding in some selective way for the satisfaction of the related need.
5. It is a goal directed activity pursued till the attainment of goal.
6. A change in goal may bring changes in the nature and strength of the motive.
7. Attainment of goal helps in the release of tension.
8. Motive is a learned response or tendency as suggested by Carroll and also an innate disposition as advocated by Fisher, Rosen, Fox and Gregory.

Understood in this way, a motive may be an energetic force or tendency working within an individual to compel, persuade or inspire him to engage in an activity for the satisfaction of his basic needs or drives. It may be innate and learned. For this reason motives, in general, are classified into two broad groups as primary and secondary motives.

The primary motives are the biological or physiological motives which ensure the preservation of life for the individual and for his race. Examples of such motives are hunger, thirst, sex, avoidance of pain, elimination of body wastes, sleep and rest etc. The primary motives are universal motives, and are found in all organisms—human or non-human—in one form or the other. They serve the basic physiological needs of the organism and are in-born and innate.

The secondary motives are the psychological or social motives. They are acquired like other forms of learned behaviour in the course of their behaviour. A need that has been satisfied is no longer a need, it ceases to be a motivating force and therefore the satisfaction of one need leads an individual to try for the satisfaction of other needs. In this way the motivational behaviour of a person is always dominated not by his satisfactions but by his unsatisfied wants, desires or needs.

## The Motivational Cycle

Motivation, as we know, is a state of the organism which involves the existence of a need that moves or drives its activities to a goal that can bring about the satisfaction of the need. Motivation, as a general term, constitutes a cycle completed in different stages as shown in the diagram.

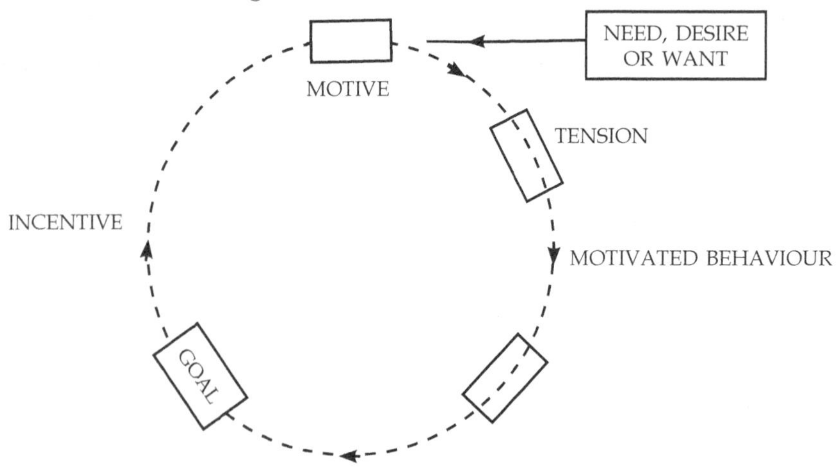


Fig. 4.1: The Motivational Cycle

In the beginning, there is a need, a desire or a want which gives to drives or motives. The drives or motives so produced bring about a state of tension and restlessness in an individual. Moved by the force of drives or motives the individual strives towards some goal. His behaviour is motivational behaviour. The journey to the goal helps in the realization of his need and provides relief in release of tension. The attainment of the goal gratifies his need and brings satisfaction and happiness to him. When the organism reaches the desired goal, he gets immediate reinforcement or encouragement. In other words, he is motivated to act further. The term 'incentive' is frequently used for this stage of motivational cycle. Incentives, in this way, are the objects or the situations satisfying the desired motives and intensifying the individual's motivation. Offering bonus to a factory worker or over-time allowance to a bank employee are examples of incentives.

## Theories of Motivation

The process or mechanism of motivation has been explained by a number of psychologists. Notable among them are Freud, Adler, Maslow and Combs Snygg.

### Freud's viewpoint

Freud's theory of motivation was based on instincts. In his last book, Outline of psycho-analysis, he asserted that Eros (life or erotic instinct) and the destructive instincts are the ultimate cause of all activities. Eros includes all sexual impulses as well as the urge for self-preservation, while the destructive instinct represents the desire to destroy even to the extent of destroying one's self. He arrived at the pleasure principle and regarded the need for sexual gratification the hard core of life instinct, as the only driving force for the human behaviour. He maintained that from birth onwards, human beings experience sex gratification. Sex, therefore, is the ultimate cause of all activity.

### Adler's viewpoint

Without agreeing with the extreme views of Freud regarding sex as the basis of human behaviour, Alfred Adler, a student of Freud, developed his own system of psychology, known as Individual psychology. He assumed that human beings are motivated primarily by social urges. While, Freud considered human beings as primary sexual, Adler considered them as primary social. He considers the need for security as the basis of all human behaviour. It is the single basic drive which motivates the individual, all his life, to act. The individual requires a margin of safety besides the simple security from danger. He achieves this margin of safety through domination and superiority. Therefore, the struggle for achievement and status or the will to dominate or power are really an outgrowth of the fundamental need for security. Thus, the motivation of human behaviour may be endorsed through a single basic drive or motive or in terms of a single need, the need for security.

### Maslow's Theory of Motivation

In his book *Motivation and Personality* Maslow emphasizes that a motivational behaviour may satisfy many needs at the same time implying that an act is multi-motivated yet it is the total organism that is stirred to activity. It is the total person motivated and not just a part. Therefore, the individual, as far as motivation of his behaviour or personality is considered, should be viewed as a whole. In this sense, we have to see that a child is motivated as a whole for learning a skill, or a worker should be motivated as a whole for doing his job and not just one or the other organs of his body and mind. He proposed five sets of basic needs in a definite hierarchical order for understanding human motivation.

According to Maslow, human needs are closely related to each other and may be arranged from the lowest to the highest development of his personality. Starting from the satisfaction of the physiological needs, every individual strives for the satisfaction of the other needs of higher order. This striving causes the motivation of their behaviour. A need that has been satisfied is no longer a need. It ceases to be a motivating force and therefore, the satisfaction of one need leads to an individual to try for the satisfaction of other needs. In this way, the motivational behaviour of a person is always dominated not by his satisfaction by his unsatisfied wants, desires or needs.

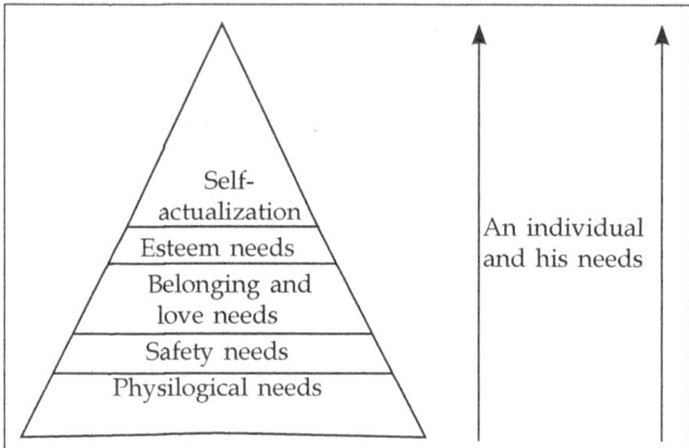


Fig. 4.2. Hierarchical structure of needs.

The motivational behaviour of most of the people fits well in the hierarchical structure of needs proposed by Maslow and consequently for them a need of a higher order does not appear until a need of a lower order is gratified. They can think of the other needs only when the food and other basic physiological needs are well gratified. A hungry person cannot think of the welfare of the society or attainment of salvation through remembering God. Similarly, one who is insecure or unsafe may hardly be motivated for the gratification of love or esteem needs.

But as it happens, there is a room for exception in Maslow's hierarchy of needs. The history of mankind may point out countless heroes, saints and other great people who have always stood for the ideals, religious or social values of life without caring for the satisfaction of biological or other lower needs.

It seems that the effects of gratification of a need are more stimulating and important than the effect of deprivation. The gratification of lower order needs motivates an individual to strive for the higher order needs. An individual, as Maslow emphasized, can actualize his potentialities as a human being only after meeting the higher level needs like love and esteem. The need of self- actualization thus seems to be the ultimate aim of human life and that is why Maslow has tried to place it at the top of his hierarchy of needs. It is the master motive which encircles all the lower order needs for motivating human behaviour.

## Combs and Snygg's viewpoint

A.W. Combs and D. Snygg advocated perceptual or the phenomenological approach for the understanding of human behaviour. Instead of explaining the individual's behaviour in terms of the situations to which he is reacting, this approach seeks to understand his behaviour from his own point of view. It attempts to observe people, not as they seem to outsiders, but as they seem to themselves. The phenomenal of perceptual field is the entire universe including the self as it is experienced by the individual at the time of action. It is unique for an individual and by all means responsible for his every behaviour. Emphasizing this point of view Combs and Snygg (1959:20) write that, "All behaviour without exception, is completely determined by, and pertinent to, the perceptual held of the behaving organism."

The perceptual field is always expressed by an individual with reference to his need and the ways of satisfying these needs. Consequently, the human need or needs decide and direct the human behaviour.

Clarifying their stand on this issue of basic human needs, Combs and Snygg (1959:46) write:

> *A man's basic need may be defined as a need for adequacy... expressed in man's every behaviour at every instant of his existence. Asleep or awake, each of us is engaged in an insatiable quest for personal adequacy. This quest may find its expression in a wide variety of behaviour aimed...at the maintenance or enhancement of our perception of personal worth and value. Other authors have spoken of this need as a need for self-actualization or self- realization. In the field of psychotherapy this need has been described as a need for growth – whenever we refer to man's basic need we mean that great driving, striving force in each of us by which we are continually seeking to make ourselves more adequate to cope with life.*

Thus, the need for adequacy is the only basic driving or motivating force. It has two principal components, (i) the maintenance of the self and (ii) the enhancement of the self. The maintenance of the self does not only involve the satisfaction of physiological needs but also the needs for maintaining one's perception of the self. An individual, from birth to death, is vitally concerned with preserving his self as he perceives that self. In accordance with this need, he selects from his perceptual field aspects which are meaningful for him, and which reinforce his picture of himself. While maintaining his self, the individual at the same time also feels the need to be more adequate, to grow, to be able to deal more effectively with life by enhancing or actualizing his self as much as possible.

The various viewpoints discussed above reveal that motivation of the behaviour is the output of the drives or motives generated by the wants or basic needs of the organism. Freud, as we have seen, over emphasized the importance of sex by declaring it as a prime motive or drive for the determination of human behaviour. He ignored man as an organism with social needs and placed his emphasis upon the instinctual and biological needs. Adler stressed upon the social urges and reduced the basic human needs to a single need for security and thus replaced Freud's sex motive by security or power motive. Maslow, while proposing five sets of basic needs, placed self-actualization at the top of his hierarchy of needs and thus emphasized the self-actualization as a prime motive for the human motivation. This was replaced by the concept of adequacy by Combs and Snygg,

It is difficult to differentiate Maslow's self-actualization from Comb's and Snygg's "need for adequacy". The American psychologist Carl Rogers has also named a similar single force "drive for growth" as a potent factor in the motivation of human behaviour. Essentially, basic human needs are nothing but demands or cravings, for which we strive hard to satisfy.

A need in its true sense does not necessarily represent a lack or involve deprivation. For example, the need for food may not necessarily be the result of hunger pangs but for the pleasurable taste sensations. Similarly, the need for sex may not necessarily be the result of the deprivation but the effect of the strong stimulus or favourable environment for seeking pleasure. Therefore, when we talk about the potentiality of needs as a generating base for the strong motives or drives, we see that our needs are not only concerned with the preservation or maintenance of the self but with the promotion and enhancement of the self also. A human being is motivated not in parts but as a whole and his entire self is involved in the process or outcome of the motivation.

Whether primary or secondary, physiological or socio-psychological, all types of needs help in the two-way task of the maintenance and enhancement of the self. Our actions or behaviour generated through needs, drives or motives are meant for the welfare of the self, that is, its preservation and promotion. The proper satisfaction of our needs helps us in actualizing our potentialities or ensuring our proper development so that we become or feel adequate.

## Summary

- Motivation may be defined as a mechanism of creating interest in a goal seeking behaviour growing out of some activating forces like needs, drives or motives.
- Needs are general wants or desires. Human basic needs may be grouped into two major heads-primary and secondary needs.
- Primary needs are concerned with our all bodily or organic needs and may include the need for oxygen, water, food, rest, sleep, elimination of waste product, physical safety and sex. On the other hand, secondary needs are psychological and social in nature and may include the need for freedom, security, achievement, affection, recognition, social company, self-assertion, and self-actualization.
- Drives are the creation of basic needs. A drive may be defined as an aroused reaction tendency or a state of heightened tension that sets up activities in an individual and sustains them for increasing his present activity level. Like needs, these may also be classified as primary and secondary drives.

- A Motive is an energetic force or tendency working within the individual to compel, persuade or inspire him towards some activity for the satisfaction of his basic needs or drives. It may be innate or acquired. Motives may also be grouped as primary and secondary motives.
- Motivational cycle in its usual way consists of the need, drive, tension, goal and incentive one giving birth to other in a cyclic way.
- The why and how of motivation may be explained from a variety of perspectives, theories or viewpoints. According to Freud, the need for sexual gratification is the only driving force for the human behaviour. According to Adler, the motivation of human behaviour may be endorsed through a single basic drive known as security drive or motive. Maslow has put forward his need based theory in this concern. According to this theory, human needs (grouped in five sets) may be arranged in a definite hierarchical order from the lowest to the highest development of the personality. The gratification of a lower order makes an individual strive for the satisfaction of other needs of the higher order which causes the motivation of his behaviour. According to Combs and Snygg, the need for adequacy is the only basis driving or motivating force. The maintenance and enhancement of the self are its two principle components.
- While drawing conclusion about the adequacy of the different viewpoints in explaining the mechanism of human behaviour it can be safely concluded that needs are the actual potent force for motivating the human behaviour. In such pursuit, however, we may provide importance to one need over the other depending on the circumstances and our own personality characteristics.

## REFERENCES

Adler, A.(1928), *Understanding Human Nature,* London: Allen & Unwin

Carroll, H.A.,(1969), *Mental Hygiene-The Dynamics of Adjustment*, New Jersey: Prentice-Hall

Combs, A.W. and Snygg, D., (1959), *Individual Behaviour* (Revised edition), New York: Harper &Row Publishers

Fisher, V.E., *An introduction to abnormal Psychology,* cited by Labh Singh & G.P. Tiwari, *Essentials of Abnormal Psychology,* Agra : Vinod Pustak Mandir, 1971, p.72.

Freud, S., (1935), *A General Introduction to Psychoanalysis,* New York: Liveright,

Maslow, A.H., (1954), *Motivation and Personality,* New York: Harper & Row Publishers.

Rosen, E., Fox and Gregory (1972), ***Abnormal Psychology,*** (2nd, International student edition) , Philadelphia: Saunder's

Shaffer, L.S. Quoted In Labh Singh & G.P. Tiwari, *Essentials of Abnormal Psychology,* Agra : Vinod Pustak Mandir, 1971, p. 72.

# 5

# PSYCHOLOGY OF ADJUSTMENT

## Meaning and Definitions of Adjustment

"Life presents a continuous chain of struggle for existence and survivals." says Darwin. The observation is very correct as we find in our day-to-day life. Every one of us strives hard for the satisfaction of our needs. While struggling to achieve something if one finds that results are not satisfactory, one either changes one's goal or the procedure. For example, if one aspires to join M.B.B.S. course, one works hard to get good marks in the Pre-Medical class. In case one is not able to get admission due to one's low percentage, one may change one's goal and feel inclined or aspire to join a B.Sc. course for medical representative job.

By restoring to such means, one protects one's self from the possible injury to one ego, failure or frustration. It is a sort of shifting to a more defensive position in order to face the challenge of circumstances after failing in earlier attempt or attempts. This special feature of the living beings is termed as adjustment. Let us now analyse this term by studying some important definitions.

*L.S. Shaffer:* Adjustment is the process by which living organism maintains a balance between its need and the circumstances that influence the satisfaction of these needs. (1961, p.511)

*Gates, Jersild and others:* Adjustment is a continual process by which a person varies his behaviour to produce a more harmonious relationship between himself and environment. (1970, pp. 614-15)

*Vonhaller:* We can think of adjustment as psychological survival in much the same way as biologist uses the term adaptation to describe physiological survival. (1970, p. 426).

Let us try to analyse, these definitions.

*Shaffer's definition* lays stress on needs and their satisfaction. One feels adjusted to the extent one's needs are gratified or in the way of being gratified. A person tries to bring changes in his circumstances in order to overcome the difficulties in the realization of his needs. Sometimes he reduces the quantum of his need so that he may feel satisfied within the limited resources of needs and in this way, he tries to keep a balance between his needs and the capacity of realizing these needs. As long as the balance is maintained he remains adjusted. The moment it is disturbed, he drifts towords maladjustment.

The second definition by Gates and Jersild takes adjustment as a signal of harmonious relationship between a man and his environment. One has to fit oneself in the prevailing circumstances. When we adjust ourselves by this means we are changing in some way to adapt or accommodate ourselves in order to fit as per certain demands of our environment. The conditions in the environment are in a continuous chain of changes. We change our nature in order to fit ourselves in the realm of nature. Thus, the process of adjustment is continuous. We try to change or modify our behaviour for bringing a perfect understanding between ourselves and our environment. For example, if an urban girl is married to a rural boy and made to live a village life, she has to change her behaviour, her habits and her way of life for accommodating herself in the changed circumstances.

The last definition by Vonhaller takes clue from the Darwin's theory of evolution. Darwin maintained that only those organisms most fitted to adapt to the changed circumstances survive. Hence, the individuals who are able to adjust themselves in changed situations in their environment can live in perfect harmony and lead a happy life. In this way, adjustment as a psychological term is a new name for the term adaptation used in biological world. In all sense, adjustment implies a satisfactory adaptation to the demands of day-to-day life.

The above discussion can lead us to summarize in the following way:

- Adjustment is a process that takes us to lead a happy and well-contented life.
- Adjustment helps us in keeping balance between our needs and the capacity to meet these needs.
- Adjustment persuades us to change our way of life according to the demands of the situation.
- Adjustment gives us strength and ability to bring desirable changes in the conditions of our environment.

Besides the demands of one's basic need, society also demands a particular mode of behaviour from its members. In case one thinks only to fulfil one's needs by setting aside the norms, ethics and cultural traditions of one's society, one is not going to be adjusted in one's environment. Here, adjustment also needs one's conformity to the requirement of one's culture and the society. In this way, adjustment does not only cater to one's own needs but also to the demands of the society. Therefore, in defining adjustment in its comprehensive way, we can conclude that *adjustment is a condition or state in which one feels that one's needs have been (or will be) fulfilled and one's behaviour conforms to the requirements of the society and culture.*

## Adjustment as Achievement or Process

Adjustment can be interpreted as both, process and the outcome of that process in the form of some attainment or achievement. When a poor child studies under the street light because he has no lighting arrangement at home he is said to be in a process of adjustment. What he attains in terms of success in his examination or the fulfilment of his ambition or pride in his achievement is nothing but the result of his adjustment to his self and his environment. Thus, adjustment as an achievement means how the effectiveness with which an individual can function in changed circumstances and is, as such, related to his adequacy and regarded as an achievement that is accomplished either badly or well (Lazarus, 1976).

Adjustment as a process describes and explains the ways and means of an individual's adaptation to his self and his environment without reference to the quality of such adjustment or its outcome in terms of success or failure. It only shows how individuals or a group or groups of people cope under changing circumstances and what factors influence this adjustment. Let us now consider some salient features of adjustment as an interaction between a person and his environment.

(*i*) *Continuous process:* The process of adjustment is continuous. It starts at one's birth and goes on without stop till one's death. A person as well as his environment is constantly changing as also are his needs in accordance with the demands of the changing external environment. Consequently, the process or nature of an individual's adjustment can be expected to change from situation to situation and according to Arkoff (1968), there is nothing like satisfactory or complete adjustment which can be achieved once and for all time. It is something that is constantly achieved and re-achieved by us.

(*ii*) *Two-way process:* Adjustment is a two-way process and involves not only the process of fitting oneself into available circumstances but also the process of changing the circumstances to fit one's needs. Emphasizing this two-way nature of the adjustment process, Robert W. White (1956) writes:

> *The concept of adjustment implies a constant interaction between the person and his environment, each making demands on the other. Sometimes adjustment is accomplished when the person yields and accepts conditions which are beyond his power to change. Sometimes it is achieved when the environment yields to the person's constructive activities. In most cases adjustment is a compromise between these two extremes and maladjustment is a failure to achieve a satisfactory compromise.*

## Areas or Spheres of Adjustment

"For an adequate adjustment one has to make oneself adjusted firstly to one's self and to one's environment. Thus, the spheres, dimensions or aspects of adjustment may be divided mainly in two categories, personal and environmental. For any individual while the adequacy of his own physical and mental health, emotional adjustment and satisfaction of personal needs are vital for the overall adjustment, his need for making adjustment with the social and occupational world can also not be overlooked. Based on this, we can categorize the overall adjustment of an individual into three spheres, namely personal, social and occupational. Let us try to know more about these three areas or spheres of one's adjustment.

## A. Personal Adjustment

Personal adjustment is concerned with an individual's adjustment to himself. Now question arises as to what does the term 'self' mean with regard to personal adjustment. The total individuality incorporating various aspects of his growth and development, personality traits and characteristics and satisfaction of his basic needs may essentially be included in the body of the term 'self'. In this sense the extent to which one remains satisfied with what he owns in terms of his physical and mental development and other personality characteristics and his basic needs remain gratified, he may be called adjusted within the sphere of personal adjustment. Let us now elaborate these components of one's personal adjustment.

1. ***Adjustment to Physical Development and Health:*** Physical growth and development follow a somewhat definite pattern. A child of a particular age is normally expected to have a certain increase in weight and height, acquire definite somatic structure and physical characteristics and have growth and development with regards to internal organs, body systems and their functioning. In case this growth and development takes place in a normal way and the individual remain satisfied, he remains adjusted otherwise it may lead to frustration and other complexes paving the way for his maladjustment. Similarly, one should keep better physical health free from stressful ailments and diseases so as to enjoy better personal adjustment. In this way, if an individual's physical growth and development as well as his physical strength, abilities and capacities are in conformity with what is expected at his age and he does not feel any difficulty in his physical functioning and general progress due to any kind of defect or inability of his physical organs, he may get along well with his adjustment to his self.
2. ***Adjustment with Regard to Mental Development and Health:*** The other major aspect of one's personal adjustment is related with his mental development and mental health. Like physical development, an individual of a particular age is expected to function at a certain level of intellectual growth and development. In case one does not acquire even the normal mental capacities and abilities expected at his age, he may feel handicapped in terms of intellectual behaviour and this deficiency (while compared to others) may lead to frustration and complexes. Similarly, one who is not keeping good mental health may turn into a maladjusted personality. Anxiety, distress, situation, pressures, complexes, frustrations all are bitter enemies of one's mental health and these may lead a person to total maladjustment with his self.
3. ***Emotional Adjustment:*** Emotions play a leading role in controlling and directing one's behaviour and providing a definite shape to his personality make-up. An individual who is capable of expressing his emotions in a proper way at a proper time may be termed as emotionally adjusted. The acquisition of such emotional adjustment may automatically help an individual to act and behave in a desired way, face the life situations properly and feel adjusted in his personal and social life.
4. ***Sexual Adjustment:*** Sex is also a personal matter like one's physical, mental and emotional adjustments. Moreover, the gratification of sex need is the most important aspect of our life. As long as this need remains in the state of satisfaction, the individual feels comfortable, satisfied and adjusted but as soon as the balance is disturbed, there arises obstacles in the path of gratification of sex needs and the individual may be drifted towards maladjustment. Studies and researches in this area have established that one's proper sexual development, his proper attitude towards sex and the satisfaction of his sex needs in a desirable and proper way are the essential factors responsible for his adjustment to his self and the environment.

5. *Adjustment with Respect to the Individual Needs:* This sphere of our personal adjustment may also include all such types of adjustments that are concerned with the satisfaction of our personal needs. Among these, we may include the needs like: (i) physiological or organic needs such as hunger, thrust, sleep and rest, etc., (ii) material needs such as need for clothes, shelter and various other material facilities and comforts, (iii) our socio-psychological needs such as need to love and to be loved, need for expression and actualization, need to dominate, get respect and regard, etc. We all, from the very beginning of our life till the end, remain busy in working and struggling for the satisfaction of these needs. In case we get success and feel satisfied, we remain adjusted or else we are compelled to drift towards maladjustment.

## B. Social Adjustment

This sphere of adjustment is concerned with one's adjustment to his social surroundings. Such adjustment is as much essential as one's adjustment with his self. In all circumstances, one should feel reasonably satisfied with what he gets in term of his social environment. By doing so, he may get along well with others and keep himself in the category of a socially adjusted person, but if it does not happen he may become a socially maladjusted person. In such circumstances, either he may cut himself off from the society or may turn into an anti-social and criminal personality. In this sense, one's adjustment with his social set up, started from his parents, home and family and extended to the neighbourhood, state, country and encircling whole world, is quite essential for the welfare of his own and the society. Let us try to know in detail about the components of one's social adjustment.

1. *Home and Family Adjustment:* One should feel the comfort and satisfaction in one's home in the spirit of 'Sweet Home'. He must have proper cordial relationships and behavioural adjustment with the members of his family. One who is fed up with his family environment and likes to spend most of the time outside the home so as to avoid the company of the family members is surely a person who is seriously lacking in terms of his home and family adjustment. Contrary to this, when the home and family environment are quite cooperative and congenial, the members of the family get proper opportunity for the satisfaction of their mutual personal needs and social obligations. In such encouraging, mutually sharing, loving and peaceful environment each member works for the progress and welfare of the others besides the development of his own. Such family environment provides a reasonable insurance for the total adjustment and well-being of all the members of the family.
2. *Adjustment with Friends and Relatives:* The social circle of one's friends and relatives is closely linked with the social environment of his home and family. One's behaviour and personality development is very much influenced, guided and patronized by one's relatives and friends. These are the persons who come to our help in the hour of our need. One may feel secure and satisfied if he has cordial, congenial and harmonious relations with (may be few) his relatives and friends. On the contrary and opposite situations, one is bound to feel lonely, insecure and perturbed at the time of distress and casualties.

In this way, the key of one's adjustment lies in getting along well with his friends and relatives.

3. ***Adjustment with Neighbours and Other Members of the Community:*** Next to our home is the neighbourhood and the community. Most of our physical, psychological and social needs are fulfilled through proper communication, exchange, goodwill and spirit of cooperation maintained with our neighbours and other members of the community. We can't live in harmony and peace with indifferent and spoiled relationships with our immediate neighbours and members of the community. The essential thing is to learn the lesson of togetherness and coexistence with the members of the community in spite of differences of opinions, living standards, language, caste, religion, etc.

   It is futile to waste our energy and resources in endless conflicts and tensions created through mutual mistrust, fear, disliking and disrespect, jealousy and envy, false pride and inflated ego. It creates a chain of reaction and ends with the state of dissatisfaction resulting in our maladjustment with our own neighbours and members of the community. Hence, it is always better to try our best to get along well with our neighbours and members of the community. Slowly, this spirit of togetherness, bond of friendship, cooperation, co-existence and peaceful living should be extended to the boundaries of one's nation and even to the world as a close-knit family.

Here the question arises as to what should one do for maintaining proper relationship with the members of his family, friends, relatives, neighbours and members of the community so that he may be well-adjusted in his social set up? The answer lies in one's proper social development and adaptability to the social environment. One should essentially learn the lesson of mutual love and respect, goodwill and trust, cooperation and sharing and other similar qualities and virtues of a social being. One should try to know the norms, modes of living and expectations of the society for adapting himself in the existing pattern of one's community and society. It does not mean that he should blindly lead to conformity, but in all his efforts he must first try to get along with the social set up and then work honestly for the desired changes and needed social progress.

## C. Occupational Adjustment

How far we are satisfied with our world of work and means of livelihood decides, to a great extent, our state or adjustment or maladjustment to our self and the environment. From the very beginning, parents aspire for a good occupation or profession for their children. They plan their education accordingly. However, entering into the profession or occupation of one's choice or being in tune with their abilities and capacities depend on a lot of factors. Whatsoever it may be, one's chosen one should learn to adjust and adapt to the needs and requirement of one's profession or occupation. His success in his field of work will depend to a large extent on the sense of satisfaction he feels in performing various duties in his job. He must be reasonably satisfied and should get along well with the men and material resources available in his world of work. Such satisfaction, adaptation and adjustment to one's occupation automatically help in attaining the desired objectives in his personal and social life leading to the overall adjustment to one's self and the environment. Now at this stage, the question may arise as to who should be termed as an adjusted individual in his field of work or occupation. For this, let us think about the possible traits and characteristics generally found in such vocationally or occupationally adjusted persons.

(i) Once entered, they feel no regret about the choice of work or occupation.

(ii) They demonstrate a sense of job satisfaction through the performance of various duties regarding their job or occupation.

(iii) They feel reasonably satisfied with the working conditions and facilities available for carrying out their job duties. They are not in the habit of unnecessarily complaining about limitations and non-availability of resources.

(iv) They get along well with their colleagues and the officials of their world of work. They try to maintain cordial relationship and harmony with them for attaining desired proficiency in their work.

(v) They are committed and have a very positive attitude towards the working and value of their occupation. They do not unnecessarily dream or plan of entering into other occupations. While respecting their own profession, they always strive to achieve a sense of satisfaction by performing their duties honestly and sincerely.

(vi) They are reasonably satisfied with the opportunities provided in their present occupation for promotion and other achievements. They do not get much perturbed despite not getting early opportunities of promotions and other incentives and believe that their work will be 'rewarded' in one way or the other.

(vii) They are usually engaged in bringing necessary improvement and modification in the methods and processes related to their occupation for qualitative improvement. They have creative sparks in them which is often reflected through their styles of functioning.

(viii) They are reasonably satisfied with their occupations in terms of economic returns. They are not found comparing their salaries and financial returns with others and complaining about their chosen occupation.

(ix) They maintain a sense of accountability for the assigned duties and try to maintain the image and respect of their profession by extending desired cooperation to colleagues and administrators.

## Characteristics of a Well-Adjusted Person

A well-adjusted person is supposed to possess the following characteristics:

1. *Physically adjusted:* A well-adjusted individual enjoys wholesome adjustment in terms of his physical health, and physiological well-being. He is physically mature and sound in relation to his age-linked physical and physiological growth and development. What he has in terms of his somatic structure physical development, strength and abilities make him feel secure and satisfied.
2. *Emotionally adjusted:* A well-adjusted individual demonstrates a well-balanced emotional behaviour. He is able to express desirable emotions in a proper amount as per the needs of the situation and his own well-being.

3. *Socially adjusted:* A well-adjusted individual is a socially mature individual. He has the necessary development in terms of social competency and social obligations. He knows his social environment and has a desire and capability to adjust his self to the demands of the social life.
4. *Awareness of his own strengths and limitations:* A well- adjusted person knows his own strengths and weaknesses. He tries to make capital out of his assets in some areas by accepting his limitations in others.
5. *Respecting himself and others:* The dislike for oneself is a typical symptom of maladjustment. An adjusted individual has respect for himself as well as for others.
6. *An adequate level of aspiration:* His level of aspiration is neither too low nor too high in terms of his own strengths and abilities. He does not try to reach for the stars and also does not repent over selecting an easier course for his advancement.
7. *Satisfaction of basic needs:* His basic organic, emotional and social needs are fully satisfied or in the process of being satisfied. He does not suffer from emotional cravings and social isolation. He feels reasonably secure and maintains his self-esteem.
8. *Absence of a critical or fault-finding attitude:* He appreciates the goodness in objects, persons or activities. He does not try to look for weaknesses and faults. His observation is scientific rather than critical or punitive. He likes people, admires their good qualities, and wins their affection.
9. *Flexibility in behaviour:* He is not rigid in his attitude or way of life. He can easily accommodate or adapt himself to changed circumstances by making necessary changes in his behaviour.
10. *The capacity to deal with adverse circumstances:* He is not easily overwhelmed by adverse circumstances and has the will and the courage to resist and fight odds. He has an inherent drive to master his environment rather than to passively accept it.

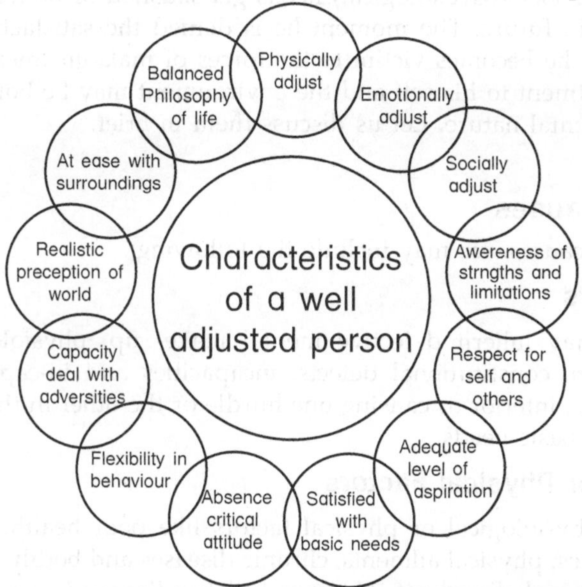


Fig. 5.1: Characteristics of a Well-adjusted Person

11. *A realistic perception of the world:* He holds a realistic vision and is not given to flights of fancy. He always plans, thinks and acts pragmatically.
12. *A feeling of ease with his surroundings:* A well-adjusted individual feels satisfied with his surroundings. He fits in well in his home, family, neighbourhood and other social surroundings. As a student, he likes his school, school-mates, teachers, and feels satisfied with his daily routine. When he enters a profession, he has a love for it and maintains his zeal and enthusiasm despite all odds.
13. *A balanced philosophy of life:* A well-adjusted person has a philosophy which gives direction to his life while keeping in view the demands of changed situations and circumstances. This philosophy is centred round the demands of his society, culture, and his own self so that he does not clash with his environment or with himself.

## MALADJUSTMENT

### Meaning of the Term 'Maladjustment'

Contrary to adjustment, *maladjustment* represents a condition or state in which one feels that one's needs are not (or will not be) fulfilled and he has been a failure in establishing harmony with his self and the environment.

Defined in this way a person suffering from maladjustment may exhibit serious behavioural and adjustment problems causing harm to the well-being of his self and others.

### Causes of Maladjustment

There is much truth in the saying that one remains adjusted as long as his basic (physiological and socio-psychological) needs get satisfied or he has some hope for their satisfaction in future. The moment he is denied the satisfaction of his needs or gets despaired, he becomes victim to the forces of maladjustment. So the causes of one's maladjustment to his self and the environment may be both of personal as well as environmental nature. Let us discuss them in brief.

## A. Personal Causes

In these types of causes, we may include the following:

### Heredity Factors

The individual may inherit defective mental make- up, physiological structure, colour of the skin, constitutional defects, incapacities and in-capabilities making him feel depressed, inferior or causing one hurdle or the other in the way of proper satisfaction of his basic needs.

### Physiological or Physical Factors

In many cases, physiological or physical factors like poor health, lack of vitality, physical deformities, physical ailments, chronic diseases and bodily defects, etc. may drift one towards maladjustment. He may feel handicapped in meeting his basic needs or may develop feelings of inferiority on account of his physical deformities, sub-normalities and in-competencies etc. which may lead to the dissatisfaction to his self and the environment.

### The Causes Inherent in the Nature of the Individual

These causes are quite inherent in the nature and temperament of an individual. The mentionable ones may be as below:

- Unrealistic aims, goals and ideals of life.
- Lack of social maturity and adjustment.
- Lack of emotional maturity and control over the emotions.
- Improper setting of the level of aspiration.
- Unresolved conflicts and contradictory desires.
- Frustrations and desperations.

## B. Environmental Causes

In most of the cases, environmental forces are said to be the greatest or sole contributor in the germination as well as perpetuation of the cases of maladjustment prevailing in our society. The forces of environment begin to play their role right from the conception of the child in the womb of the mother in the form of defective nourishment available to him. From his birth onwards the following types of defective environmental conditions may drift him towards maladjustment.

- Improper behaviour of the parents and elders towards child.
- Uncongenial and defective home environment on account of the factors like frequent quarrelling between the parents, their separation or divorce, loss of one or both the parental figures, unsocial or anti-social behaviour of the members of the family.
- The defective environmental conditions available in one's neighbourhood, community and society which may put hurdles in the proper satisfaction of one's basic needs or may force him to pick bad habits for paving the way of his maladjustment to his self and others.
- The defective and uncongenial environment available in the school in terms of the behaviour of teachers, peers, defective curriculum and methods of teaching, lack of co-curricular activities, too much rigidity or rules, punitive measures, etc.

## Detection of Maladjustment

Maladjustment must always be taken as a red signal as it may lead the individual towards serious behaviour problems, mental illness and diseases. It is always better to have its early detection and find ways and means for its rectification.

The cases of maladjustment among the individuals may be detected by following two types of measures mentioned below:

1. Use of Testing devices like Adjustment Inventory, mental health tests, youth/ child problem inventory etc.

2. Use of Non-testing devices like observation, Interview, rating scale, checklist, etc.

Let us discuss these approaches one by one.

## Use of Testing Devices

The cases of maladjustment can be better diagnosed with the help of suitable Adjustment inventories. Such inventories are available for different age groups and areas of adjustment covering a wide range of people. With the help of their administration to the individual as well as to the group, we can get the scores for being classified as adjusted or maladjusted on one or the other areas of their adjustment. Examples of these adjustment inventory are:

1. H.S. Asthana's Adjustment Inventory. (Available in two forms—Students and Adults)
2. Bell's Adjustment Inventory. (Available in two forms—Students and Adults)
3. Adjustment Inventory developed by A.K.P. Sinha and R.P. Singh.
4. Mangal Teacher Adjustment Inventory (Available in long as well as short forms)

## Use of Non-Testing Devices

The use of non-testing devices for the detection of the cases of maladjustment rests on the principle that the cases of maladjustment may be better detected through the observation of the behaviour of the people in real life situations. For this purpose, one may resort to the techniques of observation, rating scale, interview and check list being used to note down or take care of those behavioural characteristics of the students that may help in labelling them as adjusted or maladjusted. For illustration, we may name the following qualities and characteristics observable in one's behaviour for typically identifying him as a maladjusted personality.

- Lack of self -control
- Sense of inferiority
- Lack of personal security
- Nervousness and anxiety
- Aloofness and withdrawal tendencies
- Cruelty and aggressiveness
- Sarcasm and incessant scolding
- Lack of patience and tolerance
- Lack of the feelings of love, respect and affection
- Use of bizarre methods of striving to be important
- Attention-seeking behaviour
- Demonstrating problematic and anti-social behaviour
- Suffering from mental illness or diseases

## Methods of Adjustment

In order to lead a healthy, happy and satisfying life one has to learn the various ways of adjustment, i.e. coping with one's environment as effectively as possible. Also, he has to safeguard his self against turning into a maladjusted and abnormal personality. How can it be done? What are the different ways of coping with one's environment? How does one handle and face the conflicts, anxieties, pressures and stresses of one's life? To seek answers to these questions the description of possible modes, ways and methods used by the individual in his adjustment process is necessary.

The methods used for keeping and restoring harmony between the individual and his environment can be grouped into two categories, direct methods and indirect methods.

### 1. Direct Methods

Direct methods are those methods which are employed by the individual intentionally at the conscious level. They are rational and logical and help in getting permanent solution of the problem faced by the individual in a particular situation. These methods include the following:

(a) *Increasing trials or improving efforts.* When one finds it difficult to solve a problem or faces obstacles in the path, to cope with his environment he can attempt with a new zeal by increasing his efforts and improving his behavioural process.

(b) *Adopting compromising means.* For maintaining harmony between his self and the environment one may adopt the following compromising postures:

   (i) He may altogether change his direction of efforts by changing the original goals, i.e. an aspirant for I.A.S. may direct his energies to become a probation officer in a nationalized bank.

   (ii) He may seek partial substitution of goal like selection for the provincial civil service in place of the I.A.S.

   (iii) He may satisfy himself by an apparent substitute for the real thing, e.g., in the case of a child, by a toy car in place of a real car and in the case of a young boy desirous of getting married by a doll in his arms.

(c) *Withdrawal and submissiveness.* One may learn to cope with one's environment by just accepting defeat and surrendering oneself to the powerful forces of environment and circumstances.

(d) *Making proper choices and decisions.* A person adapts himself to, and seeks harmony with, his environment by making use of his intelligence for the proper choices and wise decisions particularly when faced with conflicting situations and stressful moments.

### 2. Indirect Methods

Indirect methods are those methods by which a person tries to seek temporary adjustment to protect his self for the time being against a psychological danger. These are purely psychic or mental devices – ways of perceiving situations as he wants to see them and imagining that things would happen according to his wishes. That is why these are called defence or mental mechanisms employed in the process of one's adjustment to one's self and the environment. An individual may be found to make their use in one or the other situations depending upon his needs to do so. We will be discussing about the nature and mechanism of these techniques in detail ahead in the chapter seven of this text.

## Summary

- 'Adjustment' refers to a condition or state in which one feels that one's needs have been (or will be) fulfilled and one's behaviour conforms to the requirements of his society and culture. In fact, what we understand by adaptation in the biological word is known as adjustment in the language of psychology.
- In its practical application, adjustment can be interpreted in both ways-as a process as well as the outcomes of that process in the form of some attainment or achievement.
- A well- adjusted person is supposed to be physically, emotionally and socially adjusted, aware of his own strength and limitations, respecting one' self and the others, keeping an adequate level of aspiration, feeling satisfied in terms of meeting his basic needs, not possessing critical or fault finding attitude, demonstrating flexibility of behaviour, capable of struggling in odd circumstances, realistic perception of the world, feeling at home with his surroundings and possessing adequate philosophy of life.
- The overall adjustment of an individual with his self and environment can be broadly divided into three categories or spheres namely, personal, social and occupational adjustment. Personal adjustment is concerned with an individual's adjustment to his self. Social adjustment is concerned with one's adjustment to his social surroundings and occupational adjustment is concerned with one's adjustment to his world of work and means of livelihood.
- Contrary to adjustment, maladjustment refers to a condition or state in which one feels that one's needs are not (or will not be) fulfilled and he has been a failure in establishing harmony with his self and the environment. Causes of maladjustment may lie both in the person himself (in the form of heredity, physiological factors and natures of the individuals) and his defective and uncongenial environment found in one's home, family, neighbourhood, school, society and his world of work. Since maladjustment pushes a person to a problematic behaviour, its early detection and rectification must be carried out as properly as possible. We can make use of testing devices (such as standardized adjustment inventories) and non-testing devices (like observation, rating scale, interview and check list etc.) for the detection of maladjustment among our children and can then accordingly plan for the adequate adjustment of the sufferers.
- The methods employed for keeping and restoring harmony between the individual and his environment may be described as direct or indirect. Direct methods are used by the individual intentionally at a quite rational and conscious level.

These may include one's efforts to increase the number of trials, improve efforts or adopt comprises by resetting the goal or level of aspiration etc. Indirect methods of achieving adjustment are used at the unconscious level. Their aim is to provide temporary adjustment to the individual by protecting him against the psychological dangers. Various types of mental or defence mechanisms like compensation, rationalization, projection, identification, repression, regression, withdrawal, sympathism, etc. are indirect methods which provide temporary relief from the psychological tension, conflicts and stresses and make one able to seek adjustment for the time being.

## REFERENCES


Adams, H.E., *Psychology of Adjustment*, New York: Ronald, 1972.

Arkoff, Abe, *Adjustment and Mental Health*, New York: McGraw-Hill, 1968, p. 6.

Asthana, H.S., *Manual of Direction and Norms of Adjustment Inventory*, Varanasi: Rupa Psychological Corporation, 1968.

Bell, Hugh M., *The Adjustment Inventory (Adult form) – Manual, Alto*, California Consulting Psychologist Press, 1958.

Carroll, H.A., *Mental Hygiene: The dynamics of adjustment*, N.J.: Prentice-Hall, 1967.

Gates, A.S. and Jersild, A.T., *Educational Psychology*, New York: Macmillan, 1970.

Heston, Joseph, C., *Heston Personal Adjustment Inventory*, Hudson: World Book Company, 1949.

Joshi, M.C. and Pandey, Jagdish, *Adjustment Inventory* (Mimeographed information), New Delhi: NCERT.

Katkowsky, Walter and Leon, Corlow (Eds.), *The psychology of Adjustment*, New York: McGraw -Hill, 1976.

Lazarus, R.S., *Patterns of Adjustment*, Tokyo: McGraw-Hill (3rd ed.), 1976.

Lahner, George, F.J., and Ella Kube, *The Dynamics of Personal Adjustment*, New Jersey: Prentice-Hall, 1964.

Mangal, S.K., *Dimensions of Teacher Adjustment*, Kurukshetra: Vishal Publications, 1985.

Mangal, S.K., *Teacher Adjustment Inventory* (short and long version), Agra: National Psychological Corporation, 1987.

Morgan, C.T., *Introduction to Psychology*, New York: McGraw-Hill, 1961.

Patty, W.L. and Johnson, L.S., *Personality and Adjustment*, New York: McGraw-Hill, 1963.

Ramamurti, P.V., Adjustment Inventory for Aged, *Indian Journal of Psychology*, 1968, Vol. 43, pp. 27–29.

Saxena, M.S.L., *Vyaktitva Parakha Prashnavali, Siksha*, Vol. 23, July, 1962.

Sinha, A.K.P. and Singh, R.P., *Manual for Adjustment Inventory for College Students*, Agra: National Psychological Corporation, 1971.

Shaffer, L.F.'s Article in Boring, Langfield &Weld (Eds.), *Foundations of Psychology*, New York: John Wiley, 1961.

Shaffer, L.F., *The Psychology of Adjustment*, New York: Houghton Mifflin, 1936.

Vonhaller, Geuner, B., *Psychology*, New York: Houghton International, 1970.

Waltin, J.E.W., *Personality, Maladjustment and Mental Hygiene* (3rd ed.), New York: McGraw-Hill, 1951.

White, Robert W., Abnormal Psychology, New York: Ronald Press, 1956.

# 6

# FRUSTRATION, CONFLICTS AND STRESS

## INTRODUCTION

Needs, drives and motives play a decisive role in the motivation of the human behaviour which helps an individual to attain the goal set for the satisfaction of needs or motives. This apparently simple process does not always bring positive or favourable results. Frequently, there are possibilities that the path of attaining the goal is blocked leading to ultimate failure. Repeated failure in attaining the goal further aggravates the situation leading to frustration that may end in the person's maladjustment, abnormality and mental illness.

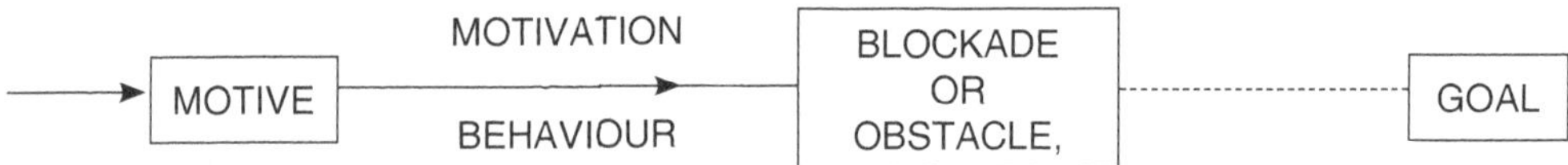


Fig. 6.1 Repeated failures in the attainment of goal may result in frustration leading to abnormality and mental illness.

In addition to such frustration, the behavioural abnormalities and mental illness may also be caused through some other unique states known as conflicts (typical fights going on in between one' needs or motives) and stresses. All these typical mental and psychological states involving frustration, conflicts and stress are quite detrimental to the well-being of the suffering individual. In the present chapter, we would be dealing with them one by one.

### Frustrations – Meaning and Definitions

Man is ambitious by nature. He has so many aspirations and desires to be fulfilled. He plans and strives hard for their realization but it is possible that despite his best planning and efforts, he may not get the desired success. At times he may find himself in the state of utter confusion and bewilderment. All the paths for going ahead seem to be blocked. Such state of affairs, along with the repeated failure in the attempts, puts one into a state or condition that can be termed as frustration. For making the term much clear, let us take the help of some definitions coined by eminent writers.

*Carroll:* A frustration is the condition of being thwarted in the satisfaction of motive (1967,p.33).

Good: Frustration means emotional tension resulting from the blocking of a desire or need (1959).

*Kolesnik:* Frustration is the feeling of being blocked or thwarted in satisfying a need of attaining a goal that individual perceives as significant (1970, p.397).

*Barney and Lehner (1953):* Frustration refers to failure to satisfy a basic need because of either condition in the individual or external obstacles (1953, p.28).

These definitions reveal the following facts about the nature and meaning of the term frustration:

- Frustration is that stage or condition in which failure dominates the attempts.
- In this state one feels a major obstacle in the satisfaction of one's basic needs or in the attainment of one's cherished goal.
- The significance of the goal and strength of the "blockade" increases the degree of frustration.
- The cause of frustration lies both in the individual himself and his environment.

## Causes of Frustrations

The cause of frustration may be divided into two major heads namely (i) External factors, (ii) Internal factors.

## External Factors

External factors are also called *Environmental factors.* These are the situations or conditions which are present in one's own environment. They affect the individual from outside. The main external factors are as follows:

1. **Physical factors:** Natural calamities, obstacles or events in the environment may try to block the path of an individual in the attainment of some important goal or in the satisfaction of one's basic needs and desires. In this way, they become the potential source for frustrating motivated individuals. For example, particular society and community may impose bar on the marriages of school mistresses and this may cause frustration to a young school mistress who is in deep love with a handsome boy and wants to marry him. Similarly, a young man with bright prospects may feel frustrated when he is denied admission to a course simply because he does not fulfil the condition of a bona fide resident.
2. **Social factors:** Social factors also include the part played by other persons in blocking the path of the motivated individuals. A child may feel frustrated when he is denied to go to a movie with his friend or to a dance party or picnic. Similarly, an employee may feel frustrated when he is thrown out instead of meeting his demands for salary hike.

3. **Economic factors:** Economic and financial factors contribute much in frustrating many of the individuals particularly in developing countries like India. Often there are news items that a young man killed himself because he was suffering from depression due to a long spell of unemployment or a mother has killed herself along with her children by jumping into a well due to the utter frustration caused by the continuous denial of the basic need—food. Similarly, men who revolt against the social, political set-up witness the results of frustration suffered due to severe economic deprivation.

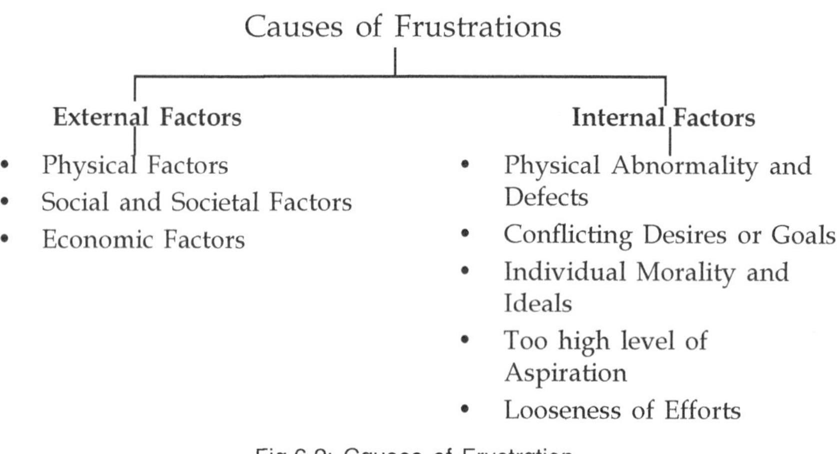


Fig.6.2: Causes of Frustration

## Internal Factors

Internal factors are the factors that frustrate an individual from within. These are also called personal factors as the person himself is the cause of such frustration. The main factors in this category are as follows:

1. **Physical abnormality or defects:** Too small or big stature, very heavy or lean and thin body, an ugly face or dark complexion, some glandular or bodily defects (such as being one-eyed, blind, lame, deaf or dumb) may constitute a source of thwarting and thereby cause frustration. Deficiency in one's intelligence or backwardness in a particular subject may also frustrate an individual who is motivated to learn a particular course or choose a particular vocation.
2. **Conflicting desires or aims:** Frustration is also caused by mutually conflicting desires or aims. Suppose a man wishes to marry a girl to whom he is in love with but also wishes to avoid it as it interferes with his ambition of going to U.K. for higher studies. Now he has to make a choice and a choice of one at the cost of the other may become a cause of frustration to him. A similar frustration may be felt by a young woman who aspires to become a mother but avoids it due to the fear of losing her job or spoiling her career.
3. **Individual's morality and high ideals:** Individual's moral standards, code of ethics and high ideals may become a source of frustration to him. He is always caught between his super-ego and Id. At the time when his ego fails to maintain

a balance between the two, he becomes frustrated. Due to the weight of the moral standards of his conscience, he possesses the unnecessary feeling of guilt or an unusual fear of punishment. For example, he may like to have friendship with some girl but his moral standard does not allow him to do so. Similarly, one may be denied to smoke, to wear broad-based trousers or to see a sex movie only because of his code of ethics or high ideals. The inhibitions and possible conflicts may give birth to emotional tension within him and consequently he may feel frustrated.

4. **Level of aspiration too high:** One may let one's aspiration fly to a very high level in spite of one's in-capabilities or human limitations. For example, a young man may aspire to become the captain of the Indian cricket team in the next year despite the fact that he does not even know how to play cricket. Such aspirations are bound to lead to frustration.
5. **Lack of persistence and sincerity in efforts:** Frustration may be caused by one's own weakness in putting continuous and persistent efforts with all his courage, enthusiasm and will power. For example, suppose one reads a book with no sincere willingness to understand it. After sometime he takes another book and does the same thing with it. He complains that he is not able to grasp anything even after reading so much. This thus gives birth to the feeling of inadequacy that ultimately leads to frustration.

## Reactions to Frustration

Frustration results in various types of reactions according to its intensity and nature of the individual experiencing frustration. Some have frustration tolerance to the extent that they bear the consequences with a little injury to the self or the society; while others (or the former in the special situations) become too violent and aggressive. In this way the reactions to frustration may be classified into two major categories, (i) Simple reactions and (ii) Violent reactions.

## Simple Reactions

Under these, we may include the following four types of reactions:

**Increasing trials or improving efforts.** During the period of frustration, some individuals undergo introspection and to overcome the obstacles they either increase their efforts or bring improvement in their behaviour or procedure.

**Adopt Compromising Means.** Repeated failure in one direction may lead organisms to change the direction of their efforts. For example, an I.A.S. aspirant in case of failure may direct his energy to the Provincial Civil Service examination. A girl's mother failing to marry her daughter to a fair and handsome boy may be contented with a boy of dark complexion.

**Withdrawal.** An individual learns to be away from the situations that cause him frustration. A child withdraws himself from the game he does not know. A young man refuses to marry because of his sexual incompetency due to some physiological deformities.

**Submissiveness.** Here the individual surrenders himself and accepts his defeat before the frustration causing conditions. A child may become extremely submissive after failing in his attempts in certain direction.

## Violent Reactions

In addition to the above- mentioned simple reactions, an individual may become very tense emotionally and resort to aggressive activities. This aggression is of two types—External and Internal.

**External aggression.** "The aggression," as Carroll observes "may be directed towards either the person or persons who caused the frustration or towards a substitute or substitutes." (1967, p. 34). A clerk in his frustration of not getting promotion may quarrel with his officer or resort to rebuking his wife or beating his children. A boy experiencing frustration in the playground may try to knock the boy down who is not giving him a chance to try the ball or may use his younger brother or parents as substitutes for relieving his tension.

**Internal aggression.** It is an aggression that is turned inward towards the self. Instead of releasing one's emotional tensions by attacking others, one resorts to attacking one's self. Instead of blaming others, the individual blames himself. No doubt certain amount of self -criticism does not do any harm but excessive aggression towards the self is sure to destroy the self. Eventually the person becomes a mental patient or tries to escape by committing suicide. Thus, as far as the well-being of the individual is concerned, inward aggression is more dangerous than outward aggression.

## Conflicts – Meaning and Definitions

The term 'conflict' is used in so many ways in our day-to-day setup. There may be conflicts between the two sets of ideologies, cultures, religions and organizations. Conflicts may arise between husband and wife, father and son and teacher and the taught. It may also show its presence among brothers and sisters, members of an organization or community, states of a country and countries of the world at large. Apart from these external or outer conflicts, there are inner or internal conflicts which are called 'psychological conflicts'. In the following text we will discuss such types of conflicts. Let us begin by giving some important definitions.

*Douglas and Holland*: Conflict means a painful emotional state which results from a tension between opposed and contradictory wishes. (1946, p. 216)

*Barney and Lehner:* Psychological conflict is a stage of tension brought by the presence in the individual of two or more opposing desires. (1953, p. 30)

*L.F. Shaffer:* Conflict may be defined as a state of affairs in which two or more incompatible behaviour trends are evoked that cannot be satisfied fully at the same time. (Boring, Langfield and Weld, 1961, p. 523).

These definitions help us to conclude that:

- Conflict is a painful state or condition of an individual.

- One feels intense emotional tension during this state.
- Tension is the result of the presence of two or more desires or wishes in the individual. These desires are contradictory in nature and therefore cannot be satisfied fully at the same time.
- The individual, being at the crossroads and not able to choose between the two opposing desires, becomes tense and restless.
- Thus, becoming a victim of the two opposing desires, he suffers from an inner conflict to do or not to satisfy one or the other desire.

## Types of Conflicts

**Approach-Approach Conflicts:** In such conflicts, an individual is faced with the problem of making a choice between two or more positive goals almost equally motivating and important. For example, a child may have to choose between reading an interesting comic book and going out to play cricket. A young man may experience such a conflict when he has to make choice for his marriage out of the two equally qualified, beautiful and respectable offers. The conflicts of this type are of little danger and temporary in character. After all, when a step is taken towards the realization of one goal, the attraction for the other automatically fades.

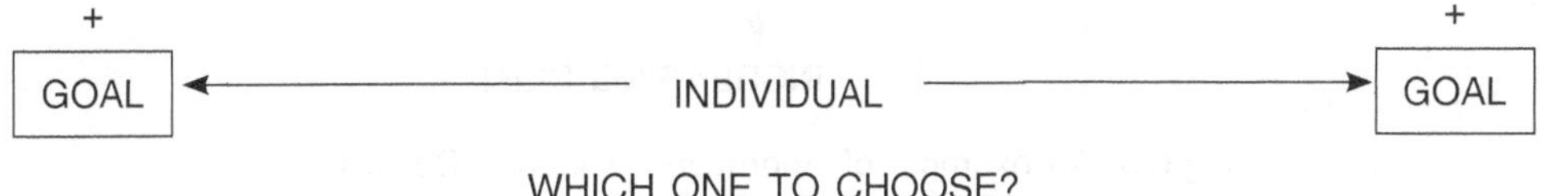


WHICH ONE TO CHOOSE?

Fig. 6.3: An Approach-Approach Conflict

However, there are occasions when one finds great difficulty in making a choice between two positive desires. For example, a young girl may be devoted to her family and all the same desire to have love marriage with a boy of another caste that is not acceptable to her parents.

**Avoidance-Avoidance Conflicts:** In conflicts of this type, an individual is caught in a situation where he must choose between two or more possible negative courses of action.

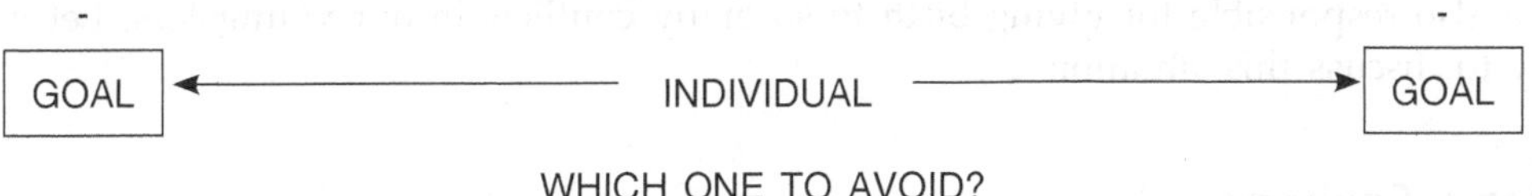


WHICH ONE TO AVOID?

Fig. 6.4: An Avoidance-Avoidance Conflict

For example, a child who does not want to study and at the time does not wish to displease parents by failing in the final examination may experience such conflict. Similarly, a boxer may have to choose between his fear of death or defeat at the hands of his rival or if he does not fight, the loss of respect from his admirers.

It is just like being caught between the devil and deep sea. Because of the threat involved in such a situation, both choices are equally unattractive and hence the natural tendency is to escape from them or to do nothing. In case one is compelled to take a decision, one is likely to suffer the conflict of Avoidance-Avoidance type. Usually conflicts of this type are more serious than the Approach-Approach type conflicts.

**Approach-Avoidance Conflicts:** In such conflicts, one is faced with the problem of choosing between approaching and avoiding tendencies at the same time. An individual may be motivated towards a kind of behaviour activity which he perceives to be wrong, evil and degrading but at the same time the attraction of behaviour is so strong that he becomes restless without doing it.

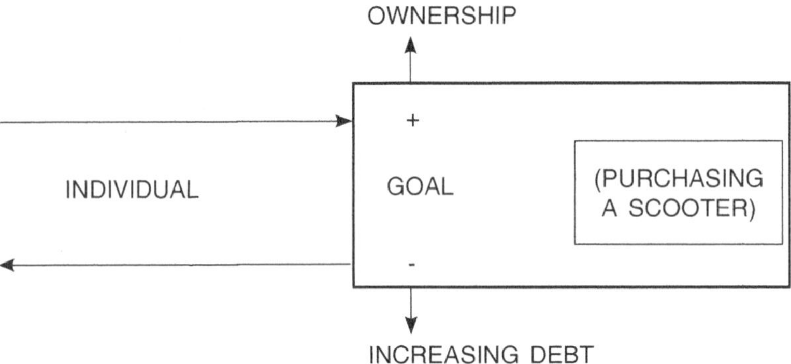


Fig.6.5: An example of Approach-Avoidance Conflict

To masturbate or not to masturbate, to marry or not to marry, to tease the girls or not are some of the situations that may repel and attract an individual simultaneously. Conflicts of this type are distinctly the most severe emotional tension and give birth to so many anxieties and complexes.

## Sources of Conflicts

We have seen that conflicts are the creation of the dissatisfaction felt by an individual due to the non-fulfillment of his two contradictory desires. The forces of the environment are in fact responsible for these conflicts as they provide necessary ground for their occurrence but at the same time we teachers, parents and society are also responsible for giving birth to so many conflicts in our youngsters. Let us try to discuss this situation.

### Home Environment

Faulty upbringing at home and unhealthy or unpleasant relationship among the family members are the potential sources of conflicts in children. A child, due to over protection, dominance, submissiveness or negligence on the part of parents, does not cope with the experiences during social contacts with other children at school and thus he may become a victim of the opposing desires in future.

## School Environment

Uncongenial school environment, dominant or submissive role of the teachers, faulty methods of teaching, denial of opportunities for self -expression, contradictory demands of the teachers and classmates are some of the bases which may give birth to conflicts.

## Social and Cultural Environment

The social environment and cultural value may also prove a potential source of conflicts. Chief among them are the sex conflicts as the demands of our culture have not been well adjusted to the sexual need of the individual. The taboos, inhibitions and the negative attitude towards sex are the cause of so many sex conflicts in the minds of our youths. The pattern of conflicting values existing in our society and culture is responsible for a number of other conflicts. For example, on one hand we give incentive to competitive gains and on the other advocate co-operation and submission. Frustration, suffered due to lack of opportunities in developing countries like India, also give birth to a number of conflicts. Similarly, non-fulfillment of the need for status, many financial worries and dissatisfaction with the working conditions and career fulfilment also prove to be the source of many conflicts.

## Conflicts Resolution

We have seen in the above discussion that sometimes we may come across with some conflicting desires producing vary taxing and complicated situations before us. Here the choice becomes quite difficult for us, which in turn, may give us a lot of anxiety and stress. At this stage, we badly need some measures of conflict resolution broadly summarized in the manner given below.

1. First of all, accept each desire as it arrives without judgement or assistance.
2. Then, remove any barrier or resistance for making your own choice out of the two conflicting desires. This barrier many times is resulted through the heightening of your own emotion. Remove the emotional blockade by adopting relaxation technique like meditation, recreational or play therapy, etc.
3. Now think with a cool mind, the goals of your life, the main purpose you want you want to serve and which one of the two desires is helpful to you in serving your life goals, (not necessarily the immediate or temporary goals), running in tune with your inner voice and may also appear socially as well as morally sound.
4. Then, opt for one of the desires and follow it with your full zeal and enthusiasm, seeking a lot of satisfaction and pleasure in doing and living with it.
5. Initially, you may choose to postpone the task of choice-making. But it should be a quite temporary phase merely for taking time in getting calm and relaxed. However, it is essential to make deliberate attempt for the proper resolution of the conflict You may find that you can do in many of the conflicting situations as exemplified below:

- If one wants to stay seated as a way of maintaining one's comfort but wants to get up as a way of getting a drink, he must search in his own context for potential ways of getting a drink without getting up.
- In case there emerges a conflict for a working teacher between watching a cricket match and setting a question paper on a holiday. The potential for compromise here lies in either limiting the time for viewing the cricket match, i.e. viewing the half game or only the important scene or managing time for both by sacrificing rest and sleep.

6. The key to the resolution between conflicting desires of opposite natures, thus lies in seeking a balanced compromise in one way or the other. However, when the desires are equally attractive or repulsive, then the choice-making may provide a great challenge to the individual concerned. At this stage, he has to analyse the greater amount of benefit received carefully or risk involved in opting one at the cost of other desire. Sometimes, it may necessitate seeking advice from elders, experienced and trusted ones and other times one has to gamble or seek direction from the Almighty. However, once a decision made, it should be followed in its strict sense to save the energy that gets wasted due to indecisiveness and half-hearted follow up.

## Stress – Meaning and Definitions

The term stress is used in a number of ways in our day to day life to represent our internal state of psychological upset or disequilibrium caused by one or the other factors named as stress. As example of such use, we can cite the following.

- Ramesh has been under a lot of stress since he got fired.
- The bank staff experienced acute stress during the ordeal of robbery.
- The people who live in Ladakh and North Kashmir experience considerable stress due to the extreme cold in winter season.
- Stress is known to cause high blood pressure, ulcer and heart attacks.

Taking clues from the above cited uses and meaning of the term stress, Morgan et al. (1986) have tried to define the term stress in the manner given below.

> *We define stress as an internal state which can be caused by physical demands on the body (disease conditions, exercise, extremes of temperature and the like) or by environmental and social situations which are evaluated as potentially harmful, uncontrollable, or exceeding our resources for coping.*

This definition given by Morgan and others makes us to think that there are some internal or external factors that may give birth to particular stressful situations proving harmful to our well-being. The nature and amount of the harm caused to our self, in this case is definitely greater than the usual amount of the wear and tear caused by day-to-day anxieties, worries, struggles, disappointments and failures. The scholar Malott and Whaley (1983) have highlighted this fact in their definition calling stress as *"conditions that cause tissue damage far beyond the daily wear and tear of living"*. It explains the reason why stress is blamed to cause fatal diseases like high blood pressure, ulcer, cancer, and heart attacks.

However, it is also true that stress does not merely results in physiological or bodily damage it also causes a wound in one's psyche resulting in the heavy loss of to one's mental health to the degree that it becomes too uncontrollable and unmanageable on the part of individual by adopting normal course of coping and adjustment.

In this sense we can define stress as *"an internal condition or state of an individual caused by one or the other internal or external factors (termed as stressors) affecting his bodily condition and psyche in a harmful way to the extent that it becomes difficult on the part of the individual to control or manage it by normal course of adaptation or damage control exercises."*

## WHAT ARE STRESSORS?

In its simple meaning, the term stressors stand for all that causes stress to an individual. In technical sense, however, it refers to *"a type of stimulus that occurs in sufficient amount to cause stress"*. (Malott and Whaley, 1983)

This definition provides a special status for the stress inducing situation. Each and every stimulus that causes day-to-day irritations or adjustment problems is not qualified for being named as stressor. In a general way, every one of us is faced many times each day with one or the other minor stress inducing situations. Breakfast or lunch is not served in time, the bus is not available, the supply of electricity or cooking gas is very poor, the Internet connection is not working, etc. such situations are very common to everyone and may cause some or other type of frustration or disappointment resulting on irritation, sadness or annoyance. But all such happenings are very much situational, momentary and manageable. These do not result in the serious setbacks or inflict heavy damage and wounds to one's body and psyche by being uncontrollable or unmanageable on the part of suffering individual. These become stressors only when they occur in such a large scale with greater intensity to cross the limit of one's normal wear and tear capacity inflicting a heavy physiological and psychological damage resulting in agony, pain, displeasure and unhappiness to him and others.

In physical sense, we may equate it to the normal wear and tear caused by the normal traffic on a crossing bridge. However, in case an eighteen -wheel truck or electric train is allowed to move on the bridge, then it may cause stress in a real sense to the bridge by crossing the normal wear and tear capacity of the bridge. Such situation may occur in one's life by facing one or the other hazards and calamities of life like losing a job, money or property, a severe illness or the death of someone close, financial liabilities beyond one's income, marital discord etc.

In his way, stressors, as we must know about them, are those stimuli that cause a serious damage to our body and psyche by crossing our limit to normal wear and tear capacity of the unhappy events in day-to-day life.

### Types of Stressors

Stressors in general may be classified into two broad categories (i) external or environmental, and (ii) internal or psycho-physiological.

## External or Environmental Stressors

Environmental stressors are those environmental stimuli that may be found to cause a heavy stress on the suffering individual. Here the stress inducing stimuli is external i.e. lying outside the individual with in his environment as illustrated below:

- These environmental stressors are found in the maladaptive and uncongenial environmental conditions at one's home, family, neighbourhood, community and work places. The mutual rivalries, fighting, clashes and struggles, improper behaviour and unnecessary bitter criticism, the disappointing and frustrating living or working conditions all may give birth to stress producing events.
- Major changes or transitions in life which compel one to cope in a totally new way may also prove a big source for the stress producing situations. We may include in such sources all the nature-and man-made catastrophes. The occurrence of earthquakes, floods, fire breaking incidence and accidents, death of the near and dear, loss of property and finances, robbery and cheating, terrorist attacks, communal violence, etc. may be said to be the glaring examples of the stress inducing situations in people's life.

## Internal or Psycho-Physiological Stressors

These stressors are found within the individual himself having a particular type of mental setup, ways of behaving and bodily conditions. We may explain them as below:

- Some people are characterized to possess a particular type of behaviour more prone and susceptible to stress than the other people. Fredman and Rosenman (1974) have named them as persons having "Type A" personality. They always remain in a hurry and noted to be very competitive, highly motivated, ambitious, workaholics, easily angered and very time conscious.
- Apart from the above, there also exist persons who have a very week psyche, with damaged self-confidence. They are always anxious, fearful and negative in their thinking. The heaven is always going to fall on them. They invite all types of worries, anxieties, pressures and stresses for the reasons unknown to them.
- Some people by nature, on the other hand, imbibe a very little stress tolerance capacity. A few minor things and decisions in life contrary to their wishes may tear them into pieces. Their capacity of wear and tear is too low and thus, they may be found to feel stressed while facing a quite minor change and adjustment problem in their day-to-day life.
- Physiological factors may contribute in a significant way as a producer and precipitator of the stress conditions. Depending upon the stress bearing capacity, the state of our body characterized with poor health, defective sensory action organ systems, illness and fatal diseases, sleeping disorder, alcoholism and drug addiction may prove a constant source of stress inducing situation to the affected parsons.
- Unhappiness and frustrations caused by one or the other factors may prove a strong psychological base for generating and fuelling the stress inducing situations in the concerned individual.

## Stress Cycle

Stress, as we have discussed, is produced or generated through a unique play or interaction between the factors or things lying within the individual himself and his environment. These factors termed as stressors are thus responsible for the stress one suffers in a particular situation. In case, the induced stressful situation persists for a longer time, then this induced and persisted stress is turned into distress for the suffering individual. This distress then itself begins to work as a source of greater stress for the individual resulting into more distress, unhappiness and sorrow.

In this way, we have a stress cycle involving stress inducing conditions, induced stress, the evil effect of stress resulting into distress, the distress felt then working as a source of greater stress which, in turn, ends in more and more distress to the suffering individual. Diagrammatically, we can represent such stress cycle, in the way depicted in Fig. 6.6.

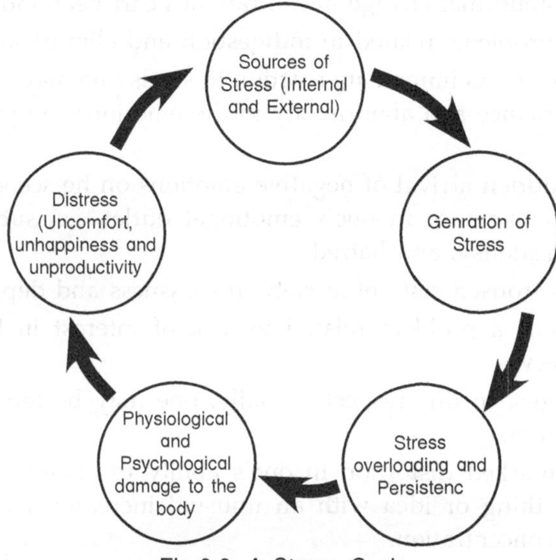


Fig.6.6: A Stress Cycle

## Effects or Outcomes of Stress

Stress when surpasses one's limit of tolerating it (termed as one's stress tolerance capacity) becomes a great harmful factor causing considerable damage to the body and the psyche of the suffering individual. We can here define one's stress tolerance "as the amount of stress one can tolerate before breaking down under the pressure of stress (much in the same way as the load and exhaustion a bridge can tolerate before demonstrating the sign of collapse)." When stress becomes overloading, at first, it results to less severe damage resulting into overall unhappiness, uncomforting, and un-productivity to the suffering individual to the extent of loss of life. We can describe these immediate and long-term effects of the stress on the body and psyche of the individual in the manner given below:

## A. Immediate Effects of Stress

1. **Behavioural changes**: The affected individual shows marked behavioural changes characterized as below:
   - Showing visible signs of nervousness, helplessness, exhaustion, and paralysed thinking.
   - Showing a state of panic reaction, running here and there, or unable to decide and do anything.
   - Developing overeating behaviour.
   - Resorting to smoking and alcoholism.
   - Exhibiting restlessness and sleeping disorder problem.
2. **Physiological changes**: In this respect, he related symptoms may be as under:
   - Level of muscular tension is increased.
   - There is an abnormal change in the rate of heart beat and blood pressure.
   - There arise problems related to indigestion and elimination.
3. **Emotional changes**: As immediate reaction to stress one may experience a lot of emotional disturbance and abnormality in the emotional output in the manner given below:
   - There is a sudden arrival of negative emotions on he scene in an abnormal and excessive amount in one's emotional outlet, i.e. sudden outburst of anger, fear, jealousy, and hatred.
   - Showing an aroused state of anxiety, restlessness and depression.
   - There happens a problem related to lack of interest in love-making and social intimacy.
4. **Cognitive changes:** In this respect, initially, one may be found to exhibit the following symptom:
   - Showing a marked distortion in one's ability to attend or concentrate on a particular thing or idea with an unusual increase in distractibility and decrease in concentration.

## B. Long-term Effects of Stress

In case if the stress inducing conditions persist for a longer time, it may lead to the worsening of the condition of the individual in the manner given below:

1. **Behavioural changes:** The affected person becomes victim of serious behavioural disorders e.g. forgetfulness, obesity, alcoholism, drug addiction, etc.
2. **Physiological changes**: The affected person becomes victim of serious physiological disorders, ailments and diseases on account of notable decrease in his immune system. In its evil effects, one's stress makes one more susceptible to infectious agents by temporarily suppressing his immune system. As a result, an individual may be seen to catch cold soon after a period of stress (such as final examination). When persisted long, the stress reactions may result in making the affected person a known victim of high blood pressure, migraine, hypertension, heart disease, skin diseases and even ulcer.

3. **Emotional changes:** The affected individual becomes victim of serious emotional disorders such as chronic anxiety and depression, fears and phobias, personality changes and mental illness.
4. **Cognitive changes**: the affected person becomes victim of serious cognitive disorders such as memory problems, obsessive thoughts and sleep disorders.

In this way, the resultant effects and outcomes of stress are quite serious and unpleasant for the well-being of the affected person. There remains no joy and happiness to him in his life. He becomes quite cut-off from the social interaction and productivity in his work output. Gradually, his life becomes miserable to him and a matter of burden to others eventually pushing him to his untimely death.

## Adaptation to Stress

The individual after receiving alarming signals about the impact of stress tries to resist the negative effects of the stress inducing situations by resorting to the mechanism of adaptation or adjustment in the manner outlined below:

### Biological Adaptation

The body adopts the required resistance by mobilizing its reserves to deal more effectively with the stressors, visible in the form of changes in the nervous and endocrine systems like increased muscles tonus, pumping of stored sugar into the blood stream, changes in breathing, perspiration and secretion of glands.

### Psychological Adaptation

In addition to biological adaptation, a mechanism of psychological adaptation is also employed by the person concerned in dealing with the situations resulted through the stress inducing factors. Such adaptations, as Colman (1970) observes, may be classified as (i) Task- oriented adaptations and (ii) Ego defence-oriented adaptations.

1. **The task-oriented adaptations:** In this type of adaptations to stress situation, one feels confident to handle it by bringing changes in oneself or one's environment or both, whatever the situation warrants. The adapted behaviour, here then, may take the following forms:
   - Attacking behaviour
   - Withdrawal behaviour
   - Compromising behaviour

Let us illustrate the mechanism of the task-oriented adaptations through its various forms with the help of a particular instance where a female child becomes victim of severe stress on account of feeling rejected and improperly treated in comparison to her brother. In this case, she may resort to one of the following types of adaptation mechanism.

(i) She may build up a high level of hostility being discharged in delinquent behaviour.

(ii) She may simply resort to withdrawal rather than attack the source of frustration. Consequently, she will be limited to herself by being an introvert and passive.

(iii) She may compromise with the situations by thinking that she is girl and has to adjust in a male-dominated society, where the sons are likely to get more affection, attention and protection and therefore, she need not to be perturbed.

2. **Ego defence-oriented adaptations**: Such type of adaptation comes into picture where one gets stressed by feeling a threat to one's integrity or phenomenon self. Here, the stressed individual often resorts to ego defence mechanisms involving attack, withdrawal or compromising stand. As a result, the person may defend himself by attacking and blaming others for his mistakes and failures. He may escape from the painful truth by denying it or pushing it to his unconscious or he may bargain compromise by admitting it in his consciousness in such a distorted way that it no longer hurts.

## Coping with Stress

The well -being of a person facing stressful situation properly lies in his ability of coping with such stress. The question here may arise what we mean by the term coping used as an encountering strategy to reduce and eliminate the effect of stress.

## What is Coping?

Lazarus and Folkman (1984) define coping as "*Constantly changing cognitive and behavioural efforts to manage external and / or internal demands that are appraised as taxing or exceeding the resources of the person*". We may clearly note that the latter portion of the stated definition reads as "external and/or internal demands that are appraised as taxing or exceeding the resources of the person" is nothing but an expression used for describing one's internal state of stress. In consequence, thus, coping is nothing but the sincere efforts made by an individual to manage or control the stress, he faces, in a given situation.

## General Coping Measures or Strategies

In managing or controlling the situations through the stress experienced by an individual the adoption mechanism (biological as well as psychological) already emphasized in this very chapter may serve a quite useful purpose. To say or suggest more in this connection, we may think to classify the needed coping strategies for meeting the stressful situations in the categories mentioned below (Cohen and Lazarus,1979).

1. **Direct action response**: The individual tries to change or manipulate his/her relationship indirectly to the stressful situation, such as escaping from/removing it.
2. **Information seeking**: The individual tries to understand the situation better and to predict future events that are related to the stressor.
3. **Inhibition of action:** Doing nothing. This may be the best course of action if the situation is seen as short term.

4. **Intra-psychic or palliative coping:** The individual reappraises the situation (for example through the use of psychological defence mechanisms) or changes the internal environment (through drugs, alcohol, relaxation or meditation).
5. **Turning to others:** One can turn to others for help and emotional support.

## Formal Coping Strategies or Techniques

Up to so far in this text, what we have discussed in the name of the adoption and coping measures represent those generalized ways and means that are employed by the affected persons in a quite spontaneous and informal way for dealing with their stress inducing situations. However, for dealing more effectively with the stress, the affected persons usually need some well-organized formal management strategies for coping with their stress. These techniques used singly or in combination (with special reference to manage stress) may be outlined as below:

1. **Information providing techniques:** Here attempts are made to provide appropriate information to the individuals about the nature of the problem causing stress. How far they are able to find the solution of their problem or in what ways, they should strive to overcome or reduce it, the required information in this concern may be properly given by the persons who are knowledgeable and experts in this field.
2. **Biofeedback techniques**: In employing such techniques, the person concerned is given appropriate medicines or treated through needed devices for providing them relief from the pain or stress inducing situations. In this way, the focus of the used techniques here purely lies in treating the symptoms of stress rather than the stressor itself.
3. **Relaxation techniques:** In these techniques of managing stress, one can make use of the technique of progressive relaxation. The technique involves alternately tensing and relaxing various muscle groups while attending closely to the sensations the person concerned is feeling when his muscles are tensed versus when they are relaxed. In this way, the person is made to learn to become sensitive to the relaxed state of tension. The methods utilized for such progressive relaxation are varied in their nature and level of difficulty such as laughing or breathing deep exercises to meditation or hypnosis. The intention of such interventions is to replace the anxious response with a response that is incompatible with anxiety.
4. **Cognitive restructuring techniques:** These techniques employ a number of specific methods (based on cognitive behaviour therapy) for the purpose of bringing desired changes in an individual's negative and pessimistic thinking or ways of responding. The main assumption lying with these techniques is the view that stress suffered by an individual is often caused by the erroneous negative thinking and "self-talks" and therefore, a suitable change needs to be brought out in one's thinking and way of interacting with the self. One must keep himself occupied with positive thinking and provide constructive and positive suggestion to his self for his welfare and improvement. As a result, a cognitive restructuring training is always focused on replacing one's negative thinking

and harmful self-talks with positive thinking and constructive internal dialogues aimed to bring desired changes in his emotional responses and behaviour.

5. **Systematic desensitization techniques**: The technique is based on the assumption that a stressful situation is caused on account of oversensitivity of an individual towards a thing or practice. If we resort to its systematic desensitization, then a thing or practice may cease to function as a source of stress for the individual concerned. Morgan et al. (1986) have illustrated the use of this technique with an example involving a young woman having intense fear of or phobia of hypodermic syringes and needles. The procedure and steps involved are summarized here as below:
   - She was taught to relax during the therapy session.
   - She was made to form a variety of images of the feared objects or situations ranked from strong to weak in terms of the amount of fear they produce. (Here in this case the therapist used real syringes and needles arranging their presentation in such a sequence that the first stimuli produced no fear and the latter stimuli produced more and more fear.)
   - Having learnt to relax in the presence of a weak stimulus the next stronger stimulus in the series was presented to her until she learnt to relax when this one was present.
   - This process continued until she could touch herself with a needle and remain relaxed.
6. **Modelling technique**: The practice to employ this stress management technique has been stemmed from the work of Bandura (1969). In his social learning theory, he has demonstrated the use and impact of modelling in learning or acquiring some or the other behaviour by observing and imitating the behaviour of a model. Accordingly, in applying this technique, the individual suffering from the stress-related problem is exposed to a model (for example on a video or film) who is coping successfully with the same stress related problem. How this is model is coping with stress, can now be learnt and practiced by the suffering individual for doing away with his stressful problem.

## Summary

- **Frustration** refers to a condition or stage reached on account of repeated failure or blockage experienced by an individual in the attainment of his basic needs or realization of an important goal. The causes of frustration may be external (like physical, social or economic factors) or internal (like one's physical abnormality or defects, conflicting desires, his morality and high ideals, unrealistic level of aspiration or lack of persistence and sincerity in efforts etc.).
- Under frustration people may react differently depending upon their own nature as well as the intensity of the frustrating experiences. They may react violently with varying intensity by resorting to aggression towards their self or the things and persons, whom they consider responsible for their frustration. Instead of it, they may also demonstrate adjustable reactions like increasing trials or improving

their efforts, adopting compromising means, surrendering and accepting their defeat or withdrawing them from the frustration giving situations.

- **Conflict** refers to a painful condition or emotionally tense state of an individual reached on account of the presence of the two equally opposed and contradictory wishes at the same time. Generally, the conflicts faced by us in our life may be of the types like Approach-approach conflicts (making choice between two or more equally attractive goals), Avoidance-avoidance conflicts (choosing between two or more possible negative course of action) and Approach-avoidance conflicts (choosing between approaching and avoiding tendencies at the same time). As a causative factor of the arousal of conflicts one's defective environment loaded with its contradictory demands may prove a potent source for the germination as well as perpetuating such conflicting situations. For seeking proper adjustment level of mental health resolution of the conflicts in a proper way is badly needed. The key to the resolution between conflicting desires of opposite nature lies well in seeking a balanced compromise in one way or the other.
- **Stress** may be defined as an internal condition or state of an individual coupled with the stressors (stimuli occurring an in sufficient amount to cause stress) affecting his bodily conditions and psyche in a quite harmful way. Stressors may be classified into two broad categories-external or environmental (such as maladaptive and uncongenial environmental conditions at home, family, social and work situations) and internal or psycho-physiological (such as mental set up, ways of behaving and bodily conditions of the individual).
- Effects or outcomes of the stress may be described as immediate and long -term effects. Both these effects are visible through behavioural, physiological, emotional and cognitive changes brought out in the stressed person. The process of coping with stress resulting in reducing or eliminating the effects of stress may be carried out through (i) adoption mechanism (biological as well as psychological) and (ii) utilizing the formal coping strategies or techniques like information processing, biofeedback, relaxation, cognitive restructuring, systematic desensitization and modelling techniques.

## REFERENCES

Bandura, A., *Principles of Behaviour Modification*, New York: Holt Rinehart &Winston, 1969.

Bandura, A. & Walters, R.H., *Social Learning and Personality Development*, New York: Holt. 1963.

Barney, Katz and Lehner, G.F., *Mental Hygiene in Modern Living*, New York: The Ronald Press Company, 1953.

Carrol, H.A., *Mental Hygiene – The Dynamics of Adjustment*, Prentice-Hall, New Jersey, 1967.

Cohen, F. and Lazarus, R.S., "Coping with the Stress of Illness", In Stone, C.G., Cohen, F. Adler, N.E. (Eds.), *Health Psychology*, A Hand Book, San Francisco, CA: Jessy-Brass, 1979.

Coleman, James C., *Abnormal Psychology and Modern Life* (3rd Indian ed.), Bombay: Tarapore Wala & Sons, 1970.

Davison, Gerald C. and Naele, John, M., *Abnormal Psychology*, 2nd ed., John Wiley, New York, 1978.

Douglas, O.B. and Holland, B.F., *Fundamentals of Educational Psychology*, New York: The Macmillan Co., 1947.

Fredman, M. and Rosenman, R., *Type A Behaviour and Your Heart,* New York: Knopf, 1974.

Good, Carter, V., *Dictionary of Education*, McGraw-Hill, New York, 1959.

Lazarus, R.S., *Psychological Stress and the Coping Process,* New York: McGraw-Hill, 1961.

Lazarus, R.S. and Folkman, S., *Stress Appraisal and Coping,* New York: Springer, 1984.

Malot, R.W. and Whaley, D.L., *Psychology,* Holmes Beach, F. L. : Learning Publications, 1983.

Messer, David & Meldrum, Claire (Eds.), *Psychology for Nurses and Health Care Professionals*, London: Prentice-Hall, 1955.

Morgan, C.T., *Introduction to Psychology,* 2nd ed., McGraw-Hill, New York, 1961.

Morgan, C.T., King, R.A. Weise, J.R. and Schopler, John, *Introduction to Psychology,* (7th ed.), New Delhi: Tata McGraw-Hill, 1986.

Selye, H., *The Stress of Life,* New York: McGraw-Hill, 1956.

Shaffer, L.F., *L.S. Shaffer's Article in Foundations of Psychology* (Ed.), Boring, Langfield and Weld, John Wiley, New York, 1961.

Shaffer, L.F., *The Psychology of Adjustment,* Houghton Mifflin, New York, 1936.

Thomas, K.W., "Conflict and Conflict Management", *Journal of Organizational Behaviour,* 13 (3), pp.265-274, 1992.

Vonhaller, Gilmer, B., *Psychology,* (International Edition), New York: Harper, 1970.

Waltin, J.E.W., *Personality Maladjustment and Mental Hygiene,* (3rd ed.), 1951.

Yarn, D.H., Dictionary of Conflict Resolution, San Francisco: Jossey- Bass Publications, 1999.

# 7

# DEFENCE OR MENTAL MECHANISMS

## What are Defence or Mental Mechanisms?

In our life, we have so many aspirations and ambitions but it is not possible to achieve all that we desire. There are many situations when we fail in our attempts and get frustrated. Our failures and frustrations may bring injury to our ego and give birth to the feelings of inferiority and anxiety. Most of us do not like to face the reality by accepting our shortcomings and failures but tend to resort to certain mechanisms for defending our inadequacies or anxieties. These mechanisms or devices are called defence mechanisms or mental mechanisms.

To understand this term more clearly, let us have a look at some of the popular definitions:

*Page:* When psychological equilibrium is threatened by severe emotional traumas, frustrations, or conflicts, the mind resorts to a variety of protective subterfuges and debtors called mental mechanisms or dynamisms. (1976, p. 39)

*Carroll:* An adjustment mechanism is a device resorted to in order to achieve an indirect satisfaction of a need so that tension will be reduced and self-respect maintained. (1967, p. 53)

*Arkoff:* Certain patterns of behaviour that are employed for protection against threat or anxiety are called defence mechanisms or adjustment mechanisms. Sometimes they are referred to as 'ego defence mechanisms' since they serve to defend the ego or the self from threat. (1968, p. 138)

*McCall:* Defence mechanisms may be defined as 'self-protective manoeuvres' pertaining to perception and motivation, mental or psychic, yet largely unconscious designed to soften or disguise what is unacceptable in or to the self (1976, p.271).

*Davison and Neale:* A defence mechanism is a strategy, unconsciously utilised, that serves to protect the ego from anxiety (1978).

On the basis of these definitions, we can draw the following conclusions about the nature and characteristics of defence mechanisms:

1. Defence mechanisms are devices in the form of a certain pattern of behaviour.
2. These mechanisms provide protection against whatever threatens our ego or self-esteem.

3. There are many situations in our environment and also within our self that threaten our psychological equilibrium. As a result, we fall victim to anxiety, frustration, conflicts or other psychological upsets. Defence mechanisms help us defend ourselves from possible injury in such delicate moments.
4. Unfulfilled desire, need or motive may bring a state of tension leading to possible injury to one's self-respect. The way out is provided by the defence mechanism in the form of indirect satisfaction of that need.
5. Defence mechanisms may be evolved by anything in conflict with our minimum ideal of what the self must be.
6. Defence mechanisms are quite temporary defence against anxiety and inadequacies. By resorting to them, one tries to deceive himself more than anybody else.
7. Since frustrations or conflicts are experienced by everyone and since everyone is compelled to maintain ego or self-respect, it follows that the defence mechanisms are used by all of us whether normal or abnormal at one time or the other.
8. Defence mechanisms are largely unconscious. They tend to operate in a machine-like or automatic way. In fact, they are always in corresponding degree, self-deceptive and thus aim at softening or disguising what is unacceptable to us in terms of our failure or inadequacies.
9. Defence mechanisms should not be confused with symptoms of neuroses or other abnormal conditions. These mechanisms are purely psychic or mental devices or ways of perceiving and desiring. Here, the individual is helped to perceive or have a matching wish to make him free of threats to his self-regard.
10. The persons employing defence mechanisms can't be labelled as abnormal or mentally deficient. In fact, a person usually resorts to such mechanisms simply for saving himself (may be temporarily) from the danger of falling in the clutches of mental illness or maladjustment with one's self or the environment.
11. The excessive use or dependence upon the mental mechanisms may lead to one or the other type of abnormalities in one's behaviour causing serious disturbances in his physiological as well as psychological functioning.

## Important Defence Mechanisms

### Rationalization

It is a defence mechanism in which a person tries to justify his otherwise unacceptable social behaviour or act by giving socially acceptable reasons for it and thus attempts to deceive others and himself by inventing good reasons to justify his conduct. Thinking on these lines a rationalizer will view and explain his idleness as "needed relaxation", his cowardice as "caution", his severe and arbitrary discipline policies "for child's own good". A child makes use of rationalization when he tries to offer lame excuses for his failure. He may blame unfairness or ambiguity of the questions, teacher or parents or his poor health and ailments and thus try to disguise his own weakness and deficiency.

The use of rationalization is almost universal. We all, at one time or the other, interpret our behaviour in an acceptable or reasonable way in order to prevent a threat to our sense of well-being and thus try to maintain or even enhance our image. We often offer the noblest of reasons for behaviour that is actually motivated by selfish desires. The game of rationalization is well played by statesmen or nations. In announcing a specific programme a government may assert that it is for the social good of all, when actually its objective stands for bringing more power to it.

The mechanism or rationalization may be well-illustrated by considering two special types of attitudes known as sour-grapes and sweet-lemon attitudes.

In sour-grapes mechanism, based on the fable of the fox and the grapes, an individual, unable to obtain what he wants, tries to avoid the bitterness of disappointment by maintaining that he did not want it any way. The young man who fails to get the job saves face and self-respect by declaring that he did not really want the job. A boy failing to win a place in his school cricket team maintains that he actually did not want to waste his time in playing cricket. Similarly, a young man rejected by his fiancée may maintain that he did not actually want to marry her as she did not meet his standards. All such justifications, explanations and excuses help the individuals in getting relief from the tension or frustration by playing down the good points and stressing on the unpalatable ones.

In sweet-lemon type reaction, the individual maintains that whatever happens is for the best or whatever he has obtained is the best he could obtain. A senior lecturer is denied promotion to the post of principal which in fact is a severe blow to him, but he adjusts to this frustration by saying that he is much happy in his present post where he enjoys comparatively more security of services and also gets to devote more time for the welfare of his family and writing. Similarly, a handicapped boy may rationalize by thinking of his broken leg as a blessing in disguise as it provides him an opportunity to catch up on his studies.

## Projection

A person may have inferior impulses, traits or motives that can involve him in a threatening situation. For his defence, he may now resort to the mechanism of projection by attributing to or observing the unacceptable motives in other persons. Arkoff points out "*Used as defence, projection implies that a person has certain thoughts or feelings or actions which are threatening to him which he then denies are his and instead attributes to others.*" (1968, p. 156)

When a person with some shortcomings observes and criticizes the failings of others, he may be said to make use of projection as defence. Similarly, a student who has been caught cheating in the examination may defend himself by saying that others have also cheated. A person with an unacceptable sexual urge may try to accuse his wife for her 'flirtations' and the wife may be considerably worried about the adultery of her husband. A boy who is tempted to be homosexual may accuse others of making indecent advances.

It is not necessary that the objects of one's projection must always be persons. Animals, natural and supernatural forces or even inanimate objects may serve as well. A student may blame his fortune for his failure. A badminton player may attribute his failure to his racket. The boy after falling from a chair may kick the chair for being responsible for his fall.

Thus, in projection what is desirable or unacceptable is neither explained (as in rationalization) nor counter-acted (as in reaction formation) or made up for (as in compensation), but one gets rid of it by projecting it (attributing or observing in) on others.

One gets satisfaction by projecting the undesirable or unacceptable on others and it may be explained through the following benefits derived:

One can get rid of the undesirable or unacceptable by denying ("I don't have such undesirable dirty thoughts.")

## Reaction-Formation

While rationalization is a kind of "refutation by argument or explanation" of implied inadequacy or unworthiness, reaction-formation is a "refutation by action". Here one strives to behave in ways that are sharply in contrast with the ways that he tends to behave for protecting his self-esteem. By utilizing reaction-formation as defence, one tries to inhibit, mark or overcome certain impulses that threaten one's self or general welfare by emphasizing the opposite or contradictory ones. A mother may hate her child, but by using reaction formation as defence she may be able to inhibit, mark or overcome unworthy impulses and thus turn into an attentive, solicitous and over protective in her behaviour towards him. A person who is strongly motivated by undesirable sex needs may react by being extremely puritanical, avoiding almost all association with the opposite sex and even criticizing others for their sexual activities. In this way, he may strive to feel, think and act in ways contradictory to his own real wishes and motives. Similarly, reaction-formation towards selfish tendencies may be manifested in extreme generosity.

Thus, by resorting to reaction-formation as defence, an individual, in spite of suspected meanness, may behave very nobly such that no one may possibly doubt the purity of his motives. It may be added that his self- reaction formation is not, however, to be confused with hypocritical pretence. The individual casually resorts to such mechanism rather than in full awareness and there is usually little doubt of the sincerity of his desire and care for the protection of his self-esteem which compels him to resort to reaction formation instead of facing the things as they are or behaving as he tends to behave.

## Repression

The automatic inhibition of a threatening impulse is called *repression*. It is an unconscious forgetting or blocking from consciousness of internal impulses, feelings or thought which are unacceptable to the conscious self. In this way, repression as a defence mechanism is that mechanism in which the threatening or anxiety producing experiences, conflicts and unfulfilled wishes are pushed down into one's consciousness and, as a result, one tries to forget the things that might be painful or threatening to one's self.

Forgetting one's date of marriage or appointment with a friend may be associated with such repression. A person who has painful experiences attached to his school or teacher may not be able to recall even the name of the school or the teacher. In another situation, a girl who has repressed the painful memories of her first love affair may not be able to write a love letter to her husband.

Therefore, repression serves by providing relief, though temporarily, from the tension or anxiety by making one believe that the tension producing situation does not exist. It saves us from distressing thoughts, feelings, and from engaging in certain actions which might prove dangerous or painful. It helps us to hide our thoughts and feelings and actions from ourselves just as we sometimes more consciously attempt to conceal certain things from others. However, in certain cases, repression as a defence may prove detrimental in the long run. What has been repressed may prove more dangerous and threatening at a later stage. Commenting on this possibility, Carroll writes *"Repressed desires, fantasies, and experiences constitute a burden sometimes light, sometimes heavy, which each human being carries. For some the burden becomes too heavy and responses are made to the strain which may be neurotic or psychotic. Such persons need professional help."* (1967, p. 75)

## Regression

*Regression* means going backward or returning to the past. It is, in a way, a retreat for an individual from the complexities of the present to an earlier and simpler form of behaviour or a more fortunate and pleasant period of one's life. Thus, used a defence, *regression may be defined as a mechanism by which an individual, longing for the earlier, happier period of life, begins to behave in a manner more appropriate to his earlier age or period of life for protecting himself from the threatening situations involving frustration, conflict, anxiety or tension.*

A man failing in his love affair resorts to regression when he exhibits his love for a doll. An older boy may regress when his new brother is born and he feels neglected or deprived. Although he has been walking for several years, suddenly he may insist that he is unable to do, that he is too small and must be carried. He may even abandon the toilet habits and insist on breast feeding. An adult earning member of the family may also show signs of regression when, after a hard day, he wants to be nurtured, pampered and otherwise cared for at home. A young woman may be said to resort to the regression mechanism when she returns to her parent's home after finding it impossible to meet the demands of her marriage and the new environment.

A person who resorts to the mechanism of regression is introvert, timid and lacks self-confidence. He feels secure only in old and tried situations and strives to avoid new experiences. He avoids adventure and is fearful of the future, turns around and retreats to the world of his past.

The extreme cases of regressive behaviour tend to develop into a disorganized personality where the individual may retreat to very early patterns of behaviour so successfully that he loses touch with reality and believes as well as behaves like a child or an infant.

## Aggression

Expression or demonstration of one's angry behaviour through verbal dialogue or physical assault or both may be termed as *aggression*. Some of us may try to adopt such type of expression as defence mechanism. Such over assertiveness may help one deal effectively with other persons, situations and problems etc. Others may get influenced or become fearful of his aggressive behaviour and thus may fall in line with him or they may avoid unnecessary dialogues or conflicts leading to spoiled relationship or bitterness with him. Reinforced by such impact of his aggressive behaviour, one may then be tempted to adopt it as an important component of one's behaviour. However, it is not essential that his resorting to such mechanism may always prove a boon to him. It has an equal chance of going otherwise. If the situation is a trying one or the rival personality is a tough guy, his aggressiveness may cost him dear.

The question arises as to from where do we pick or learn such aggressiveness. The reason lies well in our environmental surroundings where an individual from the very beginning of his life encounters or perceives the aggressive behaviour of his elders in the real life of screen. Knowingly or unknowingly, this type of aggressiveness is then transferred in one's behaviour by way of imitation and this becomes his style of coping with the environmental situations. This picked up style of ours may often get due reinforcement when we get desired success through our aggressive behaviour and consequently we may adopt it as a way of behaving with others.

As a defence mechanism, our aggressiveness may provide us temporary defence against our repressed wishes, mounted tensions and pressures, conflicting desires and frustrations etc. Our sudden outburst of foul and aggressive language or fighting may provide us a certain type of relief from the mounted pressure built up in our psyche, but the ultimate consequences are always negative and painful both to the individual as well as others who are subjected to such aggressiveness. In this way, it is always wise to give up aggression for being better adjusted to one's self and others.

## Displacement

It refers to the process of displacing or shifting of thought, feeling or action from one person or situation to another. When an individual is unable to react, or express his emotion or impulse in a particular situation, he may resort to displacement mechanism for relieving himself of the anxiety or frustration by its transfer or displacement to another situation or object—neutral, vulnerable, or less dangerous than the original. For example:

- A youngster rebuked by the mother, being unable to attack or react directly, may trample her flower-bed.
- A little boy, beaten by one of his schoolmates, may kick or slap his younger brother on returning home.
- A clerk, being ill-treated by his boss, may displace his anger towards the peon or his wife or children.

- A child who fears his father or teacher may displace his fear to animals.
- An inherent fear of committing suicide may be transferred to a fear of knives and other sharp instruments.
- A boy who is unable to get attention from his father may turn his attention to a teacher or some other adult male.

In this manner, displacement is a kind or substitution of one outlet for another, and works as a safety valve for the pent -up emotions and impulses which otherwise may prove harmful to the self and the society.

## Fantasy and Daydreaming

Fantasy or daydreaming is a kind of withdrawal of one's self in a private and satisfying world of imagination. Thus, instead of facing the realities he may become satisfied with unreal, imaginary success or satisfaction that he gets in wandering in the make-believe world of imagination. Commenting on the use of the mechanism, Arkoff writes:

"*As a defence, our fantasy life provides us with an escape from the dangers, threats, and problems of the real world. In our fantasies we can meet our unmet needs and reach our un-reached goals. We can picture ourselves as a different sort of person and the world as a different sort of world.*" (1968, p. 162)

An individual may turn to daydreaming or fantasy when the present he is living in is uninteresting and frustrating. Fantasy permits him to escape to a dream world where exciting things occur and he is able to achieve whatever he desires.

In general, there are three common types of daydreaming or fantasies – roaming in the past, conquering hero, and suffering hero or martyr type.

- In the roaming type, an individual, while considering the present as bitter and painful, tries to roam in his happy past. In such fantasies, an elderly person may relieve the happy experiences of his past, sometimes making them even more pleasant than they really were.
- In the conquering hero type, the individual imagines that he is the master of some situation. He says and does all that he failed to say and do during the actual experiences. He is the managing director of a factory, a great player of hockey, a gold medal winner in the convocation or a great cine actor. He is applauded, acclaimed and sought after. In such daydreaming a young man who fails to get married may imagine about the love affair, marriage and the affection to be shared with a beautiful girl who was once seen by him in a marriage party. Similarly, a single woman may dream that she is married, has a good husband, beautiful children and a decent home.
- In the suffering hero or martyr type of daydreams, the individual imagines himself to be the victim of some situation. It is resorted to by the individual who pities himself. As a result, a child who feels that he gets maltreatment at home may imagine himself as seriously ill or even dead. Similarly, an adult may see him undergoing great hardships or miseries and thus gets satisfaction by imaging himself a martyr or the victim of the circumstances. The suffering

hero type of daydreaming is a form of aggression turned inward and therefore may prove more dangerous than the conquering hero type.

Daydreaming or fantasy may prove detrimental when it becomes a substitute for the real world and the actual efforts for achievements. Not only does it lead to the wastage of precious time and energy but also paves the way for maladaptive behaviour and disorganization of the personality.

## Sublimation

You may have used the term 'sublimation' in your chemistry textbook as a process of purifying the solids and gases through desired heating and evaporation. That is why, it is also named as purification. In psychology, we use this term as a way or means of purifying or modifying our undesirable or unsocial desires and feelings. In this way, as a means of purification, sublimation may be considered as a special type of mental or adjustment mechanism which helps in the re-channelling or redirection of our repressed and undesirable wishes, impulses, drives, emotions or actions in some socially acceptable form and thus saving us from the mental agony and other troublesome physical consequences. As a result of the adoption of sublimation as an adjustment mechanism, one may be successful in channelling or redirecting one's so-called undesirable behaviour involving the emotion of love and lust towards love for humanity or God.

We have example of Tulsidas, the author of great epic *Ramayana* before us who successfully redirected his love or lust towards *Rama* the God after getting rebuked by his wife Ratnavali for his undesirable lust. In our day-to-day life also, we may have enough examples to demonstrate the role of sublimation. By adopting this mechanism, a woman who is experiencing trouble playing the roles of wife and mother may direct her energies to social or professional activities, a student quite brave but aggressive in behaviour may turn into a good player, boxer, wrestler, saviour of the weak, and martyrs. By re-directing and channelling his tremendous energies and strong will power, a young man may be found to write beautiful poems and sketch beautiful portraits and in this way, may discharge or sublimate some part of the strong sexual desire he was unable to discharge directly to his beloved.

## Four Additional Defence Mechanisms

1. **Isolation:** Isolation may be defined as the cutting off or blunting off what is unacceptable in the whole situation. Therefore, while resorting to isolation as defence, the individual may exhibit the following types of behaviour:
   - In spite of being in the possession of all the facts of a situation, he may not recognize them for what they are.
   - He may not view the situation to present a derogatory or painful picture.

   A mother of a severely retarded child resorts to such mechanism when she regards her child's behaviour a little different from that of other children. The long-suffering wife of a drunkard or gambler uses this mechanism when she thinks her husband's trouble only in being a little too sociable, and a dark complexioned girls by avoiding the company of her good looking friends. In such situations, isolations proves helpful in defending ourselves from the threatening situations created on account of the deficiency in ourselves or in those close to us.

The excessive use of isolation is a danger signal. It may cause great harm to the individual or those close to him, especially if it is coupled with too much day-dreaming or escapism from reality.

2. **Withdrawal:** In using this mechanism an individual tends to withdraw himself from the situation that causes frustration or failure. He makes himself safe and secure by running away from the difficulties. For example, a child may refuse participation in games for fear of failure and may deceive himself by believing that he could do well if he had participated. Similarly, there may be one or more things where he may feel inadequate or suffer from the fear of failure or criticism. In such circumstances he tries to deceive himself by not involving in the real testing situations, instead of accepting his limitations.

   In the extreme instances, the use of withdrawal as defence may lead to a condition described by James D. Page in *Abnormal Psychology* as pseudofeeble-mindedness. In this condition the policy of nothing ventured, nothing failed or punished for, is followed and the individual eventually acquires a reputation for being stupid when actually he may be of average or superior intelligence.

3. **Negativism:** It is an aggressive withdrawal to which the individual resorts for gaining attention and enhancing his self-esteem. Negativism manifests itself in various forms such as refusal to eat, refusal to listen, refusal to speak, refusal to do work, and at times, in doing the exact opposite of what has been asked or requested.

   A young child or an adolescent often uses such mechanism as a means of establishing themselves as independent persons, and to make the parents or elders feel that they are right or important. Negativism is often used by adults or mature persons. A wife may use it to revolt against the authoritarian attitude of her husband, or an unemployed youth for expressing his resentment against nearly everything in the social set-up.

4. **Compensation:** If something threatens the self-esteem by way of deficiency or unworthiness which cannot be "explained away" (rationalization) or "acted away" (reaction-formation), it can perhaps be made up or compensated for. Compensation may, thus, be described as a defence mechanism which helps an individual to balance or cover-up his deficiency or inadequacy in one field by exhibiting his strength in another field. For example, an unattractive girl who becomes a book-worm and secures the top position in the class is said to make use of such mechanism in order to command the respect and prestige that she is unable to win as a result of her looks.

   "Compensatory behaviours," Carroll maintains, is a form of aggression turned outward. It represents active resistance against frustration. It is a fighting attempt to maintain the ego, and is frequently a powerful motivating force in achievement."

   Napoleon's achievements, to some extent, are said to be the result of his compensatory behaviour for an early feeling of inferiority concerning his short stature and feminine build. Similarly, Hitler, Changej Khan and Tamoor Lang are also said to have compensated for their feelings of inadequacies. In over-compensating their feelings of inferiority, they developed a superiority complex by becoming rude, aggressive and terrible figures of their time.

The compensatory behaviour is quite common among students. While feeling inferior on being frustrated in an attempt to win recognition, one may resort to the compensatory mechanism by boastful talk, wearing peculiar clothing, affecting typical mannerism, disobeying orders and engaging in delinquencies.

Parents, guardians or teachers may be, many times, found to compensate for their own failures and frustrations through their children and students. A father who wanted to be an I. A. S officer but now serving in another profession may attempt to force his son to strive hard for the I. A. S. competition. A mother who fails to establish a harmonious relationship with her husband may bring to bear pressure upon her daughter to be careful, attentive and considerate to her husband. This type of compensatory behaviour creates serious problem for the children.

## Conclusion About Defence Mechanism

All the defence mechanisms discussed above are used unconsciously by a person to protect his self, although for the time being, from psychological dangers. They are not the permanent cure of the trouble as *Morgan* observes, but *"they merely conceal or disguise the real problem. It is still there, ready to produce anxiety again and again."* (1961, p. 143). In this way, defence mechanisms may be regarded as temporary defence against anxiety and inadequacies. Moreover, the use of such mechanisms may create new difficulties for the individual who frequently resorts to them like a person who tells a lie to save his self from a particular situation but falls on to the series of troubles on account of his telling lie.

## Summary

- Defence or mental mechanisms refers to the devices in the shape of a certain pattern of behaviour employed at the unconscious level by an individual for providing temporary relief from the psychological tensions, conflicts and stresses and make him feel adjusted for the time being. Some of the important defence mechanisms employed for this purpose may be named as rationalization, projection, reaction formation, repression, regression, aggression, displacement, fantasy and day dreaming, sublimation etc.
- In rationalization, a person tries to rationalize or justify his otherwise unacceptable social behaviour or act by providing socially acceptable reasons for it and thus attempts to deceive others and himself by inventing good reasons to explain his conduct such as blaming poor health or illness, the uncongenial conditions at home for the failure in examination.

- In projection, for seeking defence in a threatening situation one tries to project his own weakness and deficiency in others such as accusing the system allowing others to cheat after being caught for cheating in the examination.
- In adopting reaction formation as defence mechanism, a person tries to behave in ways that are sharply in contrast with the ways that he needs to behave or habitual to behave such as selfish tendencies.
- In repression, the threatening or anxiety producing experiences, conflicts and unfulfilled wishes are pushed down into one's consciousness and as result, one tries to forget things that might be painful or threatening to one's self.
- In regression, a person tries to regress i.e. behave in a manner more appropriate to his earlier age or period of life for protecting himself for the threatening situation or failure being faced at the present such as exhibiting love for a doll after meeting failure in the love affair.
- In resorting to aggression as a defence mechanism one makes use of his aggressiveness (aggressive language, assertiveness or fighting) as a way of behaving with others for making them fall in line with him.
- Displacement as a defence mechanism allows a person to get relief by displacing his anxiety or frustration to another situation or object lees dangerous than the original such as displacing his frustration in the form of beating/pushing his younger brother after being beaten by his school mate.
- By resorting to fantasy and day dreaming one tries to feel satisfied by withdrawing one's self in a private and satisfying world of imagination after getting failure or frustration in a real- life situation.
- Sublimation as a defence mechanism helps in the re-channelling or redirection of one's repressed and undesirable wishes, impulses, drives, emotions, or actions in some socially acceptable form such as redirecting one's undesirable love and lust towards love for humanity and God.
- In the adoption of isolation as defence mechanism, an individual tries to protect one's self by cutting off or blunting off what is unacceptable in the whole situation.
- In resorting to withdrawal as a defence mechanism, the individual tends to withdraw himself from the situation that causes frustration or failure.
- Resorting to negativism as a defence mechanism in one's behavior is manifested in the forms like refusal to eat, listen, speak,work, and at times in doing the exact opposite to what has been asked or requested.
- Compensation as a defence mechanism helps an individual balance or cover up his deficiency or inadequacy in one field by exhibiting his strength in another.
- However, as far as the employment of defence mechanism is concerned it is not advisable to make use of them for protecting oneself from the psychological dangers. The relief provided by them is quite temporary and resorting to such mechanisms may create new difficulties for the person.

## REFERENCES

Arkoff, Abe, *Adjustment and Mental Health*, McGraw-Hill, New York, 1968.

Carroll, H.A., *Mental Hygiene – The Dynamics of Adjustment*, Prentice-Hall, New Jersey, 1967.

Davison Gerald, C. and Neale, John M., *Abnormal Psychology* (2nd ed.), New York: John Wiley, 1978.

Kartz, Barney and Lehner, G.F., *Mental Hygiene in Modern Living*, Ronald Press, New York, 1997.

Klein, D.B., *Mental Hygiene*, Revised edition, Henry Holt, New York, 1965.

McCall Raymond J., " The defence Mechanisms Re-examined", In *The Psychology of Adjustment*, Walter Kat-Kovsky & Leon Gorlow,(Ed.), NewYork: McGraw-Hill, 1976.

Morgan, C.T., *Introduction to Psychology*, New York: McGraw -Hill, 1961.

Page, James D., *Abnormal Psychology*, New Delhi: Tata McGraw Hill, 1976.

Waltin, N.E.W., *Personality, Maladjustment and Mental Hygiene*, (3rd ed.), New York: McGraw Hill, 1951.

# 8

# SYMPTOMS AND SYNDROMES

An individual is said to be in a satisfactory mental health and considered to be normal to the extent he feels satisfied with himself and his environment. The disequilibrium of this balance leads to maladjustment, behaviour disorders, and mental illness. Defence mechanisms, as we have seen in the previous chapter, were nothing but temporary measures for defending or protecting one's self from the possible maladjustment or behaviour disorders. Temporary defences often either do not prove successful or get damaged in the long run paving way to serious behaviour disorders or mental illness.

How can one decide that an individual has become mentally ill or developed serious behaviour disorders or abnormality, is a question, which we will now attempt to answer. Every illness or disorder—physical or mental—is identified or diagnosed with the help of certain symptoms or a group of symptoms called syndromes known to be associated with that particular illness or disorder.

## Symptoms

The word "symptom" means "sign". Therefore in medicine it is an indication of sickness. In the words of Brown (1969:71), "A symptom is a surface sickness. It is the maladjusted behaviour". Let us try to analyse this definition. A person who has become physically ill may be declared so on the basis of the symptom, the fever. The fever as symptom stands to mean a surface sickness. It is not at all the actual sickness. In depth, as usually happens, there is disequilibrium in metabolism caused by an infection which is a struggle between the organism and some hostile invading forces. Similarly, headache or pain in the stomach also represents the surface sickness, the symptom of an illness or disease.

In the field of mental illness and behaviour disorders also, the diagnosis is made with the help of the related symptoms. For example, vague and unreasoned fear is a psychological symptom that represents a surface mental sickness. It is not the actual mental illness but only an indicator or sign of a sever malfunctioning of the behaviour or disorganization of the personality.

A decision has to be arrived at—whether to cure the symptom (surface sickness) or actual sickness. The cure of surface sickness or symptom as may be understood can result in a temporary cure. The removal of the symptom itself, which is in fact a mere sign of sickness, is at the best a temporary procedure. We may temporarily treat an ailing person by reducing or removing the fever, but it will not be a lasting cure. The permanent cure does not lie merely in the treatment of the fever but in the treatment of the actual illness or disease by investigating the root causes. Similarly, the treatment of the symptom, unreasoned fear in a case of mental illness, will only prove a temporary cure. The unreasoned fear is only a signal of the mental illness or behaviour disorder. Therefore, the reduction of the fear, like reduction of the fever in physical illness, may not only fail to cure mental illness or behaviour disorganization but also create more problems and complications resulting in acute mental diseases or disorders. For understanding the meaning of the term 'symptom', some of its characteristics may be examined.

## Characteristics of Symptoms

1. *Symptoms have subjective and objective nature:* Symptoms, from the point of view of diagnosis, can be referred to as subjective or objective manifestation of an illness or disorder. The condition of an abnormal or mentally ill person like depression, fear or tiredness are called the subjective symptoms, whereas objective symptoms are symptoms like faulty memory, unreasonable fear which are observed and usually revealed in his behaviour.
2. *Symptoms have cause*: A symptom is the sign or indicator of the sickness or disease which has definite underlying causes. A symptom in the form of a stomach-ache, headache or fever has deep rooted cause or causes. Similarly, psychological symptoms are the results of some situations, happenings and the destabilisation of the equilibrium of the psyche.
3. *Symptoms have significance and economy:* Symptoms are significant. Fever has a meaning. It indicates that there is disequilibrium in metabolism caused by some infection. Similarly, unreasonable fear or phobia has a meaning indicative of mental illness or malfunctioning of the behaviour. A symptom proves meaningful in indicating the state of maladjustment or illness. A specific symptom, points towards a particular disorder or disorganisation of the personality.

   Symptoms, when analysed, are the best friends of the sick. The fever is a symptom of disease within the organism and is, in fact, the process of the organ curing itself. The invading forces causing infection are destroyed through, the mechanism of fever. By developing the symptom of fever, the individual tries to protect his metabolism and his existence. It is like protecting one's self from the greater risks and troubles by facing or bearing the smaller ones.

   Similarly, the psychological symptoms of behaviour disorders or mental illness are the friends of the affected person since these save the person from the more unhappiness and sad situations. Take the case of the old maid considered to be suffering from anxiety neuroses, and habituated to looking under her bed at night for fear of someone being there. Her anxiety or fear reactions help her in seeking new equilibrium. Actually the old maid's fear or anxiety is the result of her sexual frustration. She really means that she should have someone with her at night, but she can't afford to admit the demands of her sexual urges and the social consciousness of the consequences. To protect herself from the damaging consequences of this conflict and tension, she develops the symptom of fear or anxiety which helps her to function and exist gracefully. Similarly, for a person suffering from schizophrenia, flight from reality proves helpful and economical as it prevents him from committing suicide. A physical and psychological symptom may therefore prove beneficial and economical by enabling a troubled psyche to continue at least temporarily or partially adjusted and thus make life tolerable and worth living.

4. *Symptoms hardly occur alone*: The diagnosis about the illness, mental or physical, can only be made from the symptoms. A particular symptom is a sign of a particular disturbance, disequilibrium or disorder of the body or psyche. In a diagnosis of a particular disorder or illness, therefore, help is taken from a number of symptoms related to that disorder or illness. "Symptoms", according to Brown (1969:74), "scarcely occur alone and isolated but rather occur together in fairly well organised groups." Thus cold, sore throat, headache, pain in parts of the body, high fever and certain other symptoms appear in the disease known as influenza. Similarly, rarely in actual practice do we find isolated mental symptom. In a particular mental disorder or illness it is a group of symptoms that occur together.
5. *A single symptom may appear in many disorders:* It is true that symptoms rarely occur in isolation and a particular symptom is a sign of a particular disorder or malfunctioning, but if does not mean that a symptom should occur or appear only in one disease or disorder. Any single symptom may occur in quite different disorders just as the symptom of headache or fever may occur in many organic diseases.

## The Symptoms of Abnormal Behaviour— Mental Illness and Behaviour Deviation

In the diagnosis of mental illness and behaviour disorders, the knowledge of the related symptoms is essential. The careful study of symptoms is important on account of the fact that the affected person either does not know or will not admit that he is mentally ill or abnormal. Consequently, there are little chances of getting his cooperation in the diagnosis of his case. Also, the symptom related to normality and abnormality differs in degree rather than in kind. Generally, however, somewhat fixed and persistent symptoms indicate serious abnormalities or mental illness in the affective persons. These symptoms can be classified as shown in Figure 8.1.

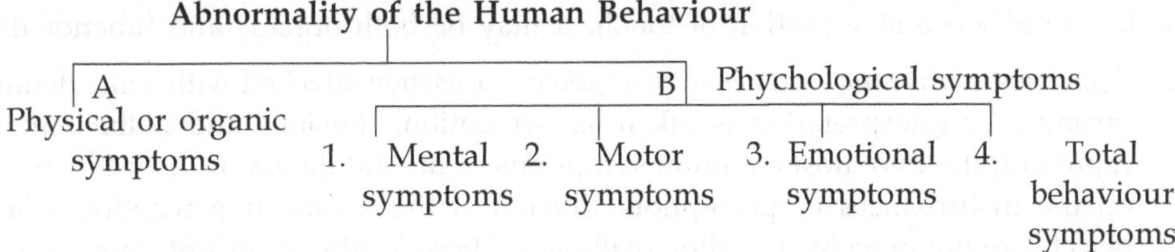


Fig. 8.1: Classification of symptoms of abnormality.

Let us try to discuss these classified symptoms.

## A. Physical Symptoms

The body and mind in an individual are always closely associated. The problems of the psyche are not only manifested through the mental symptoms, but bodily signs or physical symptoms often successfully exhibit or indicate the mental illness or disorders such as:

- Change in temperature, pulse and respiration.
- Unusual or extreme changes in the weight of the body.
- Loss of or abnormal appetite and thirst.
- Nausea, vomiting, headache and dizziness.
- Cough excessive fatigue, body pains and abnormal pupillary activity.
- Motor in-coordination.

## B. Psychological symptoms concerning abnormalities in human behaviour

The behaviour of the mentally ill or disturbed person is quite abnormal. These abnormalities in all his behaviour are found in the domains of his behaviour, that is, cognitive, conative and affective. There are definite disturbances and disorders in these processes which give rise to following definite symptoms.

**1. Mental symptoms (concerning abnormalities of the cognitive processes)**
These symptoms can be as listed below.

a. *Symptoms concerning disorder of the sensation:* Sensory processes concerning the senses of sight, hearing, smell, touch and taste may be disturbed. It may be absent, present but decreased in intensity, increased in intensity or distorted. For example, in the neurosis called conversion hysteria, the troubled person may exhibit one or the other symptom concerning disorder of his vision as under (in spite of the fact that his physical examination reveals no casual organic process to account for these symptoms).
   (i) may be completely unable to see;
   (ii) may have reduced vision;
   (iii) may complain that things are too bright and Intense; and
   (iv) may have distorted vision like double vision etc.

The disorders of the sense of touch are quite frequent in the cases of abnormality and mental illness. A common symptom, known as 'anaesthesia', is concerned with the loss or absence of sensation of touch. It may be both organic and functional.

b. *Symptoms concerning disorder of perception:* *Sensation* attached with some definite meaning or interpretation is taken as perception. Illusions and hallucinations represent; the two most common symptoms of mental illness or disorders based on the disturbances of perception. Illusion is the mistaken perception where objects are not perceived as they really are. There is, always misinterpretation of the external and real stimuli which leads to the distortion of what is seen, heard, touched, smelt or tasted. As a result, fellow patients and hospital employees are mistaken for relatives and friends, a piece of rope may become a snake, and a rustle of leaves may be misinterpreted for human voices. Hallucinations, on the other hand, represent such false perceptions where the individual perceives an object without any basis in reality. They are thus imaginary perceptions. As a result, an individual sees an object where no object is present; he hears voices, bells or other sounds but others cannot; he experiences taste sensations without food and seems to experience muscular sensations that are not present.

c. *Symptoms concerning disorders of the memory*: Loss of memory known as 'amnesia' is a well known symptom concerning disorders of memory. Amnesia usually occurs after a precipitating event such as head injury or severe emotional shock. As a result, the individual may be unable to recall events, preceding or following the shock or both. There is another symptom known as 'fuge' concerning distortion of memory where the individual losing his memory assumes a new identity and name and may start life a new by adopting new modes of living like vocation and family.

d. *Symptoms concerning disorders of thought:* These symptoms may include the following:

(1) *Flight of ideas and word hash (salad):* Flight of ideas consists of a series of rapid jumps from one idea to another. One has extreme rapidity of association of ideas but in no ordered train of thought. If the associated ideas have no logical sequence also then the term 'word hash' or 'a salad of words' is used for such symptoms. 'Neologism' is the extreme case of 'word hash' where the individual tries to coin new words such as 'radimony', a fusion of 'radio' and 'money' which are meaningless except for him.

(2) *Blocking of the thought processes or delay of the mental associations:* Blocking refers to the sudden stoppage of the sequence of thought. It is a kind of sudden failure in the sequence of mental associations. When asked, "Why did you go there ?" a mentally ill may respond, "I went there for..." Beyond the word 'for' he can say nothing. Retardation or delay differs from blocking of the mental associations in that the associations here, instead of being stopped, occur but very slowly. The patient's thinking is slow and laborious. Retardation as a symptom is usually characteristic of depression while blocking is fairly common in schizophrenia.

(3) *Agnosia:* It is related with the loss of an individual's power to perceive existing relationships in the world around him.

(4) *Aphasia:* It denotes an individual's loss of understanding or of producing language. As a result, an individual may lose his ability to use spoken language (motor aphasia), or he may be unable to use his ability to write (agraphia). In 'alexia' he may lose his ability to read the written word or, in sensory 'aphasia', the loss of ability to understand the spoken word.

(5) *Fixed ideas or obsession:* Fixed ideas denote a distorted mental association where some ideas or sequence of words or phrases are so preserved in the mental association process that it becomes very difficult to remove them. Obsessions are one step further than the preservation of fixed ideas in the association process. An obsession may be defined as persistent unwelcome thought of a fairly specific nature which the individual recognizes to be irrational but over which he has little or no control. An obsession is always unwelcome

and conflict-generating in the sense that the affected person Realizes that his belief or thought is contrary to social reality. For example, a mother may be constantly haunted by the idea to kill her little baby, or a young man may be obsessed with the idea that his hands are dirty although on looking at them he sees that they are perfectly clean. Similarly, an individual may be obsessed by the belief that certain foods are poisonous, or that the end of the world is imminent.

(6) *Delusions:* Delusions are significant disorders of judgement. They may be defined as persistent thoughts or false beliefs which the individual defends vigorously by believing them to be absolutely true despite logical absurdity or proof to the contrary, and despite their serious interference with his social adjustment. The individual never stands for the corrections in these beliefs (which have no basis in reality and are often inconsistent with the individual's knowledge and experience) by an appeal to reason. Some of the common types of delusion are as under:

(i) ***Delusion of grandeur:*** Under the influence of grandeur, the person has an unrealistic and exaggerated belief in his own attributes or achievements. Consequently, he imagines that he is a person of great power or influence. Merely by a twist of the mind, the individual, thus, becomes a millionaire, the ruler of the universe, a great inventor, a noted historian or even God. His behaviour reflects what he imagines to be, the attitudes and actions of the one with whom he identifies himself and he demands from others the attention that is appropriate to his exalted position.

(ii) ***Delusion of persecution:*** This type of delusion runs exactly opposite to that of grandeur. Here the affected person imagines himself the most incapable, unworthy or insecure creation in the world. Consequently, he may think himself as the object of hatred, jealousy, enmity and malicious influence aimed at interference with or destruction of his welfare. For example, an individual may imagine that his enemies are trying to spread malicious rumours about him, poisoning his food, and in many other ways planning to harm him. He may imagine strangers condemning him and the casual comment of a friend as a personal insult.

(iii) ***Delusion of hypochondriasis:*** In this type of delusion, the individual persistently believes and complains that he is suffering from some incurable physical or mental diseases without actually being affected by them. An individual with an intact digestive system may thus complain of his entire intestine being rotten. Others may similarly complain that their blood is turning into water, their bones becoming fragile, or they are affected with cancer or tuberculosis.

(iv) ***Delusion of melancholia:*** The person suffering from this type of delusion has a deep-rooted guilt feelings or need for punishment. As a result, the person whose behaviour has really been exemplary may persistently believe that he has committed an unforgivable crime or a moral sin. Consequently, he may spend much of his time condemning himself and attempting to set right the wrongs he never committed.

**2. Motor symptoms (abnormalities of the conative processes)**

The abnormalities of the conative processes are concerned with the motor activities of the individual in doing the opposite of what is normally expected from him. The general symptoms belonging to this type may be categorized as below:

a. *Disorders of muscular activity*: The disorders of simple muscular acts and muscular tonus may occur on an organic or on a functional basis. A significant symptom concerning this type is 'paralysis' which indicates the stage of the complete loss of motor functions of the muscles. A less complete loss is called 'pareses'. Inadequate or maladjusted muscular activity may also indicate abnormality or mental illness. In this category the, mentionable symptoms are 'tremors', 'tics' and 'choreas'. The tremors found in neurotic anxiety and hysteric reactions refer to continuous involuntary, spasmodic contractions, or trembling, in a small group of muscles. Tics are spasmodic twitching of small groups of muscles particularly of the face, neck and shoulders and are usually found in compulsion neurosis. Chorea is an irregular involuntary spasmodic movement and may be hysteric or organic in origin.

b. *Disorders of motor language habit:* The disorders of this category as specific symptoms of abnormality may be listed as below:

   (i) ***Motor aphasia:*** Loss of the ability to speak words.

   (ii) ***Agraphia:*** Loss of the ability to write.

   (iii) ***Amimia:*** Loss of the ability to express thoughts in gesture.

   (iii) ***Writing peculiarities:*** Concerning abnormalities in writing.

   (iv) ***Speech disturbances:*** Stammering, stuttering, persistent repetition of any word or phrase, halting speech or refusal to talk.

   (iv) ***Use of objectionable language:*** A display of unaccustomed vulgarity or of profane (obscene) language.

c. *Disorders of voluntary acts or motor behaviour:* This category may include the following:

   (i) ***Increased psychomotor activity:*** These symptoms relate to the condition wherein the individual is persistently engaged in a constant motion, crying, laughing, shouting or whispering.

   (ii) ***Decreased psychomotor activity:*** These symptoms manifest themselves in the slowdown of motion—hesitation or indecision (abulia), rigidity (catalepsy), and inability to walk or stand without support (astasia-abasia). The term 'abulia', closely related to the emotional symptoms of depression, refers to lack of or weakness of the will. It may be generalized where the patient does not have a will to do anything, or may cover some specific action tendency like merely not willing 'to eat' or 'to get-up'. On the other hand, rigidity refers to fixity of postures as in catalepsy. In catatonic schizophrenia, a type of catalepsy called waxy flexibility is found in which the affected person may be seen in the most unusual positions or postures for long periods despite discomfort. The arms and legs may be elevated, hands stretched out, or body bent as if the person were an automation made of wax. In rigid catalepsy, the person takes a definite postural or bodily position from which he can be removed only by extreme force.

(iii) ***Constant repetition of the same act (stereotype):*** In this category of symptoms we have 'automatism' which is a mechanical repetitive motor behaviour carried out unconsciously. Here the patient may repeatedly clench his fist, touch his lips or catch hold of his ears without being aware of what he is doing. Stereotyped mannerisms also fall in this category of symptoms in which the patient consciously or unconsciously grimaces, gestures or move his entire body stiffly and repetitively. He may sometimes shows peculiar mannerism such as queer movements of the hands and shoulders or a shuffling gait.

(iv) *Impulsive or unduly responsive motor behaviours:* These symptoms concern the motor ***behaviour*** that is impulsive or unduly responsive to external suggestion as shown by echopraxia— the persistent repetition of the movements or ***words*** of another or negativism in which the patient refuses to cooperate with ***a request*** or behaves in a manner opposite to that requested. ***For*** example, he may stand up when requested to sit down.

(v) *Compulsive motor behaviour:* One of the most common motor behaviour disturbances is known as compulsion. Compulsions are defined as acts of a persistent and fairly specific nature which the individual recognizes to be irrational, irrelevant and inappropriate to social reality but over which he has little or no- control. Compulsions are to obsessions as acts are to thoughts. As acts and thoughts should proceed side by side, therefore, compulsions and obsessions are usually present in the same patient.

An individual, after being obsessed with the idea that his hands are dirty, feels an overwhelming urge to wash his hands and consequently acts in compulsion (going and washing his hands) many times during the day even if on looking them he sees they are perfectly clean. Similarly, an individual may be compelled to return and check the lock on the door many times while proceeding to his office or market. There are some specific compulsions like kleptomania, the act of stealing regardless of value, and pyromania, the act of starting fires without any reason.

**3. Emotional symptoms (abnormalities of the affective processes)**

An irrational excessive increase in the emotional reactions (affective experiences)-conscious and unconscious form the outstanding symptoms for many mental disorders or illness. The mentionable are anxiety, the reactions concerning elation and depression, apathy, anger and fear.

*(a) Elation and depression:* Elation is related with the exaggerated feelings of well-being in an individual. Consequently, there is a display of an unnatural state of happiness that shows itself in singing, dancing, excited talking and much laughter despite the objective situation. In 'euphoria' we have extreme elation where one has no cares or worries and usually a mood to view the world through rose coloured glasses. Depression is the opposite of the individual's mood of elevation. There is a morbid sadness and dejection, an

increased perception of physical pain and guilt consciousness. The expression of worry, sighs, weeping, crying, refusal to eat or to speak are the usual signs of depression. In deep depression, the individual feels that everything is impossible and nothing in life is worth living. In extreme cases it leads to the suicidal depressions. Thus where in elated mood the individual feels fit and fine, in depressed mood he feels sick and gloomy. In some mental cases there is an unusual fluctuation of the mood between elation and depression and vice versa.

(*b*) *Apathy:* It manifests a decrease in affection where one feels neither happy nor sad. It is, in fact, a state of emotional 'flatness' with a positive attitude of indifference towards all experiences and situations. Thus events that normally evoke anger, happiness, sadness, shame or sympathy have no effect upon the person affected by apathy.

(*c*) *Anxiety:* The symptoms concerning anxiety are marked by apprehension, tension, restlessness, tremor, nausea, rapid pulse, palpitation and profuse perspiration. The individual under the affect of anxiety anticipates a danger or disaster that he may or may not be able to describe clearly. Extreme forms of such anxiety are known as 'panic' in which the whole social and physical reality is considered a possible source of danger,

(*d*) *Anger:* In a natural situation, where one is threatened by some stimuli from the environment, one may attempt to attack it with the accompanying feelings of anger, In case of pathological or abnormal anger, the person exhibits the emotion of anger as a generalised disposition to be, aggressive towards everyone and everything or it may be focused on a specific person without any reasonable basis of showing such aggressive behaviour.

(*e*) *Fear:* Pathological fear called phobia is another symptom of mental illness or disorder. Phobia is an irrational and obsessive fear and may be defined, in the words of Brown (1969:132), as "a persistent fear of something which is not objectively a source of danger but which the patient reacts to with real fear despite the fact that he realizes this reaction is inappropriate."

Some of the important phobias related to specific objects or physical situations are listed below:

(i) Acrophobia – fear of high places.
(ii) Claustrophobia – fear of closed places.
(iii) Agoraphobia – fear of open places.
(iv) Hematophobia – fear of blood.
(v) Nyctophobia – fear of the darkness.
(vi) Photophobia – fear of the strong light
(vii) Pathophobia – fear of diseases or of some particular disease.
(viii) Zoophobia – fear of animals or of some particular animal.
(ix) Hydrophobia – fear of water
(x) Toxophobia – fear of being poisoned.

**4. Total behaviour symptoms (abnormalities concerning total behaviour of an individual)**

We have mentioned the symptoms of abnormalities related to cognitive, conative and affective processes of the human behaviour. In this last category, we point out the symptoms of mental disorders of an individual's total behaviour. How does one react, in toto, to his environment or the outside world is important and should be taken into account for describing one's normality or abnormality and consequently the following types of behaviour will be taken as symptoms of behaviour disorders and malfunctioning:

(i) Antisocial acts and crimes.
(ii) Diminished, over emphasized or perverted sex-behaviour.
(iii) Alcohol and drug addiction.
(iv) Mental deficiency.

## Syndromes

We have described the various symptoms for mental illness or disorders under specific categories like mental, emotional or motor symptoms. This categorization is however quite arbitrary and should in no way be confused with syndromes,

The term 'syndrome' represents a fairly well organised group or cluster of symptoms that may be found in a particular mental disorder or disease. In actual practice, symptoms scarcely ever occur in isolation but rather occur together in organised groups or clusters. It is these clusters or complexes of symptoms which are known as syndromes.

Syndromes, in this way, are not confined to one or the other categories of the symptoms like mental, physical, or emotional described above but may include symptoms from any number of the above categories. A mentally ill person, therefore, may exhibit a definite cluster of symptoms (syndrome) drawn from the categories of physical, mental, motor, emotional or total behaviour symptoms.

Hence, in the diagnosis of a mental illness or disorder, it is the knowledge or the identification of particular syndromes that usually play the desired role and not the individual symptom as the latter may show its presence in a number of unrelated disorders or illness. The identification and classification of syndromes thus serves not only a diagnostic purpose but also provides valuable help in the classification of mental disorders or abnormalities.

## Summary

- Every illness or disorder—mental or physical—is identified or diagnosed with the help of related symptoms or syndromes.
- A symptom is a surface sickness. It is the maladjusted behaviour. In the world of medicine it is used as a sign or indicator of some sickness. Characteristics of symptoms may be stated as (i) Symptoms have subjective and objective nature, (ii)Symptoms have cause, (iii) Symptoms have a significance and an economy,

(iv)Symptoms hardly occur alone and (v) A single symptom may appear in many disorders.

- *Symptoms indicative of* serious abnormalities in one's behaviour may be broadly classified as physical and psychological symptoms. *Physical symptoms* involve signs such as change in temperature, pulse rate and respiration, unusual change in weight, state of appetite and thirst, nausea, vomiting, headache, cough, excessive fatigue, body pains, motor in-coordination, etc. *Psychological symptoms* may be grouped as mental, motor, emotional and total behaviour symptoms involving all aspects of human behaviour.
- *Mental symptoms* concerning abnormalities of the cognitive processes may include symptoms related to the disorders of perception, sensation, memory and thought (flight of ideas, word hash, delay of the mental association, obsession and delusion etc.)
- *Motor symptoms* concerning abnormalities of the conative processes may involve disorders of muscular activity (paralysis, tremors, tics etc.), motor language habit (speech or writing abnormalities), motor behaviour (increased or decreased psychomotor activities, stereotype, impulsive and compulsive motor behaviour).
- *Emotional symptoms* concerning abnormalities of the affective processes may involve anxiety and the reactions concerning elation and depression, apathy, anger and fear.
- *Total behaviour symptoms* concerning abnormalities of the total behaviour may involve maladaptive behaviour like antisocial behaviour, crime, sexual deviance and disorders, alcoholism and drug addiction, mental deficiency etc.
- *Syndromes* represent a fairly well-organised group or cluster of symptoms that may be found in a particular mental disorder or disease. In the diagnoses of a mental illness or disorder, it is the knowledge of particular syndromes that usually play the role desired and not the individual symptom. The individual symptom may show its presence in a number of unrelated disorders or illness. In addition, the syndromes also provide valuable help in the classification of mental disorders or abnormalities.

## REFERENCES

J.F. Brown (1969), ***The psychodynamics of Abnormal behaviour*** (Indian reprint), New Delhi: Asia Publishing House Pvt. Ltd.

# 9

# ETIOLOGY - THE CAUSES OF ABNORMAL BEHAVIOUR

## INTRODUCTION

The term 'etiology' in abnormal psychology concerns the study of the causes of abnormal behaviour. Why does a particular individual exhibit abnormality in his behaviour, get maladjusted and turns into a mentally ill or disorganised personality? What are the different factors or determinants that cause such trouble? The answer to such questions is the subject-matter of etiology.

The abnormal behaviour of an individual, like the behaviour reaction of any normal person, is the product of both heredity and environment. The factors causing abnormal behaviour may therefore be categorized as hereditary and environmental. Environmental factors may further be divided into psychological and sociological factors and the factors falling midway between hereditary and environmental influences may be described under biological factors. Generally, therefore, for convenience in understanding, the causes of abnormal behaviour are classified in the following broad categories:

A. Hereditary factors
B. Biological factors
C. Psychological factors
D. Sociological factors.

### Predisposing and Precipitating Causes

In the study of the causative factors of abnormality one should also be able to distinguish between the predisposing and the precipitating causes. The predisposing causes provide a fertile ground for the germination of the seeds of abnormality. They provide the base and set the stage for the triggering action of the precipitating causes by lowering an individual's adjusting ability. The predisposing causes are therefore said to be the initiator and usually occur quite remote in time from their affects. On the other hand, the precipitating causes occur immediately or shortly before their affects. They represent specific situations or conditions which prove too much for the individual to remain intact and organised. They are the immediate agents for igniting the fire (originated by predisposing causes) dormant in the individual.

It is interesting to note that one's heredity provides a base for the structure of one's personality and a strong determinant towards the normality or abnormality of his behaviour. In the study of the causes of abnormal behaviour, the heredity, therefore, serves a predisposing cause while environmental factors may serve both predisposing and precipitating causes. At a particular stage or age of an individual, one's abnormal behaviour should he supposed to be the result of the interaction between his heredity and environment. Let us try to study how it happens through the various categories of causative factors.

## A. Hereditary factors

Heredity consists of all that is transferred to the offspring from the immediate parents in the form of genes and chromosomes at the time of conception when it acquires 46 chromosomes, that is twenty- three pairs of chromosomes—one of each pair being derived from the mother and one from the father. There lies on each chromosome genes numbering one to two thousand, each of which contributes to the transmission of hereditary characteristics.

The first twenty-two pairs of chromosomes are called autosomes. They determine the physical characteristics. The remaining twenty-third pair called sex-linked pair decides the individual's sex and other sex-linked characteristics. In the male child, one member of the sex-linked pair is X chromosome (usually big in size) contributed by the mother and the other is Y chromosome (comparatively smaller than X) contributed by the father. In the female child both of these sex-linked chromosomes, one from each parent, are X chromosomes.

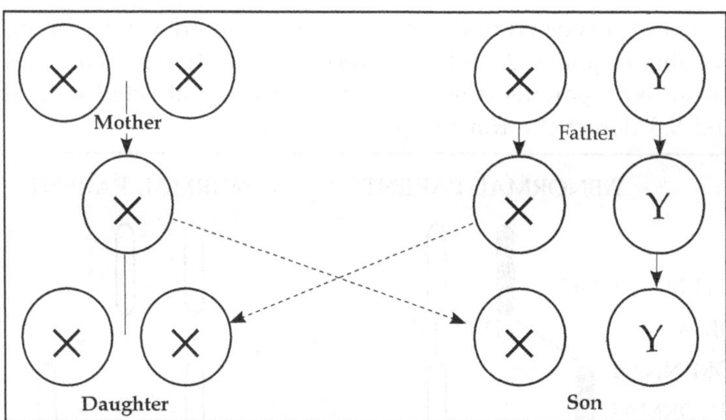


Fig. 9.1: Son or Daughter?

Abnormalities are found to be transmitted both by the sex- linked chromosomes and the autosomes. A few examples are as under.

1. One possible genetic anomaly is a missing sex chromosome. This abnormality, called Turner's Syndrome, produces a person who has the superficial anatomical appearance of a female but usually has subsequent immature sexual development (all examples of this abnormality have been XO types and no YO types have been identified).

2. The presence of extra sex chromosomes also cause abnormality diagnosed as Klinefelter's Syndrome. Here the affected person has too many female chromosomes (XXY, XXXY, XXXXY etc.) instead of the usual composition XY. Such an individual has the superficial appearance of a male and usually a normal sized penis, but very small testes, and may also possess many female characteristics, such as developed breasts, feminine face and voice, little body hair. Such males are always sterile, usually suffer from emotional difficulties and may show symptoms-of psychosis and antisocial behaviour.
3. The presence of extra chromosome in any pair of the twenty-two autosomes (three instead of the usual two) has been found to cause Mongolism—a severe form of mental retardation in which the individual has slanting eyes, a flat face and other characteristics that produce a superficial resemblance to Mongoloids.

## The Role of Genes

Genes, like chromosomes, occur in pairs. An individual may be found to derive a gene pair in one of the following forms:

- A dominant gene from one of the parents and a recessive gene from the other (Form Dr).
- Dominant genes from both the parents (Form DD).
- Recessive genes from both the parents (Form rr).

For purposes of distinction, pure DD (completely dominant) or rr (completely recessive) gene pairs are called homo-zygotes and hybrid, Dr pairs are referred to as hetero-zygotes

Defective genes transferred to the offspring are in many ways responsible for the transmission of abnormalities. A child who receives defective paired genes (dominant or recessive) from both parents runs a high risk of being affected with abnormality. Figures 9.2 and 9.3 depict the transmission of genes.

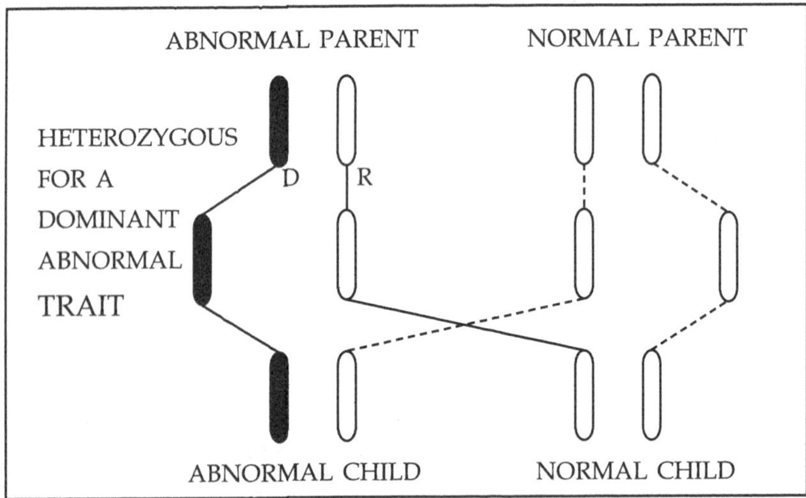


Fig. 9.2: Mating of a normal person and abnormal person

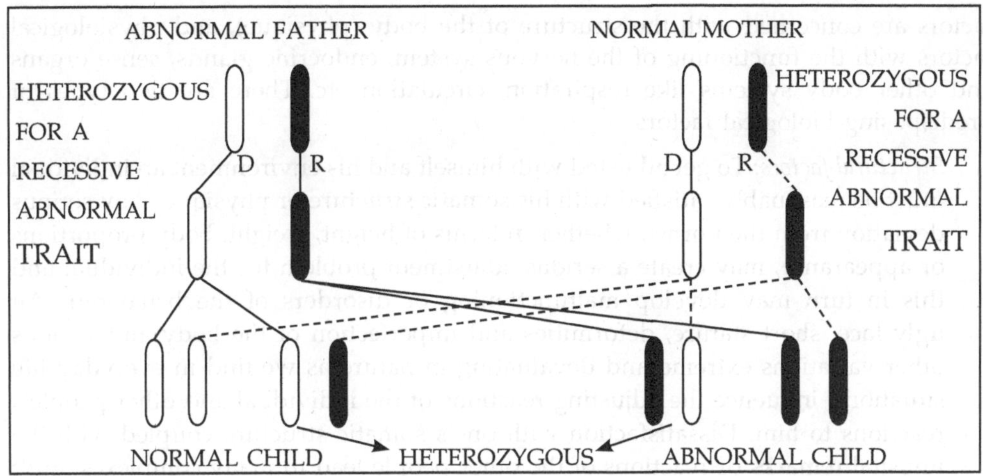


Fig. 9.3: The mating from which the great majority of abnormal persons are born

A few notable examples of the degenerations or hereditary diseases through the transmission of genes are being cited ahead.

1. *Ataxia:* It causes lack of coordination and inability to maintain balance while standing or walking.
2. *Huntington's Chorea:* This degeneration is marked by speech impairment, intellectual impairment and emotional disturbance.
3. *Idiopathic epilepsy.*
4. *Muscular Dystrophies:* A disorder involving paralysis of muscles.
5. *Neural atrophy:* A disorder of peripheral nerves.
6. *Alzheimer's disease and Pick's disease*: Both relate to presenile psychosis in which atrophy of the cerebral cortex occurs. In Pick's disease, brain degeneration occurs in localized foci, mostly in the frontal areas while in Alzheimer's disease degeneration is diffused throughout the brain.
7. *Schizophrenia.* A functional disorder in which heredity plays a part of strong predisposing factor.
8. *Psycho-physiological disorders:* Certain psychophysical disorders like hyperthyroidism, peptic ulcers and essential hypertension have been found to possess strong hereditary bases.

## B. Biological factors

While hereditary factors are more or less predisposing factors, the biological factors (falling midway between hereditary and environmental influences) constitute both predisposing and precipitating factors.

**(a) Predisposing factors**

Under this category all the factors covered by the term "constitution" arc included. There are two classes of constitutional factors- structural and physiological. Structural factors are concerned with the structure of the body (physique), and physiological factors with the functioning of the nervous system, endocrine glands, sense organs and other body systems like respiration, circulation etc. There are two types of predisposing biological factors.

1. *Structural factors:* To get adjusted with himself and his environment an individual must be reasonably satisfied with his somatic structure or physique. Any serious deviation from the norms, whether in terms of height, weight, body proportions or appearance, may create a serious adjustment problem for the individual and this in turn may develop malfunctioning or disorders of the behaviour. An ugly face, short stature, deformities and imperfection of the body and various other variations extreme and devaluating in nature as we find in everyday life situations, influence the adjusting reactions of the individual and other people's reactions to him. Dissatisfaction with one's somatic structure coupled with the unusual remarks or reactions of the other people lead to many complexes, guilt feelings and frustrating encounters. Therefore, it is true that physique or body structure does play an important role in the proper or improper functioning of the behaviour.
2. *Physiological factors:* Physiological factors within an individual also, to a great extent, influence his personality, reaction tendencies and adjusting behaviour. Some such influences can be summarized as under:
   - Individuals with a high biological energy level are inclined to discharge tension through neuromuscular activity, whereas individuals with a low energy level are more inclined to discharge tension through ideomotor or fantasy.
   - Either an excess or a deficit of autonomic reactivity may lead to abnormality. An individual who is more autonomically reactive will be more prone to develop over-action to minor stresses and formation of unnecessary conditioned fears and anxieties while the deficient emotional reactivity presumably leads to inadequate socialization characterized by impulsiveness, anti- social behaviour and a lack of inner controls.
   - Constitutional defects in the body's defences against disease and other stresses may likely cause abnormality. Normally our body produces antibodies to resist infections, but the faulty functioning of the anti-body producing mechanism may leave the body vulnerable to the degenerative diseases of the nervous system. Similarly, the tolerance capacity of an individual for psychological stress may also be lowered on account of the disruptions in the various biochemical systems involved in the functioning of the brain.
   - Over-activity or under-activity of the endocrines or ductless glands cause extreme deviations in the somatic structure, body functioning and behaviour tendencies of an individual. One may turn to be quite passive and lethargic while the other may become anxious and restless or tired and irritable on account of the endocrine imbalances. The endocrines play an important role in the growth and development of the body and mind. Any defect in their functioning leads to significant physiological anomalies which, in turn, provide fertile ground for the growth of disorganised personalities. For

example, over-activity of the secretion of adrenal glands may cause a woman to grow beard and develop masculine physique and may exhibit the physical and sexual maturity of an adult in a three or four year old child. Similarly, pituitary gland imbalances may lead to increase in height (seven to nine feet in height), dwarfs (two to four feet in height), a gorilla-like appearance and abnormal sex characteristics and behaviour. The abnormalities so produced are liable to be made an object of ridicule, jest, social isolation and harsh and unfair treatment which, in turn, cause a variety of abnormalities in the behaviour of the affected persons.

**(b) Precipitating Factors**

The mentionable biological precipitating factors are noxious agents, and deprivations of biological nature.

1. *Noxious agents*: These are the external objects or situations which are injurious to the well-being of an individual. The abnormalities resulting from noxious agents are called toxic psychoses. Disorientation of mental functioning, memory loss, difficulty in intellectual functions, visual illusions and hallucinations are some of the common symptoms of toxic psychoses. The notable noxious agents are as under:
   (i) *Microorganisms:* These are disease producing bacteria. Some microorganisms may infect the brain along with the body as in pneumonia, malaria and syphilis while the others may affect the brain directly as in meningitis.
   (ii) *Toxic chemicals:* The chemicals such as lead, methyl alcohol, carbon monoxide, carbon tetrachloride and intoxicating drugs and other material produce toxicity. They affect the functioning of the brain and may result in behaviour disorders.
   (iii) *Physical injury*: Physical injury and trauma may cause damage to the brain either directly or through interference with its blood supply and thus may result in brain disorders—structural or functional.
2. ***Biological deprivation:*** Deprivation of necessary biological necessities such as oxygen, food, water, vitamins, hormones, sleep and rest and the like may precipitate a functional disorder, or may cause structural changes in the brain. Some of the important deprivations are malnutrition, oxygen and sleep.
   (i) *Malnutrition:* Severe malnutrition during early embryonic and infantile stage has been found to lower body resistance, affect brain structure and growth of intelligence. Postmortem studies of the malnutrition death of the infant have revealed the content of their brain cells to be sixty per cent less than that of the normal content. Pellagra, a mental disorder, is found to be caused by vitamin deficiency. In the same manner, the deficiency of certain vitamins, glucose and hormones has been found to cause many abnormalities—structural or functional.
   (ii) *Deficiency of oxygen:* Anoxia—a deficiency of the oxygen supply to the tissues—has been found to cause many abnormalities. Human nerve cells are very sensitive to lack of oxygen and may result in structural damage

to the brain or life-long mental deficiency or affect drastically the complex mental functions such as immediate memory.

(iii) *Sleep deprivation:* Sleep deprivation is considered an important precipitating biological factor causing abnormality under stress. The prolonged sleep deprivation brings typical abnormal symptoms in the behaviour of an individual such as irritability, feeling of persecution, inability to concentrate and periods of disorientation and misperceptions, illusions and hallucinations. In some cases it may also bring about certain neurological changes and autonomic nervous system effects.

## C. Psychological Factors

Besides hereditary and biological factors, psychological causes often prove to be the cause for the development of abnormal behaviour and mental illness All types of frustrations, conflicts, stresses, and pressures brought about by faulty psychological development, upbringing and socialization of the child result in disorganised personality and abnormal behaviour. Truly speaking, in the satisfaction of needs lies the welfare of the individual. When one feels frustrated in the satisfaction of his psychological needs, his behaviour reactions turn into mal-adaptation and abnormalities. Let us see how it happens.

1. *Psychological deprivations of the early age:* Psychological deprivation during infancy and early childhood contributes predisposing causes for the abnormal behaviour at the later stage or sometimes works as a precipitating cause. Such situations may be cited as follows:

   (i) *Oral deprivation:* The individuals who are deprived of the opportunity of seeking gratification from sucking behaviour in infancy may be found to be emotionally unstable and disturbed at the later stage.

   (ii) *Parental deprivation:* Loss of parental affection has been found to play a very significant role in the development of maladjustment and abnormality. The loss of father or mother or both has a very damaging effect on the well-being of the child. He does not get adequate love and affection, attention and care as he should otherwise get. In such situations he feels insecure, develops neurotic or psychotic tendencies and thus becomes susceptible to stress situations in later life. The condition is more damaging in the case of separation, desertion or divorce between the parents. Here the child cannot get the appropriate psychological environment for his development and consequently develops maladaptive reaction tendencies. Inadequate mothering, due to any reason in the form of indifference, rejection, overprotection etc. may cause tense, unsatisfied and negativistic behaviour on the part of children which may develop into a deviant behaviour at the later stage.

   (iii) *Anal deprivation:* Anal frustrations on account of the early and rigorous toilet training of early age are reported to cause emotional difficulties and behavioural problems in later life.

2. *Faulty learning and horrible experiences*: Most of the patterns in our behaviour are the result of our learning and experiences. In the case of learning of habits, attitudes, interests or other acquired traits and physical mental, emotional and social competencies, where the adequate and right learning results in adjustment, inadequate and faulty learning creates difficulties in one's adjustment.

   Let us take for example the learning of sex behaviour. The child may learn that sex is shameful or fearful. He may think that he is not fit for normal sex behaviour. Such faulty acquisition, misconceptions and wrong understanding of the sex-related information are found to contribute to learning maladaptive behaviour such as homosexuality, inadequacy, withdrawal tendency etc., which may further result in serious disorganisation of the personality.

   Certain painful experiences, especially in the early age, are bound to leave psychological wounds that never completely heal. Sometimes such experiences like an encounter with a vicious dog or a bull, sexual assault, or experience with a gang of robbers may be sufficient to establish a conditioned fear response which may result in certain types of abnormality and mental illness.

3. *Defective family environment land parental attitude:* Parental attitude raid uncongenial family environment full of defective models, conflicts and stress situations prove a potent source for the causes of abnormal behaviour. In this connection the following adverse situations may be cited as examples.

   (i) *Negative models:* The parents and other senior members of the family may be emotionally unstable, inconsistent, and disturbed in their usual behaviour or antisocial. These parents and elders are destined to set negative models for their children.

   (ii) *Undesirable parental attitude:* Parental attitudes towards the child may be defective and erroneous such as (a) rejection, (b) over protection, (c) over indulgence, (d) perfectionism—unrealistic ambitions for child, (e) much dominance or strictness and (f) much leniency or carelessness.

   (iii) *Unhappy conditions:* The family environment may be uncongenial due to (a) broken homes as a result of death, divorce, desertion or separation, (b) marital discord of the parents due to continued disagreement between the parents in the form of quarrelling, bickering, nagging and general tensions, (c) sibling rivalry amounting to the feeling in a child that his brother or sister is getting more parental affection and attention than himself, and (d) poor resources involving poor economic conditions and finances, cultural and social deprivation, lack of education of the parents and bad reputation of the family.

In all the above defective situations in the family environment, the child fails to get favourable conditions for his adequate adjustment and development. He neither gets balanced love and affection nor adequate safety, security and resources for the satisfaction of his essential needs. He is therefore always starved of one or the other of his physical or emotional needs. Predisposed in this manner, the unfortunate happenings concerning the treatment towards him and the members of the family are bound to make his behaviour and reaction patterns quite deviant from the normal and thus he drifts towards abnormality and mental illness.

4. *Maladjustment in adolescence:* Adolescence is a crucial age of storm and stresses. The varying physical and socio-psychological needs of this age have to be satisfied for the adjustment moving between independence versus dependence, realism versus idealism, parental affection versus peer group norms, age temptations versus social taboos etc. The adolescent must be made to satisfy himself reasonably with his body development, somatic variations and organic and psycho-physical changes lie must be helped in the proper exercising of his emotions and channelising the stream of his valuable energy. Adolescents are very sensitive and should therefore be treated and cared for adequately according to their needs and problems of their age. An attack on their situation may invite a host of problems. Their resentment, indifference and hostility should not be misunderstood but rather they should be helped to establish self-identity and meaningful standards of conduct to follow. But this is not always possible and there starts "the conflict of the generation". Adolescents are then misunderstood, their problems are not cared for and their aspirations thwarted. It gives rise to conflicts, tensions and frustrations among the adolescents, and thus leading to abnormalities and mental disorders.
5. *Maladjustment in adulthood:* Adulthood needs a minimum level of maturity and adequate competencies for facing the problems of a responsible family life. In-competencies and inadequacies in this regard may bring frustrations and hardships which in turn result in abnormality and mental illness. Some of the devastating situations may be: (i) marital disharmony or maladjustment, (ii) marriage or sex-frustrations, (iii) poor earning, unemployment or vocational maladjustment, (iv) largeness of the family and unnecessary heavy responsibilities, (v) social maladjustment or deprivation of social interaction, (vi) lack of security and safety to one's well-being and members of the family, (vii) frustrations from the children or other dependents, (viii) continued physical illness and chronic diseases of one's own or the members of the family, and (ix) insecurity - and fear of the old age.
6. *Psychological stresses and self-devaluation:* Stress refers to a psychic condition of an individual subjected to constant failures, frustrations, tensions, conflicts and pressures. Stresses, as we have noticed, constitute the precipitating causes which disintegrate the personality of the affected person. The stress tolerance capacity of an individual is an important deciding factor and depends upon early upbringing, psychological and biological makeup, and the present favourable or unfavourable environment and psyche-state. Still the outcome of the severe stress situations causing personality disorders cannot be questioned. The central factor causing maladjustment and disorders in the stress situations is the feeling of self-devaluation. One losses faith in one's integrity, abilities and capacities and thinks himself unworthy unwanted and good-for-nothing. Some self-devaluating and devastating stress situations may be cited as under:
   (i) *Personal Imitations and shortcomings*: An individual for adequate adjustment should learn to be reasonably satisfied with his own limitations and shortcomings. No one is perfect in this world In addition to one's assets, one should know one's limitations and accept them so as not to cause

damage to oneself. The person who plans his ambitions well within his own capacities avoids the risk of undesirable frustrations, while those who aim to reach the stars with their feet on the earth are destined to suffer from self devaluation. Much of our unhappiness and the feelings of self-devaluation are the result of our ignorance and failure to appreciate our assets and unnecessary condemnation as well as worries about our limitations *such* as a big nose, short statute, dark complexion and poor vision etc.

*(ii)* *Failures and losses:* Repealed failures and accidental losses lead to strong feelings of inferiority and self-devaluation to the extent that one may "go to pieces'. A school boy may attempt suicide as a result of his successive failures, or an unemployed youth may turn into a split personality on account of his repeated failures to get a job and the subsequent sufferings. The losses relating to human or material resources are painful and frustrating in their effects especially on account of the fact that there is nothing one can do about them once they have occurred. As a result of an appreciable financial loss, damage to one's, property, loss of social status, loss of friendship and company of our dearest and death of the loved ones, one may feel frustrated, even to the extent of losing the will to live.

*(iii)* *Guilt feelings:* The feelings of guilt leading to self-devaluation are associated with the cases of abnormal behaviour and mental disorders. The lady who is washing her hands under compulsive neurosis reactions does so, on account of some inherent guilt feelings. Similarly, early sexual experiences and tragedies may lead to feelings of guilt, sinful attitude and self devaluation and thus cause abnormality of sex behaviour and other personality disorders.

*(iv)* *Unreasonable comparisons*: We are more sad, unhappy and unworthy on account of the fact that we are in the habit of making unreasonable comparisons of our gains and status with other people of resources and capabilities. We seldom realise that in this world of great diversities and differences there are people who appear to enjoy more facilities than ours, but there are others also who are not fortunate enough to make both ends meet. Therefore, one has to be content with a level suited to his own resources and capabilities, People who fail to develop such maturity and reasonable outlook are bound to suffer from self devaluation, inferiority feelings and frustrations which lead them to abnormality.

*(v)* *Severe conflicts:* Many times conflicts in the form of what to do or what not to do, out of the given choices or alternatives, become sources of frustrations and stresses that ultimately lead to the development of abnormality and behaviour disorders. The central idea behind any conflict—the choices to make—is the inability to determine what is good or bad, desirable or undesirable. Sometimes the conflicting situations are loaded with extreme anxiety, feeling of threat insecurity and indefiniteness. Under such stresses one is likely to fall victim to abnormalities or mental disorders.

*(vi)* ***Severe pressures:*** Stress situations affecting our behaviour are often generated through severe pressures stemming from inner or outer source. While mild pressures may be tolerated with or without strain, the excessive and

severe one's lead to the disorganisation of behaviour. Some of the pressure-generating situations are cited here:

a. The desire of excelling others or reaching the top in competitive endeavours.
b. The unreasonable and excessive demands of the work environment—educational or occupational.
c. The stressful demands of the marital or family life.
d. The stressful demands of living as an efficient and adjusted citizen in the complicated and demanding conditions of modern age.
e. The hazards and calamities of life.

## D. Sociological Factors

It is difficult to separate sociological influences from the psychological ones as the sociological factors rooted in the social and cultural environment of an individual cast their impact on the behaviour of an individual through the organic and psychological channels of one's personality and behaviour. However, for the sake of convenience we would be dealing with some of the social and cultural factors and stress situations responsible for the faulty development and disorganisation of one's personality and behaviour.

An individual's social and cultural environment consists of all the external factors within his home, family, neighbourhood, school and college, world of work, society and community, caste and religion, state and the country etc. His personality and behaviour at any stage of his development is a product of the interaction of his biological and psychological make-up with his sociocultural environment.

It is true that much of our abnormal behaviour is an acquired disposition or learned behaviour. As a result of what an individual experiences or for what he becomes conditioned to through formal and informal contacts in his sociocultural environment, his behaviour patterns get fixed accordingly. Consequently, the abnormalities and mental disorders are the cause and result of the defective and unfavourable sociocultural environment. Most of the maladaptive and abnormal behaviours like antisocial behaviour, alcoholism, drug addiction, sexual deviations and disorder, neurotic and psychotic disorganisation, if analysed, may be found to possess deep-rooted sociocultural causes. Let us cite a few devastating situations particularly lying within our defective and pathogenic sociocultural environment for the growth and perpetuation of abnormal behaviour.

1. *Problems related with earning of living:* The world of work provides many times strong stress situations for an individual. Particularly in the developing countries like ours, the earning of one's living is a source of all frustrations and stresses. Millions of our youth face the problem of unemployment and under-employment. It is bound to push them into so many troubles and complications and personality disorders. Frustration coupled with strong urges of the satisfaction of the basic needs either makes them aggressive towards their sociocultural environment or turns their aggression inward for the development of suicidal tendencies and neurotic or psychotic split-up of the personality. The rising corruption, nepotism, favouritism, provincialism and day-to-day interference of the political bosses is

adding to occupational problems. Under these circumstances it is no surprise to find the cases of mental illness or behaviour disorders among the frustrated employed as well as unemployed individuals. Such abnormalities of behaviour are the result of emerging sociocultural conditions related with the earning of one's livelihood.

2. *The caste considerations and minority status: The conscious*ness about minority status and socioeconomic factors attached with the caste considerations in our country may be said to be a major source of frustrations, conflicts and stresses. Linguistic, religious and cultural minorities face a great deal of adjustment problems particularly in a specific and awkward situation when majority groups are in the grip of linguistic, religious or sectarians sentiments and divisive forces. In such a situation, their security and safety is threatened and their self-esteem injured. It leads them to un- adjusting defensive behaviour resulting in malfunctioning of their behaviour. The caste groups falling into specific lower categories in the hierarchy of castes, besides their low socioeconomic status, are maltreated and become victims of apathy and even scorn from the upper caste groups. This creates in them the feelings of inferiority, frustration, resentment and other behavioural disorders.

   A new dimension has been emerging from the problems created by caste considerations in our country. It concerns the reservation of seats for the backward and scheduled classes in educational institutions and career openings. The youth belonging to the upper castes are giving rise to a peculiar frustration, resentment and feelings of self-devaluation on account of this policy of reservation. They get more disturbed in a situation when the facilities of reservation are enjoyed by the wards of more privileged and economically sound members of the lower castes.

3. *Effect of urbanisation and modernization:* Heavy industrialization, increasing urbanisation, and rapid modernization have disturbed our usual sociocultural pattern. The family structure has shrunk, the village culture is being trounced by the typical urban ways, old cultural values are being lost and the new generation has adopted the ways of the western culture in the name of modernization. All this has created a new sociocultural environment without caring for its ill effects which are obvious. The gulf between the poor and the rich, or the privileged and the unprivileged has widened. The village farmers have been forced to become factory workers and labourers and live in the most un-hygienic and depressive conditions. The emotional feedback and feelings are missing today in our society. A next- door neighbour or even inmates of the same building are strangers to each other. Nobody is there to listen or sympathise for the sufferings and inadequacies. The parents have no time for their own children and sons have no time or resources to look after their aged parents. Urbanisation, industrialization and modernisation have been the causes of insecurity, emotional cravings, self-devaluation, conflicts and frustrations leading towards the disorganisation of behaviour and personality.

4. *Cultural and social evils:* Cultural setting profoundly and widely affect the development of personality and behaviour. Every culture through its established norms of traits and behaviours shared by most of its members provides a basic

model of living. The cultural patterns like the child rearing practices, the family organisations, the sex practices, marital status, beliefs and traditions, restrictions and taboos, ways of treating the elders or youngsters, superstitions etc., differ from culture to culture. These patterns cause frustrations, complexes, feelings of guilt and self-devaluation depending upon emotional conflicts and stresses generated by them. The social evils attached to our society like dowry system, the preferential treatment to the son over the daughter, the maltreatment of a widow, typical superstitions and orthodox views, unreasonable dominance of religions in many cases provide a generating or precipitating factor for the development of abnormality and behaviour disorganisation.

5. *Marital discord and family instability:* Marital adjustment is a key to happiness. The reverse is also true. Marital discords, as may be witnessed in day-to-day happenings, are bound to result in utter disillusionment, self-devaluation and severe psychological wounds. These situations are harmful not only to the well-being of the marriage partners but are destined to prove devastating to their children also. The stability of family life depends upon marital harmony. Divorce, separation, and desertion lead to destabilize the equilibrium of the mental peace. Similarly, untimely death of a spouse brings severe stress situations to the other partner. Economic fluctuations and staying away of the father or mother on account of earning the living may disrupt the usual family pattern. All such situations often prove detrimental to the parents and their dependents.
6. *Natural and national catastrophes:* The catastrophes like floods, fires, earthquakes, droughts, hailstorms, wars, economic depressions and acute national crisis create severe stress situations to the affected groups or individuals. Huge losses of property, deaths, physical deformities, disorganisation of the social institutions brought out by such catastrophes disturb the lives of unfortunate millions. It has far reaching consequences resulting in the pathological sociocultural environment for the development of the behaviour disorganisation of the victims and their dependents.

## Conclusion

It must be emphasised that both predisposing and precipitating causes, work in the development of maladaptive behaviour. The predisposing factors of heredity, pathogenic biological makeup, defective family patterns and sociocultural settings lower the stress tolerance capacity of an individual by contributing towards inadequate personality development and maladaptive behaviour. The precipitating factors either initiate or intensify the distress. Most of the psychological and sociocultural factors generating severe stress situations, frustrations, conflict, feeling of guilt and self-devaluation and suicidal tendencies come into this category. Mental illness or abnormality of behaviour is rarely caused by a single causative factor. It is generally the result of the interaction between or among the multiplicity of factors—hereditary, biological, psychological, and socio-psychological. What a person inherits and afterwards acquires in the form of his physical and psychological makeup as a result of the interaction with the various environmental forces decides the normal or abnormal functioning of his behaviour and mental set-up.

## Summary


- *Abnormal behaviour* is caused as a result of the interaction between predisposing and precipitating causes. Predisposing causes provide the base and stage. Precipitating causes prove the immediate ignition agent for the causation of abnormalities. Causative factors responsible for abnormal behaviour may be grouped as hereditary, biological, psychological and sociological.
- *Hereditary factors* provide predisposing causes. Chromosomal deviations may cause abnormalities like Turner's syndrome, Klinefelter's syndrome and Mongolism. Similarly, defective genes transferred to the offspring are in many ways responsible for the transmission of abnormalities like Huntington's chorea, Alzheimer's and Pick's disease, schizophrenia, ataxia, idiopathic epilepsy and certain psycho-physiological disorders like peptic ulcer, hyperthyroidism etc.
- *Biological factors* may provide both predisposing and precipitating causes. Predisposing causes are provided by structural and physiological factors, while the structural factors are concerned with the structure of the body (physique), physiological factors involve the functioning of the nervous system, endocrine glands, sense organs and other systems like respiration, circulation etc. The proper or improper functioning of one's behaviour depends upon the normality or abnormality of these structural and physiological factors. Some biological precipitating factors are noxious agents and deprivations of biological nature like malnutrition, deficiency of oxygen and sleep deprivation.
- *Psychological factors* may provide both predisposing and precipitating causes. They may be studied under various heads such as (i) Psychological deprivations of the early age (in the form of oral, parental and anal deprivations), (ii) Faulty learning and horrible experiences, (iii) Defective family environment and parental attitudes, (iv) Maladjustment in adolescence and adulthood and (v) Psychological stresses and self-devaluation.
- ***Sociological factors*** involve devastating situations within our defective sociocultural environment such as (i)Problems related with earning or living, (ii)The caste considerations and minority status, (iii) Effect of the urbanisation and modernization, (iv) Cultural and social evils,(v) Marital discord and family instability and (vi) Natural and national calamities.
- In essence, one's maladaptive behaviour is the interaction of the predisposing and precipitating causes generated through the combination of different factors.


## Suggested Readings


Barlow, David (2012). *Abnormal Psychology: An Integrative Approach*. Belmont, CA, USA: Wadsworth Cengage Learning.

Hansell, James and Lisa Damour (2005). Abnormal Psychology. New Jersey: John Wiley and Sons

Kring, A.M, Johnson, S.L., Davison, G.C., and Neale, J.M., (2012), Abnormal Psychology (12th edition), New York: John Wiley & Sons.

Rosenhan, D. L., & Seligman, M. E. P. (1989), *Abnormal Psychology (Second Edition)*, New York: W.W. Norton.

Nolen-Hoeksema, Susan (2013). Abnormal Psychology (6th ed.). Boston: McGraw-Hill.

# 10

# CLASSIFICATION OF MENTAL DISORDERS

There is no limit to human variance. The abnormalities of behaviour, therefore, are innumerable. However, for the sake of diagnosis, prevention and treatment of these disorders it becomes essential to put them into some definite categories. The attempts for classification of mental disorders, abnormalities and diseases, therefore, have been the right steps in this direction.

## Development of the Classification System

A. *The old era:* The historical evidences of establishing some classification of behavioural disorders take us to the attempts made by Hippocrates, nearly 2,500 years ago. He divided behavioural disorders into three categories—mania, melancholia and phrenesis, and developed a theoretical account of their appearance. In India too, the *rishis*, much earlier than the Hippocrates' era, gave a far reasonable classification of the abnormal behaviour in terms of disequilibrium in the three *gunas* (*Satguna, Rajoguna* and *Tamoguna).*

   However, the credit for giving a formal systematic classification of mental disorders as prevalent today goes, in the later part of nineteenth century, to the German psychiatrist Emile Kraepelin. He linked all forms of disorders and mental illness to hereditary and biological factors and provided a classification based on causes, prognosis and symptoms of mental diseases.

B. *The modern era:* The two world wars tore apart millions of families, social organisations and individuals. With such increased cases of mental disorders and diseases and the subsequent expansion of psychiatric services all over the world, the need for a standardized classification system was widely felt. The American Psychiatric Association in 1948 set up a committee to develop such a system for classifying mental disorders. This system was further refined and an official *Diagnostic and Statistical Manual of Mental Disorders* (DSM-I) was published in 1952. It acknowledged three main groups of disorders as indicated in Table 10.1.

**Table 10.1: DSM-I**

A. Disorders of brain tissue function
   a. Acute
   b. Chronic
B. Mental deficiency
   a. Familial or hereditary
   b. Idiopathic
C. Disorders of psychogenic origin (no clearly defined physical cause)
   a. Psychotic disorders
      (i) Involutional reaction
      (ii) Affective reactions
      (iii) Schizophrenic reactions
      (iv) Paranoid reactions
      (v) Other
   b. Psychophysiologic
   c. Psychoneurotic
   d. Personality disorders
   e. Transient situational personality disorders.

(Adapted from: American Psychiatric Association, (1952), *Diagnostic and Statistical Manual of Mental Disorders*, Washington D.C.: American Psychiatric Association)

The problems concerning adequacy and universality of the system DSM-I, created the need for modified systems. As a result, in 1965, the World Health Organisation (WHO) brought out a classification system known as the International Classification of Diseases (ICD-8) containing Section V on behaviour disorders. **Table 10.2** presents a summary of this section of ICD.

**Table 10.2**

**Summary of ICD-8 (Section V) classification**

| 290-315 | Mental disorders |
|---|---|
| 290-299 Psychoses | |

290. Senile and presenile dementia
291. Alcoholic psychosis
292. Psychosis associated with intracranial infection
293. Psychosis associated with other cerebral condition
294. Psychosis associated with other physical condition
295 Schizophrenia
296. Affective psychoses
297. Paranoid states
298. Other psychoses
299. Unspecified psychoses,

*300-309 Neurosis Personality Disorders and other non-psychotic mental disorders.*

300. Neuroses
301. Personality disorders
302. Sexual deviations
303. Alcoholism
304. Drug dependence
305. Physical disorders of presumably psychogenic origin
306. Specified symptoms
307. Transient situational disturbances
308. Behaviour disorders in childhood
309. Mental disorders not specified as psychotic associated with physical conditions.

*310-315 Mental retardation*

310. Boarder-line mental retardation
311. Mild mental retardation
312. Moderate mental retardation
313. Severe mental retardation
314. Profound mental retardation
315. Unspecified mental retardation.

*Source:* Adapted from WHO (1965), International Classification of Diseases, 8th Revision, (ICD-8), Geneva: World Health Organization.

Dissatisfied with their earlier classification DSM-I the American Psychiatric Association, in 1968, brought out a more comprehensive system of classification known as DSM-II. It gave ten major categories of mental disorders, instead of three given under DSM-I as shown in Table 10.3.

**Table 10.3 DSM-II**

1. Mental retardation
2. Organic brain syndromes
3. Psychoses
   - **a.** Schizophrenia
   - **b.** Major affective disorders
   - c. Paranoid states
   - **d.** Other psychoses.
4. Neuroses.
5. Personality disorders
   - **a.** Personality disorders
   - **b.** Sexual deviations
   - c. Alcoholism
   - **d.** Drug dependence.
6. Psycho-physiologic disorders
7. Special symptoms
8. Transient situational disturbances
9. Behaviour disorders of childhood and adolescence
10. Conditions without manifest psychiatric disorder.

Adapted **from:** American Psychiatric Association, (1968), *Diagnostic and Statistical Manual of Mental Disorders* (2nd ed.), **DSM-II,** Washington **D.C.:** American Psychiatric Association.

In the years to follow, ICD-**8** and DSM-II were subjected to wide criticism on account of their specific limitations and shortcomings. To provide a more uniform pattern of classification and common terminology for the different countries of the world, WHO brought out, towards the end of 1977, an improved classification known as ICD-9

Table 10. 4: gives a summary of the Section V of ICD-9 dealing with the classification of mental diseases.

**Table 10.4**

**Summary of ICD-9 (Section V)**

| | |
|---|---|
| 290-319 | Mental disorders |

290-294
Organic
Psychotic
Conditions

| | |
|---|---|
| 290 | Senile and presenile psychiatric conditions |
| 291 | Alcoholic psychosis |
| 292 | Drug psychosis |
| 293 | Transient organic psychotic condition |
| 294 | Other organic psychotic conditions (chronic) |

*295-299 Other Psychoses*

| | |
|---|---|
| 295 | Schizophrenia |
| 296 | Affective psychoses |
| 297 | Paranoid states |
| 298 | Other organic psychoses |
| 299 | Psychoses with origin specific to childhood |

*300-302 Neurotic, Personality and Other non-psychotic disorders*

| | |
|---|---|
| 300 | Neurotic disorders |
| 301 | Personality disorders |
| 302 | Sexual deviations and disorders |

*303-305 Psychoactive substance*

| | |
|---|---|
| 303 | Alcohol dependence syndrome |
| 304 | Drug dependence |
| 305 | Non-dependence, abuse of drugs |

*306-311 Other Mental Disorders (primarily adult onset)*

| | |
|---|---|
| 306 | Physiological malfunctioning arising from mental disorders |

| | |
|---|---|
| 307 | Special symptoms or syndromes not classified elsewhere |
| 308 | Acute reaction to stress. |
| 309 | Adjustment reaction |
| 310 | Frontal lobe syndromes |
| 311 | Depressive disorders not classified elsewhere |
| *312-316 Mental disorders diagnosed in childhood* | |
| 312 | Disturbance of conduct not classified elsewhere |
| 313 | Disturbance of emotions specific to childhood and adolescence |
| 314 | Hyper kinetic syndrome of childhood |
| 315 | Specific reading retardation |
| 316 | Specified arithmetical retardation |
| 317-319 | Mental retardation. |

*Source:* Adapted from WHO (1977), International Classification of Diseases, 9th revision, (ICD-9), Geneva: World Health Organization

On the lines of WHO, the American Psychiatric Association, also tried to improve its DSM-II classification by setting up a new committee. It resulted in the emergence of DSM-III. The new system was named as "multiaxial classification system" because it allowed classification on five separate dimensions (axes) as shown in Table 10.5.

**Table 10.5: DSM-III**

*Axis I:* Clinical psychiatric syndrome(s) and other conditions

1. Organic mental disorders
2. Drug use disorders
3. Schizophrenic disorders
4. Paranoid disorders
5. Affective disorders
6. Psychoses not elsewhere classified
7. Anxiety disorders
8. Factitious disorders
9. Somatoform disorders
10. Dissociative disorders

*Axis* 11: Adult personality disorders and specific developmental disorders

1. Personality disorders
2. Psycho-sexual disorders
3. Disorders usually arising in childhood or adolescence
4. Reactive disorders not elsewhere classified
5. Disorders of impulse control not elsewhere classified
6. Sleep disorders
7. Other disorders and conditions

*Axis III:* Nonmental medical disorders

*Axis IV:* Severity of psychosocial stressors

*Axis V :* Highest level of recent adaptive functioning.

---

Adapted from: American Psychiatric Association, (1980), ***Diagnostic and Statistical Manual of Mental Disorders*** (3rd ed.), DSM-III , Washington D.C.: American Psychiatric Association.

After the emergence of the classification systems known as ICD-9 and DSM-III at the hands of WHO and American Psychiatric Association, there have been continued efforts on the part of these two bodies for improving and bringing new classification systems. In this concern, where WHO, has brought the classification systems known as ICD-10, ICD-11 in the years 2010 and 2019 respectively, the American Psychiatric Association is credited to bring the classification systems Known as DSM-III-R, DSM-IV, DSM-IV-TR, and DSM-V in the subsequent years. The different classification systems brought out by American Psychiatric Association with their increased vision and years of publication have been presented in the Table 10.6.

**Table 10.6: The Evolution and Developments in DSM**

| *Nomenclature of DSM* | *Number of Mental Disorders for which Diagnoses have been provided* | *Year of Publication* |
|---|---|---|
| DSM-I | 128 Disorders and Diagnoses | 1952 |
| DSM-II | 193 Disorders and Diagnoses | 1968 |
| DSM-III | 228 Disorders and Diagnoses | 1980 |
| DSM-III-R | 253 Disorders and Diagnoses | 1987 |
| DSM-IV | 383 Disorders and Diagnoses | 1994 |
| DSM-IV-TR | 383 Disorders and Diagnoses | 2000 |
| DSM-V | 541 Disorders and Diagnoses | 2013 |

Here in the text now we will be discussing about the latest developed classification systems of DSM, namely, DSM-IV-TR and DSM-V brought out in the years 2000 and 2013 respectively.

**DSM-IV-TR** was brought out in 2000. It consists of a total of five Axes. The first two Axis I and Axis II provide the necessary classification and diagnoses for 383 disorders. Among the rest three, where the third one Axis III mentions about General Medical Conditions and Axis IV about Psychosocial and Environmental Problems, the Axis V presents The Global Assessment of Functioning Scale (GAF Scale).

The classification of disorders provided in Axis-I and Axis-II is now presented in the Table 10.7 given below:

**Table 10.7: DSM-IV-TR**

---

**Axis I:**

1. **Disorders Usually First Diagnosed in Infancy, Childhood and Adolescence**
    - *Learning Disorders* (Reading Disorder, Mathematics Disorder, Disorder of Written Expression)
    - *Motor Skill Disorder* (Developmental Coordination Disorder)
    - *Communication Disorders* (Expressive Language Disorder, Mixed Receptive/ Expressive Language Disorder, Phonological Disorder, Stuttering)
    - *Pervasive Developmental Disorders* (Autistic, Rett's, Oppositional defiant and Asperger's Disorder)
    - *Attention-deficit and Disruptive Behaviour Disorders* (Attention-deficit/ Hyperactivity Disorder
    - *Feeding and Eating Disorders of Infancy or Early Childhood*
    - *Tic Disorders* (Tourette's Disorder, Chronic Motor or Vocal Tic Disorder, Transient Tic Disorder)
    - *Elimination Disorders* (Encopresis, Enurisis)
    - *Other Disorders of Childhood and Adolescence* (Separation of Anxiety Disorder, Selective Mutism, Reactive Attachment Disorder of Infancy or Early Childhood, Stereotypic Movement Disorder)
2. **Delirium, Dementia, and Amnestic and Other Cognitive Disorders**
3. **Substance-Related Disorders**
    - *Alcohol –Induced Disorders*
    - *Amphetamine -related Disorders*
    - *Caffeine- related Disorders*
    - *Cannabis –related Disorders*
    - *Caffeine- related Disorders*
    - *Cocaine- related Disorders*
    - *Hallucinogen- related Disorders*
    - *Inhalant- related Disorders*
    - *Nicotine- related Disorders*
    - *Opioid- related Disorders*

- *Phencyclidine- related Disorders*
- *Sedative, Hypnotic, or Anxiolytic - related Disorders*
- *Poly-substance - related Disorders*

4. **Schizophrenia and Other Psychotic Disorders**

- *Schizophrenia* (Paranoid Type, Disorganized Type, Catatonic Type, Undifferentiated Type, Residual Type)
- *Schizophreniform Disorder*
- *Schizoaffective Disorder*
- *Delusional Disorder*
- *Brief Psychotic Disorder*
- *Shared Psychotic Disorder*
- *Psychotic Disorder Due to a General Medical Condition*

5. **Mood Disorders (***Depressive, Bipolar, Mood Disorder due to a General Medical Condition and Substance-Induced Mood Disorder)*
6. **Anxiety Disorders**

- *Panic Disorder*
- *Agoraphobia without History of Panic Disorder*
- *Specific Phobia*
- *Social Phobia (social Anxiety Disorder)*
- *Obsessive-Compulsive Disorder*
- *Post-traumatic Stress Disorder*
- *Acute Stress Disorder*
- *Generalized Anxiety Disorder*
- *Anxiety Disorder Due to a General Medical Condition*
- *Substance-Induced Anxiety Disorder*

7. **Somatoform Disorders (***Somatization,Conversion ,Hypochondriasis,Body Dysmorphic and Pain Disorders)*
8. **Factitious Disorders**
9. **Dissociative Disorders (***Amnesia, Fugue, identity or Multiple Personality Disorder)*
10. **Sexual and Gender Identity Disorders**

*Sexual Dysfunctions* (Sexual Desire Disorders: Hypoactive Sexual Desire Disorder, Sexual Aversion Disorder, Sexual Arousal Disorder: Female Sexual Arousal Disorders: Male Erectile Disorder, Orgasmic Disorder: Female Orgasmic Disorder, Male Orgasmic Disorder, Premature Ejaculation, Sexual Pain Disorder, Sexual Dysfunction due to a General Medical Condition, Substance- Induced Sexual Dysfunction.)

*Paraphilias* (Exhibitionism, Fetishism, Frotteurism, Paedophilia, Sexual Masochism, Sexual Sadism, Voyeurism, Transvestic Fetishism)

*Gender Identity Disorders* (Gender Identity Disorder: In children, In Adolescents and Adults)

10. **Eating Disorders (***Anorexia Nervosa, Bulimia Nervosa and Eating Disorder Not Otherwise Specified*

11. **Sleep Disorders**
12. **Impulse Control Disorders Not Elsewhere Classified**

**Axis II**

1. **Mental Retardation**
2. **Personality Disorders** (*Paranoid, Schizoid, Schizotypal , Antisocial, Borderline, Histrionic, Narcissistic, Avoidant, Dependent and Obsessive-Compulsive Personality Disorder)*
3. **Other Conditions that may be a Focus of Clinical Attention**

---

*Source:* Adapted from American Psychiatric Association (2000), *The Diagnostic and Statistical Manual of Mental Disorders,* Washington D.C.: American Psychiatric Association.

## DSM-5

DSM-5 is the latest version of the Diagnostic and Statistical Manual of Mental Disorders brought out by the American Psychiatric Association (APA) in the year 2013. It is a 947 page manual that lists 541 diagnose. The classification of mental disorders provided in DSM-5 is presented in brief below in the **Table 10.8**.

**Table 10.8: DSM-5: Classification of mental disorders**

---

1. **Neurodevelopmental Disorders** (Intellectual Disability; Communication Disorders; Autism Spectrum Disorder; Attention-Deficit/Hyperactivity Disorder; Specific Learning Disorder; Motor Disorder; and Other Neurodevelopmental Disorders)
2. **Schizophrenia Spectrum and other Psychotic Disorders** (Schizotypal -Personality Disorder; Delusional Disorder; Brief Psychotic Disorder; Schzophreniform Disorder; Schzophrenia Bipolar and Depressive type; Substance/ Medication-Induced Psychotic Disorder; Psychotic Disorder Due to Another Medical Condition -With delusion or with hallucinations; Catatonia Associated With Another Mental Disorder; Catatonic Disorder Due to Another Medical Condition; Unspecified Catatonia; Other Specified Schizophrenia Spectrum and Other Psychotic Disorder; Unspecified Schizophrenia Spectrum and Other Psychotic Disorders; Bipolar and Related Disorders - with manic, hypomanic or mixed features; Other specified or unspecified bipolar and Related Disorder)
3. **Depressive Disorders** (Disruptive Mood Dysregulation Disorder; Persistent Depressive Disorder -Dysthymia; Permanent Dysphoric disorder; Depressive Disorder Due to Another Medical Condition; Other specified or Unspecified Depressive Disorder)
4. **Anxiety Disorders** (Separation Anxiety Disorder; Selective Mutism; Specific phobia; Social Anxiety Disorder-Social Phobia; Panic Disorder, Agoraphobia; Generalized Anxiety Disorder; Anxiety Disorder Due to Another Medical Condition; Other Specified or Unspecified Anxiety Disorder)
5. **Trauma -and Stressor- Related Disorders** (Reactive Attachment Disorder; Disinhibited Social Engagement Disorder; Post-traumatic Stress Disorder; Acute

Stress Disorder-with Depressive mood or anxiety, with disturbance of conduct or emotions or both, unspecified; Other Specified or Unspecified Trauma and Stress related Disorder

6. **Dissociative Disorders** (Dissociative Identity Disorder; Dissociative Amnesia; Depersonalization/ Derealization Disorder; Other Specified or Unspecified Dissociative Disorder)
7. **Somatic Symptom and Related Disorders** (Somatic Symptom Disorder; Illness Anxiety Disorder; Conversion Disorder-Functional Neurological Symptom Disorder, Psychological Factors Affecting Other Medical Conditions; Factitious Disorder; Other Specified or Unspecified Somatic Symptom and Related Disorder)
8. **Feeding and Eating Disorders** (Pica in Children or Adults; Rumination Disorder; Avoidant/ Restrictive Food Intake Disorder; Anorexia Nervosa; Bulimia Nervosa; Binge-Eating Disorder; Other Specified or Unspecified Feeding or Eating Disorder)
9. **Elimination Disorders** (Enuresis; Encopresis; Other Specified or Unspecified Elimination Disorder-with Urinary or Fecal symptoms)
10. **Sleep-Wake Disorders** (Insomnia Disorder; Hypersomnolence Disorder; Narcolepsy; Breathing-Related Sleep Disorders; Parasomnias Sleepwalking, Sleep Terror, Nightmare, Rapid Eye Movement Sleep Behaviour Disorder, Restless Legs Syndrome; Substance/Medication-Induced Sleep Disorder; Other Specified or Unspecified Insomnia Disorder; Other Specified or Unspecified Hypersomnolence Disorder; Other Specified or Unspecified Sleep -Wake Disorder).
11. **Sexual Dysfunctions** (Delayed Ejaculation; Erectile Disorder; Female Orgasmic Disorder; Female Sexual Interest/ Arousal Disorder; Genito-Pelvic Pain/ Penetration Disorder; Male Hypoactive Sexual Desire Disorder; Premature Ejaculation; Substance/ Medication- Induced Sexual Dysfunction; Other Specified or Unspecified Sexual Dysfunction)
12. **Gender Dysphoria** (Gender Dysphoria in Children or Adolescence and Adults; Other Specified or Unspecified Gender Dysphoria)
13. **Disruptive, Impulsive-Control, and Conduct Disorders** (Oppositional Defiant Disorder; Intermittent Explosive Disorder; Conduct Disorder; Antisocial Personality Disorder; Pyromania; Kleptomania; Other Specified or Unspecified Disruptive, Impulse-Control, and Conduct Disorder)
14. **Substance-Related and Addictive Disorders** (Alcohol- Related Disorders; Caffeine- Related Disorders; Cannabis- Related Disorders; hallucinogen- Related Disorders; Inhalant-Related Disorders; Opioid- Related Disorders; Sedative, Hypnotic or Anxiolytic- related Disorders; Stimulant- Related Disorders; Tobacco-Related Disorders; Other or Unknown Substance-Related Disorders; and Non-Substance Related Disorders)
15. **Neurocognitive Disorders** (Delirium; Major or Mild Neurocognitive Disorder Due to Alzheimer's Disease;

    Major or Mild Frontotemporal Neurocognitive Disorder; Major or Mild Neurocognitive Disorder with Lewy Bodies; Major or Mild Vascular Neurocognitive Disorder; Major or Mild Neurocognitive Disorder Due to

Traumatic Brain Injury; Major or Mild Neurocognitive Disorder Due to HIV Infection; Major or Mild Neurocognitive Disorder Due to Parkinson's Disease; Major or Mild Neurocognitive Disorder Due to Huntington's Disease ; Major or Mild Neurocognitive Disorder Due to Another Medical Condition ; Major or Mild Neurocognitive Disorder Due to Multiple Etiologies ; and Unspecified Neurocognitive Disorder)

16. **Personality Disorders-** ((i)*Cluster A Personality Disorders*-Paranoid, Schizoid and Schizotypal Disorders; (ii)*Cluster B Personality Disorders*- Antisocial, Borderline, Histrionic, and Narcissistic Personality Disorders; (iii) *Other Personality Disorders*- Personality Change Due to Another Medical Condition, Other Specified and Unspecified Personality Disorder)
17. **Paraphilic Disorders** (Voyeuristic Disorder; Exhibitionistic Disorder; Frotteuristic Disorder; Sexual Masochism Disorder; Sexual sadism Disorder; Paedophilic Disorder; Fetishistic Disorder; Transvestic Disorder; Other Specified or Unspecified Paraphilic Disorder)
18. **Other Mental Disorders** (Other Specified Mental Disorder Due to another Medical Condition; Unspecified Mental Disorder Due to Another Medical Condition; and Other Specified or Unspecified Mental Disorder)
19. **Medication-Induced Movement Disorders and Other Adverse Effects of Medication** (Neuroleptic-Induced Parkinsonism; Other Medication-Induced Parkinsonism; Neuroleptic Malignant Syndrome; Medication-Induced Acute Akathisia; Tardive Dyskinesia; Tardive Dystonia; Tardiv Akathisia; Medication-Induced Postrul Tremor; Other Medication-Induced Movement Disorder; Antidepressant Discontinuation Syndrome; and Other Adverse Effect of Medication)
20. **Other conditions That May Be a Focus of Clinical Attention-** (Problems related to Family Upbringing; Other Problems Related to Family, the Primary Support Group; Child Physical Abuse; Child Sexual Abuse ; Child Neglect, Child Psychological Abuse; Spouse or Partner Violence-Physical; Spouse or Partner Violence-Sexual; Spouse or Partner Violence-Psychological; Adult Abuse by Non-spouse or Non-partner; Educational and Occupational Problems; Housing and economic Problems; Other Problems Related to the Social Environment; Problems Related to Crime or Interaction with the Legal System; Other Health Service Encounters For Counselling and Medical Advice; Problems Related to Other Psychosocial. Personal, and environmental Circumstances; Other Circumstances of Personal History; Problems Related to Access to Medical and Other Health Care; and Non-adherence to Medical Treatment)

---

*Source:* Adapted from American Psychiatric Association (2013), *Diagnostic and Statistical Manual of Mental Disorders* (5th ed.), Washington, DC: American Psychiatric Association.

How does and in what way the latest classification DSM-5 stands distinguished from the previous ones? It may be briefly summarized as below:

**A. Nomenclatures for certain categories have been changed in DSM-5**

| *New Name given in DSM-5* | *Old Name* |
|---|---|
| Intellectual Disability | Mental Retardation |
| Major Neuro-cognitive Disorder | Dementia |
| Illness Anxiety Disorder | Hypochodriasis |
| Delayed Ejaculation | Male Orgasmic Disorder |
| Gender Dysphoria | Gender Identity Disorder |

**B. A few categories appearing in previous DSMs have been dropped in DSM-5**

(i) Dissociative fugue (sub- category of Dissociative Disorders in DSM-IV-TR)

(ii) Asperger's Disorder (sub-category of Pervasive Developmental Disorder in DSM-IV-TR)

(iii) Sexual Aversion Disorder (sub-category of Sexual Dysfunctions in DSM-IV-TR)

(iv) Substance Abuse and Substance Dependence (Both of them previously categorized separately have been submerged in the category Substance Use Disorder in DSM-5)

**C. A few new categories (not appearing in previous DSMs) have been added in DSM-5**

(i) Hoarding Disorder (a conscious, ongoing urge to accumulate possessions, as well as corresponding feelings of anxiety or mental anguish whenever those possessions get thrown away).

(ii) Excoriation Disorder (repeated picking at one's own skin which results in skin lesions and causes significant disruption in one's life).

(iii) Persistent Depressive Disorder (a consolidation of DSM-IV defined chronic major depressive disorder and dysthymic disorder)

(iv) Premenstrual Dysphoric Disorder (a severe form of premenstrual syndrome)

(v) Disruptive Mood Dysregulation Disorder (a childhood condition of extreme irritability, anger, and frequent, intense temper outbursts)

(vi) Somatic Symptom Disorder (characterized with distressing somatic symptoms along with abnormal thoughts, feelings, and behaviours in response to these symptoms).

(vii) Binge Eating Disorder (Recurrent and persistent episodes of binge eating)

(viii) Mild Neurocognitive Disorder (characterized by modest declines in memory or other cognitive functions)

## ICD-10 classification of mental and behavioural disorders

ICD- 10 is the Tenth Revision of the International Statistical Classification of Diseases and Related Health Problems brought out in the year 1994 by WHO. It includes in its Chapter V, a detailed classification of over 300 mental and behavioural disorders. ICD-10 is available in its two main versions (i) *Clinical Descriptions and Diagnostic Guidelines* and (ii) *Diagnostic Criteria for Research.*

The former provides clinical descriptions detailing the principal signs and symptoms of each disorder, together with other important but less specific associated features, as well as comprehensive guidelines for their diagnosis. The latter version is intended to help those researching specific disorders to maximize the homogeneity of study groups. To this end, it sets out criteria that allow the selection of individuals with clearly similar symptoms and other characteristics.

Here we are presenting the classes or main categories of mental disorders specified in ICD-10

**Table 10.9: Classification of Mental Disorders in ICD-10**

| Broad Class | Categories included |
|---|---|
| F00 to F09<br>**Organic, Including Symptomatic Mental Disorders** | F00 Dementia in Alzheimer's Disease<br>F01 Vascular Dementia<br>F02 Dementia in other diseases classified elsewhere<br>F03 Unspecified Dementia<br>F04 Organic amnestic syndromes, not induced by alcohol and other psychoactive substances<br>F05 Delirium, not induced by alcohol and other psychotic substances<br>F06 Other mental disorders due to brain damage and dysfunction and to physical disease<br>F07 Personality and behavioural disorders due to brain disease, damage and dysfunction<br>F08 Unassigned<br>F09 Unspecified organic or symptomatic mental disorder |
| F10 to F19<br>**Mental and Behavioural disorders due to Psychoactive substances use** | F10 Mental and Behavioural Disorder due to the use of Alcohol<br>F11 Mental and Behavioural Disorder due to the use of Opioids<br>F12 Mental and Behavioural Disorder due to the use of Cannabinoids<br>F13 Mental and Behavioural Disorder due to the use of Sedatives or Hypnotics<br>F14 Mental and Behavioural Disorder due to the use of Cocaine<br>F15 Mental and Behavioural Disorder due to the use of other stimulants including Caffeine<br>F16 Mental and Behavioural Disorder due to the use of Hallucinogens |

| | |
|---|---|
| | F17 Mental and Behavioural Disorder due to the use of Tobacco<br>F18 Mental and Behavioural Disorder due to the use of Volatile solvents<br>F19 Mental and Behavioural Disorder due to the use of multiple drug and of other psychoactive substances |
| F20 to F29<br>**Schizophrenia,**<br>**Schizotypal and Delusional Disorders** | F20 Schizophrenia<br>F21 Schizotypal disorder<br>F22 Persistent delusional disorders<br>F23 Acute and transient psychotic disorders<br>F24 Induced delusional disorder<br>F25 Schizoaffective disorders<br>F26 Unassigned<br>F27 Unassigned<br>F28 Other non-organic psychotic disorders<br>F29 Unspecified non-organic psychosis |
| F30 to F39<br>**Mood**<br>**(affective)**<br>**Disorders** | F30 Manic episode<br>F31 Bipolar affective disorder<br>F32 Depressive episode<br>F33 Recurrent depressive disorder<br>F34 Persistent mood (affective) disorders<br>F35 Unassigned<br>F36 Unassigned<br>F37 Unassigned<br>F38 Other mood (affective) disorders<br>F39 Unspecified mood (affective) disorders |
| F40 to F49<br>**Neurotic,**<br>**Stress related**<br>**and**<br>**Somatoform Disorders** | F40 Phobic anxiety disorders<br>F41 Other anxiety disorders<br>F42 Obsessive-Compulsive disorders<br>F43 Reaction to severe stress and adjustment disorders<br>F44 Dissociative (Conversion) disorders<br>F45 Somatoform disorders<br>F46 Unassigned<br>F47 Unassigned<br>F48 Other Neurotic disorders<br>F49 Unassigned |

| | |
|---|---|
| F50 to F59<br>**Behavioural syndromes Associated with Psychophysical disturbances and Physical factors** | F50 Eating disorders<br>F51 Non-organic sleep disorders<br>F52 Sexual dysfunction, not caused by organic disorder and disease<br>F53 Mental and behavioural disorders associated with the puerperium, not elsewhere classified<br>F54 Psychological and behavioural factors associated with disorders or diseases classified elsewhere<br>F55 Abuse of non-dependence producing substances such as vitamins, steroids or hormones and antidepressants<br>F56 Unassigned<br>F57 Unassigned<br>F58 Unassigned<br>F59 Unspecified behavioural syndromes associated with psychological disturbances and physical factors |
| F60 to F69<br>**Disorders of Adult Personality and Behaviour** | F60 Specific personality disorders- paranoid, schizoid, dissocial personality disorder<br>F61 Mixed or other personality disorders<br>F62 Enduring personality changes, not attributable to brain damage and disease<br>F63 Habit and Impulsive disorders such as pathological gambling, pathological stealing (Kleptomania)<br>F64 Gender Identity disorders such as Trans-sexualism<br>F65 Disorders of sexual preferences such as fitishism, exhibitionism<br>F66 Psychological and behavioural disorders associated with sexual development and orientation such as sexual relationship disorders<br>F67 Unassigned<br>F68 Other disorders of adult personality and behaviours<br>F69 Unspecified disorder of adult personality and behaviour |
| F70 to F79<br>**Mental Retardation** | F70 Mild<br>F71 Moderate<br>F72 Severe<br>F73 Profound<br>F74 Unassigned<br>F75 Unassigned<br>F76 Unassigned<br>F77 Unassigned<br>F78 Other Mental retardation<br>F79 Unspecified Mental retardation |

| | |
|---|---|
| F80 to F89<br>**Disorders of Psychological Development** | F80 Specific developmental disorders of speech and language<br>F81 Specific developmental disorder of scholastic skills<br>F82 Specific developmental disorders of motor function<br>F83 Mixed specific developmental disorder<br>F84 Pervasive developmental disorders<br>F85 Unassigned<br>F86 Unassigned<br>F87 Unassigned<br>F88 Other disorders of psychological development<br>F89 Unspecified disorder of psychological development |
| F90 to F98<br>**Behavioural and Emotional Disorders with Onset usually Occurring in Childhood and Adolescence**<br><br>F-99<br>Unspecified<br>Mental Disorders | F90 Hyper Kinetic Disorders<br>F91 Conduct disorders<br>F92 Mixed disorders of conduct and emotions<br>F93 Emotional disorders with onset specific to childhood such as separation anxiety, sibling rivalry<br>F94 disorders of social functioning with onset specific to childhood and adolescence<br>F95 Tic Disorders such as chronic motor or vocal tic disorders<br>F96 Unassigned<br>F97 Unassigned<br>F98 Other Behavioural and emotional disorders with onset usually occurring in childhood and adolescence such as stammering, feeding disorders<br>F99 Unspecified mental disorders, not otherwise specified |

*Source:* Adapted from World Health Organization (2010), *The ICD-10 Classification of Mental and Behavioural Disorders: Clinical Descriptions and Diagnostic Guidelines,* 10th ed. Geneva: World Health Organization.

## ICD-11

ICD-11 is the latest version of the WHO classification system meant for bringing needed improvement in the diagnosis and classifications of mental diseases, mental and behavioural disorders and health problems on the global basis. In this concern, a final draft of the **ICD-11** system has been submitted in this very year, 2019 to WHO's World Health Assembly (WHA) for official endorsement. The overall significance of ICD -11 over the existing ICD-10 may be briefed as below:

- ICD-11 is much easier and simple in its use than ICD-10
- It is more clinically relevant on account of the systematic reliance on the use of code combinations and extension codes
- It has a very much multilingual in character existing in 43 languages in electronic versions

- It is capable of providing description of each disease entity (category) in a quite clear terms aiming to help users in understanding the meaning of the category in human-readable terms. It is a quite mentionable advancement over ICD-10, which had only title headings.

All these above discussed ICD and DSM classification systems provided by WHO and American Psychiatric Association are however, somewhat technical and cumbersome. Their comprehension may be difficult for the beginners especially the students of degree classes in the subject abnormal psychology. For doing away with this difficulty and also for a comprehensive discussion of the mental disorders, and abnormalities in this text, we are hereby producing a relatively simple and functional classification (**Table 10.10**) for being employed to the discussion carried out in the coming chapters of this text.

**Table 10.10**

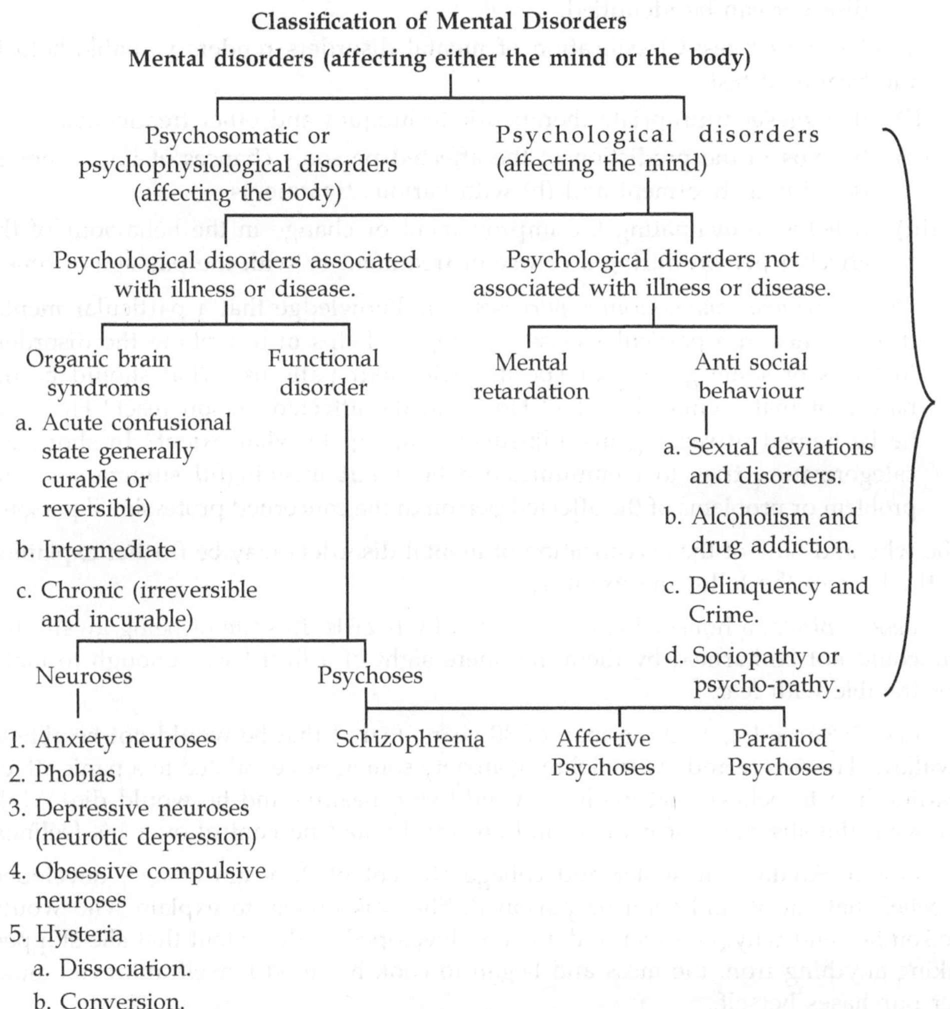

## The Necessity and Purposes of Classification

The classification of mental disorders of diseases is based on the following similarities.

(i) Similarity of the symptoms and syndromes.

(ii) Similarity of the treatment techniques.

(iii) Similarity of the possibilities of improvement.

In the light of the above the commonly recognised functions or purposes of the classification of mental disorders or diseases may be summarized as below:

1. *Diagnosis purposes:* The classification of mental disorders helps the diagnosis on the following grounds.
   (i) Symptoms and syndromes related to the specific class can be properly investigated,
   (ii) The possible factors contributing in the development or maintenance of the disorder can be identified.
2. *Treatment purposes:* Classification of mental disorders renders valuable help in the treatment task:
   (i) It suggests appropriate therapeutic techniques and other treatments.
   (ii) It helps in the prediction of the affected person's chances of improvement (a) without treatment and (b) with various treatments.
   (iii) It helps in evaluating the improvement or change in the behaviour of the affected person during a course of treatment or with the passage of time.
3. *Descriptive and communicative purposes:* The knowledge that a particular mental disorder lies in a particular class or category helps in describing the disorders in terms of some general or specific behaviour patterns. What should be the nature of that mental disorder? How can the affected person react? How can he be helped in seeking his adjustment and up to what extent? In short, the categorization tries to communicate a brief but meaningful summary of the problem or problems of the affected person to the concerned professional persons.

The why and how of the classification of mental disorders may be further explained in the light of the following examples.

*Case 1*: Bimla, a housewife, was terrified by lizards. In spite of being aware that she could not be harmed by them, the mere sight of a lizard was enough to make her tremble with fear.

*Case 2:* Surendra, a young man of 30 years, feared that he would not be able to swallow. The severe and overwhelming anxiety sometimes escalated to a panic attack leading him to believe that his heart would stop beating and he would die. While knowing the absurdity of his fear and anxiety he had no control over his feelings.

*Case 3:* Savita, a hosteller and college student of 22 years of age, developed a belief that she would soon be poisoned. She was unable to explain who would poison her and why. Her fear and anxiety developed to the extent that she stopped taking anything from the mess and began to cook her food herself and even make her purchases herself.

*Case 4 :* Prem Singh, a retired army personnel, believed that the British government was after him as he had been in association with Azad Hind Fauj. The government of free India should now take full responsibility of protecting him from being kidnapped and killed by many people in police uniform spying for the British government. He wrote to the D.I.G. police for appropriate screening of the district police to identify the British spies. He also wrote to the Prime Minister and President of India, requesting them for his adequate protection. Gradually, his anxiety and fear became so intense that he confined himself in a locked room closing all the windows and ventilators so that none could get at him.

*Case 5:* Ramesh Chandra, 23 years of age, reported for psychiatric help. He believed that he would be unable to perform normal sexual act as he was impotent. Therefore, his fiancée should not suffer unnecessarily on account of him. He insisted on her forgetting him and to marry someone else. On medical examination it was found that there was nothing wrong with his sex organs and his fear had no organic cause.

All the five cases cited above are obviously the cases of mental disorders. Their diagnosis, understanding and treatment definitely requires some classification since it would be futile to group them in a broad category—mental disorder. The cases have some similarities and also dissimilarities. Let us classify them on this basis.

The symptoms of fear and anxiety are common to all. In the cases of Savita and Prem Singh, the disorder is in the thought process (delusion or hallucination). They have beliefs which are irrational and baseless. There is a gross distortion or misrepresentation of external reality in both these cases which is significantly absent in the remaining three cases. These two cases may then be classified as psychotics.

The other three cases show neurotic symptoms but the last one typically differs in some characteristics with the cases of Bimla and Surendra. The behaviour patterns in the case of Ramesh Chandra are significantly attached to his sex behaviour. In the absence of any organic cause his problem is concerned with psychic impotence—the common psycho-physiological disorder associated with sex. The remaining two cases of Bimla and Surendra may then be classified as neurotics.

On further classification, we may differentiate the cases of Bimla and Surendra by distinguishing the particular type of neurosis. Similarly, the psychotic cases of Savita and Prem Singh may also be further differentiated.

The problem of differentiation and classification is a typical one in any attempt of the diagnosis and treatment of the mental diseases and disorders. The symptoms often overlap. Even different diagnoses may have symptoms in common. Take the case of schizophrenia. Here a particular patient may have delusions and hallucinations but along with these psychotic symptoms the neurotic symptoms like excessive fear, anxiety, hysteria, depression and obsessive-compulsive reactions may also be present. Typically, the anxiety symptoms may occur in all cases of mental disorders.

Therefore, a mere diagnosis of anxiety reactions will not serve any useful purpose for some classification. The other symptoms related to the similarities and differences typical to a particular class or category of mental disorders have therefore definitely to be searched out for an appropriate classification.

## Summary

- Attempts for the classification of mental disorders may be studied in terms of the old era, modern era and contemporary position. In the old era, Hippocrates' classification (mania, melancholia and phrenesis), Indian classification (*Satguna, Rajoguna* and *Tamoguna*) and Kraepelin's classification are important. However, these are of purely historical interest.
- The modern era witnesses the development of a number of classification systems Developed by two agencies—American Psychiatric Association and WHO. The systems developed by the former are named as DSM (Diagnostic and Statistical Manual of Mental Disorders) and by the latter as ICD (International Classification of Diseases). Up to this time, American Psychiatric Association has brought out a number of manuals in the name of DSM-I, DSM-II, DSM-III, DSM III-R, DSM-IV, DSM IV-TR, and DSM-5 from the year 1952 to 2013. In comparison to the use of DSM's, ICD's developed by WHO are in wide use throughout the world on Global Basis on the part of clinicians, practitioners, health workers, students and researchers in the field.
- The contemporary position witnesses the development of DSM-5 and ICD-11 in the years 2013 and 2019 respectively at the hands of APS and WHO.
- **The classification** of mental disorders helps in the diagnosis process and treatment task, it also communicates a brief but meaningful summary of the problem of the patient to the concerned professional persons.

## REFERENCES

American Psychiatric Association (1952), *Diagnostic and Statistical Manual of Mental Disorders,* Washington D.C.: American Psychiatric Association.

American Psychiatric Association, (1968), *Diagnostic and Statistical Manual of Mental Disorders* (2nd ed.), **DSM-II,** Washington **D.C.:** American Psychiatric Association.

American Psychiatric Association, (1980), *Diagnostic and Statistical Manual of Mental Disorders,*(3rd ed.), DSM-III Washington D.C.: American Psychiatric Association.

American Psychiatric Association (2000), *The Diagnostic and Statistical Manual of Mental Disorders,* Washington D.C.: American Psychiatric Association.

American Psychiatric Association (2013), *Diagnostic and Statistical Manual of Mental Disorders* (5th ed.), Washington, DC: American Psychiatric Association.

WHO (1965), International Classification of Diseases, 8th Revision, (ICD-8), Geneva: World Health Organization.

WHO (1977), International Classification of Diseases, 9th revision, (ICD-9), Geneva: World Health Organization.

WHO (1992), International Statistical Classification of Diseases and Related Health Problems, 10th revision (ICD-10), Geneva: World Health Organization.

World Health Organization (2010), *The ICD-10 Classification of Mental and Behavioural Disorders: Clinical Descriptions and Diagnostic Guidelines,* 10th ed. Geneva: World Health Organization.

# 11

# PSYCHO-PHYSIOLOGICAL DISORDERS

Psycho-physiological disorders have been known as psycho-somatic disorders which implies that the mind (psyche) determines the disease or disorders of the body (soma). In fact, this wider conception regarded "mind" and "body" as inseparable aspects of the whole functioning organism and established a close relationship between psychological state of the mind and bodily sickness. This relationship may be studied in the light of the following two aspects.

1. *The effect of psychological attitude on body sickness:* The positive psychological attitude reflected in "fighting spirit" and "faith healing" helps recovery in serious diseases and accidents. Even in such diseases as tuberculosis or cancer the favourable attitude of the patient increases the chances of his recovery. On the other hand, the negative altitude reflected in the belief that he cannot get well or his inherent intention for not getting well cast the negative effect.
2. *The effect of body sickness on psychological attitude*: The persons who are seriously ill or suffering with acute or painful body diseases are often seen mentally upset and emotionally disturbed. In their cases the anxiety and pessimism, resulting from their bodily sickness, is readily displaced to other situations making them disturbed and maladjusted.

In this way, there seems a close body-mind relationship in determining the causes and treatment of mental disorders or disabilities suffered by an organism. Where bodily diseases may have psychological origin, the psychological ailments may also arise from organic diseases. Generally, such diseases or disorders may be divided into the following three categories:

1. *Predominantly organic or physiological:* The diseases like tuberculosis, cancer and physical injuries like a broken leg belong to this category. They have no psychological origin but their treatment, to a great extent, is influenced by the psychological state or attitude of the patient.
2. *Predominantly psychological or psyche:* The disorders having no significant organic cause and predominantly affecting the psychological functioning of the organism (such as defence ***mechanisms)*** may be included into this category. A close analysis of the disorders belonging to ***this category*** may reveal that they are not at ***all*** uninfluenced by one's bodily state—normal or abnormal health.

3. ***Both organic and psychological factors equally significant:*** This category includes disorders or maladjustment of the behaviour or personality of an individual in which both organic and psychological factors are conspicuously significant in their origin and in their treatment. These disorders are termed as psycho-physiological disorders.

According to the American Psychiatric Association publication (1968:46),

*"psycho-physiological disorders are characterized by physical symptoms that are caused by emotional factors and involve a single organ system, usually under autonomic nervous system intervention. The physiological changes involved are those that normally accompany certain emotional states, but in these disorders the changes are more intense and sustained."*

This definition leads us to the following characteristics of psycho-physiological disorders:

1. Psycho-physiological disorders always exhibit one or the other typical physical symptoms like pain, vomiting, difficulty in breathing, diarrhoea etc. It is the severity of the distress caused by these symptoms that usually compels the individual to seek medical help.
2. Although the physical symptoms developed on account of the psycho-physiological disorders appear similar to those reflected in certain emotional states (anxiety, anger etc.). Yet the visceral effects of emotional conflict in these disorders are so pronounced that actual and irreversible damage may be done to the body's structure. In this way a so-called psychological illness or disorder turns into "a real" illness or disorder with identifiable tissue pathology.
3. In psycho-physiological disorders the emotional conflicts affect the viscera through the autonomic nervous system which has two main divisions known as sympathetic and parasympathetic systems. These two systems of the autonomic nervous system are controlled by the brain in such a way that in normal conditions the effects of the two systems are kept in approximate balance. It results in the predominance of either sympathetic or parasympathetic activity flooding a single organ system-respiratory, circulatory, etc.
4. The psycho-physiological disorders are neither exclusively caused by psychological factors nor by the organic but in all cases, they are brought about by an interaction of psychological and organic factors.

## Distinction Between Psycho-Physiological Disorders and Conversion Neurosis:

Both these disorders involve bodily symptoms and are the consequences of poorly handled emotional conflicts. However, the following distinctions may be made between these two disorders,

1. In psycho-physiological disorders the physical disturbances are related to the autonomic nervous system and hence are not fully under one's voluntary control, while in conversion neurosis physical symptoms involve the sensory and motor nerves of the central nervous system and are hence subject to voluntary control.

2. Conversion neurosis produces physical disabilities that lack an adequate organic basis, while in the psycho-physiological disorders the "adequate organic basis' is present.
3. In psycho-physiological disorders the physical disturbances are real enough and not merely symbolic in nature as in the case of conversion neurosis.
4. Whereas psycho-physiological disorders result from the prolonged effect of natural reaction to emotional stress, the conversion neurosis often results from an unconscious symbolic expression of emotional conflicts.
5. Psycho-physiological disorders may very often result in actual and irreversible damage to the body's structure which can be life-threatening, whereas such happenings are quite rare in conversion neurosis.

## The Main Psycho-Physiological Disorders

The classification system DSM-II of the American Psychiatric Association has mentioned the following ten categories of psycho- physiological disorders:

1. Respiratory disorders
2. Cardiovascular disorders
3. Gastro-intestinal disorders
4. Genito-urinary disorders
5. Skin disorders
6. Endocrine disorders
7. Hemic and lymphatic disorders
8. Muscular-skeletal disorders
9. Neurological disorders
10. Sensory disorders.

1. **Respiratory Disorders:** Respiratory disorders are concerned with the malfunctioning or dysfunction of the respiratory system. A few common psycho-physiological disorders are as following:
   (a) *Asthma:* The main symptom involves difficulty in breathing (wheezing) and a sense of constriction of the chest. In psycho-physiological cases of asthma, the muscles in the walls of the bronchi (tubes in the lungs) contract because of the relative under activity of the sympathetic system or of the relative over-activity of the parasympathetic system.
   (b) *Common cold:* It consists of the inflammation of the muscular membranes of the nose and throat with profuse discharge.
   (c) *Rhinitis:* It involves noninfectious inflammation and swelling of the nasal mucosa with itching, sneezing and profuse watery secretion from the nose.
   (d) *Hay fever:* It concerns with some sort of allergic reaction in which the mucous membranes of the nose become inflamed.
   (e) *Hyperventilation*: Literally it means "over breathing". It consists of episodes of fairly deep breathing with the mouth open or rapid shallow breathing

and results in the sensations of dizziness, chest pain, blurred vision and tingling of or numbness in the extremities.

What causes such disorders of the respiratory system has been a matter of wide investigation. Some of the common causes are given below.

(i) *Genetic influences (hereditary cause):* One may inherit a tendency towards respiratory weakness which may make one prone to allergies and infections of the respiratory system.

(ii) *Allergies and infections* Respiratory disorders are often caused by allergies and infections of the respiratory system. Physiologically, allergies are sensitivity reactions that occur when certain substances come in contact with body tissues. In the case of respiratory disorders, it concerns with the hypersensitivity to substance (like dust, ragweed, smoke, a particular odour or smell, food or drink etc.), which are inhaled or ingested.

(iii) *Psychological factors*: Psychological factors work both as predisposing as well as precipitating causes for the respiratory disorders. Many individuals learn to be ill by feeling the utmost necessity of falling ill as their becoming ill may gain them attention or affection (from whom they wish to secure it) and or freedom from some demands. Emotional disturbances and unfavourable state of mind like anxiety, depression, anger, irritation, neglect or isolation and frustration may create respiratory disorders through intervention of autonomic nervous system. For example, rhinitis may be caused by the congestion growing out of the emotional disturbances. These psychological factors work as precipitating causes by lowering the resistance of an individual and thus making him susceptible to the various respiratory disorders or hindering treatment, and secondly by increasing the trouble or worsening the state of the individual especially under stress situation.

2. **Cardiovascular Disorders:** Today the cases of disorders and diseases of the heart and vascular system are on the increase. The major cardiovascular disorders with psycho-physiological factors are hypertension, angina pectoris, migraine and coronary disease.

   a. *Hypertension:* It is a chronic stale of high blood pressure. It may have organic causes in the form of the interference with the circulatory function of the kidneys. When no such organic cause can be found the condition is referred to as essential hypertension, indicating that it is caused by emotional factors.

   b. *Angina pectoris:* It is severe pain in the chest. In the form of organic cause, it is related with an insufficient supply of oxygen to the heart muscles. But in many cases, the individuals experiencing anginal pain and a feeling of being stabbed in the heart, usually, do not show any signs of organic disturbances indicating that they may also be caused by psychological factors.

   c. *Migraine*: It involves extremely painful headaches. The pain usually occurs on the side of the head. Sometimes it is associated with nausea and blurred vision. The attack rarely lasts more than twenty-four hours and is often much briefer. It is generally caused by the sympathetically innervated contraction followed by dilation of blood vessels in the brain. The present emotional disturbance, the early psychological experiences and the genetic influences may be the other causes of migraine disorders in addition to or absence of the known bodily causes.

d. *Coronary diseases:* Diseases of the heart like clotting of blood (thrombosis) blocking one of the vessels serving the heart involves both physiological and psychological factors. On account of the psychological stress situations, the rate of blood clotting is usually increased. Anxiety, anger and excitement result in the increase of heart palpitation which in turn increases resistance to the flow of blood and speeds up blood clotting. The presence of such psychological factors, thus, may work as predisposing or precipitating causes for the coronary diseases or heart disorders.

3. **Gastro Intestinal Disorders:** According to Mahoney (1980:243) disorders of the gastro-intestinal system may be roughly divided into three types (a) anorexia nervosa, (b) digestive problems and (c) peptic ulcer and colitis.

a. *Anorexia nervosa:* Loss of appetite is known as anorexia. In the absence of organic disorder when it is caused by emotional factors it is referred to as anorexia nervosa. The more severe cases of anorexia nervosa are characterised by weight loss to the point of emaciation. This disorder is much more frequent among girls and young women of the middle and upper socioeconomic classes with symptoms of menstrual disturbances, slow heart beat rate and constipation. Its onset often occurs during or shortly after adolescence, at which time the young girl becomes very conscious of her weight. She goes on "crash" starvation diets. As she starves herself ever thinner, she may adamantly deny that she is underweight and may seem almost phobic about weight gain. Consequently, she resorts to a kind of voluntary self-starvation many times complaining that food disgusts her, or that she is afraid of choking on it or of vomiting after eating. In some cases, self-induced vomiting are frequent rituals to cleanse one's body of food alter the 'sin' of eating. According to some writers, anorexia nervosa is often related to sexual events in the patient's life history—the onset of puberty, guilt felt in connection with sexual activity or fantasy etc. A desire to remain undeveloped and being a favoured child than a responsible adult, an unconscious association of food with impregnation, continuation of childhood negativism created by parents over the child's health and nourishment may be some other psychological factors contributing towards this malfunctioning of gastrointestinal system.

b. *Disorders related with digestive problems*: Emotional factors are responsible for the serious alteration of a delicate balance of digestive enzymes and acids in our body which in turn, as Mahoney (1980:245) observes, give rise to the following digestive problems.

(i) Diarrhoea—frequent liquid bowel movements.

(ii) Constipation—infrequent and occasionally painful bowel movements.

(iii) Nausea—loss of appetite and feeling of imminent vomiting.

(iv) Gastritis – an inflammation of the lining of the stomach often associated with an excess stomach acid and a burning sensation.

c. *Peptic ulcer and colitis:* Peptic ulcer and colitis represent the disorders associated with structural damage to the stomach and intestines.

*Peptic ulcer* is an open sore (an inflamed wound) on the lining of the stomach or more frequently in duodenum (the upper portion of the small intestine). An important symptom is pain which a person experiences after meals and which can be eased only by eating. There may be nausea or vomiting along with pain. There is bleeding in severe cases. It is caused by the corrosive action of the overactivity and excessive secretion of the digestive acids on the protective mucous membranes of the stomach and small intestine. The ulcers arise from a complex interplay of emotional and organic factors. Emotional states are closely related to the physiological factors responsible for the cause of ulcer. A strong and sustained conflict evokes a chronic emotional response usually of hostility or anxiety. The inability to reduce the emotional tension in some harmless ways (like defence mechanisms or proper channelisation) causes the stomach or duodenum to be susceptible to injury by its own acid secretions. It has often been found that the persistent emotional stress and the resulting autonomic nervous system activities are responsible for the over-activity and excessive secretion of digestive acids. They cause ulcer by weakening the mucous membranes and breaking down the digestive tissues. It is also significant to note that the people having a higher achievement motivation, aggressive nature, resentment and higher anxiety level are more susceptible to ulcer. This supports the role of emotional tensions and stresses in the development of ulcers.

***Colitis*** is an inflammation of the colon (large intestine). Its first sign is often the presence of mucus in the stools. If the inflammation continues over a long period of time, the colon may suffer structural damage in the form of lesions developing into ulcerative colitis. This psycho-physiological disorder has been recognised to have a strong emotional episode like death of some dear ones, separation or divorce, loss of a job or property etc. Similarly, anger, hostility and strong resentment, lack of emotional maturity have also been found to play a decisive role in the development of colitis.

4. **Genito-Urinary Disorders:** Many psycho -physiological disorders are connected with the genito-urinary system of our body. Some of them are urinary disorders, menstrual disorders and disorders associated with sex.

   a. *Urinary disorders*: The frequency of urination is known to increase in a state of anxiety or nervousness. Similarly, under psychological stress bladder function in some persons is inhibited. The urinary tract is connected with autonomic fibres and therefore it is quite possible that the emotional difficulties may prove an important causative factor of urinary disorders. Psychological conflict and emotional state of the child has been found the sole factor in many cases of enuresis (bed wetting), the most common urinary disorder of childhood. The validity of the psychological factors causing urinary disorders may be sufficiently proved on the basis of the findings of the researches conducted at the time of war in U S. A, which noted a very common prevalence of enuresis among men in army recruiting centres.

b. *Menstrual disorders:* Menstrual disorders in women are often caused by the emotional factors. Dysmenorrhea or painful menstruation is one such disorder which may have autonomic basis. Similarly, amenorrhoea, related with the failure of menstruation for several months, may be caused by psychological factors like intense desire for pregnancy, a bodily defence against sexuality, emotional shocks, tension created by marital discord or sexual conflicts.

c. *Disorders associated with sex:* Two of the major psychophysiological disorders connected with sex are impotence in men and frigidity in women. Only a few cases of these disorders are found to have an organic cause while in most cases psychological factors play a key role. Hostility towards the partner, anxiety and fear of disease, injury or pregnancy and guilt feeling concerning sex are the major sources of such disorders. As a result, the impotent male is unable to perform the sexual act and derive pleasure out of it. Similarly, in the frigid female there is either a pathological lack of sexual desire or a diminished desire for sex. In chronic cases it leads to dyspareunia (painful intercourse) in which the establishment *of* normal heterosexual relationships becomes difficult or impossible on account of the local neuromuscular reaction in the form of vaginal spasms.

5. **Skin Disorders**: In day-to-day life our skin may be seen to mirror many of our emotions. The stages of embarrassment, anger, tension and stresses may exhibit some typical states of our skin. The skin, in fact, is so richly supplied with small blood vessels controlled by the autonomic nervous system that it becomes a sensitive indicator of the emotional behaviour and consequently psychological factors may successfully lead to various skin disorders. Some of the most common skin disorders are.

- *Acne:* It is a disorder in which oily secretions clog pores or form pimples.
- *Dermatitis or eczema (allergic):* It involves inflammation of the skin often associated with an itching sensation. In neurodermatitis there is specific inflammation of the skin with cause of the emotional origin.
- *Hives:* It is an allergic reaction in which affected skin areas may become inflamed and itchy.
- *Dandruff:* It involves an accumulation of greasy scales in the hair.
- *Herpes simplex:* In this disorder there are inflamed blisters (cold sores) usually around the mouth.
- *Hyperhidrosis:* It involves excessive perspiration which is sometimes accompanied by blisters, rash, or infection.

All these skin disorders may have organic as well as psychological causes.

Emotional disturbances and stressful events are observed to cause various skin disorders. For example, high stress situations may lead to typical emotionally linked sweat responses (hyperhidrosis) quite different from the heat related perspiration. Similarly, the acne and eczema disorders may get precipitated or increased substantially during emotional strains and stresses. It has been also observed that skin disorders can be learned like other autonomic and visceral symptoms. Commenting on this aspect Kisker (1964:222-223) writes.

*Disorders of the skin usually cannot be hidden. The evidence of the sufferer's distress is quite evident to everyone. For this reason, there are immediate and considerable expressions, of attention and concern from friends, family members and physicians. Environment support is strong, and if the person affected perceives the symptoms as being rewarding in any way, they are reinforced and autonomic learning occurs.*

## Other Psycho-Physiological Disorders

In addition to the five types of major psycho-physiological disorders described in above, we have the following categories of disorders:

*Endocrine disorders* are related to the disorders of the glandular functioning. The functioning of these glands has a close relation with the autonomic nervous system. Disturbance or deviations from the normal conditions in one, automatically upsets the other. That is why emotional stresses have been found to cause over-activity or under-activity of the endocrine glands (for example, excessive activity of the thyroid gland in hyper thyroid disorder). On the other hand, glandular dysfunction caused by hereditary, biological or environmental factors may lead to the emotional problems and behaviour disorders.

*Hemic and lymphatic disorders* are related with the disorders of the blood and lymph systems of our body. Psychological factors are found to play a substantial role in these disorders. For example, anemia is known to be caused or precipitated by emotional disturbances and stressful events.

*Musculoskeletal disorders* are associated with the bones and voluntary muscles of our body. Some of the important psycho- physiological disorders of this type are backache, muscle cramps, psychogenic rheumatism and arthritis. In these disorders of emotional origin, the individual experiences pain localized in the bones or voluntary muscles of the back, or the rest of the body. For example, in arthritis (pain due to inflammation of a joint), emotional factors play their part through the autonomic system by inducing the blood supply to the affected part.

In all types of psycho-physiological disorders discussed above, we have found a close association between psyche and body factors affecting each other. Truly speaking, these disorders are always the result of a close interaction between organic (genetic and other biological factors) and psychological factors. Psychological factors sometimes work as predisposing causes and at the other times as strong precipitating ones. The role of causative factors may be analysed through the case studies of a few disorders.

***Case 1 (A case of asthma):*** Kavita, a young woman of 22 years of age, was reported for the treatment of asthma. The patient was the only child of a happy marriage. She had a history of asthma since the age of six. Her mother was a patient of asthma and her father and other members of the family were very sympathetic and attentive to her mother. The patient was severely handicapped by the disease until she was fourteen years. This attack then ceased until the honeymoon, which was her first night away from her parents. In the subsequent year her condition got too serious. In the interview she revealed that interaction with her husband had become very strained and that she often experienced difficulty in breathing when confronted with her domestic unhappiness.

***Case 2 (A case of peptic ulcer):*** A young man was admitted for the treatment of peptic ulcer. As a child he was quite submissive and was always in the company and protection of his brother five years older than him, and parents who provided him much attention. When he was thirteen, his brother died and about two years later he lost his father. Following the death of his father, his mother became psychologically dependent on him, consulting him about important problems and requiring him generally to substitute for both his older brother and his father, a situation for which he was completely unprepared intellectually and otherwise. While maintaining a secure outer appearance, he was aroused emotionally and his emotional reactions were repeatedly intensified by the excessive expectations of his mother. At the age of eighteen he experienced a short period of stomach discomfort which was followed by the initial haemorrhaging of a duodenal ulcer. (Adapted from Davison and Neale, 1978).

*Case 3: (A case of anorexia nervosa)* A young girl Kamini 25 years of age, reported for medical help. She was an emaciated girl weighing 28 kg and a height of five feet. She was depressed and seemed to be totally preoccupied with not becoming fat and her parents could not reason well with her about her diet. Historically she was traced to be normal until she was 21 years of age. With an occasional remark of her friend and family members, she began to feel that she was too fat and not as attractive as her friends. Her parents were in search of a good match for her. Her belief about her figure became more pronounced after going through a few matrimonial interviews. She rigorously started to slim and became fussy about her diet. Her periods stopped after a year and gradually she became weak and thin. For the last six months she had been emaciated to work and felt difficulty carrying out her daily routine.

*Case 4: (A case of frigidity):* A woman, Kanchan, 30 years of age, complained to a lady doctor that she derived no satisfaction from the sexual act. After examination it was found that she did not have any organic cause for the same (any mental or physical abnormality). Her husband was also found normal. It was revealed that the patient had an affair before marriage from which she had derived some pleasure. Her parents found out about the affair and made life impossible for her lover, who left the place. At the age of 22, she married a teacher who was obsessional and rigid in all matters. She got no pleasure from intercourse throughout her marriage of eight years and often objected to his mechanical approach. Intercourse took place two or three times in a month at his insistence. She certainly never made any advances. There were no children.

*Case 5: (A case of skin disorder):* Kamla, a married woman 22 years age approached for the treatment. At the age of three she had developed eczema on both arms and hands. This condition remained problematic for two years then cleared up at the age of seven, when her mother was pregnant. Her hands and arms again had eczema with the onset of her first menstruation for a period of three months. Recently she had severe skin eruption associated with the impending absence from her husband. As the date of his departure approached, her symptoms gradually worsened and eventually she was hospitalised.

*Case 6: (illustrating the impact of stresses):* Richard Nixon the President of America, suffered with the repeated attacks of phlebitis in 1974 soon after his resignation on account of the Watergate scandal. He developed a number of blood clots in his left leg and one large clot required emergency surgery to prevent further complications. Historically, it was revealed that President Nixon suffered his first phlebitis attack in 1965. Predisposed to such disorder, his phlebitis was probably aggravated by the stressful situation like sudden loss of power, position and prestige on account of his forced resignation. (Adapted from G.W, Kisker, 1977).

An analysis of these cases reveals the following facts:

1. Genetic or hereditary factors play some part in the development of psycho-physiological disorders.
2. Body structure, its chemical functioning, allergies and infections may initiate and precipitate many of the disorders.

Apart from these organic factors, psychological factors, by all means, initiate, control, precipitate and determine the severity and occurrence of these disorders. Many psycho-physiological disorders can be caused through conditioning and reinforcement. For example, a child who is repeatedly allowed to stay home from school when he has an upset stomach may learn to be rewarded from chronic indigestion. Similarly, a housewife may suffer chronic backache or asthma on account of her conditioning to get sympathy and attention due to her illness.

Emotional factors and psychological stresses have always been found to play a significant role in all types of psycho-physiological disorders. They may relate to the patient's childhood experiences, behaviour and treatment got from the parents, the early inconveniences, deprivation and accidents in one's life, the uncongenial familial environment, unhealthy parent-child relationships and unhappy family life of the parents. All of them prove to be great predisposing factors for these disorders. In the subsequent years, the newly emerging demands and perplexities of the adolescents' life and many of the stresses and strains of adulthood pose problems and conflict situations for the perpetuation of the psycho-physiological disorders. These stressful situations have been found to contribute towards psycho-physiological disorders in the following ways:

(a) By affecting unfavourably the autonomic nervous system and thus the body chemistry and metabolism.

(b) By reducing the fighting capacity of an individual against the disease spreading virus and bacteria.

(c) By creating a precipitating and immediate cause to the already predisposed individual. In such cases the physical damage is said to be triggered by the intense emotional stress of the life events.

(d) By providing a good reasonable escape through developing and intensifying a desire to be ill.

## Prevention and Treatment of the Psycho-Physiological Disorders

The psycho-physiological disorders are caused by the interaction of the organic and psychological factors. Therefore, the prevention and treatment of these disorders lie in caring for these factors.

As far as the genetic influences are concerned, they are beyond one's control. Hence, their presence as a predisposing factor can never be ruled out. For the other biological factors and psychological factors we may adopt a good number of preventive measures in the form of the provision of better environmental facilities and education for good physical and mental health and satisfactory living. Regarding treatment of these disorders various approaches have been suggested:

1. *Biomedical measures:* In psycho-physiological disorders the illness is real and not apparent. There are real organic problems, disturbances in the body which require medical-cum-biological treatment. Depending on the therapist's specific beliefs and diagnosis the treatment may range from surgery to medication. In many cases of psycho-physiological disorders like heart diseases, bleeding ulcers, severe urinary disorders emergency medical treatment is urgently required. While in the others also, it becomes desirable at a certain stage when various types of drugs and medicines are used to control the severity of the disease. Sometimes the physical health is restored by changing the diet, modifying the environment and removing unfavourable biological conditions causing the growth of virus and bacteria.
2. *Psycho-analytic measures:* From the psycho-analytic point of view, a painful and health damaging psycho-physiological symptom represents some sort of symbolical aggression or self-punishment for the unacceptable impulses associated with unconscious conflicts. Therefore, in psychoanalytic treatment, the patient is helped to confront and resolve the unconscious conflict which lies at the root of the symptom.
3. *Behaviour modification measures:* Psycho-physiological disorders are also caused by the learning of maladaptive behaviour. In behaviour modification therapy attempts are made to unlearn the unfavourable learning through extinction and differential reinforcement. For example, there was a case of a child who happened to exhibit symptoms of asthma (heavy coughing and wheezing) at bed time. The parents were prepared to induce behaviour therapy in the following two ways:
   (i) to ignore systematically (extinguish) the child's asthmatic responding,
   (ii) to reward more normal breathing with some incentive (love and affection, good food and sometimes money).

   The results were encouraging as the child gradually got rid of the maladaptive responses.
4. *Psychotherapy measures:* Emotional factors and psychological stresses prove predisposing as well as precipitating causes for the psycho-physiological disorders. A proper training of the emotions and helping the patient to learn well adaptive normal ways to cope with his conflict and stressful situations may bring favourable results. As far as possible, attempts should be made to improve the patient's life situations by modifying his environment so as to reduce daily stress. Measures like short term psycho-therapy may also help the patient for the release of his tension, anxiety and similar other factors making him unhappy. These measures prove helpful at least in decreasing the patient's vulnerability to subsequent stress and improving his mental health.

5. *Biofeedback measures:* Recently, biofeedback measures have been studied to control many of the psycho-physiological disorders like headaches, back aches, irregular heartbeats, asthma, muscular spasms, teeth grinding, epilepsy, sexual impotency etc. Biofeedback refers to procedures in which selected biological processes such as heart rate, muscle tension etc., are amplified via special instruments so that the individual may be made aware of them (in the form of signals such as lights or sounds) and then may be trained to control their occurrence. For example, blood pressure or pulse rate can be measured and amplified so that the person knows them through suitable signals. By getting training in lowering down the tones of such signals, the person may learn to exercise voluntary control over these functions and thus may be helped in the treatment of related disorders.

## Summary

- The term psycho-physiological disorders include those disorders or maladjustment of the behaviour or personality of an individual in which both organic and psychological factors are conspicuously significant in their origin and in their treatment. These disorders differ from conversion neurosis in terms of the involvement of nervous system, presence of adequate organic basis reality of physical disturbances, reaction to emotional stress and damage to the body's structure.
- Respiratory disorders involve malfunctioning of the respiratory system. Asthma, common cold, rhinitis, hyperventilation, hay fever etc. are such disorders.
- Cardiovascular disorders (disorders of the heart and vascular system) include the disorders like hypertension, angina pectoris, migraine and coronary disease.
- Gastrointestinal disorders (disorders of the gastrointestinal system) include the disorders like anorexia nervosa, digestive problems, peptic ulcer and colitis.
- Genito-urinary disorders (disorders of Genito-urinary system) include urinary, menstrual and sexual disorders.
- Skin disorders include the disorders like acne and eczema (allergic).
- Endocrine disorders (disorders of the glandular functioning) involve the under-activity or over-activity of one or the other endocrine glands.
- Hemic and lymphatic disorders are related with the disorders of the blood and lymph systems. Musculoskeletal disorders are associated with the bones and voluntary muscles of the body such as backache, muscle cramps and arthritis.
- As far as the causes related to Psycho-physiological disorders are concerned, these are the outcomes of a close interaction of genetic and other biological factors (like body structure, its chemical functioning, allergies and infections) and psychological factors, (like conditioning and reinforcement, early deprivations, emotional problems and psychological stress).
- Regarding the prevention of the Psycho-physiological orders it can be properly said that genetic influences are beyond one's control. However, reasonable control may be exercised over biological and other psychological factors for their prevention. For the treatment of these disorders there are measures like biomedical, psycho-analytic, behaviour modification, psycho-therapies and biofeedback.

## REFERENCES

American Psychiatric Association (1968), DSM-II, quoted by Mahoney, Michael J. (1980), ***Abnormal Psychology,*** San Francisco: Harper & Row.

Davison, Gerald C. & Neale, John M. (1978), Abnormal Psychology, (second edition), New York: John Wiley & Sons

Kisker, George W. (1964), ***The Disorganised Personality,*** (3rd International Students Edition), New York: McGraw-Hill.

Mahoney, Michael J. (1980), ***Abnormal Psychology,*** San Francisco: Harper & Row.

# 12

# PSYCHONEUROTIC DISORDERS

Psychoneurotic disorders are purely psychological disorders. There is no relevant organic pathology present in these disorders of the behaviour and thus may be clearly distinguished from the psycho-physiological disorders which are known as the disorders of the psyche as well as body. The illness diagnosed in the psycho-physiological disorders is more real than apparent as in the case of psychoneurotic or psychotic disorders. Thus a neurosis by no means may be labelled as a disease entity.

In the sequence of the disorders of behaviour, neurosis falls midway between minor emotional maladjustment and psychotic disorders. Consequently, it is known as more serious than a minor emotional maladjustment and less serious than a psychotic disorder. Neurotic disorders in a real sense represent the typical ways of dealing with frustrations and conflicts and the anxiety which results from these frustrations and conflicts.

"Anxiety," as described in DSM-II (1968:39), "is the chief characteristic of neuroses. It may be felt and expressed directly, or it may be controlled unconsciously." It is in this context that George W. Kisker (1977:194) has defined neurosis as "a pattern of maladaptive behaviour in which a person responds to life stress with persistent anxiety or other behaviour representing attempts to control the anxiety."

Anxiety is closely linked to an individual's needs and motives. If the essential needs linked with affection, security, self esteem, achievement and freedom are not satisfactorily gratified it may give rise to the feeling of excessive anxiety or guilt which in turn results in a neurotic behaviour. But it should not be concluded that every anxiety reaction leads to neurotic behaviour. We are occasionally quite anxious, irritable, down or restless, but it does not mean that we are neurotic. It is only when the anxiety behaviour patterns become more persistent and interferes with our ability to lead a normal life and thus depict "break downs" in the adjustment mechanism, that they are usually labelled "neurosis."

In spite of its extreme anxiety content neurotic behaviour is not disorganised nor is neurotic personality is a split personality. It can be safely distinguished from the psychotic behaviour or personality in the manner discussed ahead.

## Distinguishing Neurotic Behaviour from Psychotic Behaviour

1. The relation of a neurotic person to reality is not defective. He talks rationally and does not show marked distortion of external reality. He perceives his

environment well within the normal range. Since he is not affected with bizarre ideas, hallucination or illusion, it is not difficult to follow his train of thought.

2. In neuroses, there are no deep and lasting disturbances of affect. In other words, emotional distortions in neuroses are mild and not so severe as in psychoses. For example, a neurotic may at times be depressed, but his depression is not so severe as to affect seriously his thought processes and general behaviour as in the case of psychotic personality. The Characteristics like sever agitation or stupor are not found in neurotic depression.
3. The cognitive distortion is relatively mild in neuroses. The intellectual potentialities in a neurotic personality more or less remain unaffected, whereas in psychotic behaviour the cognitive distortion is severe and causes impairment of the intellectual functioning.
4. The social relations in neurotic behaviour are not much disturbed as in the case of psychotic behaviour. A neurotic, although disturbed and disorganised, does not live in some other world as a psychotic does. He is not much handicapped by his behaviour pattern as to make his social adjustment impossible.
5. In neuroses no severe disorganisation of personality, as in psychoses, is found. A neurotic therefore remains relatively well integrated. In comparison to a psychotic, the neurotic proves less harmful to others and the symptoms of his behaviour deviation are not severe to cause anxiety to others. The need for care and attention in a mental hospital is not usually felt in the case of neurotics as it is for psychotics.

## Specific Forms or Types of Neurotic Behaviour

The major types of neurosis as mentioned in the classification system DSM II-are as follows:

1. Anxiety neurosis
2. Hysterical neurosis—(a) Conversion type, and (b) Dissociative type.
3. Phobic neurosis
4. Obsessive compulsive neurosis
5. Depressive neurosis
6. Neurasthenic neurosis
7. Depersonalization neurosis
8. Hypochondriacal neurosis

Let us discuss them one by one.

### 1. Anxiety Neurosis:

The anxiety neurosis represents a behaviour dominated by anxiety reactions which interfere with the individual's personal and social adjustment. The anxiety involved here is a free floating anxiety characterised by the following:

(i) It is irrational in the sense that no relevant or justified explanations can be given by the individual for his anxiety reactions.

(ii) Quite often, a very minute danger or stress situation gives rise to disproportionately strong anxiety reactions in the individual

(iii) In anxiety neurosis, unlike other neurosis, the anxiety is experienced directly and not indirectly in the form of phobias or compulsions.

*Symptoms:* An individual suffering from anxiety neurosis, may exhibit the following symptoms for no apparent reason:

(a) *Physiological*

(i) Mild nausea, loss of appetite and some loss of weight.

(ii) Heart palpitations, feeling of heart burn, elevated blood pressure and increased pulse rate, suffocation and difficulties in breathing.

(iii) Cold Sweat, headaches, muscle tension or pain, dryness- of the mouth, trembling of hands and lips and frequent sighing.

(iv) Speech disorder, sleep disturbances, and sexual dissatisfaction.

(v) Inappropriate eating habits, chronic mild diarrhoea, frequent urination and difficulties in digestion,

(vi) Excessive use of alcohol, tranquillizing drugs or sleeping pills.

(b) *Psychological:*

(i) *Disturbances in thinking:* The neurotically anxious, individuals often complain of lack of concentration in work and interest in life. They are always uncertain and fearful of making mistakes. As a result they prefer making no decision than making a wrong one.

(ii) *Disturbances in feeling:* Anxiety neurosis is characterized by extreme and generalized apprehension by a feeling of helplessness and resentment. The anxiety neurotics are likely to have pronounced feelings of dread and apprehension no matter how well things seem to be going. They are convinced of something terrible happening but can't tell what it will be or even why it should happen. The length to which they go to find things to worry about is remarkable. As soon as one cause for worry is removed, they find another until their kith and kin lose patience with them. Similarly, while suffering from the feeling of helplessness, an anxiety neurotic does not know which way to turn. He is sure that anything he attempts will result in failure. He is likely to be dependent on others, which he does not like to do. So, resentment wells up within him and ultimately results in aggression towards the self as he does not possess enough courage to attack those upon whom he is dependent.

## Examples of Anxiety Neurosis

*Case 1:* A married working woman, 37 years of age, reported for help. She was unable to go out on her own and always felt brightened. She felt uneasy at work and anxious if left alone at home by her husband. She usually worked with a tense feeling and occasionally had a sense of doom. Medical examination revealed that she had no physical disease. Her pulse rate was 100 per minute at rest and she was extremely tense and fearful.

Her case history revealed that she was the second of five siblings. Her parents had frequent quarrelling when she was a child. She was married at the age of 20 and had a girl child at the age of 22. She reported that illness came on at the age of 24. She reported that intercourse had been reduced since the daughter's birth. It occurred two or three times in a year and then without orgasm. Her husband, a busy businessman reported that she had been ill for some time, possibly two or three years, but she had become worse in the past few months, when at times she developed a cancer phobia. Before that she worried over everything —"you name it, she worries about it—I can't understand it. At times she's nasty but I understand that and put up with it." He was completely self-contained and introverted.

*Case 2:* An engineer, 50 years of age, sought help for his problem. He was anxious, frightened, tense and sweating. He began to worry about his heart, which had speeded up to a rate of 102 per minute. At times he felt as if chocking. He had diarrhoea. His hands trembled and his mouth was dry. He had a deformed penis.

The case history revealed that he had been married for 26 years, but had never been capable of sexual intercourse. His wife and he had an almost continuous life of clubs, parties and theatres together and they had been perfectly happy. Two months ago he had been by-passed for promotion. He became concerned and he and his wife stopped going to social functions and theatres (Adapted from Psychiatric Investigation, J.H. Price, London: Butter Worth, 1972, pp. 18-21).

*Case 3:* An 18 year-old girl was referred to a psychiatric clinic. She first came to the attention of the authorities eight months earlier, when she attempted suicide. At the time of interview, she was found under considerable tension. The anxiety lessened somewhat in the face of repeated encouragement and reassurance. Eventually, she told a story which revolved for the most part around her father. She said that he had told her that her mother had frustrated him sexually. At another time, he kissed her, but she denied any further advances. She admitted having frequent dreams and night- mares most of which involved the father.

Her anxiety became so great that she insisted that her mother should sleep with her. Before going to bed, she went through a ritual of barricading the bedroom door. She could sleep as long as her mother kept an arm over her. At the same time she was afraid of the mother and occasionally hesitated to eat anything she had prepared, and was sometimes so fearful that she remained awake all night in order to watch her mother. The problem got intensified by the father's advances when he attempted to molest her and by the mother's passive reaction to the situation. The girl had deeply ambivalent feelings about both her father and her mother. In spite of her repeated expressions of fear and hatred for the father, she was found to be preoccupied with thoughts of him both in her waking fantasies and her dream life (Adapted from Kisker, 1977, p. 197).

## 2. Hysterical Neurosis

Hysterical neurosis represents such neurotic reaction in which the person resorts to conversion or dissociation for controlling his anxiety or solving psychological conflicts. As a result, hysterical neuroses are said to be of two major types—conversion type and dissociative type.

*Conversion hysteria:* This type of hysterical neurosis represents behaviour disorder in which a person's anxiety or psychological conflict is converted into a physical symptom like paralysis of legs or inability to hear. Actually, it is a sort of learned reaction to frustration in which the individual tries to seek a neurotic defence by a psychogenic impairment of bodily sensation or action. Here a distinction needs to be made between conversion hysteria and psycho-physiological disorders discussed in the previous chapter. In the words of Kisker (1977:206), it may be summarized as below:

*When the symptom is expressed through the sensory or motor pathways of the central nervous system, the condition is called a hysterical conversion neurosis. However, when neurotic Symptoms involve the autonomic nervous system, the maladaptive behaviour is called psycho-physiological disorder.*

**Symptoms:** Conversion symptoms appear mainly in two areas, namely sensory and motor.

1. *Sensory symptoms:* Conversion symptoms may involve any of the senses. Anaesthesia (lack of skin sensation) is one of the most common conversion reaction. As a result, the person no longer feels pain even when sharp objects are pressed in the affected parts. Contrary to anaesthesia, a person may feel painful sensations that are difficult for him to describe in some areas of the body especially when the area is stimulated. In the conversion reactions involving visual and auditory senses, the person may become blind or deaf for being unable to see or hear things, which he actually does not like to see or listen to. It is natural for a soldier to develop the conversion blindness (even though the eyes and optic nerves are normal) after seeing a very close friend blown apart by an exploding shell. Similarly, a traumatic experience may give such a shock to an individual that he may not dare to use his ears for fear of what he may hear and, consequently, he develops the conversion deafness.
2. *Motor symptoms:* Conversion hysteria frequently involves motor symptoms of the voluntary controlled muscles like tremor or shaking, tick-like movements, minor cramps, contraction of muscles disorders of speech, paralysed limbs and convulsive seizures etc.

In conversion paralysis, a limb becomes useless and so makes it possible for the individual to escape from what is to him an impossible situation. Thus in many cases, the conversion paralysis becomes a preferred way of reaching to stress. As an example we may cite the case of a soldier who became paralysed when the order was given to attack the enemy or a person whose arms got paralysed when he could not protect his wife from the clutches of the antisocial elements.

The interesting thing to note with the conversion paralysis is that it usually amounts to a functional disorder. Here too, the loss of the function may be selective. Similar is the case with another conversion disorder known as writer's cramp. Persons suffering from writer's cramp cannot write but are able to use the same muscles for other activities, for example, to shuffle a pack of cards or to play a harmonium.

Disorders of speech constitute one of the most common motor manifesting of conversion hysteria. In aphonia the person is able to speak only in whispers. Stuttering, in the majority of cases, is known to result from the psychological reasons. In such cases, the individual, afraid of saying the wrong thing, sets up inhibitions which interfere with the normal functioning of the speech organs.

A convulsive seizure, in many respects, resembles epilepsy. The individual falls and may become unconscious. This usually happens when others are present. Although he may throw himself around, his pupillary reflex to light remains unaffected, he does not bite his tongue as usually happens in epilepsy, and he is nearly always careful not to injure himself.

In addition to these two types of conversion symptoms, some writers try to include visceral symptoms as the third type. But it is proper to classify symptoms like headaches, choking, sensations, and coughing spells, difficulty in breathing, belching, and nausea in psycho- physiological disorders rather than neurotic disorders as these symptoms also involve the autonomic nervous system along with involuntary muscles of the body

In some cases of conversion hysteria, there exists an exaggeration of actual organic symptoms. Thus, an individual who has a minor organic disorder may build a hysterical superstructure on this foundation. Therefore, in actual sense, all hysteric individuals attempt to convert their psychological disturbances into physical disorders or diseases and thus seem to resort to an escape mechanism for justifying their otherwise unjustified behaviour. The following example illustrates the mechanism of the conversion reactions.

A fifty year-old successful businessman, married to an attractive and considerably young wife, suddenly developed a paralysis of his arm. On medical examination no organic cause was found for his disorder. The psychological evaluation of the patient revealed that while he seemed anxious to be cured of his disorder, he displayed his arm with some satisfaction, demonstrating the lack of sensation by touching his lit cigarette to the affected part. With the possibility of a conversion reaction, psychotherapy was recommended. It resulted in the removal of the symptom but it returned a few days later. However, the psychological nature of the disorder had been proved and psychotherapy was continued. It became clear to the therapist that the patient had been using his neurotic symptoms to solve his problems. His young and attractive wife was fond of night clubs, while the patient merely wanted to come home at night, have dinner, read his paper and go to bed. The difference in age and interests resulted in serious conflict. Finally, the wife began to go out without her husband and it was at this point that the symptom appeared.

The therapist concluded that his paralysis was serving a number of purposes such as (i) good excuse for staying home at night, (ii) forcing the wife to spend more time with him at home in the evenings, (iii) seeking sympathy and attention of friends and relatives, and (iv) a good excuse for coming home from his office at any hour of the day as he was jealous of his wife and suspected her fidelity.

Interestingly, the eventual cure in this case was brought about by the sudden disappearance of his wife with a police officer. When he was convinced that his wife would never return to him, his symptom disappeared spontaneously as he had no problem of living with his wife now (Adapted from Kisker, 1977, p. 208).

*Dissociative hysteria:* The hysterical dissociative neurosis is maladaptive cognitive behaviour in which a person tries to control his anxiety or psychological problem by the dissociation of his self. Disturbances in consciousness and /or loss of personal identity are the main characteristics of such dissociative reactions. The four major types of such reactions are (i) somnambulism, (ii)amnesia, (iii)fugue and (iv)multiple personality.

*Somnambulism* refers to a condition in which a person sometimes carries out specific acts at specific times during the night in a sleep-like state after he has gone to sleep in a normal manner. During sleep-walking, his eyes are open and he responds more or less well to commands, yet he is not awake. The person finally returns to his bed and to sleep and in the morning remembers nothing of the events of the night. In their sleep-walking, persons are known to travel long distances and do many complex activities.

*Amnesia* refers to the loss of memory. In dissociative amnesia, the individual forgets temporarily all experiences which are associated with the kind of self which he intends to forget. It may be partial or complete. In its complete form the person cannot remember anything about his earlier life—not even his name. He cannot recognize his family and friends, forgets his actual age or residential address, yet his basic habit patterns such as the ability to walk, talk, read and reason remain intact. He may remain in a state of amnesia for just a few minutes, for hours, or for days.

A *fugue* is a combination of amnesia and physical flight. In this state the loss of identity continues for a long period of time (may be for several years) and it is accompanied by actual flight from the customary surroundings. The person may suddenly leave home, travel to another area and sometimes begin a "new life."

The following example may illustrate the happenings in a state of amnesia or fugue.

A married woman was brought for medical help by her husband. She was in a very much confused and tense state. Her husband reported that she had left home two weeks ago while he was away from his work. He took the help of police but she could not be traced. One day he received a report that a woman of her description had been arrested in another city. When he went there and identified her, she did not at first recognize him, did not know her name, and could not remember what had happened to her or anything about herself. According to the police, she had been arrested for "resorting" after a motel owner had called the police to complain that several different men had visited the motel room she had rented three days before in the company of a sailor. The young woman seemed unable to remember any of these alleged events. On the use of psycho-therapy, gradually she came to recognise her husband, wept bitterly and requested him to take her home (Adapted from Mahony, 1980, p. 261).

Psychologically speaking, in the above case the person resorts to the state of amnesia or fugue for a neurotic escape from an intolerable situation. In actual sense, the loss of identity or physical flight is utilized as a solution against the un-manageable neurotic anxiety growing out of severe conflicts.

Multiple personality is an extreme and rare form of the dissociative type of hysterical neurosis. It refers to a condition in which the person may alternately behave in two or more distinctly different patterns. He is usually unaware of this multiplicity of his personality. He may change from one personality to another for periods ranging from a few hours to a few years. The different personalities are often extreme opposites, that in one he may he an extrovert and the other an introvert. In such a case, while asking the patient his name, (who was in real sense Sudarshan a reserved, gentle and tradition bound person) he may reply that he is Mr.------- and thus may behave differently exhibiting altogether a different personality (a vocal and fashionable youth). Sometimes, a person may experience change of personality of three, four or more different characters within a span of time (days, months or years). In these cases the person usually does not remember what happened in the other case and thus multiple personality mechanism proves a complete escape from one's real- self for keeping away the intolerable anxiety, fear or conflict situations. It should be remembered that in multiple personality disorder reaction, the person never assumes the identity of a famous person (Jawahar Lal Nehru, Napoleon or Cleopatra) and it is in this sense that it may be differentiated from split personality (schizophrenia).

## 3. Phobic Neurosis:

The term "phobia" comes from the Greek word *'photos'* which means panic, flight or fear. Phobic neurosis may be defined as a disorder of the behaviour in which a person experiences persistent, intense, irrational fear of a specific situation or object. In spite of his rational knowledge that his fear is unrealistic and overwhelming, he is forced to experience great apprehension and anxiety symptoms while in contact with the phobic object or situation. In a natural sense fear reactions are very common to every one of us. It is normal and indeed adaptive to be fearful of situations which pose real danger. Fear does not become a phobia unless it is irrational. It turns into neurotic disorder when it becomes too intense to interfere with the person's normal activities and to affect his mental health. Some of the common phobias with their technical names and inherent meaning are listed below:

Acrophobia – fear of high places.
Agoraphobia – fear of open places.
Aichmophobia – fear of short and pointed objects.
Algophobia – fear of pain.
Astraphobia – fear of storms, thunder and lightning.
Claustrophobia – fear of closed spaces or confinement.
Hematophobia – fear of the sight of the blood.
Hydrophobia – fear of water.
Lalophobia – fear of (public) speaking.
Mysophobia – fear of dirt or contamination.
Nyctophobia – fear of darkness.

| | | |
|---|---|---|
| Ochlophobia | – | fear of crowds |
| Pathophobia | – | fear of disease or illness. |
| Photophobia | – | fear of intense light. |
| Pyrophobia | – | fear of fire. |
| Thanatophobia | – | fear of death. |
| Toxophobia | – | fear of being poisoned. |
| Xenophobia | – | fear of strangers. |
| Zoophobia | – | fear of animals or some particular animal. |

It is clear that phobias may involve any situation or object surrounding one's life. Moreover, they have no respect for age, intellectual level or social position. Henry III of France had a peculiar phobia concerning eggs and became terrified at the sight of them. Schopenhauer, the German philosopher, had a fear of razors and thereby preferred to singe his beard rather than shave it.

All phobias are essentially morbid fears. They put a person in a typical abnormal feature.. The nature, symptoms and causation of the phobic neurosis may be understood through some of the following illustrations:

*Case 1:* A young woman had ochlophobia-fear of crowds.Whenever there were many people around her, she was afraid that she would be crushed or died from suffocation. In spite of the knowledge that her fear being irrational, she was not able to travel by train or bus, go shopping in a market, attend social parties or visit movies. This kept her a virtual prisoner in her home. On free association, her phobia was traced to her early childhood. As a child she had been granted permission to watch the circus parade go by her house but was strictly warned not to follow it into town. On account of the excitement she forgot this and followed the parade into the centre of the town where she soon found herself crowded on all sides. She became frightened and began to cry. A kind gentleman helped her out of the crowd to a front row. After a time her fear subsided and she returned home. Due to fear she could not discuss her terrifying experiences with her parents. The entire experience was repressed into the unconscious, giving rise to an irrational fear of crowds. Due to its free association, the early experience was recalled and the knowledge of the source of fear gradually helped her to get rid of her phobia (Adapted from Page, 1970, p. 142).

*Case 2:* A young woman 30 years of age had agoraphobia —the fear of open places. The phobia became so serious that she had to give up her job and remained home at all times. Psychological investigation revealed that in early teens she had been sexually promiscuous with several boys in the neighbourhood. In her later life she experienced intense guilt feeling about her behaviour and repressed all memories of it. The phobia which developed later in her life was based on the fear that she might lose contact of herself and be led into a life of prostitution. These repressed memories were revived by the sight of a group photograph and the knowledge of the source of her phobia made her treatment quite possible (Adapted from Kisker, 1977, p. 200).

*Case 3:* A young man had a phobia of being grasped from behind. In social gatherings he arranged to have his chair against the wall. It was impossible for him to enter crowded places or go to a movie. When walking on the road, he would look back over his shoulder at intervals to see if he was closely followed. Psychological investigation revealed that as a young boy he used to steal peanuts from a grocery store. The owner, determined to know who was stealing his peanuts, hid himself behind a barrel. Just as the boy put his hand in the pile of peanuts, the owner jumped out and grabbed him from behind. The boy screamed and fell fainting on the side walk. The terrifying experience was repressed into consciousness and the present phobia was the result of that earlier repressed experience (Adapted from Davison & Neale, 1978, p. 138).

## Causes of Phobias

As may be evident from the above three cases, the real cause of the phobia is either unknown to the patient or forgotten on account of being repressed into his unconscious. In general, there are three main causes of phobia:

1. ***A forgotten terrifying fear experience of early age:*** In case one above the young woman had a phobia concerning crowds on account of her terrifying childhood experience. Similarly, an individual frightened by an accident involving a dog, horse or an insect in his childhood may develop a zoophobia
2. ***Neurotic defence against anxiety generated by unconscious conflict:*** According to psychoanalysts, phobias are merely defence reactions against the anxiety generated by unconscious conflicts related to sexual and aggressive feelings and impulses. In case two above the young woman was using her phobia of open places as a defence to save her from the situation of being led into a life of prostitution. Similarly, a housewife may develop aichmophobia, fear of sharp and pointed objects, and refuse to keep kitchen knives and scissors in the house on account of her repressed impulses to cut her husband's throat. A husband may develop hydrophobia so that he may keep himself away from rivers because of his repressed feelings of drowning his wife.
3. ***Learned pattern of maladaptive behaviour:*** Phobias, to a great extent, represent the learned pattern of maladaptive behaviour either on account of conditioning or social learning. A conditioned response to a fear producing situation (usually experienced during early childhood) may result in a peculiar phobia. In case three, the young man may be seen to develop phobia of being grasped from behind on account of classical conditioning. Similarly, a child with a fearful reaction to an unpleasant experience associated with a cat may learn to be afraid of the cat. Afterwards, he may develop an irrational fear of the cats which may include the word cat as well as the sight of it or other animals ***resembling*** it. Operant conditioning in which inadequacies or avoidance of something may be reinforced by the positive reinforcer like sympathy, attention, help and assistance from others, means of controlling or dominating others or excuse for the failure may also be responsible for many phobias. Besides this, fearful parents, members of the family or teachers serve as model for social learning of phobias. A mother who

becomes terror-stricken on account of lightning and thunder may communicate her fears to her children and later on, after being reinforced in the later years of one's life, she may develop astraphobia—fear of thunder and lightning.

## 4. Obsessive-Compulsive Neurosis

Obsessive behaviour represents maladaptive behaviour in which an individual is haunted with the persistent recurrence of unwelcome, absurd and disturbing idea or thought. For example, a wife may have an obsessive idea of stabbing or poisoning her husband, a mother of hurting her little girl, a son of wishing his mother's death, a husband of pushing his wife down a flight of stairs. Although the patient realizes the absurdity and irrelevance of such thoughts, still he is unable to get rid of them. The more desperately he tries to rid himself of them, the more they persist.

Obsessive behaviour, in the step further, becomes compulsive behaviour. Compulsion is in fact an overt manifestation of the obsessive thought or an idea. In other words compulsions are obsessions translated into action. Compulsive behaviour, in this way, may be defined as maladaptive behaviour in which a person is seen to perform repeated acts of unreasonable and irrelevant nature such as washing his hands again and again, checking the alarm clock several times to ensure it has been wound, or returning to his house again and again to be certain that the door has been locked or following an elaborate ritualistic sequence in detail before going to sleep. Such patterns of behaviour are maladaptive in the sense that they are unnecessary and irrational. Even the person realizes the absurdity of his compulsive acts, but he feels uncomfortable unless he performs the compulsive act.

While obsessive behaviour may exist without compulsion, compulsive behaviour can't even originate without obsession. It is true that thoughts or ideas must compulsorily precede action. But as far as obsessive-compulsive neurosis is concerned, the symptom of both obsessive and compulsive behaviour are present in such neurosis as may be evident from the following definition given in DSM-II (1968)

In this reaction the anxiety is associated with the persistence of unwanted ideas and of repetitive impulses to perform acts which may be considered morbid by the patient. The patient himself may regard his ideas and behaviour as unreasonable but nevertheless is compelled to carry out his rituals.

## Some Examples of Obsessive-Compulsive Behaviour

1. An adolescent boy was found to have a unique obsessive-compulsive behaviour concerning fire, technically known as *pyromania*. He was preoccupied with the idea of fire and possessed an overwhelming urge to set fires without caring for the consequences. He admitted setting innumerable fires causing damage to properties and lives but could not give any reason for his strange criminal behaviour.
2. A pretty young woman of a rich family was found to be suffering from an obsessive compulsive behaviour, kleptomania (uncontrollable urge to steal). Whenever she attended dinner parties she could not resist herself from putting

selected spoons in her handbag. She had a record of 300 stolen spoons. At one time when 'She was seen picking the spoons by a friend and asked why she did it, she felt humiliated but replied, "I don't know why it happens but something compels me to do it."

3. Samuel Johnson suffered from an obsessive-compulsive behaviour, *coprolalia.* He had a strong urge to utter obscene words for which he was often humiliated. He had no explanation for his strange conduct.
4. A principal of a Girls college was found to suffer from an obsessive-compulsive behaviour related with contamination and cleanliness. She used to wash her hands and take baths several times a day. After going outside it was necessary for her to change her clothes. Whenever a visitor came to her drawing room, she had the room cleaned and sprayed with disinfectant.
5. As reported by Freud, an eleven year-old boy was found to be engaged in a typical obsessive-compulsive ceremony every night before going to bed. He did not sleep until he had told his mother in the minutest detail all the events of the day, there must be no scraps of paper or other rubbish on the carpet of the bedroom, the bed must be pushed right to the wall, three chairs must stand by it and the pillows must lie in a particular way. In order to get to sleep, he first kicked about a certain number of times with both legs and then lay on his side. When asked why he did these things, he was unable to give a satisfactory reason.
6. A middle-aged man was found to suffer with an obsessive- compulsive-behaviour related with the drinking of tea. He could not drink his tea for fear that a pin might have been dropped into it. He was forced to pour his tea back and forth several times to make certain that it did not contain any pin.
7. A school boy, thirteen years of age, was brought for help on account of his obsessive-compulsive rituals. When he urinated, he had to wash four times, if he had to put on his socks, he washed seven times, and if he touched something with one hand, he had to touch it with the other, He could give no reason for observing such methodical ritual.

## A Few New Varieties of Obsessive–Compulsive Behaviour Brought in Light in DSM-5

In the latest classification of mental disorders, DSM-5 provided by American Psychiatric Association in the year 2013 a significant mention has been made about Obsessive-Compulsive-Related Disorders, i.e. particular patterns of repetitive and excessive behaviour that greatly disrupt the lives of the people in a variety of ways. DSM-5 has assigned four of these patterns to that group of disorders namely (i) hoarding disorder, (ii) trichotillomania (hair- pulling disorder),(iii) excoriation (skin picking) disorder and (iv)body dysmorphic disorder. Let us know about them.

## Hoarding Disorder

Individuals suffering from the obsessive-compulsive disorder named as Hoarding disorder are found to feel that they must save items, and they become very distressed if they try to discard them (APA.2013). Hoarding or making collection of objects or things is an inborn instinctive phenomenon distinctly visible in the behaviour of the small children. It is also a good hobby as well. However, it may turn into a big problem or mental disorder when it becomes an obsession as well as compulsion to acquire and hoarding on the things not at all needed on their part at present. In Brief a person suffering from hoarding disorder may be found to be characterized as below:

- They have inherent craving for collecting and accumulating a host of things and as a result it is common for them to wind up with numerous useless and valueless items, from junk mail to broken objects to unusual clothes.
- They are extremely unaware of the severity of their behaviour. People with hoarding disorders are extremely attached to their possessions, and they are very resistant to efforts to get rid of them. (King et al, 2012:207)
- The compulsion for the people to remain away from giving up their possessions, results in an extraordinary accumulation of items that clutters their lives and living areas.
- In all its way, this pattern causes the individuals significant distress and may greatly impair their personal, social, or occupational functioning. Part of their homes may become inaccessible because of the clutter. In addition, it often results in fire hazard, unhealthy sanitation conditions, or other dangers.

## Trichotillomania (Hair- Pulling Disorder)

The term trichotillomania is derived from the Greek for "frenzied hair-pulling". Accordingly, the people suffering from trichotillomania are found to demonstrate the typical behavioural characteristics summarized as below.

- They are in the habit of repeatedly pull out hair from their scalp, eyebrows, eyelashes, or other parts of the body (APA, 2013).
- Typically, those with the disorder pull one hair at a time.
- Some sufferers follow specific rituals as they pull their hair, including pulling until the hair feels "just right" and selecting certain types of hairs for pulling.
- There lies a strong emotional element in the shape of sizable anxiety or stress responsible for triggering or accompanying the hair-pulling behaviour.
- The demonstration of such undesirable behaviour causes much distress, impairment, or embarrassment to the affected individual.
- Despite taking resolution not to engage in such behaviour and trying to reduce or stop the hair-pulling for the time being, the sufferers may find them helpless in getting rid of this practice.

## Excoriation (Skin-Picking) Disorder

Individuals suffering from Excoriation (skin-picking) disorder are found to demonstrate the behaviour characterized as below:

- Much alike the practice of hair pulling from a particular body part, the people suffering from skin picking disorder are engaged in using their fingers to pick on one area of their body, most often the face.

- Most of the time the preferred area or body part chosen for skin picking remains one's face. However, the other common areas of the body used for this practice may include the arms, legs, lips, scalp, chest and extremities such as fingernails, and cuticles.
- Keep picking skin on one of the area of their body results in significant sores or wounds (APA, 2013).
- Like hair-pulling, the skin-picking behaviour is also typically triggered or accompanied by anxiety or stress.
- It is designated as an obsessive-compulsive behaviour in the sense that the affected person is so much habituated to do it again and again despite the agonies, impairment and embarrassment suffered, resolutions made and attempts done for leaving this bad practice.

## Body Dysmorphic Disorder

Individuals suffering from the obsessive-compulsive disorder named as body dysmorphic disorder are found to engage in the behaviour characterized as below:

- They become preoccupied with the belief that they have a particular defect or flow in their physical appearance. Actually, the perceived defect or flaw is imagined or greatly exaggerated in the person's mind (APA, 2013).
- The perception or belief that there is definitely something wrong with their body part or appearance, drive the individuals to engage in obsessive -compulsive acts such as repeatedly checking themselves in the mirror, grooming themselves, picking at the perceived flaw, comparing themselves with others, seeking reassurance, or performing other similar behaviour activities.
- Of course, it is quite natural and common in our society for the teenagers, and young adults to worry about their appearance and body make-up. The concerns of people with body dysmorphic disorder, however, are extreme. Sufferers may severely limit contact with other people, be unable to look others in the eye, or go to great lengths to conceal their "defects"-say always wear sunglasses to cover their supposedly misshapen eyes. As many as half of people with the disorder seek plastic surgery or dermatology treatment, and often they feel worse rather than better afterward. A large numbers are housebound, and more than 10 percent may attempt suicide. (Comer,2015:171)
- It is also quite common to witness the people suffering with Body Dysmorphic disorder to experience difficulties, distress, impairment and embarrassment on account of their repetitive undesirable behaviour.
- The people affected by the Body dysmorphic disorder, according to the researchers in this area are generally found to focus on some or the other specifics such as wrinkles on the face; spots on the skin; excessive facial hair; swelling of the face; a misshapen nose, mouth, jaw, or eye brow; appearance of their feet, hands, breasts, penis, or other body parts or even concerned about bad odours coming from sweat, breath, genitals, or the rectum as witnessed in the case history depicted below:

*A woman of 35 had for 16 years been worried that her sweet smelled terrible... For fear that she smelled, for 5 years she had not gone out anywhere except when accompanied by her husband or mother. She had not spoken to her neighbours for 3 years...She avoided cinemas, dances, shops, cafes, and private homes... Her husband was not allowed to invite any friend home; she constantly sought reassurance from him about her smell...Her husband bought all her new clothes as she was afraid to try on clothes in front of shop assistants. She used vast quantities of deodorant and always bathed and changed her clothes before going out, up to 4 times daily (Marks,1987:371, Quoted by Comer,2015:171).*

## The Causation of Obsessive-Compulsive Neurosis

What causes such maladaptive behaviour is a thing of concern. Hereditary or other biological factors are not observed to contribute anything to the development of obsessive-compulsive neurosis. This maladaptive behaviour is predominantly a learned reaction pattern. Conditioned learning, in a variety of environmental learning situations, provides enough opportunities for the origin and development of the many obsessive-compulsive rituals. The beginning in such maladaptive behaviour patterns may be the result of one of the following possibility:

1. An obsessive compulsive act may be a direct expression of an undesirable motive or impulse. What is not accepted by the ego and thus repressed in the unconscious may become conscious but the individual is not aware that it represents fulfilment of his own desire. For example, pyromania (compulsion to set fire), homicidal-mania (compulsion to kill) may be interpreted behaviourally as a revenge reaction arising out of the basic frustrations and conflicts. These reactions provide opportunities for the satisfaction of hostile thoughts, outlet for the aggressive feelings and achievement of some kind of power and a sense of satisfaction.
2. The feelings of guilt and self-condemnation associated with the past, or sometimes with the present misdeeds may also give rise to an obsessive-compulsive behaviour. As a result, an individual may be forced to counteract or cleanse himself of guilt by means of compulsive rituals, for example, the compulsive hand washing ritual. It may be taken as a symbolic attempt to wash away a feeling of guilt relating to sexual or other undesirable behaviour. In literature, compulsive hand bashing behaviour of Lady *Macbeth,* the prime character *in* Shakespeare's *Macbeth* illustrates the dynamics of such behaviour. She had an excessive guilt feeling on' account of her participation in the murder of the king Duncan and her compulsive hand-washing was nothing but an attempt to cleanse her hands of the imaginary blood spots.
3. Many times obsessive-compulsive reactions are generated as defence reactions based on the reaction-formation mechanism. In such situations, the individual behaves in ways which are directly contradictory to his unsocial or otherwise dangerous thoughts or impulses. As a consequence, one may defend himself from abnormal sexual desire by developing a strong attitude of condemnation towards such behaviour. Similarly, one may defend himself against his hostile impulses towards his wife or son by becoming obsessively thinking and compulsively doing some acts demonstrating concern for their safety.

4. Indecisiveness coupled with the feeling of inadequacy may be the reason for certain obsessive compulsive behaviour. It may breed compulsive doubts and one may be forced to engage in such rituals such as returning again and again to check the lock on the door or cleaning the plates again ami again before eating. The compensatory behaviour for his feeling of inadequacy or helplessness may also force an individual to resort to such compulsive behaviour as compulsory stealing, killing or protecting himself from the unknown enemies and dangers.

The basic element in obsessive-compulsive behaviour is the personal satisfaction which an individual derives in performing such acts. In doing so he gets himself relieved of the immediate anxiety tension or pressure. He feels satisfied with a sense of achievement in the form of fulfilment of his desires which, in turn, further reinforces his compulsive behaviour and gradually a reaction pattern involving obsessive-compulsive neurosis is developed and the person becomes fixed to behave in a peculiar way in spite of being aware that his behaviour is irrational.

## 5. Depressive Neurosis

This is a neurotic disorder characterized by disproportionate reactions to distressing stress situations like the death of a loved one, an occupational failure or a financial set-back. In such distressing stress situation, there is nothing abnormal to have feelings of grief and despair in a reasonable amount. It is when these feelings become much exaggerated in intensity and duration and begin to interfere with personal or social adjustment of an individual that they turn into behavioural disorder—neurotic and psychotic.

Neurotic depression may be considered halfway between normal depression and psychotic depression. Neurotic depressive reactions are neither too severe in degree or in duration as the psychotic depressive reactions nor as mild and simple as in normal depressive reactions.

Time is found to be a great healing factor in normal depressive reactions. The memories of normal stress situation become hazy with the passage of time, coupled with the creation of new interests. Life becomes worth living once more. In neurotic depression, however, the depressed mood does not return to normal even after a reasonable period of time as it ordinarily does in normal depressive reactions. Here the symptoms concerning depression of mood are also severe. The patient may have intensive feelings of dejection, discouragement and sadness. There is a high level of anxiety and apprehensiveness and extreme feelings of self-condemnation. The person is unable to concentrate and his level of activity and initiative is lowered. In its more severe form, the anxiety and desperations are heightened to such an extent that the person is unable to work, and sits in despair viewing the dark side of life alone and sometimes thinks of committing suicide.

However the situation is not much severe and incurable as in psychotic depression. The symptoms like delusions, hallucinations, marked retardation of the thought process, severe agitation and actual suicidal attempts etc. often found in psychotic states are significantly absent in neurotic depression.

Depression may be viewed as hostility or anger directed against the self instead of being turned outward. Instead of blaming others, the person blames himself for the loss and the distressing situation. This consciousness of guilt raises his level of anxiety and apprehensiveness and forces him to relieve his tension through the mechanism of self-criticism and a relatively continued mood of depression. Thus the formula for neurotic depression is self-condemnation plus an external loss precipitated in the case of predisposing personality traits as inability to express hostility and aggression directly and outwardly, submissiveness, dependence, sensitivity to criticism and self-criticism. In case of neurotic depression, the person may be viewed as punishing himself by feeling responsible for the loss or for the distress situations.

The following examples reveal the characteristics of depressive neurosis.

*A young woman was found to be suffering from neurotic depression. Hardly had she been married for one year when her husband died of poisoning by drinking milk he had taken at night before going to bed. A lizard was found in the milk pot and this convinced the young woman that she was to blame for the death of her husband. She often thought that she had murdered her husband since she had not covered the milk pot while boiling the milk. Thus instead of experiencing normal grief or sadness, she developed neurotic depression.*

The dynamics of neurotic depressive behaviour in the above example reveal that the process starts when there is considerable emotional loss for which the person thinks his self-responsible. He begins to condemn himself and is overwhelmed with the feelings of intense guilt. The depression then employed is a defence which satisfies the person when he inflicts punishment on himself through a continued period of depression. In some cases it turns out to be the last resort and is adopted as an illness especially when the person sees no silver lining among the dark clouds of despair and frustration in his life. The seriousness of this illness increases with the intensification of despair when many patients attempt suicide.

## 6. Neurasthenic Neurosis

The literal meaning of the term "neurasthenia" is "nervous exhaustion" or "nerve weakness". It is characterized by complaints of easy fatigability (mental and physical), irritability, lack of energy, chronic weakness and pains and aches in different parts of the body. However, the chief feature of neurasthenic fatigue and weakness is its selective nature. Its patient has all the energy to do things of his interest but feels fatigued and exhausted when asked to do something that does not interest him. This type of neurotic disorder is common among women particularly house- wives who are bored and feel neglected by their husbands. That is why it has often been called "housewives' neurosis". Their neurasthenic neurosis is a psychological disorder which serves to provide secondary gains and relief from unpleasant situations.

## 7. Depersonalization Neurosis

This type of neurotic behaviour is characterized by the feelings of unreality and "estrangement from the self, body or surroundings". Consequently, the patient does not feel real or feels that what is being done by him is a play rather than an actual life event. In case of a young man suffering from depersonalization neurosis, reported by an investigator, one of the most bizarre experiences during his illness was the unique feeling described thus : "I am two separate persons—one that thinks and one that acts. When I feel like this it's like being in a bad dream and 1 didn't know what is real and I don't know if I am the thinking person or the acting one."

## 8. Hypochondriacal Neurosis

This type of neurosis is characterized by an excessive concern for physical health and persistent intense fear of illness, disease or dysfunction. The symptoms of this neurotic disorder are given below:

(i) The patients believe that they have physical illness or disease even when there is no such evidence.

(ii) Patients often detail how extensively their illness has affected them, and they seldom discuss anything but their symptoms.

(iii) They are often frustrated when medical examinations are negative and feel convinced that the doctors have erred. As a result, they move from one doctor to another seeking "better" treatment.

(iv) The patients are anxious and found to exhibit obsessive- compulsive behaviour with regard to their supposed illness.

(v) In severe cases the patient has a strong conviction that he will not recover.

(vi) The symptoms concerning non-existent illness are nourished by the patient like valuable assets for seeking desired attention, care and sympathy from his family and also as convenient means for wish fulfilment.

## Causes and Treatment of Psychoneurotic Disorders

The most important causative factors of all neuroses are psychological. We see that psychoneurotic reactions often represent learned maladaptive behaviour patterns. The faulty upbringing, improper childhood experiences, uncongenial home and school environment, and the stresses and strains suffered in the later life provide sufficient predisposing and precipitating causes for learning neurotic reactions. An individual feels satisfied in behaving neurotically as it helps him to fulfil his otherwise unsatisfied needs. He derives pleasure in seeking sympathy, attention and care from his well-wishers or even strangers for his limitations on account of his illness or disease. Thus his neurotic symptoms are reinforced and make his disorder more severe in intensity and duration.

The psychoneurotic disorders vary in respect of their nature (characteristics and symptoms) and causation. Therefore no common treatment may be prescribed for all such disorders. However, in general, neurotic patients are curable. They respond more favourably to behaviour therapy and psychotherapy than patients suffering from conduct disorders or functional psychoses. The treatment adopted for major types of neurosis may be summarized below. Details of various therapies are discussed in a separate chapter.

*Anxiety neurosis:* Neurotic anxiety patients may be readily helped by chemical therapy, sedatives or mild tranquillizers. In chronic cases insulin therapy may be given. They may also be given psychological treatment through (i) supportive psychotherapy; (ii) insight therapy; (iii) group psycho-therapy; and (iv) finding other outlets for the patient's drives.

*Hysterical neurosis:* The symptoms of many hysterical neuroses may be alleviated by hypnosis. The release of an individual from an emotionally stress situation and intensive psychotherapy like supportive psychotherapy, group therapy and re-educative therapy are the measures needed for better results.

*Phobic neurosis:* The following therapeutic measures are adopted for the treatment of these disorders:

a. Insight therapy
b. Relaxation and desensitization (de-conditioning)—The patient is relaxed sometimes with the help of drugs, and then gradually introduced to the phobic situation, starting with the least terrifying kind.
c. Implosion (or flooded) therapy—The patient is immediately immersed in the most frightening phobic situation until he no longer experiences fear.
d. Adaptation therapy—The patient observes (in real life or film) someone else handling his phobic situation.

*Obsessive-compulsive neurosis: "Thought stopping" is a* technique which is of help in such disorders. Even lobotomy, ***a*** brain operation, in which the nerve pathways between the frontal lobes of the brain and the thalamus and hypothalamus are cut, has often resulted helpful in this neurosis. Psychotherapy measures are the other better alternative.

*Depressive neurosis:* The following methods, often in combination, are useful in the treatment of neurotic depression:

- Drug therapy
- Electroconvulsive therapy (ECT)
- Psychotherapies like supportive psychotherapy and insight psychotherapy.
- Modifying the stress environmental situation. In extreme cases of depression electric shock therapy is used.

*Hypochondriacal neurosis:* This disorder is difficult to treat as the person resists recognizing that the problems are not physical. He derives satisfaction in being ill. The circle can be broken and the person no longer remains a hypochondriac when he no longer needs the symptoms concerning his self-created illness. However, the psychological treatment proves useful.

## Summary

- Psychoneurotic disorders or neuroses are purely psychological disorders. There is no relevant organic pathology present and the illness is more apparent than real as in the case of psycho - physiological disorders.
- Among psychological disorders, they are more serious than minor emotional maladjustment and less serious than a psychotic disorder. The feeling of excessive anxiety or guilt makes the central core of a neurotic behaviour. However, this

behaviour is not disorganised and a neurotic personality is not a split personality as in the case of psychosis.

- Psychoneurotic disorders or neuroses may be classified as (i) Anxiety neurosis, (ii) Hysterical neurosis, (iii) Phobic neurosis,(iv) obsessive -compulsive neurosis, (v) Depressive neurosis (vi) Neurasthenic neurosis and (vii) Depersonalization neurosis and (viii) Hypochondriacal neurosis.
- Anxiety neurosis represents a behavior dominated by a free floating anxiety interfering with the individual's personal and social adjustment. Apart from the anxiety ridden physiological symptoms, the person also exhibits definite psychological symptoms in terms of disturbance in thinking and feeling.
- Hysterical neurosis represents neurotic reaction in which the person resorts to conversion or dissociation for controlling his anxiety or solving psychological conflicts. There are two types of hysterical neurosis—conversion hysteria and dissociative hysteria. Dissociative hysteria may further be classified as somnambulism, amnesia, fugue and multiple personality.
- Phobic neurosis represents disorders in which a person experiences persistent intense irrational fear of a specific situation or object which interferes with his normal activities and affects his mental health. They are generally caused by early terrifying experiences and unconscious conflicts or learned on account of conditioning or social learning.
- Obsessive compulsive neurosis represents maladaptive behaviour in which a person is haunted by the recurrence of absurd thought or idea and as a result may be compelled to act upon it.
- Obsessive-compulsive-related disorders pointed out in DSM-5 are the disorders in which obsessive like concerns drive one to engage repeatedly and excessively in certain patterns of behaviour resulting into a great disruption in their life. The people suffering from hoarding disorder are compelled to save items and become very distressed if they try to discard them, resulting in an excessive accumulation of items. Trichotillomania (also called as hair pulling disorder) is a type of disorder in which people repeatedly pull out hair from their scalp, eyebrows, eyelashes, of other parts of the body. Excoriation disorder (also called skin-picking disorder) is a disorder in which people repeatedly pick at their skin resulting in significant sores or wounds. Body dysmorphic disorder is a disorder in which people become preoccupied with a type of imagined or greatly exaggerated belief that they have certain defects or flaws in their physical appearance.
- *Depressive neurosis* is a neurotic disorder characterized by disproportionate depressive reactions to some distressing stress situations, so intense as to interfere with personal or social adjustment of an individual. *Neurasthenic neurosis* is characterized by complaints of easy fatigability, irritability, lack of energy, chronic weakness and pains and aches in different parts of the body. *Depersonalization neurosis* is characterized by the feelings of unreality and estrangement from the self, body or surroundings. *Hypochondriacal* neurosis is characterized by an excessive concern for physical health and persistent intense fears of illness,

disease or dysfunction.

- The most important *causative factors* of all neuroses are psychological. The early unhappy experiences, repressed wishes and unresolved conflicts initiate the process. Later, the unfavourable circumstances, stresses and strain provide sufficient cause for learning neurotic reactions. In many cases psychoneurotic reactions often represent learned maladaptive behaviour patterns.
- *The treatment of* the psychoneurotic disorders varies from each other in relation to their nature and causation. No common treatment can therefore be prescribed for all these disorders. However, neurotic patients are curable. They respond more favourably to behaviour therapy and other psycho therapies than the patients suffering from conduct disorders or functional psychosis.

## REFERENCES

American Psychiatric Association, (1968), *Diagnostic and Statistical Manual of Mental Disorders* (2nd ed.), DSM-II, Washington D.C.: American Psychiatric Association.

Comer, Ronald J. (2015), *Abnormal Psychology* (Ninth Edition), New York: Worth Publishers (A Macmillan Education Imprint)

Davison, Gerald C. & Neale, John M. (1978), *Abnormal Psychology,* (second edition), New York: John Wiley & Sons

Kisker, George W. (1964), ***The Disorganised Personality,*** (3rd International Students Edition), New York: McGraw-Hill.

Mahoney, Michael J. (1980), ***Abnormal Psychology,*** San Francisco: Harper & Row.

Marks, I.M. (1987) Fears, Phobias and Rituals: Panic, Anxiety, and Their Disorders. Oxford University Press, Oxford.

Page, James D. (1976), ***Abnormal Psychology,*** New Delhi: Tata McGraw-Hill.

Price, John Harding., (1972), *Psychiatric investigations,* London: Butterworths.

# 13

# PSYCHOTIC DISORDERS

Psychotic disorders or psychoses are more "serious disorders" of the mind and in this sense represent major illness in comparison with the minor illnesses of neurotic disorders. A psychotic behaviour is characterized by a serious form of personality disturbance in which the patient shows periodic or prolonged loss of contact with the world of reality. The legal and social term "insanity" is frequently used for the psychotic disorders. A person who is judged insane is considered unable to act consciously and therefore, lawyers often plead the insanity of their clients for saving them from being punished for crimes committed by them.

The general characteristics of the psychosis as summarized by Thorpe and Katz (1948:449) are as follows:

1. The individual's mental functions are usually so disturbed that he is incapable of carrying out his daily activities.
2. The individual manifests symptoms of severe nature, often in the form of delusions, hallucinations, stupor, incoherence, or violent reactions.
3. The individual is more or less out of contact with reality.
4. The individual usually lacks insight; that is, he does not appreciate or realize the psychological nature of his symptoms and disabilities.
5. The individual's behaviour may be injurious to himself or to society, or both; he usually must be placed under guardianship or in confinement, as in a mental hospital.

## Psychotic and Psychoneurotic Disorders

1. Psychoneurotic disorders affect the whole personality of the individual by completely disorganising or splitting it, while neurotic disorders affect only parts of one's personality and as a whole the neurotic personality remains intact.
2. Psychoneurotic disorders are major illnesses and involve such serious disorders of the mind where the patients lose contact with reality. Neurotic patients, on the other hand, never lose contact with reality and are able to make a reasonably adequate adjustment with their environment.
3. Psychotics are considered to be a potential danger to themselves and others. Very often their behaviour is unpredictable and uncontrollable. For this reason, their hospitalization is essential irrespective of the fact whether the patient wants to go to a hospital or not. In the case of neurotics hospitalization is seldom

4. Neurotics build castles in the air, while psychotics actually live in them. It signifies that in contrast to neurotics, the world of psychotics is unreal. While a neurotic does not deny reality but merely attempts to ignore it, the psychotic, on the other hand, substitutes the reality with something else by completely denying it.
5. Psychotics get completely caught in their disturbances and lose perspective. They rarely have insight into the nature of their behaviour. Neurotics, on the other hand, usually have insight into the nature of their behaviour. They are likely to be aware of the symptoms, if not why they exist.
6. Psychotic behaviour is characterized by the symptoms of severe nature like delusions, hallucinations, coma or stupor and severe agitation. Significantly, such disorder of thoughts, perceptions and affects are seldom present in neurotic behaviour.

## Classification of Psychotic Disorders

Psychotic disorders are generally classified into two major groups—the organic and the functional.

The organic psychoses are associated with, and are most likely due to, some demonstrable organic pathology. These disorders cause considerable damage to the central nervous system. While in all other psychiatric disorders the brain tissue remains intact, in the organic brain disorders, there is actual physical damage of the brain tissue.

The functional psychoses are not associated with any demonstrable or observable organic pathology. They are not caused by any observable organic defects. While in organic psychoses abnormality can be distinguished in terms of the structural changes in the brain, in functional psychosis there is no demonstrable abnormality of the structure of the brain. What is important in such psychoses is the abnormality of its function, and that is why they are known as functional psychoses.

## Organic Psychoses

Organic psychoses disorders are also known as organic disorders of the brain, organic mental disorders or organic brain syndromes. These disorders of the brain may be classified as acute, intermediate or chronic. An acute disorder is likely to be temporary and reversible, whereas a chronic disorder is irreversible because of permanent damage to the nervous system. In general, a disorder takes the form of acute, intermediate or chronic in proportion to the tissue loss and impairment of the function of the brain.

An acute disorder is likely to be temporary and reversible, whereas a chronic disorder is irreversible because of permanent damage to the nervous system. In general, a disorder takes the form of acute, intermediate or chronic in proportion to the tissue loss and impairment of the function of the brain.

*General symptoms:* Disintegration caused by the brain damage is generally characterized by the following symptoms:

a. *Impairment of the mental* processes: Impairment of the all cognitive functions, for example, impairment of concentration, memorization, comprehension, judgement, planning, learning ability, numerical ability and impairment of orientation related with time, place and person etc.

b. *Impairment of affective responses*: Depression, irritability, crying and laughing without adequate cause.

c. *Impairment in general behaviour:* Carelessness and negligence of personal appearance, neglect of and failure to assume duties and responsibilities, loss of normality or deterioration of character.

*Causative factors:* The most frequent factors which cause organic psychoses may be listed as under:

1. Infection
2. Trauma, natal and post-natal physical injuries affecting the central nervous system.
3. Mal-nutrition
4. Intoxication—drugs, poisons, alcohol etc.
5. Endocrine disturbances
6. Circulatory dysfunctions
7. New growth formation in the brain tumours cancers etc,
8. Progressive degeneration of the portions of central nervous system either due to age factor or by some other unknown causes.

For convenience, the common organic mental disorders can be grouped in different classes.

**(a) Infection of the Nervous System**

Mental disorders may be caused due to infection of the nervous system and brain resulting from bacteria or viruses which invade the brain and damage the nerve tissue. Some such mental disorders are neurosyphilis, encephalitis and meningitis.

Syphilis is an infectious disease caused by microscopic organisms called spirochetes which enter the body through minute breaks or scratches in the skin or directly through mucous membranes such as the lining of the mouth or the genital track. Syphilis spreads from person to person during sexual intercourse, kissing or from direct contact with open syphilitic sores or lesions. The infection can be transmitted from an infected mother to the child in her womb. The infection causes damage to any tissue or organ of the body.

The term neurosyphilis indicates that the syphilitic infection has been transmitted to some part of the brain or the spinal cord. General paresis is an example of neurosyphilitic disorder. It is caused by the progressive infiltration and destruction of brain tissue by the spirochetes of syphilis. It is also known as general paralysis of the insane or paresis. The brain of a paresis patient looks different to the naked eye. This disorder develops only in about five per cent of untreated syphilitics and is found to be more common among men than among women. Its onset occurs when the infected person is about fifty years old.

*Symptoms:* A person suffering from paresis usually manifests the following physical or psychological symptoms:

*Physical*:

(i) A shaky, crude and illegible handwriting with a lot of mistakes.

(ii) Speech disturbances involving stumbling, stuttering, omitting important syllables, mispronunciation and slurred speech.

(iii) Non-contraction of the eye lids to light.

(iv) Tremors of the muscles, arms, eye, tongue and lips.

(v) Disorders of the movement such as dragging of feet, walking with a shuffling gait, having trouble in keeping balance, absence of the knee jerk reflex etc.

(vi) Peculiar mannerisms such as grimacing, dancing about, ceaseless rubbing and picking, smacking of lips, grunting, chewing and sighing.

*Psychological:*

(i) Impairment of memory and judgement.

(ii) Deterioration of personal habits and moral social behaviour.

(iii) Emotional instability and unpredictability.

(iv) Loss of abstract thinking.

(v) Delusions and hallucinations.

*Treatment:* For all the purposes efforts should be made in the society for the adoption of positive preventive measures against infection. It is always better to have an early detection and treatment where infection has taken place. Examination of the serum and the cerebrospinal fluid is necessary for diagnosis of neurosyphilis. At present penicillin therapy (a full course of the antibiotic penicillin) is considered an effective and preferred treatment for neurosyphilis. Penicillin is highly effective in large doses, is expensive and is practically without risk and the course of treatment is also short.

In encephalitis, there is inflammation of the brain tissue while meningitis involves an infection of the thin protective membranes that cover the brain and spinal cord. In both encephalitis and meningitis the infection may be caused by a wide range of microorganisms—such as bacteria, fungi, protozoa and viruses—some of which are carried by insects. For example, one form of encephalitis is transmitted by mosquitoes.

Symptoms of encephalitis usually involve fever, drowsiness, and ocular-pupillary disturbances, insomnia, restlessness, agitation, irritability and excitability. Similarly, meningitis is characterized by a wide range of symptoms involving the central nervous system, resulting in coma, delirium, emotional instability, convulsions, and disturbances of mobility. In the acute phase of encephalitis the patient is lethargic and appears to be sleeping all the time. Because of this symptom, the disease is sometimes referred to as the "sleeping sickness."

**(b) Disorders Associated with Brain Tumours**

Brain tumours or neoplasms involve abnormal growths of the tissue or masses of cells in the brain. Even a relatively small brain tumour may cause behavioural disorders directly through damage to brain centres and thus disrupting normal intellectual functioning or indirectly through disturbances in blood circulation or increased intracranial pressure of cerebrospinal fluid.

Psychological symptoms are usually the first signs of tumours of the brain and therefore, the disorder may be mistakenly diagnosed as functional rather than organic in nature. Hence, a great care is needed for the diagnosis of the possibility of a brain tumour in psychiatric as well as general medical case.

*Symptoms:* The usual early symptoms involve persistent headache, vomiting, mental confusion and memory impairment. As the tumour enlarges and the intracranial pressure increases, there may be carelessness in personal habits, loss of all concepts of time and place, irritability, convulsive seizures, sensorimotor losses, hallucinations, apathy and an overall impairment of intellectual functions. The severity of a brain tumour depends upon the location, size and rapidity of growth. Serious brain tumours, especially those with psychiatric complications, are most common in the frontal, temporal and parietal lobes. In the well advanced stage of brain tumours, the treatment becomes difficult.

*Treatment:* Brain tumours are treated primarily by surgical operations and the chances of recovery rest upon the size, location of the growth and on the amount of the brain tissue which need to be removed with the tumour.

**(c) Disorders Due to head Injuries**

Head injuries may be considered as one of the major causes of mental disorders. The common causes of such injuries are: (i) usual accidents like automobile accidents, plane crashes, train wrecks and industrial blows; (ii) falls and blows (iii) incidents involving surgical removal of brain tissue; and (iv) a birth injury during an instrumental delivery.

The above cited accidents or incidents usually cause damage to the brain which as a result of (a) tiny hemorrhages over large areas of the brain, (b) rupture of major blood vessels, (c) swelling of the brain tissue, or (d) direct damage to brain centres through penetrating wounds.

*Symptoms:* The immediate acute symptom of any serious head injury is likely to be a disturbance of consciousness. In more severe cases it may involve delirium, in-coherence and hallucinations. Usually, these symptoms clear up in a few days or weeks leaving irritability and weakness as a residual, but there are also possibilities that they may develop into chronic disorders causing impairment of intellectual and motor functions or bringing serious personality changes.

*Treatment:* The patient suffering head injury must be given immediate treatment. In severe cases, medical treatment must be supplemented by long range re education and rehabilitation. The patient may be made to adjust in accordance with his impaired subnormal capacities through psychotherapy. Environmental as well as personality factors also play an important role in such treatment. The versatility, compensatory abilities and will to recover and the significant factors in one's ability to regain former levels of functioning are important. Similarly, an appropriate re-education and rehabilitation programme and favourable life situation in which to return are other favourable factors for returning to the community with relatively minor impairments.

### (d) Disorders associated with epilepsy

The term 'epilepsy' is derived from the Greek word meaning seizure. In the past, epilepsy was called the 'scared' or 'falling' disease caused by some divine sources or evil spirits. Epilepsy in general refers to a disorder of the nervous system with or without convulsive behaviour mainly characterized by sudden and recurring episodes of clouding or loss of consciousness accompanied by disturbances in the electrochemical activity of the brain.

*Symptoms* of this disorder may range from a slight lapse of awareness to loss of consciousness with severe convulsions. The genuine epileptic seizures can be differentiated from hysterical convulsions on the grounds that they can occur at any time and at any place while hysterical convulsions generally occur only in the presence of others, as a means of gaining sympathy. The symptoms like frothing at the mouth and papillary disturbances present in genuine seizures are also not found in hysterical convulsions.

*Types of epilepsy:* On the basis of the area and the degree of brain damage the epileptic seizures can be classified into the following four main types:

1. *Grandmal (Great illness):* It represents the most dramatic and common form of epilepsy consisting of four phases, namely, the 'aura' phase, the 'tonic' phase, the 'clonic' phase and the 'coma' phase.

The 'aura' phase is a sort of warning or signal stage consisting of psychological, sensory or motor symptoms in the form of illusions and hallucinations, fear and dizziness, unpleasant ideas, thoughts or impulses to do strange acts. This period gives the person enough time to sit or lie down. The 'tonic' phase is characterized by actual convulsions in which the entire body becomes rigid, the consciousness is lost, breathing is suspended, the jaws are clenched, the eyes become wide open and the pupils dilate. Fortunately, this phase lasts for about half a minute only. In the 'clonic' phase, there are spasms of the muscles alternating between contraction and relaxation. It creates intensive jerking movements as a result of which the patient may foam at the mouth, bite his tongue, strike his head against the ground and lose sphincter control. In the 'coma' phase, the individual still remains unconscious but the convulsions stop and the patient sleeps for a few minutes or hours. After gaining consciousness, there is no recollection of the events in epileptic phases.

2. *Petit mal (Small illness):* In such type of epilepsy there is a loss or diminution of consciousness without convulsions, which lasts only a few seconds. The patient stops all his activities, and stares vacantly ahead or towards the floor. He maintains his posture during the attack or he may slip and fall. He, however, resumes his normal activities after a few seconds. The patient may not even be aware of the attack. He may think that his mind has gone blank for a few seconds. Usually, this type of epilepsy is most common in children and teenagers.
3. *Psychomotor epilepsy:* In psychomotor epilepsy there is a typical EEG disturbance in the region of the anterior temporal lobe. The main feature of this type of epilepsy is a psychic disturbance, which varies greatly from one patient to another. It may or may not involve loss of consciousness. Under such attacks, persons may be seen to be engaged in routine tasks or unusual acts like climbing up a table

or a chair or undress in public. Some patients may become violently assaultive and may be seen either to mutilate themselves or injure other people. However, they show no memory of acts performed during the period of attack which may last from a few minutes to several days. This type of epilepsy is most difficult to treat.

4. *Jacksonian:* Named after its discoverer an English neurologist H. Jackson, this type of epilepsy is much like a modified Grandma seizure. The attack begins in one part or one side of the body, for example, one side of the face or one arm or a finger with muscle twitches or numbness, or a burning sensation. These muscular or sensory disturbances then spread over the side of the body on which they originate and even sometime the other side also. There is a gradual loss of consciousness and then the attack usually becomes similar to grandmal seizure.

*Causes of epilepsy:* There is evidence that heredity plays an important role in the etiology of epilepsy. Many investigators have reported that typical epileptic brain waves are to be found in close relatives of epileptics.

Other biological factors like congenital deformity, birth trauma head injury, toxins and drugs have also been found to be associated with the causation of epilepsy. According to a neurologcial theory called the 'irritation theory', epilepsy is brought about as a result of direct stimulation or irritation of the cerebral cortex.

The psychological factors in the form of conflicts, frustrations and stresses usually act as a trigger in precipitating seizures in many persons. Originally predisposed to epilepsy, very often the convulsive behaviour of an epileptic represents a reaction to his frustration or a form of escape from an intolerable situation.

*Treatment*: A combination of medical treatment and psychological therapy works well for epileptics. In some cases surgical treatment has been found the only effective remedy. Many of the newly discovered drugs like ethosuximide, phenyl thylacetylurea, carbamazepine, chlordiazepoxide and diazepam are found to be effective with many cases of epilepsy. For better results, the proper orientation of the patient to his disorder is very much needed. To bring necessary modification in his environment is another necessity and to help him to adjust to his world of work and environmental situation is the further task that should be satisfactorily accomplished.

In recent years some of the advanced preventive techniques like pocket size radio device are proving quite effective in preventing as well as controlling epileptic seizures. The person is warned so that he may be able to find a place to rest or to take appropriate medication. In the more advanced techniques like brain pace-maker, the patient may be adequately helped in controlling the seizures. When he feels the warning signal of a seizure, the device is switched on and an electrical stimulus for stalling the attack is sent to the brain.

**(e) Disorders associated with toxic reactions**

Mental disorders may be caused by the ingestion of a variety of toxic substances such as alcohol, drugs, gases and heavy metals.

Every tissue and organ of the body is affected by the consumption of alcohol. It is believed to cause five major types of brain disorders, namely (1) pathological intoxication, (2) delirium tremens, (3) alcoholic hallucinosis, (4) alcoholic deterioration, and (5) Korsakoff's syndrome.

The disorder pathological intoxication often named as "crazy drunk" is found among the people who are emotionally unstable. A small amount of alcohol is sometimes enough to throw the susceptible persons into a state of violence, confusion, agitation and excitement.

Delirium tremens develops after prolonged periods of heavy drinking. It is marked by delirium and hallucinations. There is a marked tremor of the hands and tongue and sometimes of the facial muscles as well. Hallucinations are primarily visual but they may be tactile as well. Unpleasant creatures like cockroaches and spiders may appear to be crawling up the wall or all over the alcoholic's body.

The major symptom in alcoholic hallucinosis is the auditory hallucination, in which the person responds by attacking his or her supposed tormentors after listening voices seem to be making insulting accusatory and derogatory remarks.

The disorder alcoholic deterioration is found among the chronic alcoholics who share progressive deterioration over the years. It is probably caused by impairment of the nerve cells of the cerebral cortex. The symptoms of this disorder range from mild personality disorganization to serious states of dementia.

Korsakoff's syndrome associated with the chronic state of alcoholism involves psychological symptoms like memory disturbances, confabulation, delirium and emotional instability in addition to organic symptoms in the form of multiple neuritis. This disorder is usually caused by the degeneration of cells in the cerebrum and the peripheral nerves.

The excessive and indiscriminate use of many drugs and chemicals affecting the tissues may develop an organic brain disorder. For example, morphine (an opium derivation) addiction results in a variety of organic and psychological problems. The addict becomes indifferent, negligent, forgetful, loses his sense of conscience, feels difficulty in sleeping and develops hallucinations and a breakdown of morale. Similarly, amphetamine drug (Benzedrine) addiction results in tension and apprehension, trembling, sleeplessness, marked loss of appetite, disturbances in intellectual functioning, delusions of persecution and auditory hallucinations. The sleep inducing drug barbiturates (bromides, barbital) addiction is found to cause irritability arid lethargic attitude slowly resulting in an intellectual deterioration, personal inefficiency and general deterioration of the personality.

Other toxic agents such as lead, mercury, manganese, carbon- monoxide, copper and arsenic can seriously impair brain functioning.

In serious cases of lead poisoning there may be definite psychotic symptoms such as headaches, tremors, convulsions, hallucinations, delirium, and progressive deterioration of both brain and behaviour. It may result in extensive cortical damage and blindness in children (often victims of chewing old toys and lead based paints) the chronic lead poisoning may result into convulsive seizures and mental retardation, in cases of mercury and manganese poisoning, the brain and spinal cord are badly affected. The first signs are irritability, memory loss and difficulties in concentration. Then the gait and speech are affected. The patient becomes restless and emotionally upset leading towards irreparable psychological and personality disturbances.

**(f) Disorders associated with endocrine disturbances**

The endocrine glands secret their hormones directly into the bloodstream. Either over secretions or under secretions of these glands may cause various mental disorders.

*Thyroid disorders:* An over secretion of the hormone thyroxin by the thyroid gland may cause hyperthyroidism or Graves' disease (named after an Irish physician Robert Graves) marked by the symptoms like loss of weight, tremors, sleep disturbances, tenseness, insomnia and emotional excitability. Chronic cases may lead to neurosis or even psychosis marked by hallucinations and delusions.

Hypothyroidism, an under secretion of thyroxin hormone may bring about a condition called myxedema in adults marked by the symptoms like physical and mental sluggishness, memory defects, increase in weight and even delirium. As the disorder progresses, the skin becomes dry and brittle and hair is lost from the eyebrows and the genital area. At more severe stage the depression may become highly pronounced leading to psychosis. In children, this disorder may cause mental retardation.

*Adrenal disorders:* An under-secretion of cortisone secretion by the adrenal cortex produces Addison's disease (named after an English physician Thomas Addison). It is marked by symptoms like loss of weight, lowering of blood pressure, irritability and headaches, fatigue, reduced sex drive, darkening of skin and mucous membranes, moderate depression, loss of vigour and lack of ambition, and even hallucinations and delusions in some cases.

An over-secretion of the hormone cortisone may lead to a number of rare and dramatic changes in secondary sex characteristics like masculine physical appearance in females or development of female characteristics in males. Such changes lead to complications in the individual's life adjustment and thus may eventuate in a wide range of psychopathological reactions. More particularly, a rare disease Cushing's syndrome (named after Harvey Cushing, the American neurosurgeon) affecting young women has been found to be caused by over secretion of cortisone. The patient shows symptoms of severe unpleasant mood swings and depression which may lead to a state of anxiety, agitation and irritability. Physical symptoms may include obesity, muscle wasting, changes in skin, colour and texture and bone porosity which may cause spinal deformity.

**(g) Disorders associated with degeneration**

Some of the mental disorders are known to be associated with advancing age or degeneration and deterioration of the brain tissue. The brain and the central nervous system deteriorate abnormality fast in such circumstances causing varying degree of personality disorganisations. Generally, such disorders of advancing age can be classified into three groups—presenile disorders, senile disorders and cerebral arteriosclerosis.

*1. Presenile disorders*: The mental disorder occurring before 65, the senile age (usually between 45 and 60 years), are referred to as presenile disorders or presenile dementias. Alzheimer's disease, Pick's disease, Parkinson's disease and Huntington's chorea are such disorders. We would be discussing these disorders in detail later on in a separate chapter in this text. However, here also we are presenting some essentials related to these disorders.

*Alzheimer's disease:* This disease was first described by the German neurologist, Alois Alzheimer in 1860. In this disease, the brain tissue deteriorates rather rapidly than in Pick's disease. Generally, its termination in death comes within an average of four years. It is three times more prevalent among women than among men. In this disorder the patient manifests a gradual intellectual deterioration, loss of memory, absentmindedness, illogical reasoning, anxiety and depression, irritation, occasional hallucinations and labile effect with periodical episodes of forced laughter and tears. The patient blames others for personal failings and has delusions of persecution. In the sensillum (after 65 years of age), it would be indistinguishable from arteriosclerotic dementia.

*Pick's disease:* This presenile disorder was first described by a Czechoslovak psychiatrist, Arnold Pick in 1891. It is a degenerative disorder of the central nervous system, mainly involving frontal and temporal lobe atrophy. It usually has its onset between 45 and 50 years of age and is more prevalent in women than men in the ratio of about 3 to 2. Life expectancy after onset is usually four to seven years. In a degenerative process, the total weight of the brain may be reduced. The patient usually exhibits difficulty in remembering, inability to deal with new problems and situations, loss of interest and attention, restlessness, easy fatigability, irritability, speech disturbances, and lack of insight into his condition.

*Parkinson's disease:* This disorder was first described by James Parkinson in 1817. It is a chronic progressive disease of the central nervous system involving particularly the thalamus, basal ganglia, and reticular activating system. Its usual onset is between 50 and 65 years of age. The symptoms described by Davison and Neale (1978) are:

*The primary symptoms are severe and continual muscular tremors usually occurring at a rate of four to eight movements per second, which rhythmically agitate the limbs, hands, neck and face. The tremor may begin in one hand or arm, spread to the leg of that side, then to neck, jaw, and face, and finally to the two other limbs. Only muscles that are at rest are subject to tremors, however, not those that are engaged in a coordinated movement. But manual skills may eventually be lost, and speech, swallowing, and chewing are laborious. Other physiological effects include muscular rigidity, akinesia - an inability to initiate movements – and defects in balance. The face later becomes masklike and expressionless, the gait stiff and distinctive, with the upper part of the body moving forward ahead of the legs. The individual may have difficulty in concentrating, become apathetic, and withdraws from social contact. About 90 per cent of patients with Parkinson's disease are depressed, and in 30 per cent intellectual deterioration is evident.*

*Huntington's chorea:* This disorder was first described by an American neurologist George Huntington in 1872. It usually begins when the individual is in the thirties and thereafter deterioration is progressive over a period of 10 to 20 years eventually ending in death. This disease is attributable to defective genetic inheritance and thereby runs in families from generation to generation. The actual brain pathology in this disease consists mainly of atrophy or degeneration of small ganglion cells of the corpus striatum. The physical symptoms consist of the choreic or choreiform movements (uncontrollable involuntary irregular spasmodic twitching and jerking of the limbs, trunk and head). The patient has difficulty in speaking and walking. Eventually, there is a total loss of body control. The behaviour symptoms are characterized by violent outbursts, depression, irritability, confusion, poor memory, euphoria, poor judgement, vagrancy, prostitution, delusions, suicidal ideas and attempts, and hallucinations. At present there is no effective treatment for Huntington's chorea. However, a variety of drugs like chlorpromazine and thiopropazate hydrochloride appear most effective in controlling the violent choreic movements.

2. *Senile disorders:* Senile dementia is chiefly a characteristic of the senile age group in which there is a gradual decrease in mental and physical abilities. The brain of the senile patient shows considerable atrophy, especially in the frontal lobes. There is a reduction in brain size, the cortical convolutions narrow, the fissures between them widen and functional cells are replaced by scar cells. The senile patients exhibit a marked decrease in intellectual ability and forgetfulness for recent events. Other symptoms are perseveration (telling the same thing again and again), circumstantiality and rambling speech. The individual becomes careless in personal hygiene and may display unusual or unexpected behaviour. The lessening of alertness, incoherent speech, disorientation, intolerance for change, losing control of sexual impulses, agitation, psychosomatic disorders, amnesia are some of the other symptoms. In some cases, the deterioration leads to severe psychotic or neurotic reactions. Gradually, the physical and intellectual deterioration increases to a stage where the patient is bed ridden incontinent and incoherent.
3. *Cerebral arteriosclerosis:* This is another major mental disorder of old age. Men are affected about three times more frequently than women. It is characterized by hardening and thickening of the walls of blood vessels, large arteries and small arterioles and capillaries which reduce the supply of blood to the brain resulting in intra-cerebral bleeding. The actual onset of the disorder may be sudden or gradual. When the onset is a sudden stroke due to blockage of or an artery, the symptoms include headache, dizziness, loss of contact with surroundings, clouding of consciousness, incoherence, disorientation, restlessness, seizure or paralysis of one side of the body, emotional liability etc. In cases where the onset is gradual, the symptoms are similar to those of senile psychosis. The duration of this disorder varies from person to person. In some cases, it is fatal after a short period, while in others the chronic illness may last many years. However, the average duration is considered to be about three to five years after which death usually occurs.

## Functional Psychoses

Mental disorders exhibiting a change only in the function of the brain and not in the brain structure like organic psychoses are included in the functional psychoses. The three major disorders of this category are:

- Schizophrenia
- Affective disorders
- Paranoid disorders.

*Schizophrenia:* In frequency, schizophrenic disorder leads all psychoses, functional and organic. When compared to other functional psychoses in terms of severity or seriousness, it may be considered as the most serious or severe of the functional psychoses. Consequently, the hospitalisation of schizophrenic patients is longer (ten to forty-five years) than that for any other group.

The term schizophrenia literally means splitting of the mind. Here splitting of the mind does not mean a split personality as in amnesia and multiple personality, but a marked separation of the self from reality. "The term schizophrenia." according to Coleman (1970:275), "is now used to include a group of psychotic reactions in which there are fundamental disturbances in reality relationships and in emotional and intellectual processes."

Schizophrenics as a rule manifest a number of symptoms, the significant ones of which are:

1. Lack of coherence in the thought process.
2. Disorganised patterns of thinking and feeling,
3. Apathy absence of feeling.
4. Disorganised patterns of speech.
5. Peculiarities of movements or bizarre actions.
6. Autism – preoccupation with private fantasy.
7. Withdrawal from reality or seclusiveness.
8. Neglect of conduct and personal habits.
9. Delusions and hallucinations.

*Types of schizophrenia:* For the purpose of diagnosis as well as treatment, the schizophrenic disorders may be sub-divided into the following four major types:

- Simple schizophrenia
- Hebephrenic schizophrenia
- Catatonic schizophrenia
- Paranoid schizophrenia.

*Simple schizophrenia:* Simple schizophrenia is characterized by an attitude of indifference, or in advanced stages by extreme apathy. The disorder usually begins with a decreased interest in the normal activities of life during adolescence or early adult life and then gradually develops into loss of ambition, emotional indifference and withdrawal from social relations. The individual becomes increasingly indifferent and seclusive and begins to obtain his satisfaction through day-dreaming and eventually sinks into an apathetic state. At this stage he does not care at all. There is nothing to wish for, nothing to fight for. He has no connection with realities to assume responsibility and is content to lead a simple, irresponsible, indifferent and dependent life.

Simple schizophrenic disorder may be distinguished from other types of schizophrenia on the ground that it rarely shows the more dramatic symptoms such as disorientation, delusions, hallucinations, or disturbances of language or action. Simple schizophrenics are sometimes mistaken for mentally retarded on account of their apathy, indifference, Jack of concentration, low level of motivation and intelligence. Psychological tests, however, may reveal that they are not mentally retarded. Another difficulty is encountered in differentiating simple schizophrenia from inadequate personality. The difference between the two is that those with inadequate personality may appear to try to function effectively while schizophrenics do not try at all.

*Hebephrenic schizophrenia*: The onset of this disease usually occurs in adolescence and develops gradually. In this disorder the affected person retreats from the stresses of life by regressing to a silly, childish level of behaviour and by withdrawing into a fantasy world of his own, with accompanying emotional disintegration of the personality with most dramatic psychotic symptoms like symbolic language disturbances and symbolic actions hallucinations, particularly auditory, and delusions of a sexual, religious hypochondriacal and persecutory nature.

Hebephrenia represents withdrawal in an extreme form. The patient no longer remains interested in the world around him. His silly and inappropriate giggling, weeping or laughing behaviour does not result from external stimuli but from stimuli from within the imaginary world in which he lives. In severe cases the withdrawal and regression is so extreme that the person behaves in many ways like an infant. It is an incurable stage and the patient continues to exist on the level of his choice in the strange world of his own creation.

*Catatonic schizophrenia:* The catatonic schizophrenia is diagnosed mainly on the patient's behaviour fluctuating between stuporous depression and wild excitement. Consequently, his motor behaviour may be inhibited (stupor) or alternately he may break out into an inexplicable burst of over-activity (catatonic excitement). During, his periods of stupor the patient may remain for hours in a bizarre posture. For example, he may sit, stand, or keep his limb in a particular position for hours on end or he may manifest symptoms like muscular rigidity (rigidity of the muscles and a general resistance to movement), waxy flexibility (remaining in any position in which he is put), echopraxia (mimicry or imitation of what others do), echolalia (automatic repetition of words said by another) and negativism (resisting even the simplest request). He may repeatedly carry out complicated stereotyped movements such as hanging the parts of his chair in a certain sequence symmetrically with both-hands or walking endlessly up and down the ward; some steps in one direction and an equal number of steps in the other.

In the excited phase of catatonia, the patient becomes extremely over active, agitated, aggressive and destructive. During such periods he may shout, throw himself around, tear his clothes, assault others, or injure and mutilate himself The violence of the catatonic patient is unbridled. In addition to the motor symptoms, the catatonic patients display typical schizophrenic thinking and affect. They may frequently experience fears, hallucinations and delusions involving ideas of grandeur and of persecution.

The genesis of catatonia may be searched into some sound psychological basis. The meaningless behaviour, the stereotyped physical activity, the stupor or violence are actually never senseless in the light of the patient's inner conflicts and repressions. Any psychological trouble arising out of conflicts and frustrations (for example sex frustrations and feelings of guilt concerning sex behaviour) may become a potent source for the catatonic functional psychosis.

*Paranoid schizophrenia*: The term paranoid literally means 'beside on self.' Consequently, a paranoid is said to be a person who believes for himself to have a special relationship with other people. The paranoid patient is intensely preoccupied with his relationship to other people, bad though this relationship may be. As a result, paranoid schizophrenia is diagnosed mainly by the disorders of thought content involving systematic delusions and hallucinations frequently of persecutory nature resulting in loss of critical judgement and an unpredictable behaviour,

In the beginning, the individual who develops paranoid schizophrenia feels unworthy and suffers from the feeling of inferiority. He resorts to the defence mechanism of blaming others for his failure to achieve. He carries this defence to extremes by distrusting everyone to the extent that he feels certain that they have designs against him. Suspicions of others gradually grow into ideas of reference and ideas of reference, in turn, become delusions of persecution.

Hallucination and the delusions of persecution of the paranoid schizophrenic may take many forms sometimes of very peculiar nature. The patient falsely believes that an event has a particular significance for him individually. He may believe that the events described by the news reader on the television are oblique references to his own life; the newspapers say things about him in code; there is a special meaning for him in the nods and glances exchanged by others on the train.

The persecutory beliefs and the element of mystery combine to produce a preoccupation with plots to kill or injure the patient. A businessman was sure that his partner was trying to get rid of him and take over the company. Another patient used to wear a rubber suit at home to protect himself from the rays of an "influenced machine" which a spiteful neighbour was directing against him. A labourer declared that some people were going to lower him into hot acid and make hot iron out of him. The more interesting case is of a woman patient who remarked that "one of the doctors has stolen my mind out of my head and he is going to use it to make a lot of money".

The paranoid schizophrenic is inclined to be very verbal about his or her ideas and beliefs. Such patients are generally alert, agitated, talkative, aggressive but also confused and afraid. At times when they believe that someone wants to destroy them, they destroy them first in order to save themselves. The hostile attitude and aggression shown by some of the paranoid patients reflects such trends. However, as the personality deteriorates with time, the paranoid schizophrenics tend to become withdrawn and apathetic rather than aggressive.

## Etiology of Schizophrenia (Causation)

*Genetic factors (heredity):* There have been many studies to support the claim that schizophrenia is inherited. These studies may be grouped into three major types: family-risk studies, twin studies, and studies of adopted children.

It has been observed in family-risk studies that the families of schizophrenics had a disproportionately large number of schizophrenic cases. The fact that the disorder runs in families has led to the conclusion that schizophrenia is inherited.

In twin studies where one of the twin pair has schizophrenia, then the chances of the other twin having schizophrenia are higher when he is identical than when he is non-identical. Since identical twins are genetically the same in comparison with the non-identical ones, the findings suggest that hereditary influences play a part in the inheritance of schizophrenia.

The studies carried out with the children of schizophrenic parents adopted by normal parents and children of normal parents adopted by schizophrenic parents also suggest that there are genetic influences in schizophrenia. It was noticed that when the child of schizophrenic parents was separated from his family soon after birth and nurtured in a proper environment by normal parents, he was still found to be affected with this disorder.

In spite of the evidence put forward by hereditarians, the hereditary influences provide only the necessary causes but not the sufficient ones. Genetic influences are not the sole cause of schizophrenia. The children belonging to schizophrenic parents of families are not bound to become schizophrenics. There are instances of one of the identical twins not being schizophrenic though both- parents or one of them were schizophrenic. If schizophrenia itself is inherited, then its emergence in one identical twin should always be accompanied by its emergence in the other identical twin. We may conclude that schizophrenia is not exclusively the product of hereditary influences. On the other hand, there are some psychiatrists who would deny that the genes and chromosomes may be loaded for schizophrenia in the children of schizophrenics. Therefore, the controversy lies not in the existence of hereditary influences in schizophrenia but on the extent of this influence.

We may conclude that genetic influences provide some genetic predisposition to schizophrenia. This explains why the disorder seems to be hereditary, and also why it is not essential for the identical twins to be schizophrenics. Genetic influences, thus, may be the first step in the process of making of a schizophrenic by providing a relatively weak constitution which may not be able to resist the many stresses of life.

In summary, heredity influences appear to be relatively unimportant in the development of schizophrenia. Whether a child predisposed to schizophrenia through his genetic influences will become schizophrenic or not depends upon the environmental influences to which he shall be exposed in future,

*Environmental factors:* Besides genetic influences, researchers have tried to link schizophrenia with the biochemical disturbances and metabolic errors in the body. But this possibility has not made much headway. The accepted causal theory of schizophrenia in the recent years speaks of the psycho social causes inherent in one's environment. It asserts that schizophrenic reactions are learned patterns of behaviour and are acquired in the same way in which normal behaviour is acquired. These patterns arc the results of defective up-bringing, faulty environment, improper models of imitation and emotionally traumatic experiences of life.

A schizophrenic flying from reality may learn to withdraw into a private world of fantasy and social isolation where he feels safer in his private world or in his state of regression. The schizophrenic withdrawal often represents an avoidance of threatening interpersonal relationships, criticism and failure. Family environment plays an important role in the development of schizophrenic behaviour. The improper relationships prevailing in familial situations, particularly between the mother and father on one hand and between parents and the child on the other, may provide sufficient ground for the development of schizophrenia.

In many cases the behaviour of the mothers towards their children may be considered as a sufficient cause. The non-verbal behaviour of these mothers does not match their verbal behaviour. They may appear to be rejecting, stressing on independence and at the same time may show affection, over-protection and self-sacrificing attitude. This "double bind" dilemma coupled with discord between parents may result in an irrational and maladaptive behaviour of the offspring. Consequently, a child may learn:

- to avoid close interpersonal relationships;
- improper emotional behaviour;
- indecisiveness and suspicious nature; and
- thought disorders.

All such learning patterns in the early life gradually develop into schizophrenic behaviour.

Stress situations at any stage in early or later life may be considered as one of the most important precipitating factor for causing schizophrenia. In genetically predisposed brain and nervous system, the stress events trigger biochemical and metabolic changes which result in schizophrenic symptoms. The stresses (the miseries of one's life in the socio-culture context) in the majority of the cases cause abnormality in the patterns of interpersonal relationships. They also cause feelings of inferiority, frustrations, tensions, anxiety and fearful attitude in the individual who may lose confidence in his abilities, isolate him and become suspicious of everything in his environment and may learn to attack others in imaginary self- defence.

In conclusion, it can be said that genetic influences are a necessary, but not sufficient cause, for the development of schizophrenia. What is acquired as predisposition to the disorder in the form of genes and biological structure is further subjected to environmental influences. The early childhood experiences and family situations coupled with the stress events of later life act as causative as well precipitating factors in the development of schizophrenic behaviour. The likelihood of an individual becoming a schizophrenic depends upon the magnitude or degree of the genetic predisposition (heredity) and stress (environment).

*Treatment*: Schizophrenic reactions, besides being a learned behaviour, have a hereditary and biological base. The treatment of this disorder, therefore, involves the physical as well as psychological methods. No time should be lost in commencing treatment as delay may leave the patient a schizophrenic forever.

Physical methods involve the use of insulin coma therapy, electric shock, psychosurgery and chemotherapy, that is, the use of tranquillizers, energisers and anti-anxiety drugs. In view of the risk involved, insulin coma therapy is rarely used. Psychosurgery is also rarely performed on schizophrenics unless all other available forms of treatment have failed. Physical treatment is usually performed through medication (use of drugs). It is often supplemented by electroconvulsive therapy (ECT) for better results. However, ECT is reserved for cases where drugs are not successful, or for patients who are particularly agitated or distressed. Since schizophrenia is a disorder of arousal, drug therapy works well as most of the drugs like phenothiazines, butyrophenones, the rauwolfia alkaloids, trifluoperazine (stela zine) and diazepam (valium) and other tranquillizers decrease arousal.

It is to be remembered that the principal characteristic of the schizophrenic behaviour is withdrawal. It follows that the principal ingredient in its psychological treatment should therefore be relationship. The classical form of psychoanalytically oriented psychotherapy should not be used. The removal of defences and use of un-covering techniques involve great risk of precipitating overt schizophrenia in previously borderline or latent cases. Individual and group psychotherapy may work well with the schizophrenics if the personal relationships between the patients and the therapist are properly established. The therapist has to win the confidence of his patient and should try to remove suspicion and distrust originated with the first inter-personal relations. The therapist has to trust and like the patient and not fear him. At times the schizophrenic may attempt to hurt the therapist merely on the assumption that he wishes to destroy him (as he has been hurt in other relationships). In such a delicate situation, a good therapist must exercise patience, tolerate the hostility of the patient without fear and without counter hostility. Persons who care for the treatment of schizophrenics should always remember that schizophrenics are after all human beings. Like normal persons, they respond negatively to punitive treatment and positively to warmth and understanding. They should be sympathetically understood and, as far as possible, their ideas and beliefs should never be challenged, but they should be gradually made to come to terms with reality.

## Affective Disorders

Affective disorders of psychotic origin are characterized by severe disturbances of mood (or affect, as the emotional state is known technically). The patient is either excessively- elated and high in spirits (manic state) or excessively depressed and low in spirits (depressive state). Sometimes he may show a combination of ups and downs of mood resulting in manic-depressive slate. Disturbances in emotional state, that is, the mood, arc accompanied with changes in the patient's thought process. Consequently, the patient may be preoccupied with unpleasant thoughts concerning disease, poverty, unworthiness or guilt or develops ideas, of grandeur. He may suffer from misrepresentation of reality, delusions or hallucinations. Changes in mood and thought contents lead to changes in the patient's behaviour. He may show signs of abnormal over-activity, sometimes harming others or himself.

## Schizophrenic and Affective Disorders

In spite of much overlapping of symptoms, the differences between schizophrenic and affective disorders are:

(i) In schizophrenia there is a complete retreat from reality. The patient adopts it as a simple means for his adjustment. On the other hand, in affective disorders, the individual appears to be desperately trying to do something about the situation. The reaction is that of fighting as seen in manic state. Even in depression, there is an element of aggression.

(ii) Schizophrenic disorders are more frequent than the affective disorders. The percentage of schizophrenic patients entering mental hospitals is three to four times more than the patients with affective disorders.

(iii) The patients with affective disorders are more extroverted and less withdrawn than schizophrenics.

(iv) A large percentage of affective disorder patients are married. In contrast, most of the schizophrenics never marry.

(v) In comparison to affective disorder patients, schizophrenics remain hospitalized for a long period of time. The possibility of their improvement is much less than the manic-depressives.

(vi) Affective disorders are more common in women than in men while most of the schizophrenics are found to be men.

## Classification of Affective Disorder

According to DSM-1I, affective disorders may be classified into three categories:

- Manic disorder
- Depressive disorder
- Bipolar affective disorder (Manic-Depressive disorder)

1. *Manic disorder:* Manic disorder or mania is associated with the elation of mood and excessive excitement. The patient is high in spirits, overactive and bursting with energy. Manic behaviour is of three degrees: hypomania, acute-mania, and hyperacute or delirious mania.

*Hypomania* is a relatively mild form of excitement which manifests itself through a state of apparent happiness coupled with unusual restlessness or nervousness. An individual suffering from hypomania is found doing something at high speed. For example, in conversation he speaks rapidly or engages himself in drumming with his fingers or keeps moving his feet while others are talking. The patient appears quite friendly, self-confident and energetic. His thoughts are usually on pleasant topics or wish fulfilling fantasies. While the depressed patient has ideas of unworthiness, the patient with hypomania has ideas of grandeur. Instead of worrying about illness, he denies the fact that he is currently ill. Similarly, instead of remaining within his means, he is liable to spend lavishly. All seems to be going well with such individuals. But over-activity, excitement, high spirits, and ideas of grandeur compel an individual to behave foolishly and impulsively. This is so because the patient is out of touch with reality. He must therefore be saved from the stage when he starts cursing himself for his behaviour and being frustrated by excessive irritations leading to acute stages of this disease.

The acute mania is a more severe form of manic disorder in degree. While hospitalization is rarely needed for persons suffering from hypomania, the acute manic is always a case for hospital care when restlessness or excitement is more marked and elation more extreme. There is a quickening of thought process, speech and motor excitement. The patient is extremely gay and confident. As a result of his over confidence and excitement he loses the little self-control that he has and becomes unfriendly, uncooperative, insensitive, careless (even of his appearance and surroundings), irritable, vulgar, aggressive, and even assaultive to others. He resents any form of restraint or criticism and wants to have his own way. He frequently has delusions and hallucinations, usually of the grandeur type for maintaining his feeling of self-importance.

Hyperacute or delirious mania is the most extreme form of manic disorder. The patient becomes very restless and excited. He experiences hallucinations and delusions of both persecution and grandeur and loses all contacts with reality. In his wild excitement, the patient may shout and laugh constantly, tear his clothes and is likely to become dangerous both to himself and to others. He, then, has to be kept isolated in a room.

2. *Depressive disorder:* Depression is the polar opposite of mania. The patient remains in low spirits, feels discouraged and sad. He loses his interest in things around him and may even neglect appearance and body care. The patient's movements become slow. He may either sit doing nothing or even remain in bed in a form of stupor ignoring his surroundings and need for food and hygiene. There is a marked retardation of thought process, and he has difficulty summoning enough energy to think. He talks slowly and hesitantly or not at all. By contrast, some patients with severe depression may also show signs of agitation. They pace up and down restlessly wringing their hands in despair. Agitation and retardation have some common elements also. The element of anger (rage) is likely to be present in both as the depressed individual may express hostility inwardly and outwardly. The other common feature exhibited through retarded or agitated behaviour is a severe lack of useful energy. Loss of appetite, loss of weight and constipation are common. Sexual desire tends to diminish and the patient is likely to become frigid or impotent. The patient suffers from insomnia. Early morning wakefulness is a characteristic found in severe forms of depressive disorder.

   Depressive disorder also involves delusions and hallucinations usually associated with feelings of guilt. The patient may hear voices accusing him of sins that he has committed. The ideas related with disease, unworthiness and poverty are also found. The patient may be preoccupied with disease and retains his convictions despite medical examination. Feelings of depersonalisation are coloured by the mood in depressive illness. Declarations like "my mind is dead," "my legs have been turned to lead", "my liver has been taken away", often reflect the state of affective disorder in individuals. Another common feature of depressive disorder is loss of confidence and pessimistic outlook. The world looks gloomy for the patients and nothing gives delight. The profound helplessness and ideas of unworthiness may lead to suicidal attempts or to the passive contemplation of suicide.

*Sub-types of depressive disorder*: Based on the degree of severity of the symptoms, the depressive disorder may be classified under three subheads: (i) mild (simple), (ii) acute, and (iii) depressive stupor.

*The mild or simple depression* characterizes the initial stage of the disorder. *In acute depression* the symptoms characterizing depression are more marked and reach their peak in depressive stupor. *The depressive stupor* is the most extreme form of depressive reaction where the patient is unresponsive, lies motionless and usually requires forced feeding. While a mild depressive requires no hospitalization and is often treated as an out-patient, the acute depression needs hospitalization and supervision for guarding against suicidal attempts. In the stupor stage the need for looking after the patient becomes much pronounced and the treatment becomes most difficult.

3. *Bipolar affective disorder (manic-depressive disorder):* This category of affective disorder involves reactions which are neither manic nor depressive, but a blend of the two with the mood of elation (excitement and over-activity) accompanying morbid ideas and despair. The classical signs of manic depressive illness as suggested by J.H. Price (1972:57) are listed below:
   - (i) Sudden, unexplained, often profound changes in mood to either sadness or elation, with no degree by degree shift.
   - (ii) The illness occurs without any appropriate external stimulus.
   - (iii) Depression is at its worst in the early morning.
   - (iv) When ill, the patient is out of touch with reality. At such times one cannot reason with him.
   - (v) The manic phase has the appropriate characteristics– ecstasy, euphoria, flight of ideas, over-activity and expansiveness.
   - (vi) In the depressive episode, patients often resign from their jobs or may give up all their possessions.
   - (vii) Illness is known to respond to electroconvulsive therapy.
   - (viii) Manic-depressive psychosis is classically a genetic illness, and inheritance follows the dominant single autosomal gene.
   - (ix) The additional clinical features are somatic delusions and vague hypochondriacally complaints such as, "My bowels are blocked, I have not defecated for years."
   - (x) The major risk of the illness is suicide, particularly in the early morning when the patient has no one with whom he may share his problems.

***Causes and treatment of affective disorders:*** A number of studies have established that mania and depression, either separately or combined, are more frequently encountered in families than schizophrenia. But this is not sufficient reason for providing a genetic basis for affective disorders. The possibility of learning this type of behaviour as a consequence of environmental influences from early childhood cannot be eliminated. However, the latest researches in this field have helped in establishing the genetic and biochemical factors responsible for affective disorders.

Apart from genetic and biochemical conditions, psychological factors appear to be by far the most significant in the development of affective disorders. Somehow the affective reactions are the learned reaction patterns that an individual adopts to cope with his adjustment and satisfaction of his basic needs. For example, when the child learns that his depressed state catches attention brings sympathy and support from friends and relatives, he adopts depression as a preferred pattern of behaviour. The early life experiences and stress events of the later years often trigger incidences of the affective disorder. The inherent guilt feelings, lack of love and affection, frustrations, situations giving rise to conflicts, tensions and stresses all produce hostility which may compel an individual either to seek its outward expression or inward sufferings as found in most of the affective psychoses.

The treatment of affective psychosis involves both the physical as well as psychological methods. Electroconvulsive therapy medication constitutes the physical methods of treatment. In depressive disorder, antidepressant drugs (mostly the tricyclic anti-depressants) are widely used, while the use of tranquillizers is recommended in the manic disorder. In the agitated type of depression a combination of tranquillizing and antidepressant drugs is sometimes useful.

In psychological methods of treatment of depressive disorders psychotherapies like supportive therapy, insight oriented therapy, and listening therapy may effectively used.

In the case of mania, neither supportive nor the insight oriented therapy works well. Hospitalization is just the first need for such patients. A well organised psychological approach known as management of interpersonal relationship between therapist and the patient has been found useful in the treatment of manic patients.

## Paranoid Disorders

In this chapter the term paranoid has been used while describing paranoid schizophrenia. The distinction between paranoid disorder and paranoid schizophrenia may be summarised as under:

1. Like paranoid schizophrenia, paranoid disorders are also characterised by delusions, but the delusions here are more systematized and closely interrelated than in paranoid schizophrenia.
2. In paranoid schizophrenia there is splitting of the mind, that is, disorganisation of the personality showing a marked separation of the self from reality, but in paranoid disorders, there is no such disorganisation of the personality. Besides, there is no deterioration in intellectual functioning and the patient does not cut himself away from reality. He pretends to be rational and normal in a particular area.

Paranoid disorders are sub-divided into two groups (i) paranoia and (ii) paranoid state.

Paranoia, sometimes called true paranoia, is rare. This disorder develops gradually and has been found to be characterized as below:

*Nature of Delusions*

(i) The patient shows highly systematized and stable delusions of persecution and of grandeur.

(ii) The delusion system in paranoia is skilfully and logically operated by the patient. In fact the paranoiac has a high intelligence to give logical and convincing reasons for his behaviour.

*Personality Organisation*

(i) There is little or no general personality disorganisation present in the paranoiacs,

(ii) The patient is sensible and coherent in his thinking and behaviour and features like hallucinations and gross disturbances in memory and conduct are lacking.

Thus the paranoid individual is very well integrated. In fact he is better integrated than normal individuals, He is cool, calculating and a well-controlled individual. He knows his enemies and plans aggression with great care and cunning. It is in this sense that he *is* to be taken as dangerous. His emotional reactions are in accordance with expressed ideas. The majority of them are self-supporting and capable. They often go unidentified in general population and usually try to maintain their 'crazy' behaviour despite hospitalization and treatment. It is in this sense that paranoia is considered a continuous and incurable disorder.

*Paranoid state*: In comparison with paranoia, a person passing through paranoid state remains in it for a brief period, and then recovers. It is in this sense less dangerous than true paranoia. The paranoid state lies between paranoia and the paranoid schizophrenia with respect to abnormalities in behaviour and resistance to deterioration. A paranoid state is neither very logical nor complex as true paranoid behaviour nor does it compete with paranoid schizophrenia. Delusions are less bizarre and changeable than those observed in schizophrenia, and less reasonable and logically elaborate than those found in paranoia. Although thinking here is somewhat disconnected and hallucinations are common, yet the patient does not show any sign of impairment in intellectual and emotional spheres with the passing of years.

*Causation and treatment:* Hereditary and constitutional factors definitely contribute towards the causation of a predisposition for the development of paranoid disorders in individuals. However, the most important causes of this disorder are found within one's environment. The paranoid reactions, to a large extent, are the learned pattern of one's behaviour for which there are certain socio-psychological causes. First, the process of paranoid reactions may be initiated by the resulting frustration as a consequence of failures accompanying excessive ambition. It creates resentment and feelings of hostility. The individual learns to adjust in this situation by denying his own hostility and utilizing the mechanism of projection.

Secondly, it may happen that at a deeper level, there are strong but unconscious feelings of inferiority. The paranoids predisposed to ego-centric nature are compelled to make up for their inferiority by superiority or tend to rationalize it by persecutory delusions.

Thirdly, for counting the deep rooted feelings of resentment the paranoid may learn aggressive behaviour. With high intelligence and being a well controlled individual he may plan aggression against his known enemies (according to his belief) with great skill. His behaviour then results in dangerous consequences. Sometimes he may resort to sex offences and develop character disorders.

Fourthly, the paranoids, long before the development of this disorder, are very selfish, unsocial human beings. They always consider themselves right and all who disagree become personal enemies for them. Their jealous, suspicious and morbid sensitive nature leads to their social isolation. They fail in gaining status and recognition which creates a serious threat to their self-esteem. Consequently, they are forced to resort to projection as a defence mechanism and adopt delusion reactions for satisfying their inner needs. As there is no deterioration of the intellectual powers and the person exercises remarkable self-control, the delusions of grandeur or persecution are highly systematized. The individual, on the basis of his critical judgement, tries to provide some superficially factual basis or reasoning for his otherwise unjustified responses and behaviour.

Whatever be the form of learning of paranoid behaviour, it involves a gradual and systematic development. For example, the development of delusion of persecution according to Page (1976) may follow the sequence: "He flees, he defends himself and finally he attacks." If a person is relentlessly persecuted by his enemies who follow him everywhere and despite his best efforts, he is unable to run away or hide from them, and then he is compelled to defend himself against them. He may appeal to the police and state authorities, write letters to newspaper editors, and purchase weapons to defend him. At last, in desperation, he turns and attacks his persecutors or attempts to take his own life.

Thus, predisposed as paranoid personality by the genetic or constitutional factors, an individual may gradually learn to behave as paranoid under the influence or stress of socio-psychological factors.

*Treatment and prognosis*: The paranoid disorders involve highly systematized and very stable delusion of persecution and grandeur. Once these delusions are developed, they remain fixed. It is then futile to alter them. The prospects of producing a remission by any form of therapy are therefore much less in the case of paranoid disorders. These illnesses are relatively incurable and non-progressive. On account of fixed beliefs and delusions, the patient is unable to trust the therapist. He regards himself superior to the therapist and refuses to cooperate. That is why psychotherapy becomes tedious with paranoids. Physical measures like drug therapy or ECT also do not show much results except for patients with whom the treatment is undertaken before the fixation of delusion system. However, hospitalization of the paranoids is essential. Although it works as a punitive measure than a therapeutic one, it brings favourable results by exerting a restraining influence.

## Summary

- *Psychotic disorders* represent the "serious disorders" of the mind in which the patient shows periodic or prolonged loss of contact with the world of reality, manifests symptoms of a severe nature in the form of delusions, hallucinations, stupor, incoherence or violent reactions, and requires compulsory hospitalization. They may be broadly classified as organic and functional.
- *The organic psychoses* are associated with, and are most likely due to, some demonstrable organic pathology. In these disorders, there happens to be a considerable damage to the brain tissue. These disorders of the brain may be classified as acute, intermediate or chronic depending upon the tissue loss and impairment of the function of the brain. Symptoms, in general, involve the impairment of the mental processes, affective responses and general behaviour.
- *Causative factors and treatment*
  1. Organic mental disorders may be caused due to infection of the nervous system and brain resulting from bacteria or viruses which invade the brain and damage the nerve tissue. Examples are neurosyphilis, encephalitis and meningitis. Treatment should be made with the adoption of positive preventive measures against infection followed by the early detection and treatment. For such diseases penicillin therapy is effective.
  2. Brain tumours may cause behavioural disorders. The treatment is primarily surgical.
  3. Head injury may cause mental disorders. The treatment consists of medical as well as psychotherapeutic measures.
  4. Mental disorders in the form of epilepsy are generally caused by the multiplicity of factors like genetic, biological and psychological. The treatment lies in a combination of medical and psychological therapy.
  5. Organic mental disorders may be caused by the ingestion of a variety of toxic substances such as alcohol, drugs, gases and heavy metals.
  6. The over-secretion or under-secretion of the endocrine glands may cause various mental disorders.
  7. The disorders classified as presenile disorders, senile disorders and cerebral arteriosclerosis are associated with advancing age or degeneration and deterioration of the brain tissue. The notable presenile disorders are Alzheimer's disease, Pick's disease, Parkinson's disease and Huntington's chorea.
- *Functional psychoses-* The term functional psychoses includes mental disorders which exhibit a change only in the function of the brain and not in the brain structures like organic psychoses. They are broadly classified as schizophrenia, affective disorders and paranoid disorders.
- Schizophrenia literally means splitting of the mind involving fundamental disturbances in reality relationships and in emotional and intellectual processes. For diagnosis as well as treatment, these disorders are usually classified as simple,

hebephrenic, catatonic and paranoid schizophrenia depending upon the severity of the symptoms and incurability of the disease. The likelihood of an individual becoming a schizophrenic depends upon the magnitude or degree of genetic predisposition (heredity) and stress (environment). The treatment involves the physical as well as psychological methods.

- Affective disorders of psychotic origin are characterized by the severe disorders of mood or affect exhibiting extreme changes in emotional state and thought contents. These disorders may be subdivided as manic disorder, depressive disorder and manic-depressive disorder. The genetic biochemical conditions and psychological factors have been found to be associated with the development of affective disorders. The treatment involves the physical as well as psychological methods.
- Paranoid disorders involve highly systematized and stable delusions of persecution and grandeur. There is no splitting of the mind as in the case of paranoid schizophrenia. They may be subdivided as paranoia and paranoid state depending upon the severity of the disorder. While the genetic or constitutional factors work as predisposing, the influence or stress of socio-psychological factors may force an individual to behave as paranoid.
- The prospects of producing a remission by any form of therapy are much less in the cases of paranoid disorders. The illnesses are relatively incurable and non-progressive. However, hospitalization, working as a punitive measure brings some favourable results.

## REFERENCES


Coleman, James C. (1970), *Abnormal Psychology and Modern Life*, Bombay: D.B. Taraporewala & Sons.

Davison, Gerald C. & Neale, John M. (1978), *Abnormal Psychology,* (second edition), New York: John Wiley & Sons

Kisker, George W. (1964), ***The Disorganised Personality,*** (3rd International Students edition), New York: McGraw-Hill.

Mahoney, Michael J. (1980), ***Abnormal Psychology,*** San Francisco: Harper & Row.

Page, James D. (1976), ***Abnormal Psychology,*** New Delhi: Tata McGraw-Hill.

Price, John Harding., (1972), *Psychiatric Investigations* , London: Butterworths.

Thorpe, Louis P. & Katz, Barney (1948), *The Psychology of Abnormal Behaviour,* New York: The Ronald Press Company.

# 14

# MENTAL DEFICIENCY

We have seen that all the important systems of classification discussed in the chapter 10 of this text take mental deficiency or retardation to be essentially an abnormal behaviour. A more functional view presented through table 10. 09 of the same chapter, shows that mental deficiency or retardation is a psychological disorder. Although it is not associated with any specific illness yet it certainly affects the development and functioning of the mind and behaviour of the affected person. It is in fact an arrested or incomplete development of the brain beginning usually at birth and leading to a diminution of intellectual powers relative to the chronological age. The frequently used terms 'mental retardation', 'feeble mindedness', 'subnormal child' and 'mental sub- normality' carry the same meaning as 'mental deficiency". The other less commonly used terms are 'amentia', and 'oligophrenia'. We will therefore use these terms interchangeably in this text. Some of the definitions explaining the meaning of these terms are reproduced below.

*Page*: Mental deficiency is a condition of subnormal mental development, present at birth or early childhood and characterized mainly by limited intelligence and social inadequacy. *(1976:354)*

*Rosen, Fox and Gregory*: Mental retardation refers to a chronic condition present from birth or early childhood which is characterized by both impaired intellectual functioning as measured by standardized tests and impaired adaptation to the daily demands of the individual's social environment. *(1972:356)*

*American Association on Mental Retardation* : Mental retardation refers to significantly sub-average intellectual functioning existing concurrently with deficits in adaptive behaviour and manifested during the developmental period (Grossman, 1983, p.11).

*British Mental Deficiency Act (1929)*: Mental retardation is a condition of arrested or incomplete development of mind existing before the age of 18 years whether arising from inherent causes or induced by disease on injury. (Cited by Shanmugam, 1981:197-98)

All these definitions reveal that:

(i) Mental retardation is a condition or state of mind.
(ii) It is not a disease or illness of the mind.
(iii) It is related to the subnormal development of the mind or brain.
(iv) It is also related to one's inadequate adjustment or adaptation with the environment.

(v) The deficiency may be observed at birth or in early childhood.
(vi) Both the inherent and external factors may cause mental retardation.

In this way, mental deficiency, retardation or sub-normality may be considered a retarded, subnormal or deficient growth and development of one's mind or brain exhibiting his subnormal intellectual capacities or inadequate adaptation to the environment on account of some inherent or external factors.

## Classification

### Intelligence Test as a means of Classification

The concept of IQ and scores on intelligence tests was found useful in labelling the individual as gifted, average (normal) or subnormal (retarded). Terman, using Standford Binet Scale, tried to label the individual with IQ between 90 and 100 as normal or average and persons with IQ below 90 as below average or subnormal. The subnormal were further categorized as under:

(i) IQ from 76 to 90 (border line and the dull)
(ii) 51 to 75 (morons)
(iii) 25 to 50 (imbeciles), and
(iv) Below 25 (idiots).

As a consequence of later developments the category involving borderline and dull was dropped as the individual belonging to this category had equal chances of drifting towards subnormal and normal categories.

It may be seen that the categorization of sub-normal or retarded as morons, imbeciles and idiots is arbitrary and there are differences of opinion regarding the range of IQ and its corresponding category since different intelligence tests result in varying range in terms of their numerical scores. For doing away with this difficulty a consensus was reached, at least for segregating the normal from the subnormal or the retarded that for declaring one as sub-normal it is better to have measurement of one's IQ in relation to the mean standard deviation of the tests used.

However, the later researches in the field of sub-normality raised doubts about the creditability of IQ scores. It was felt that a certain level of IQ score *does* not by itself designate an individual a mental retardate. He must also be capable to adapt to the natural and social demands of the environment. Consequently, the importance of assessment of adaptive behaviour in the identification and demarcation of the level was soon realized.

### Adaptive Behaviour as a means of Classification

This criterion describes one's adaptive behaviour expected of his age and cultural group, in two ways for the required assessment, namely (i) the degree to which the individual is able to function and maintain himself independently, and (ii) the degree to which he meets satisfactorily the culturally imposed demands of personal and social responsibility.

Attempts have been made to devise measures for the assessment of deficiency in adaptive behaviour through Vineland Social Maturity Scale, Adaptive Behaviour Scale (AAMD), and Max- held Buck *Holz* Social Maturity Scale.

The consideration of deficiency in adaptive behaviour along with the very low scores on an intelligence test resulted in the development of an altogether new classification of sub-normality, the terms moron, imbecile, or idiot are now completely avoided for determining the level of retardation. The new terminology in-terms of obtained IQ on different tests scale is represented below.

**Table 14.1: Level of Retardation**

| *Level of retardation* | *Intelligence* | *Quotient* |
|---|---|---|
| | *Standford Binet* | *Wechsler scales* |
| Profound | Under 20 | Under 25 |
| Severe | 20–35 | 25–39 |
| Moderate | 36–51 | 40–54 |
| Mild | 52–67 | 55-69 |

In view of their typical subnormal intelligence and deficient adaptive behaviour these categories are described below.

*Mild retardation:* A majority of approximately eight-five per Cent of the retarded belong to this category. In adult life, these individuals attain intellectual levels comparable to that of the average ten year old child. Their social adjustment may be compared with that of the adolescent. Here too they lack the innovative and vigorous nature of normal adolescents. They show signs of delayed development early in life, and learn to walk, talk, feed and toilet themselves a year later than the average. They may be identified in schools as slow learners and are frequently required to repeat early grades. Speech disturbances are common among them.

In comparison with normal individuals, the mildly retarded exhibit immature behaviour, have poor control over their impulses, lack judgement, and fail to anticipate the consequence of their actions. Their sexual behaviour and adjustment, in spite of the normal sexual development and fertility, is unpredictable and leads to a variety of problems and difficulties.

The mildly retarded individuals generally do not show any organic pathology and require little supervision. They are considered to be educable. With early diagnosis, parental assistance, and aid of special classes, they can be expected to reach a reasonable degree of educational achievement and to make an adequate social and economic adjustment in the community.

*Moderate mental retardation*: Approximately ten per cent of the totally mentally retarded belong to this category. In adult life these individuals attain intellectual level similar to that of the average six year old child. Physically they appear clumsy, suffer from motor in-coordination and present an affable, dull and somewhat vacuous personality. As a result of their inadequate development and deficient capacities and abilities they are regarded as 'trainable' instead of being 'educable' like the mildly retarded. From early infancy or childhood they show signs of retardation in almost all areas of development, and though they manage to speak, their, rate of learning is too slow. They are unable to do any work that requires initiative, originality, abstract thinking, memory or consistent attention, and cannot be expected to acquire the basic skills of reading and writing.

However, with early diagnosis, parental help and adequate training and support, most of the moderately retarded can achieve considerable independence in all spheres of life. Nevertheless, they require constant supervision and support and need institutionalization depending on their general level of adaptive behaviour.

*Severe mental retardation:* Nearly 3.5 per cent of the total retarded individuals-- mostly children and adolescents—belong to this category. They never attain an intellectual level greater than that of the average four year old child. The mortality rate due to high susceptibility to disease is quite high among these individuals. They are grossly retarded in development from birth or infancy on- word and show severe motor and speech retardation. Sensory defects and motor handicaps are common. The majority of them display relatively little interest in their surroundings and many of them never master even the necessary skills and functions like feeding and dressing themselves, or bladder and bowel control.

The severe mental retardates are neither 'educable' nor 'trainable' and the majority of them remain dependent on others throughout their lives. They need care and supervision of others with a great need for institutionalization. They may profit with proper care, timely treatment and specialized training and managing their own physical well-being and doing manual labour.

*Profound mental retardation*: This group makes 1.5 per cent of the total mentally retarded population. If is characterized by the most severe symptoms of mental retardation. The individuals belonging to this category never attain in adult life an intellectual level greater than that of the average two year old child. They are severely deficient both in their intellectual capacities and adaptive behaviour. The symptoms associated with them arc retarded growth, physical deformities, pathology of the central nervous system, mutism, severe speech disturbances, motor in-coordination, deafness and convulsive seizures. They are unable to protect themselves against common dangers and are unable to manage their own affairs and satisfy their physical needs. Their life span, as a result of their low resistance, is too short. Such individuals are completely dependent on others and need the care and supervision given to an infant. Essentially, they need to be institutionalized as their condition deteriorates on account of the biased attitude of the parents and stress demands of their environment.

## Common Clinical Types of Mental Retardation

The knowledge of well-known categories of mental deficiency or retardation based on a number of clinical symptoms and syndromes is useful in the identification, treatment and care of the retardates.

*Mongolism:* The mental deficient whose facial characteristics bear a superficial resemblance to members of the mongolian race are classified as mongols. The retardation in them ranges from moderate to severe (IQ approximately 20-50).

The Mongoloids tend to be short in stature with small round heads, abnormally short neck, thumbs and fingers, with slanting almond shaped eyes, and short flat noses. They usually have a small mouth, fissured and dry lips and tongue. Their hands and feet are broad and clumsy, and they have a deep voice. Motor coordination is awkward. They are handicapped in any learning or training but most of them can learn self help skills, acceptable social behaviour and routine manual skills.

The causes of mongolism are faulty heredity (possible chromosomal anomalies, and metabolic factors (glandular imbalance often involving pituitary glands). But once it occurs, it is irreversible. There is no effective treatment or workable preventive measures.

*Cretinism:* This mental deficiency ranging from moderate to severe retardation results from thyroid deficiency. The severity of the disorder depends on the age at which the deficiency occurs as well as the degree and duration of the deficiency.

The physical symptoms in the case of persons suffering from cretinism consist of a dwarf-like, thick-set body, coarse and thick skin, short and stubby extremities, abundant hair of wiry consistency and thick eyelids that give a sleepy appearance. Other pronounced symptoms include a broad, flat nose, large and flabby ears, a protruding abdomen and failure to mature sexually. Early timely treatment in the form of injection of thyroid gland extract produce favourable results in all cases except those of long standing where the damage to the nervous system and to general physical development is beyond repair.

*Microcephaly:* It refers to mental deficiency associated with failure of cranium to attain normal size on account of the impaired development of the brain. The microcephalic has an unusually small head which rarely exceeds a circumference of seventeen inches, as compared with the normal of approximately twenty-two inches. In addition, he is short statured with the usual cone-shaped skull and receding chin and forehead. Depending upon the degree of severity of mental retardation, micro-cephalic fall into the profound, severe and moderate categories of mental retardation. Both genetic as well as non-genetic factors impair development of the brain and thus cause microcephaly. There is no proper medical treatment available for microcephaly if there has been impaired brain development.

*Hydrocephaly:* This mental deficiency results from the accumulation of an unusually large amount of cerebrospinal fluid within the cranium, causing damage to the brain and enlargement of the skull. The degree of mental retardation in this disorder varies from moderate to profound depending upon the extent of neural damage which, in turn, depends upon the age of onset, the duration and the size of the skull. The chief symptom in hydrocephaly consists of the gradual increase in the size of the skull. The causes seem to be genetic as well as non-genetic. In some cases the disorder is present at birth or the head begins to enlarge soon after birth op account of prenatal disturbances. More often, the disorder develops during infancy or early childhood on account of intracranial neoplasm or acute inflammatory brain disease. An early diagnosis and proper surgical treatment shows favourable results in checking further damage of the brain tissue. However, the advanced acute stage does not respond to any treatment and eventually results in death.

*Phenylketonuria (PKU)*: This disorder has a genetic base and is assumed to be transmitted through a recessive gene carrying metabolic disturbance. As a result the child at birth lacks an enzyme needed to breakdown phenylalanine, an amino acid found in protein foods. Consequently, there is an abnormal accumulation of phenylalanine in the blood causing damage to the brain tissue.

The symptoms such as vomiting, a peculiar musty odour, infantile eczema and seizures, motor in-coordination, signs of mental retardation and neurological manifestations relating to severe brain damage are found to be common with this disorder. However, the diagnosis of the disorder is primarily made on the basis of the presence of phenyl pyruvic acid in the urine. The treatment of PKU depends on early detection. Special diet, low in phenylalanine, is recommended to the affected infants. Timely treatment helps in restraining or preventing brain damage.

*Amaurotic idiocy*; It is a rare hereditary disorder of fat metabolism transmitted as a simple recessive characteristic. It is never transmitted directly from patient to offspring, because death generally occurs before puberty. The only mode of transmission is through the mating of persons who, although free of overt symptoms, are carriers of the defective genes. This disorder has been described to occur in two different forms-infantile and juvenile– depending on the ages at which it occurs. The major symptoms of this disorder include muscular weakness, inability to maintain normal posture, loss in the ability to grasp objects, visual difficulties leading to progressive blindness, seizures and neurologic manifestations.

Infantile amaurotic idiocy, also known as Tay-Sachs disease is common among infants. The disorder appears at about six months of age and death occurs between the ages of two and three years. Juvenile amaurotic idiocy occurs at five or six years of age and the patient may live up to thirteen years.

## Causes of Mental Retardation

It is difficult to postulate standard causes for mental retardation applicable to every such case. A number of factors are believed to cause mental retardation which may be divided into two broad categories–

A. Organic or biological factors

B. Socio-psychological factors.

### A. Organic or biological factors

Causes listed in this broad category are described below.

1. *Genetic factors:* Mental deficiency may be established by genetic factors operative at the time of conception in two ways– either through transmission of some defective genes in the chromosomes of one or both parents, or on account of chromosomal aberrations.

   The transmission of defective genes gives rise to many disorders causing mental deficiency. Mental retardation or deficiency attributable to a dominant gene is very rare because the persons affected are generally incapable of reproduction. It is often the result of the pairing of two defective recessive genes. When defective recessive genes are paired, as in PKU, the production of an enzyme, necessary for an important metabolic process, is usually disturbed. This in turn, affects the development of the embryo and causes menial deficiency. In some cases, like Tay-Sachs disease, mental deficiency may also be transmitted by the pairing of single recessive genes.

Several chromosomal anomalies determine mental retardation at the time of conception. Down's syndrome or mongolism is one such disorder which is said to be caused by chromosomal aberrations. The majority of the mongoloid children are found to have 47 chromosomes instead of the usual 46. The number of chromosomes increases as a result of tripling of chromosomes 21 (during the fertilization of the egg the chromosomes of pair 21 become three instead of two). Another example of chromosomal abnormality is Klinefelter's syndrome in which an extra X chromosome is usually at fault. This disorder occurs only in males and symptoms are usually noticed at puberty when the testes remain small and the boy develops feminine secondary sex characteristics such as enlarged breasts and round hips.

2. *Infection:* Mental retardation can also be the result of many infectious diseases like syphilis, rubella (German measles) toxoplasmosis, or encephalitis which can damage brain tissue and the nervous system resulting in severe mental deficiency or retardation. If the mother suffers from one or the other of these infectious diseases, she may transmit infection to the developing fetus. A child at birth or afterwards may be infected with diseases which cause life-long mental subnormality. Encephalitis and meningococcal meningitis cause irreversible brain damage and even death if contracted in infancy or early childhood. Besides directly damaging brain tissues, such infectious diseases may indirectly lead to mental abnormality by causing congenital physical defects such as blindness, deafness, paralysis and epilepsy.
3. *Intoxication:* Mental retardation may be caused by intoxication. A number of toxic agents like carbon monoxide, mercury, lead and various immunological agents like anti-tetanus serum or the use of small pox, rabies and typhoid vaccine may result in brain damage during development after birth. Similarly, large doses of X-ray in radio therapy in the abdominal region of the pregnant mother, drugs administered to the mother during pregnancy, incompatibility in blood types between mother and fetus, an overdose of drugs administered to the infant also lead to toxicity and brain damage.
4. *Trauma:* Mental retardation may be caused on account of physical damage to the brain in the form of injuries prior to birth, at the time of delivery, or following birth in the manner as below.

- Prenatal injuries adversely affect the brain and the nervous system of the fetus. One of the main causes of such damage is asphyxia which results from oxygen deprivation and consequently causes suffocation of the tissues. It is accounted for by the compression of the umbilical cord which supplies the fetus with blood carrying oxygen and nutrition from the mother. Another example of prenatal injury is the damaging effects of irradiation on the uterus of the pregnant mother.
- Abnormal delivery and birth injuries make for another cause of mental retardation.

Difficulties during labour result in damage to the infant's brain. Any abnormal delivery also involves the risk of brain injuries. An abnormal position of the fetus, breech extraction, the use of forceps and other obstetrical procedures cause haemorrhage of the brain and thus lead to mental retardation.

- Premature birth exposes the child to an increased risk of brain damage from mechanical trauma and anoxia (condition associated with the changes in oxygen supply). Similarly, post-mature birth also results in an increased risk of anoxia for the child, during the later weeks of pregnancy and child birth.
- Another birth trauma in the form of anoxia resulting from delayed breathing of the newborn infant or as a result of anaesthetic accidents may also damage the brain. Anoxia may also occur after birth as a result of cardiac arrest associated with operations, heart attacks, gas poisoning or near drowning.
- Accidental brain injuries received in infancy, childhood or later in life, causing damage to the brain also lead to serious mental retardation.

5. *Metabolic and endocrine disorders: Mental retardation* may be caused by various disturbances in metabolism by which body cells are built up and broken down, and by which energy is made available for their functioning. The chemical errors involving metabolism of fat cause Tay-Sachs disease while disturbed protein metabolism causes PKU. Both these disorders lead to severe mental retardation. Similarly, metabolic disorders like galactosemia involving an inability to metabolize galactose and maple syrup urine disease, involving chain amino acids lead to mental retardation. Several metabolic disorders involving endocrine imbalances may also result in various degrees of mental retardation. Hypothyroidism (usually referred to as cretinism) is one of such metabolic disorder.
6. *Tumours:* Mental retardation may be caused by brain damage associated with brain tumours and other new growths. Tuberous sclerosis or epiloia is characterized by numcous nodules and tumours throughout the brain and other parts of the body. A butterfly shaped rash initially appearing on the face, spreads over a wider area. It may finally lead to convulsions and mental retardation. Similarly, macrocephaly (large headedness), microcephaly (small headedness) and hydrocephalus (accumulation of an abnormal amount of cerebrospinal *Audi* in the cranium) are some of the other conditions resulting in mental sub-normality that may be caused by tumours.

## B. Socio-Psychological Factors

Psychological factors coupled with adverse sociocultural environment play a leading role in the causation as well as perpetuation of mental retardation. Children who are denied the satisfaction of their psychological and social needs become over sensitive to psychological stress in the same way as the patient with vitamin deficiency is susceptible to infection. The early childhood deprivation like lack of adequate mothering and parental care results in a retarded rate of development.

In an inadequate sociocultural environment the children are deprived of the basic necessities of life for their proper physical, intellectual, emotional and social development. A poverty ridden, deprived, crowded and uncongenial family environment provides sufficient as well as necessary grounds for the germination and perpetuation of mental sub-normality. The deprived members tend to marry spouses like themselves and their poverty compels them to suffer. The severe environmental deprivation in the form of physical, cultural, emotional and intellectual poverty especially during infancy and childhood results in the retardation of the child's intellectual development even when his potential at birth is normal. The child may have difficulty in developing verbal ability on account of such unfavourable environment or may suffer from lack of emotional and social maturity and thus may not be able to adapt to the needs of his environment.

In some cases, the failure of the school system has adverse affects. School maladjustment tends to retard the development rate of the Child who, once labelled as a slow learner or retarded on the basis of speech, IQ scores, achievement test scores and observable behaviour, becomes subnormal on account of the perpetuation of inferiority feelings and complexes.

## Detection or Identification of Mental Retardation

Mental retardation is concerned with the retarded or arrested growth and development of one's intellectual functioning or with the inability to adapt one's behaviour to the environmental needs. The causes may range from a genetic basis to biochemical, neurological, accidental, infectious and socio-psychological determinants. Whatever the degree of severity of the retardation, its prevention and treatment involves detection and identification at an early stage.

1. *Detection before birth:* By means of certain tests in which a small amount the fluid surrounding the developing foetus is examined, it is possible to screen metabolic diseases or the incurable chromosomal abnormalities affecting the developing foetus.
2. *Detection at the time of birth:* Most of the metabolic diseases and developmental defects causing mental retardation may be detected soon after birth. For example, Phenylketonuria (PKV) may be easily diagnosed through the detection of phenyl pyruvic acid in a new born infant with the help of the urine test or a relatively simple blood test. Similarly, congenital cerebral defects causing biological disorders for the mental retardation like macrocephaly, microcephaly, and hydrocephaly may be detected soon after birth.
3. *Collecting history of the causation or development of mental retardation:* Useful information about the history of the causation and development of mental retardation can help in the identification of disabilities among the retarded. This may be in the form of genetic information, the prenatal history of the child and the mother's condition and experiences during pregnancy, history of labour and delivery, blood group incompatibility, exposure to infections and chronic diseases, happenings in the form of accidents, seizures and impairment in motor and intellectual development, emotional episodes and psychological stresses.
4. *Assessment of intellectual functioning:* Intelligence test scores in terms of IQ are used not only for identifying or segregating individuals with subnormal intellectual

capacities but also for classifying the severity of their mental retardation into various categories (like moron, imbecile and idiot) or degrees (like moderate, severe and profound). However, the diagnosis of subnormal intellectual capacity cannot be made merely on the basis of a relatively low IQ. The following characteristics should also be kept in mind.

(i) Mentally subnormal children lack much in the power of observation, imagination, thinking and reasoning, and ability to generalize.

(ii) They are poor at abstraction and can only think in terms of concrete objects and situations.

(iii) They are slow learners. It has been found that they take longer to learn a skill.

(iv) They are poor at following general verbal instructions, unless these are repeated at frequent intervals.

(v) Their rate of intellectual development is too slow in comparison with children of their own age.

(vi) The areas of their interest, aptitudes and choices are limited.

(vii) The creativity aspect is almost absent in such children.

5. *Assessment in terms of adaptive behaviour:* In addition to the criterion of subnormal intellectual capacities, an assessment of one's deficiency in terms of adaptive behaviour and personality problems may also prove helpful in the diagnosis of mental retardation. The mental retardates are socially as well as emotionally maladjusted personalities. They do not realize their rights and obligations towards others and often have deficient moral judgement and suffer from character disorders.

Most of these retardates are dependent and experience difficulty in managing their affairs. In some severe cases the extent of personal independence is so limited that they are incapable of protecting themselves against common physical dangers. Personality problems and deficiency in terms of adaptive behaviour may be accessed through a keen observation, or with the help of tests like Adaptive Behaviour Scale and Minnesota Developmental Programming System.

## Prevention of Mental Retardation

Prevention is said to be better than cure. Attempt should therefore be made to adopt preventive measures for exercising control over the occurrence and development of mental retardation. Some preventive measures are listed below.

1. *Genetic counselling and voluntary birth control.* Genetic factors play a significant role in the causation of mental retardation. Chromosomal aberrations as well as pairing of defective recessive genes prove detrimental for normal brain development and functioning. This knowledge may be helpful for the wise parents. There are tests to identify parents who have chromosomal anomalies or defective and inferior genetic material. For example, fluorescent blood test may help in determining whether one or the other prospective parent is genetically normal or is a carrier of the recessive gene causing Tay-Sachs disease. Similarly, there are tests that reveal whether the developing foetus will be the victim of

some specific mental retardation or not. They should be informed about the problems to be faced in raising a mentally retarded child. Such parents may be counselled about the risk they run in begetting children.

2. *Proper care of the mother and child:* Adequate care of the mother and the new born infant is essential for the prevention of mental retardation. In general, there should be a provision of adequate diet for all expectant and nursing mothers. All routine health measures should be adapted for the mothers and the infants. Proper care should be taken for the prevention of possible physical damage in the form of injuries prior to birth, at the time of birth or immediately
3. *Providing normal and stimulating environment after birth:* Uncongenial and unfavourable conditions present in one's sociocultural environment and psychological deprivations especially in early childhood may cause or perpetuate mental retardation. For the prevention of such consequences, there is a great need for educating the parents and other responsible members of the society. As far as possible, the children should get normal as well as stimulating environment for the proper growth and development of their innate capacities. Illiteracy and poverty of the parents, and poor defective family environment should not come in the way of the satisfaction of their basic needs. They should not be allowed to develop inferiority feelings, complexes, and frustrations on account of their limitations.
4. *Provision of public education:* An attempt should be made for arousing the public into adopting preventive measures for controlling mental retardation. For example, by giving the right information about the correlation of mother's age and mongolism, public opinion may be built in favour of avoiding children after forty. Similarly, retardation caused by toxic agents may be prevented by providing information and education to the public so that they may be saved from their evil effects. In the field of environmental modifications, and pollution control, programmes of public education may bring effective results which, in turn, may prevent and control mental retardation. Public education can also help in educating the masses about the need and importance of nutritious and balanced diet, controlling infectious diseases and taking measures for the welfare of the mother and infants. The hazards of accidents may also be controlled by making the public aware about the possible safety measures.

## Remedial Measures for Mental Retardation

Whatever preventive measures we may adopt, it is neither possible nor feasible to eliminate completely the possibility of the occurrence of mental retardation. Neither can we exercise much control over hereditary influences nor can we avoid accidental hazards, and traumas. Moreover, we also feel handicapped in controlling the evil influences of defective sociocultural environment and are unable to overcome the deficiency of psychological deprivations. Therefore cases of mental retardation are bound to exist and hence we have to think and plan the treatment and remedial measures for the mental retardates.

One thing which should be made clear while seeking treatment of mental retardation is the fact that there is no cure for mental deficiency. Mental retardates are essentially incurable in the sense that they cannot be given more intelligence and made normal. No amount of training or medical care can transform a mental retardate into a normal individual. Mentally sub-normal should never be confused with the persons who are mentally ill or suffer from a mental disease. In this connection, the observation of Wechsler (1979) is worth quoting:

*"Mental deficiency unlike typhoid fever or paralysis is not a disease. A mentally deficient is not a person who suffers from a specific disease process but one who by reasons of intellectual arrest or impairment is unable to cope with his environment to the extent that he needs special care, education and institutionalization."*

It will be appropriate to consider the treatment or remedial measures for the adjustment, rehabilitation and education of the mentally retarded, in the light of the above observations.

1. *Medical or physical measures:* Mental retardation, to some extent, is said to be a medical problem. The following medical measures may prove helpful in some cases:
   (i) *Cretinism:* This mental retardation resulting from deficiency in thyroid secretion, if recognised at birth or in its early manifestations, may be corrected or controlled by the institution of thyroid therapy.
   (ii) *Congenital syphilis:* Children infected with congenital syphilis are usually found to be suffering from severe mental sub-normality. An early detection and prompt penicillin therapy is found to be helpful in the preventing as well as control of many effects of congenital syphilis.
   (iii) *Phenylketonuria (PKU):* On early detection with the help of a simple urine test, PKU, a metabolic disorder causing mental retardation may be checked or controlled, to a great extent, by placing the infant on a special diet relatively free of phenylalanine found in most protein foods.
   (iv) *Hydrocephalus*: Hydrocephalus, resulting from the accumulation of an abnormal amount of cerebrospinal fluid within the cranium results in mental retardation. Surgical treatment is found to be very effective in the treatment of this disorder. It is aimed at the reduction of the normal production of cerebrospinal fluid or to the channelling of the fluid by removing blockade or obstruction resulting from congenital malformations or post-natal infections.
   (v) *Epileptic seizures*: In the case of patients subject to epileptic seizures, the administration of anti-convulsant medication may prove helpful in controlling and minimizing intellectual deterioration.
   (vi) *Controlling disturbed behaviour*: The administration of tranquillizers proves useful in controlling hyperactive and disturbed behaviour among mental retardates.
2. *Psychological treatment* ; Often on account of the link between mental sub-normality and psychological factors, psychological treatment in the form of individual or group psychotherapy is found to be useful in providing remedial measures for mental retardation. Children can be helped in solving problems of their emotional and social maladjustment and resolving their mental conflicts through psychological measures.

3. *Educating the parents*: Parents can also help in the welfare, care as well as treatment of the mental retardate. For this purpose, there is a need for proper counselling services for them. Moreover, on account of their emotional involvement the patents do not realize the shortcomings and deficiency of their children and waste a lot of time and money in the hope that some magic cure will he found or the deficiency will be automatically eliminated with the lapse of time. Sometimes, they become disturbed by the responsibilities of looking after their mentally retarded child. Such disappointed, insecure and guilt-ridden parents begin to demand behaviour and intellectual achievement beyond the abilities of the child who is often abused, snubbed and punished for no fault of his. Some parents adopt an over protective approach in their effort to shield the child from challenging situations and thus make him completely dependent by interfering with the development of whatever abilities or capacities he may have. It is therefore essential that:
   - Parents should first realize the truth about their child. They should accept the child's limitations and the mental deficiency in the sense that the child cannot be given more intelligence and made normal.
   - Secondly, they should be educated to behave normally with their mentally subnormal child without being over protective or rejecting the child.
   - Thirdly the parents should be given training and education for handling the emotional and social adjustment problems of their children. They should never compare their achievements and abilities with their normal siblings or other children in the home and neighbourhood. It should be seen that he is not to be unnecessarily criticized or ridiculed by others.
   - Fourthly, they should be educated to provide essential training at home to their mentally retarded child. How to train him to manage his affairs independently, how to make the child to develop and seek maximum utilization of his subnormal capacities are some of the areas where useful education and training can be provided by the parents.
   - Finally, the parents should be made to realise that if needed there is no harm in sending their children to special schools meant for the mental retardates. It is the best place for their education and training.
4. *Provision of special education and training:* It is a cardinal educational as well as psychological error to educate or train the mental retardates with the normal. The involved attitude of the parents at home also interferes with the development of the retarded child. The remedy lies in the provision of special education or training for them. The institutes or boarding schools meant for subnormal children serve a useful purpose in this direction. For better results, the special institutes or schools must be managed keeping in view the following considerations
   (i) There should be proper grouping and classification of the mentally retarded children on the basis of the degree of the severity of their retardation.
   (ii) The 'educable' should be educated and the 'trainable' should he trained. Those who are neither easily educable nor trainable should be cared for and efforts should be made to train them for managing their essential day-to-day affairs.

(iii) The schools should provide essential environment for maximum development of the abilities and capacities of all mental retardates. Curriculum, methods of teaching, and tools for evaluation should be adjusted according to the individual needs.

(iv) There should be a provision for specially trained teachers able to utilize new materials and techniques for their education or training. They should be able to deal with the special problems of these children, understand them sympathetically, and help them to grow with their deficiencies.

(v) In these schools, greater emphasis should be placed on co-curricular experiences and the children should be provided opportunities for learning the ways of their emotional and social adjustment, imbibing moral virtues and desirable personal habits.

(vi) These institutions should have the provision for vocational education and training. The mental retardates should be trained for manual work, crafts and specialized vocations according to their abilities. The general attitude towards the mentally handicapped need to be changed. They are not to be sympathized, protected, and ridiculed but to be helped in growing and developing within their strengths and limitations. Their education or training should begin at home. Thereafter special schools or institutions may be involved for their education and training. The society and the state, then, should take responsibility for their rehabilitation and adjustment.

## Summary

- Mental deficiency, retardation or sub-normality may be understood as a retarded, subnormal or deficient growth and development of one's mind or brain exhibiting subnormal intellectual capacities or inadequate adaptation to the environment on account of inherent or external factors.
- The terms moron, imbecile, idiot for the classification of sub-normality have been replaced by new terms like mild, moderate, severe and profound retardation. The new classification is based on the consideration of deficiency in adaptive behaviour along with the considerable low scores on an intelligence test. Some well-known classified categories of mental retardation based on a number of distinguishable clinical symptoms and syndromes may be listed as mongolism, cretinism, microcephaly, phenylketonuria (PKU), and amaurotic idiocy.
- As about its causation, mental retardation may be the result of organic and socio-psychological causes. The organic causes include factors operative at the time of conception, infection, intoxication, trauma, metabolic and endocrine disorders and tumours. Besides this, psychological factors coupled with adverse sociocultural environment arc said to play a significant role in the causation as well as perpetuation of mental retardation.
- The detection and identification of mental deficiency requires efforts in the form of (i) the tests before birth, and at the time of birth, (ii) collection of the history of the causation or development of mental retardation, (iii) assessment of intellectual functioning, and (iv) assessment in terms of adaptive behaviour.

- Preventive measures taken for mental deficiency may be listed as (i) genetic counselling and voluntary birth control, (ii) proper care of the mother and the child, (iii) providing normal and stimulating environment after birth, and (iv) provision of public education.
- Treatment regarding mental deficiency involves (i) medical or physical measures, (ii) psychological treatment, (iii) providing education to the parents, and (iv) provision of special education and training to the sub-normal.

## REFERENCES

British Mental Deficiency Act (1929), Quoted in Shanmugam, T.E., *Abnormal Psychology,* New Delhi: Tata McGraw Hill, 1981

Grossman, H.G. (Ed.) (1983), *Classification in Mental Retardation,* Washington, DC: American Association on Mental Retardation.

Kisker, G.W., The Disorganized Personality (International Student Edition III), New York: Mc Graw Hill,

Page, James D. (1976), ***Abnormal Psychology,*** New Delhi: Tata McGraw-Hill.

Rosen, E., Fox and Gregory (1972), ***Abnormal Psychology,*** (2nd, International Student Edition), Philadelphia: Saunders

Wechsler, D. Quoted by Dutt, N.K. , ***Psychological Foundations of Education,*** Delhi: Doaba House, 1979.

# 15

# SOCIOPATHY

According to the American Psychiatric Association (1968), antisocial behaviour is "characterized by impulsive, irresponsible actions satisfying only immediate and narcissistic interests without concern for obvious and implicit social consequences". Such behaviour is not only harmful for the adequate personality development and well-being of the individuals but also affects their social adjustment and proves detrimental to the society. The following are the four types of antisocial behaviour.

- Sociopathy or psychopathy
- Criminal behaviour-delinquency and crime
- Alcoholism and drug addiction
- Sexual deviations and disorders.

Sociopathy is a new name for characterizing the antisocial behaviour of personalities instead of the term psychopathy. The new terminology stresses the fact that antisocial behaviour is a social rather than a psychological maladjustment. Actually, both the terms carry the same meaning and are therefore often used interchangeably.

According to DSM-II (1968:43), sociopaths or antisocial personalities may be defined as *"individuals who are basically un-socialized and whose behaviour pattern brings them repeatedly into conflict with society. They are incapable of significant loyalty to individuals, groups, or social values. They are grossly selfish, callous, irresponsible, impulsive, and unable to feel guilt or to learn from experience and punishment. Frustration tolerance is low. They tend to blame others or offer plausible rationalizations for their behaviour. A mere history of repeated legal or social offences is not sufficient to justify this diagnosis."*

In the subsequent editions of DSM brought out by American Psychiatric Association in the name of DSM III, DSM IV, DSM IV-TR and DSM V, the antisocial behaviour or sociopathy has been placed in the category of Anti social Personality Disorders. In its latest version DSM V brought out in the year 2013, it has been diagnosed and assigned to individuals who habitually and pervasively disregard or violate the rights and considerations of others without remorse. Accordingly, people with Antisocial Personality Disorder may be habitual criminals, or engage in behaviour which would be grounds for criminal arrest and prosecution, or they may engage in behaviours which skirt the edges of the law, or manipulate and hurt others in non-criminal ways which are widely regarded as unethical, immoral, irresponsible, or in violation of social norms and expectations.

## Characteristics of Sociopaths

Based on the research findings and writings of some well- known psychologists and sociologists like Cleckley (1959), Thorne (1959), Heaton ward (1963), Coleman (1964), and Rosen, Fox & Gregory (1965), the characteristics of sociopaths may be summarized as below:

1. *Superficial charm and intelligence:* A sociopath shows his charm. He talks well and gives the impression of being alert and clearheaded. His pleasant manners and a good sense of humour help him in exploiting others through superficial charm and tall tales.
2. *Lack of control:* A sociopath exhibits a complete lack of control through his emotionally unstable, ego-centric, impulsive and irresponsible behaviour. His interest lies in immediate pleasure and he has no absolute purpose or long range goals. He is unable to exercise his responsibility and is impatient of routine work and thereby changes his jobs or fields of interest frequently. He may drift into sexual deviations, crime, alcoholism or drug addiction not because of an urge to do such antisocial acts but because of his lack of control, false adventurism, absence of long range perspective and regard for consequences.
3. *Lack of anxiety, shame or guilt*: Sociopaths also exhibit complete absence or minimal outward evidence of anxiety, shame or guilt. They commit an antisocial act, but are not ashamed of it nor do they repent for the harm done to other people or the society by their antisocial behaviour. Instead of feeling guilty they try to justify their conduct. Sociopaths generally do not exhibit any symptom of unusual anxiety or guilt during or after their antisocial behaviour. This unique characteristic combined with innocent and sincere appearance enables sociopaths to escape suspicion and detection for their antisocial activities.
4. *Inability to profit from social rewards or punishments*: General behaviour responds favourably to social rewards and is often corrected through punishments. But in the case of sociopaths, social rewards or punitive means fail to produce desirable results. A sociopath never takes his behaviour seriously and does not respond emotionally after committing an act. The lack of effective reaction results in the sociopath's inability to learn from experience particularly to avoid punishment or get a reward.
5. *Inadequate and improper social adjustment:* In a socio-psychological sense, sociopaths are victims of social maladjustment. Their antisocial personality and selfish behaviour results in their inadequate social adjustment and defective social relationships. The self is always great for them and this makes them self centered. Outwardly they may show friendship and concern for others but true loyalty, sincerity and intimacy are alien to their nature. They are usually un-sympathetic, ungrateful, insensitive, incapable of love and remorseless in their dealings with others. They suffer from insincerity and incapacity for love and attachment.
6. *Hostility towards authority and discipline*: Sociopaths are unusually aggressive and hostile towards authority and social regulations. They come into conflict with authority right in their childhood. They feel hostile towards their parents, particularly the father. Later, their hostile attitude creates difficulties with school and college authorities, employers, police, military and other law enforcement

authorities. Their maladjustment leads to truancy, job instability, nomadism (pathological roaming from place to place) and their hostility towards law and discipline causes them to drift into criminal activities.

7. *Low frustration tolerance*: Sociopaths exhibit a very low level of frustration tolerance. They are quickly bored by almost any serious and sustained efforts that give no- immediate result or pleasure. A little frustration causes much resentment leading to hostile action and deep depression in them. As a result, they threaten to harm themselves or destroy others.
8. *Early onset and long persistence*: Antisocial behaviour is, to a great extent, a learned reaction pattern and as such it usually starts early in life. In no case its onset goes beyond early twenties. Once caught in antisocial behaviour, it becomes difficult to get rid of it.
9. *No genuine suicide attempts*: Sociopaths, generally, don't have a history of genuine suicide attempts. They threaten suicide or make a suicidal gesture in order to manipulate the behaviour of others for achieving their personal ends. In fact, sociopaths rarely commit suicide. In case it happens it is more often impulsive than planned.
10. *Deviant sex life and behaviour:* Sociopaths suffer sexual maladjustment and abnormalities. Their incapacity for love and attachment, selfish nature, defective super ego, insincerity, lack of remorse or shame and hostile attitude towards social conventions and regulations, make them lead on unconventional and unrestrained sex life. They lead tribal, impersonal, poorly integrated promiscuous lives, and are in the habit of changing their life partners.
11. *Use of rationalization and projection for defending anti- social behaviour*: A sociopath is an expert in defending his socially disapproved and unjustified behaviour by using the mechanism of rationalization and projection. He is a pathological liar and lies readily even when it is obvious that he will be found out. He justifies his behaviour by inventing excuses or reasons apparently reasonable and at times blames others (persons or situations) for his antisocial activities.
12. *Absence of symptoms of psychosis and neurosis*: Sociopaths apparently look like neurotics or psychotics. But sociopathy is different from these functional disorders. Sociopathy never affects the body of an individual as in neurosis or psychosis. In sociopathy there is absence of nervousness neurotic anxiety, or other psychoneurotic manifestations. Similarly, irrationality, delusions, hallucinations and other common symptoms of psychosis are absent in sociopathy.
13. *Absence of ideals and goal of life:* Sociopaths live in the present for the satisfaction of the immediate needs, they have no absolute ideals or goals in life and seldom plan for the future. Their life style is haphazard which suits their self interest. Their life is disorganised and unplanned.
14. *Addiction to alcohol and drugs:* Sociopathy usually leads to alcohol and drug addiction. Social maladjustment, defective relationships, adventurism, law tolerance for frustration, absence of ideals, hostility towards social regulations, and bitterness in life created by selfish nature compels a sociopath to take to alcohol and drugs, gradually leading to addiction.

15. *Absence of judgement and insight*: The main characteristic of a sociopath is the absence of judgement and the inability to act intelligently. He is unable to reach at a decision based on logic. This illustrates the emotional development of the illness which prevents him from acting in a logical manner.

The presence of all the above symptoms or characteristics is not essential for identifying an individual as sociopath. However, the severity of the sociopathic behaviour, to a large extent, depends upon the multiplicity and the severity of these characteristics.

## Etiology of Sociopathy

### Heredity and Biological Factors

Defective genes, physique and body constitution, defective intelligence, mental deficiency, brain disorders and similar other biological determinants have been held responsible for sociopathic behaviour. But there is no convincing evidence of heredity being responsible for sociopathy. Behaviour, in all aspects, is an acquired characteristic and learned pattern. Nothing substantially is known about the role played by genes and chromosomes in the transmission of sociopathic reaction. Similarly, there is dearth of research and experimental evidence for proving the positive correlation between sociopathy and defective biological make up like a poor physique, ill health, glandular imbalance, low intellectual capacity and brain pathology. At the most, biological factors lead to emotional and social maladjustment leading to uncontrolled, unconventional antisocial behaviour. In some cases of sociopathy, biological factors may play a significant role but they are in no way the sole cause for such behaviour.

### Environment or Socio-Psychological Factors

Sociopathy as a behavioural problem involves social and psychological maladjustment. A sociopath learns other personality traits and behaviour characteristics. Like every one of us sociopaths have a unique life style. They follow a consistent learned pattern of living (defensive or retaliatory) which tends to be self perpetuating. Since learning is environmental in character, sociopathy as a learned pattern of behaviour is liable to be caused by environmental factors inherent in one's family, neighbourhood, school, society or community.

*Parents and family* : Uncongenial family environment characterized by sociopathic behaviour of the parents or other members of the family, unhealthy relationships prevailing between the parents and other members of the family, lack of emotional and social security, denial of the facilities for the satisfaction of essential primary and secondary needs, poverty, emotional and social traumas within the family may lead a child to learn specific reaction pattern of antisocial behaviour which enables him to lead an anxiety free, egocentric, self-perpetuating life. All this may happen in some of the following ways.

1. The children of sociopaths are likely to be antisocial in their behaviour not due to hereditary transmission but on account of the indelible impressions that are left on the young minds. The child imitates the role of his or her sociopath father or mother by accepting it as a model and is gradually conditioned to behave antisocially.

2. The elder members of the family can become a model for sociopathic behaviour. An economically and socially deprived family may be engaged in domestic violence, street brawls, drunkenness, drug addiction, promiscuity and other antisocial behaviour. The children in such families are conditioned to learn the behaviour of adults who reject the norms of the wider society and exemplify self interest and a disregard for the rights of others.
3. Broken homes on account of the death of one of the parents, separation, desertion, divorce or prolonged parental absence are likely to breed sociopathy. In such situations the child, placed in a foster home or orphanage, or brought up by a single parent or relatives in severe economic, social and emotional deprivations has no chance to develop primary emotional relationships with the parents and other members of the family. As a result his emotional and social needs may be frustrated and, in a desperate bid for perpetuating himself, he may adopt a sociopath life style.
4. Homes that are not broken but emotionally disturbed also germinate and perpetuate a large number of sociopaths. The parents with different opinions about the rearing, education and career of their children may frequently quarrel leading to marital disharmony and strained relationship between them. The parents may also be careless, over indulgent, over-bearing with their children. In some cases rejection or inadequate supervision of the child by the parents may lead to disaster. In such circumstances, the child is unable to develop the identification needed for an adequate super ego or the empathy for close human relationships. He feels neglected, rejected and unwanted, and turns to antisocial elements, or sociopaths from his peer group or other members of the society from whom he gets attention, admiration and reward for his undesirable behaviour.
5. Similarly, over indulgence of the parents may also prove harmful. Such parents allow the child to express his aggression and other needs without inhibition, The child who is not taught to give and share but only to take and snatch from others lacks control and becomes a sociopath,
6. On many occasions, double standard or the inconsistencies shown by the parents in their behaviour, especially in dealing with their children, may lead a child to sociopathy. The child may encounter inconsistencies in the behaviour of one or the both parents. At one time he may be punished for a particular behaviour but rewarded another time tor the same. He may be scorned and disliked by one of the parents for a particular habit or act but appreciated by the other. In such circumstances the child does not learn to develop reliability and consistency of behaviour. With a defective super ego and lack of control he does not imbibe values and ideals. He is likely to suffer lack of judgement and insight leading to antisocial behaviour.

## Environmental Factors Outside the Family

The consequences of defective family environment are further perpetuated and nourished in the environment outside the home. The neighbourhood, peer group and the antisocial climate in one's community become a substitute for what is denied to a child at home and he learns what comes to him in the form of undesirable or sociopathic behaviour of his associates. Sometimes the availability of cheap literature, movies and mass media provide models of thrilling and undesirable experiences to the youngsters in an already vitiated environment.

## Treatment

Sociopathy, besides being a legal problem, is a behavioural disorder and social problem. Hardened measures in the form of capital punishment, depriving them of the essential needs, or housing in maximum custody prisons do not show any favourable results. Proper medical and socio-psychological measures need to be taken for providing them relief from their problems and rehabilitating them into becoming useful members of the society.

Sociopaths are emotionally disturbed personalities. During the episodes of perturbed behaviour, some anticonvulsant or depressant drugs like phenothiazine, phenobarbitone, dilantin, carbamazepine, chlordiazepoxide may help in stabilizing their behaviour and reducing antisocial trends. But drug administration can cause side effects. Every sociopath's reaction to drugs and situations must be noted and recorded. A particular drug should be continued only if it has no side effects and leads to positive progress.

Under psychological measures, psycho-therapy has been tried for the treatment of sociopathy but the results have not been encouraging. The failure of psychotherapy largely stems from the lack of a sociopath's cooperation with the therapist who is unable to win the sociopath's confidence as the latter does not trust him and considers the therapist as another representative of authority like parents, teachers, policemen and jailors. Moreover, sociopaths generally have a defective ego, poor judgement, and lack of insight. They seldom feel the need for a change in their life style. The realisation of the usual therapeutic goals like establishing identifications with acceptable models, developing controls and satisfying emotional bonds with others is therefore difficult with the sociopaths.

The treatment or reform of sociopaths can neither be undertaken in mental hospitals nor in jails. In fact, they need behaviour modification with consistent self imposed discipline carried out in a controlled and well supervised special institutions Behaviour therapy shows favourable results in behaviour modification of sociopaths. One such measure has been suggested by Bandura (1977) through the following three steps:

- Withdrawal of reinforcement as a sort of punishment for antisocial behaviour.
- Modelling of desired behaviour by changing agents and the use of a graded system of rewards or reinforcers for imitating such behaviour.
- Reduction of material incentives and rewards as the individual's behaviour is increasingly brought under control of self-administered symbolic rewards.

Evidently, the above approach aims to help the sociopaths to develop inner control by reducing dependence on external control. The change in behaviour takes place slowly but steadily and an improved sociopath serves as a model to other sociopaths by acting as agent of change.

The task of behaviour modification and supervision of the sociopaths in the institutions needs great skill, patience and effort on the part of the therapist and other institution personnel. The therapist and nursing staff should be prepared to tolerate the sociopath's behaviour involving repeated aggression, abuse, threats, assaults, fights with staff and public, negativistic behaviour, refusing medication, absconding, drunkenness and thieving. The progress in treatment can be judged from the development of emotional attachment or the sociopath's interest in others; and by not committing criminal, social or moral offences.

It should be remembered that it is the stage by stage progress which is more fruitful in the treatment of sociopathy. Speedy progress exposes them to unmanageable stresses resulting in disaster. The treatment is stopped when the patient is observed to react ably to normal life situations and can support himself.

It has been found that the sociopaths in many cases abandon their customary mode of behaviour on reaching the age of forty even when no treatment is given. This is perhaps due to a decrease in the strength of instinctual biological drives, to the gaining of some insight into their own behaviour, and to the accumulated effect of social conditioning. They are then termed as "burnt out" sociopaths as they give up their undesirable mode of living and become better socialized. However, it is undesirable to wait for this natural burning of antisocial designs through aging, for much damage of the society may be caused by them before they burn out. Attempts should, therefore, be made for their early treatment and rehabilitation.

## Summary

- The terms sociopathy and psychopathy carry the same meaning. These are used for the antisocial behaviour of individuals who are basically unsocialized and whose behaviour pattern brings them repeatedly into conflict with society.
- The persons characterized as Sociopaths are found to exhibit the characteristics, like (i)Superficial charm and intelligence,(ii)Lack of anxiety, shame or guilt, (iii) Lack of control and false adventurism, (iv)Inability to profit from social rewards or punishment, (v)Inadequate social adjustment and improper social relationships, (vi) Hostility towards authorities and discipline, (vii) Low frustration tolerance, (viii)Early onset and long persistence of the anti-social behaviour, (ix)No genuine suicide attempts,(x) Deviant sex life and behaviour, (xi)Using rationalization and projection for defending antisocial behaviour, (xii) Absence of accepted symptoms of psychosis and neurosis , (xiii) Absence of ideals and goal of life, (xiv)Addiction to alcohol and drugs, and (xv) Absence of judgement and insight.
- Regarding the etiology of sociopathy there seems to be no significant positive correlation between sociopathy and defective heredity and biological make up. Sociopathy is a behavioural problem involving social and psychological maladjustment and, as a learned pattern of behaviour, is liable to be caused by environmental factors inherent in one's family, neighbourhood, school, society or community. The child may imitate the antisocial behaviour of his father, mother or other members of the family by accepting it as a model. The uncongenial

and defective family environment on account of poverty, broken or emotionally disturbed homes, faulty parent child relationships, improper up-bringing, and denial of the basic needs may put a child on the track of antisocial behaviour. Thereafter, environmental factors outside the family perpetuate and nourish this tendency by encouraging and luring him into learning sociopathic behaviour.

- Regarding the treatment of anti-social behaviour or sociopathy it can be well inferred that punitive measures show no favourable results. Here, proper medical or socio-psychological measures need therefore to be taken. Anti-convulsant or depressant drugs may be used for relief in the episodes of perturbed behaviour of the sociopaths. It helps in stablizing behaviour and reducing antisocial trends. Psychotherapy, under psychological measures, does not prove much effective with sociopaths. However, for behaviour modification of the sociopaths, behaviour therapy shows favourable results. This measure should be taken in a controlled and well- supervised special institution instead of a jail or a mental hospital.

## REFERENCES

American Psychiatric Association (1968), *Diagnostic and Statistical Manual of Mental Disorders, (2nd ed.),* Washington, DC: American Psychiatric Association.

American Psychiatric Association (2013), *Diagnostic and Statistical Manual of Mental Disorders, (5th ed.),* Washington, DC: American Psychiatric Association.

Bandura, Albert, (1977), Quoted by Shanmugam, T.E., *Abnormal Psychology,* (1981:244-45), New Delhi: Tata McGraw Hill, 1981.

# 16

# CRIMINAL BEHAVIOUR – DELINQUENCY AND CRIME

The terms sociopath or sociopathy in contrast with the legal base of the terms criminal or crime have psychological and psychiatric grounds. Whereas all sociopaths generally exhibit criminal behaviour, it is not essential that all criminals (adults or minor) should be sociopaths. The following points make a distinction between criminals and sociopaths:

**Table 16.1 Distinction between Criminals and Sociopaths**

| Criminals | Sociopaths |
|---|---|
| 1. Criminals usually show normal or extraordinary concentration. | 1. Sociopaths exhibit complete lack of concentration |
| 2. Criminal offences are planned and well organized. | 2. The offences are usually impulsive, often poorly carried out. |
| 3. Criminals operate under a conscience peculiar to themselves and are loyal to each other, but not to society, by whom they frequently feel rejected. They may be hostile to one particular group of people or section of the society, but may be generous to others. | 3. There is no evidence of a conscience in sociopathic behaviour. Sociopaths even do not hesitate to steal from fellow patients. They may be observed to wander from woman o women, having many children and supporting no one, not even themselves. |
| 4. It is not essential for the criminals to be inadequate in all forms of behaviour. | 4. Sociopaths are usually inadequate in all forms of behaviour. |
| 5. Criminals exhibit skill and proficiency and develop sophistication in committing a crime. They are ruthless in their approach which is their work. They act with judgement and keen insight. | 5. Sociopaths are not very serious about their criminal behaviour. They repeat the same offences and never learn from their past experiences. They suffer from poor judgement and lack insight. |
| 6. Criminals have an affect; this means that they commit an offence with a motive and frequently care for their family and children. They get upset and punish children if they commit crimes. | 6. Sociopaths have only the shallowest affect. They show no serious concern for their life partners, family or children. For them self is always great. |

## Delinquency and Crime

The terms 'crime' and 'delinquency' are legal ones and their meaning varies from country to country and in the same country from one state to another. In India, any person of 18 years and above convicted by the court for violating the provision of Indian Penal Code (IPC) and the Criminal Procedure Code (CPC) is a criminal. Of course, there are state laws which vary from state to state. For example, in some states or part of a state, liquor consumption, except for medical reasons, may be considered a crime, whereas in others it may not be so.

Similarly, for legally labelling an individual who has not completed 18 year of age as delinquent, he must be convicted by the court for violating the provisions of the Children's Acts, the IPC and the CPC.

## Delinquency

Criminal behaviour or tendency to commit crime in any society or nation is not only found among the adults, but minor children and adolescents also. These individuals are known as juvenile or young delinquents. (Juvenile delinquents, therefore, are criminals minor in age below the age of eighteen in our country) and usually referred to as minors with major problems.

In this connection special mention may be made to the legal provision available in our country in the from of Acts. In its latest development we have now The Juvenile Justice (Care and Protection of Children) act 2015 operating in our county since 15th January,2016. It replaces the previously enforced Juvenile Justice (Care and Protection of Children) Act, 2000. In the previously enforced act,2000, the term Juvenile was defined as "a person who has not completed eighteenth year of age" and thus those below the age of 18 were not tried as adults for committing offences. In the revised Act 2015, however, there is a provision to try the persons of the age group 16-18 as adults if they are involved in heinous offences ( the offences for which the minimum punishment under the Indian Penal Code or any other law is imprisonment for seven years or more).

The individuals (minor in age) labelled as delinquents are found to violate the law of the land and commit offences like thefts, gambling, cheating, pick-pocketing, murder, robbery, dacoity, destruction of property, violence and assault, intoxication, vagrancy, begging, kidnapping, abduction, and sexual offences. The term 'juvenile delinquent' or 'young delinquent' means a child or youth (minor in age) who deviates seriously from the norms of his culture or society and commits offences such as murder and robbery or those that are strictly age related such age drinking liquor and sexual activities. Juvenile delinquency should, therefore, be considered a serious challenge to the well-being of the society. The young delinquents, if not handled properly, become a source of concern for the society.

## Causes of Delinquency

1. *Hereditary factor:* The early researches held heredity responsible for delinquency. The claim of hereditarians like Henry, Maudsley, Tredgold, and Dugdale that

delinquency is inherited was tested by William Healey, Cyril Burt, Conrad and Jones, Wingfield and Sandiford. They concluded that delinquency is not inherited and therefore it is unjustified to blame heredity for delinquent behaviour.

2. *Constitutional or physiological factors:* Defective constitution or glandular systems were also thought to be the cause of delinquent behaviour. Udai Shanker (1958:30) observes that *"poor health, short or too big stature or some deformity which gives rise to feeling of inferiority, dispose one to more aggression, as a compensatory reaction for his inadequacies."* Consequently, this leads to delinquent behaviour. Apparently this alienation seems to be well founded but it is not so, for not much scientific evidence has been reported in its support so far. However, in some cases, it may be taken as one of the causes of delinquent behaviour.

3. *Intelligence factor:* While earlier writers like Lombroso and Goddard emphasize that the most important cause of delinquency and crime is low grade mentality, Burt, Healey, Bronner, Merrill and others deny that delinquents are mentally retarded. In fact, a direct causal relationship between intelligence and delinquency is doubtful. High intelligence is no guarantee for good behaviour. Often persons with superior intelligence have been found to be the leaders of notorious gangs, and antisocial organisations. Sometimes it is argued on the basis of the statistics that since the majority among the delinquents possesses low intelligence, defective intelligence therefore causes delinquency. But this conclusion is not well founded. The collected statistics, in such cases, may represent an unreal picture. An intelligent individual may not be caught red handed, whereas someone with low intelligence may always be taken in custody. Moreover, defective intelligence may lead to delinquency in one situation and may be a barrier to it in another situation. Hence, low intelligence alone cannot be held responsible for delinquent behaviour.

4. *Environmental and social factors:* It has been proved that delinquent behaviour is a learned reaction. Delinquents do not inherit delinquent characters from their parents or ancestors but are made so by the uncongenial environment and social conditions, Udai Shanker (1958:30) observes that *"delinquency is not inherited; it is the product of social and economic conditions and is essentially a coefficient of the friction between the individual and the community. The most important causes of antisocial behaviour are environmental and sociological in character."* It is therefore the uncongenial environment of the family, school, neighbourhood and society which should be blamed for the delinquent behaviour of the child since he picks up delinquent traits in such situations. We shall now see how environment is responsible for the delinquent character formation among minors.

**a. Home environment and delinquency**

A defective and deficient family environment is a fertile ground for the germination of delinquency. As a matter of fact, family life and delinquency are closely related. Findings of various studies indicate that the family environment, where the following relationships or conditions prevail, is most susceptible to delinquency.

(i) Broken home – where the family is incomplete due to death, desertion, separation or divorce.

(ii) Improper parental control.

(iii) Unusual jealousy and rivalry among the siblings or children within the family and reactions like, "My parents gave him more love than they gave me".

(iv) The delinquent and criminal behaviour of the parents or other family members.

(v) Domestic conflicts.

(vi) Economic difficulties and poverty of the family.

(vii) Dull, monotonous and uninteresting home environment.

(viii) Denial of reasonable freedom and independence to the youngsters.

(ix) Maltreatment and injustice done, to the youngsters

(x) Lack of proper physical and emotional security.

In these situations and environment the child does not get the opportunity for the satisfaction of his basic needs. He becomes victim of the emotional problems like inferiority, insecurity, jealousy or being thwarted which make him a maladjusted individual and consequently turn him into a hostile, rebellious and antisocial personality. Thus, uncongenial home conditions deserve to be blamed for juvenile delinquency and in all circumstances the root cause of delinquent behaviour must be investigated in family background and home environment.

**b. Uncongenial environment outside the home**

Whereas home provides the roots for the delinquent behaviour, the social environment outside the home nourishes it by supplying some substitute for the satisfaction of unsatisfied basic needs and urges. For example, the peer-group or gang presents itself as a substitute for family love and belongingness. It also satisfies the need for recognition and gives an individual the opportunity for self-dependence and adventurism. Delinquent acts of peer-group lead him to delinquent behaviour and engage in delinquent acts. Neighbourhood and the places of social contracts and situations where the elder members of the society engage in antisocial activities, or the mass media like newspapers, books, magazines and cinema that acquaint children with immoral and anti social acts, provide temptation for the youngsters to become delinquents.

**c. Maladjustment in school**

In many cases of delinquency, uncongenial school environment can be a significant emulating factor. It brings about serious maladjustment and consequently increases the probability of delinquent character formation. Such environment may involve the following elements:

- Defective curriculum.
- Improper teaching methods.
- Lack of co-curricular activities.
- Lack of proper discipline and control.
- Slackness in administration and organisation.
- Antisocial or undesirable behaviour of the teachers.
- Maltreatment and injustice done to the child.
- Failure or backwardness.

To conclude, delinquency is an environmental and social disease. Delinquent acts are learned and acquired acts. No child is born delinquent nor is delinquent behaviour the product of genes. Thus delinquents are not a specific type of human beings born with innate, physical, mental or emotional characteristics. They are normal individuals with normal needs and desires. Like other normal children they also want to love, to be loved and to satisfy the need for security and recognition. The denial of these basic needs leads to maladjustment and makes them hostile and rebellious. Thus delinquent behaviour is a reaction or resentment against the prevailing social and environmental conditions. It is a revolt against parents, teachers or social organisations which do not provide them the essential environment for the satisfaction of their basic needs and urges.

## Prevention and Treatment

Delinquency, besides being a legal problem, is basically a psycho-social problem. All delinquents are essentially maladjusted personalities and the result of faulty up-bringing and maltreatment. The solution of the problem requires preventive and curative measures.

### *Preventive Measures*

Initially these involve improvement of the social or environmental conditions which thwart the satisfaction of the basic needs of the individual. Some of the following suggestions may work well in this direction.

*Parental education:* Parents should be aware of the psychology of delinquency so that they can treat and handle their children with understanding and provide them an environment for the satisfaction of their basic needs and urges. It requires parental education which may be provided through guidance services, clinics and voluntary social services.

*The child's company*: Parents, family members and school authorities should keep a close watch on the activities and social environment of the children and take care so that they do not fall in bad company. Antisocial elements and criminals often seek out youngsters for their own purposes. Attempts should be made to save the children from them and they should be educated in keeping away from such elements.

*Substitute environment:* It is difficult to bring a change in the defective family environment or the influences of the neighbourhood and peer- group. In such circumstances children should be removed from their original environment and placed either in foster homes or well-managed reformatories and special schools so that they may be provided with healthy environment for their emotional and social adjustment.

*Rectifying school education and environment: School* environment should be healthy and congenial. The curriculum, methods of teaching, discipline, class-room behaviour of the teacher and the social atmosphere of the school should be rectified so that children do not involve themselves in emotional and social maladjustment problems.

The attitude of teachers who impose their authority on children and do not understand their basic needs should be changed. The headmaster as well as the teachers should be familiar with the psychology of individual difference and delinquency.

### *Curative Measures*

The problem of juvenile delinquency should not be regarded as panel problem. It is an educational and welfare problem. Juvenile delinquents should not be put behind bars and treated through the panel system. Delinquents require rehabilitation and re-education for which special legal provisions should be made. The legal dealings with the juvenile delinquents have been changed in the progressive communities of the world. The "Children's and Young Person's Act" of U K. is a good example of dealing with delinquents in an appropriate way. In our country also, a number of good provisions of this act have been maintained by making constitutional provisions for this purpose in the preceding years. The special mention on this ground may be made to The Juvenile Justice (Care and Protection of Children) act,2000 and the presently operative "The Juvenile Justice (Care and Protection of Children) Act, 2015.

The essentials involved in relation to the dealing with delinquents may be summarised as below:

(i) Establishment of special juvenile courts with trained magistrate to deal with the juvenile delinquents.

(ii) Appointment of trained social workers or probation officers for taking charge of delinquent cases.

(iii) Taking help from clinical psychologists and psychiatrists for understanding the delinquent behaviour of children.

(iv) Establishment of special schools where the education, correction and rehabilitation is possible.

(v) Provision of keeping the children in the custody of responsible persons or social agencies.

(vi) Establishment of remand homes where juvenile delinquents are placed while they wait for their trial or for approved school placement or for being given to the custody of responsible persons or as asked by probation officer before employment on being discharged from the approved schools.

The provision of 'special schools' or 'approved schools' needs special mention in this programme. These schools have specially trained staff. The curriculum is flexible and provides opportunities for self expression, recreation, manual work and learning of useful crafts. Provisions are made to satisfy the basic needs and urges of the children and thus they are helped in their social and emotional readjustment. In this way the children are helped to get rid themselves of the delinquent behaviour and learn to respond meaningfully to social situations and conditions.

The attitude towards delinquency in our country is also changing. It has now been realized that children who are called delinquents are ill primarily in their inability to conform to the social milieu. Consequently, in most of the states, the Children

Act has been enforced and some have gone ahead in the work of rehabilitation and re-education of the young offenders. Separate child welfare boards for dealing with the problem of delinquency have been established and approved schools have come into existence. Some states encourage voluntary organisations to take custody of the delinquent children. Provisions for the care of the neglected and destitute children are also made so that they do not become delinquents. Some states have started foster care programmes which envisage the court giving custody of a child to a responsible person. There is, however, the need to arouse public consciousness on this problem. No government can solve a social problem without public cooperation. Therefore, there *is* a need for a change in our attitude towards delinquents so that they may be helped in their readjustment and rehabilitation.

## Crime

Crime may be defined as an act prohibited by law of a country or state or a failure on the part of an individual to perform an act that is prescribed by that law. In a legal sense, person of 21 years and above convicted by the court of Jaw for violating the provision of I PC and CPC is labelled a criminal in our country and the illegal act for which he is convicted is known as crime. Any behaviour like pickpocketing, gambling, burglary, robbery, theft, dacoity, rape, kidnapping and abduction, attempts at suicide, murder, riots, destroying another's property, sexual assault, prostitution, cheating, counterfeiting, failure to deposit taxes and revenue etc., arc termed criminal behaviour.

## Causes Underlying Crime

Although it is not essential for a delinquent to become a criminal yet, in many cases, adult crime has been found to show a history of juvenile delinquency. Both delinquency and crime have a similar tendency characterized by unique reaction pattern of aggression against the social set-up. The causes underlying crimes are therefore similar to those of delinquency.

The biological factors like- defective heredity and intelligence, poor constitutional make-up or glandular disturbances, have not been found to play any substantial role in the causation of criminal behaviour. The view that a criminal is born has almost been discarded in favour of the socio-psychological environmental factors being responsible for the criminal tendency in an individual.

It should be observed that criminal behaviour may have a variety of forms and degree of severity. It may range from an offence which is committed once in a life-time to a life style of criminal behaviour. Hence the pathology involving socio-psychological causes also varies from crime to crime and criminal to criminal. A criminal behaviour is not necessarily generated and developed by a single factor or factors.

The criminals are always the victims of social maladjustment arising out of the defective environmental conditions and unfavourable circumstances of life. Some of these situations may be summarized as below:

1. *Learned as a professional art: Criminal behaviour may be* learned like any professional act or art like tailoring, wood work, or haircutting from the parents or the members of the family, community or race. The perpetuation of a particular criminal behaviour like burglary, prostitution, theft, or bootlegging among certain tribes, castes or races are some other examples.
2. *The impact of defective family environment:* The uncongenial home environment contributes to criminal character formation. It is often the result of broken homes through desertion, **divorce,** separation or the death of one or both parents. Moreover, the defective and deficient environment created by unfavourable intra-familial tensions and conflicts, lax parental control, poverty, sibling rivalries and maltreatment is insufficient to fulfill the basic physiological and psychological needs of children in the family. In order to gratify their physical, social and emotional needs they are lured and sometimes forced on to the path of crime.

   Not only the young members of the family may but adults be forced to lead a life of criminals on account of the frustrations caused by deficient family environment and unhealthy interpersonal relationships. For example, sex frustration may lead one to promiscuity, prostitution or even causing murder, rape or other similar offence.
3. *Economic factors:* Poverty, unemployment, desire for the pleasures of life, competition to earn money by any means, evils of industrialization all contribute in pushing an individual towards criminal behaviour,
4. *Degradation of moral values:* The crisis of character and degradation of moral values in the society also cause criminal- character formation. Crimes such as the call-girl rackets in posh colonies and luxury hotels, adulteration of food and drugs, forgery, counterfeiting of money, bank robberies, black money transactions, smuggling, bribery and selling secrets of one's own country can be attributed to lack of moral values.
5. *Environment outside the family:* Whereas defective home environment and circumstances provide the basic causes for criminal behaviour, the criminal environment outside the home nourishes it by providing substitute for the gratification of unsatisfied needs and cherished goals. Neighbourhood, community, places of social contacts where there are opportunities for mixing with criminal characters attract and even push the individuals into the world of crime. The unhealthy impact of the mass media, especially cheap literature, obscene pictures, photographs and films encourage individuals towards crime.
6. *Social system and denial of justice:* The defective social system and traditions lead to circumstances where an individual learns criminal behaviour. For example, the dowry system, dominance of men in the social set up, the status of a widow, give rise to complications leading towards crime. The gulf between the rich and the poor, caste differences, hatred towards other communities, races, linguistic groups, sects and religions, the exploitation of labourers and landless farmers by landlords often lead to strained relationships and crimes.
7. *Mental illness and abnormal state of mind:* ***Sometimes*** crimes are committed by the

mentally ill persons in an abnormal state of mind. The compulsive behaviours like kleptomania of the neurotics and abnormal behaviour of the sexual deviants may lead to crime. Similarly, psychotic individuals classified as criminally insane may commit a variety of offences depending upon the situation and the state of their mind. Under the influence of liquor and drugs, offences are committed not by the professional criminals *m* socially and emotionally maladjusted individuals but by normal people. Individuals suffering from senile brain degeneration and mental deficiency may also be found responsible of certain offences committed in an abnormal state of mind without realizing the consequences of their behaviour.

## Prevention and Treatment

The remedy for criminal behaviour demands preventive and curative measures.

**Prevention:** The preventive measures involve improvement of Social factors and environmental conditions that are responsible for the germination and perpetuation of criminal behaviour. The problem is a gigantic one and needs the cooperation of parents, members of the family, neighbourhood, community, school or college authorities, religious heads, police and government officials responsible for the social and psychological environment of the inhabitants of a society. The following measures may be fruitful in the prevention task:

1. Since today's delinquents are tomorrow's criminals, maximum efforts should therefore be made for the prevention,, control and treatment of all the identified delinquents.
2. There is a great need for social reforms and breaking social and caste barriers.
3. The task of narrowing the gulf between the rich and the poor, linguistic groups and religious sects should be given priority.
4. The importance of moral values should be inculcated. There should be an end to the crisis of character threatening the existence of the moral base and legal codes of our society.
5. The system of education and national planning need rethinking and re-modification for minimising economic difficulties of our youth and adults.
6. The problem fo unemployment has to be checked and the professional dissatisfaction as well as frustration affecting the vast population of the younger generation should be curbed.
7. Attempts should be made to minimize undesirable influence of literature, films and other mass media.
8. The parents, elders, government authorities, social, religious, educational and political leaders should be such that they become ideals of socially desirable behaviour.
9. The society should feel the necessity of providing social and legal justice to it citizens. In case of environmental deprivations and hazards of life, the affected individual should be helped, protected and rehabilitated.

Thus there is a need for modifying the environmental conditions so that one does not fall victim to social and emotional maladjustment or lured by the criminals and drifted by instinctive behaviour to commit crimes.

**Treatment and Rehabilitation:** The old notion that a criminal is born and nothing can be done for reforming and rehabilitating him still holds its ground. The law enforcement is still largely punitive and revengeful. Even in many civilized societies and developed countries the treatment meted out to criminals is still in terms of tooth for tooth and eye for eye. The criminals are isolated from society, kept in prisons and punishments such as lashing, severing of hands and legs, hanging are given in public not to deter the criminal from further offences but also to prevent others from indulging in such acts. However, as a result of an increase in the knowledge of human behaviour and criminal psychology, there have been changes in the attitude of the general public, police officials and government authorities towards criminals and crime. It is now felt that for most criminals, their behaviour is a part of the larger pattern of personality maladjustment. Criminal behaviour is nothing but a social disease and criminals are ill primarily in terms of their inability to conform to the social milieu. With serious psychological and psychiatric problems, they need hospitalization, medical and psychological treatment as curative measures for their illness.

The change in attitude has ushered a new era in the management of jails which are now called correctional institutions. The progressive prison authorities are now adopting a constructive attitude towards criminals. In addition to the custodial care, the responsibilities in terms of the possible attempts to re-socialize, readjust and rehabilitate the criminals are clearly felt. The emphasis is on the study of each prisoner as an individual, as a victim of circumstances and to provide him the medical aid and psychological treatment, training and help needed for his restoration to society as a self-supporting and law-abiding citizen. The effectiveness of the curative and reformatory measures lies in modifying the behaviour of a criminal and equipping him with the necessary art and skill for playing a useful role in the society.

Some of the measures used in this new constructive reformatory approach are:

1. The crimes committed by delinquents or young offenders and also by the relatively normal adults during periods of acute stress and deprivation have very little chances of being repeated unless they are compelled to do so again. Also, the majority of new criminals are accidental criminals who commit an offence by chance or mishap. The environment of the prisons, coupled with their association with hardened criminals, often convert them to a life criminal. Attempts should be made to keep them out of prisons by granting probation and making provisions for their adequate supervision by competent probation officers.
2. The constructive approach calls for change in the environment of the prison and treatment of prisoners as human beings in need of sympathy and affection in understanding their behavioural problems.
3. Many countries are now experimenting with open prisons which do not have fence or outer walls and their dormitories are neither locked nor guarded. There are open fields with situations where prisoners are provided opportunities to work for which they are paid. Their expenses are met out of their earnings which arc partly sent to their families. Occasionally, they too are sent to meet their families. There is an environment of mutual love, understanding and trust prevailing in the

prison providing sufficient opportunities for the modification of their behaviour. They are made to learn useful social skills and readjustment in the society.

4. The ideal humanitarian approach that all prisons should be converted into hospitals—the criminals are usually mentally ill, socially maladjusted and psychologically handicapped individuals— is taking root in prisons of many countries. Efforts are also being made to study criminal behaviour, to investigate its causes, and to find ways modifying it. The cooperation of the physician, psychiatrist, social worker, legal authorities is well sought by prison authorities for the treatment of abnormal and antisocial behaviour of the inmates.
5. In some countries useful rehabilitation programmes are being adopted for the welfare of criminals. In our country, the rehabilitation of the dacoits of the Chambal valley by Sarvodaya leaders may be cited as a good attempt in providing opportunities for leading a self-supporting and law-abiding life.

## Summary

- Criminal behaviour involving the terms criminal or crime has a legal base in contrast to the psychological and psychiatric grounds of the terms sociopath or sociopathy. The violation of the law of the land and committing legal offences is termed criminal behaviour and the person who exhibits such behaviour is termed a criminal, when such offences are committed by individuals, minor in age—in legal sense from seven to eighteen years in our country—they are termed delinquents and not criminals, and their criminal behaviour is known as delinquency.
- Causes of delinquency are inherent in one's defective and uncongenial home, family and other sociocultural environmental conditions instead of hereditary or biological factors. While the causes for the delinquent behaviour are provided by uncongenial home and family environment, the social environment outside the home nourishes it by supplying substitute for the satisfaction of unfulfilled desires and needs.
- While seeking measures for the prevention and treatment of delinquency, it should be well remembered that delinquency is not so much a legal problem as it is a psycho-social problem arising out of the faulty upbringing and maltreatment of the youngsters. We should, therefore, begin with preventive measures.
- Preventive measures aim at improving the social or environmental conditions and may involve parental education, protecting the child from bad company and antisocial environment, providing substitute for the defective environment and rectifying the school education and environment.
- Curative measures aim at rehabilitation and reeducation of the delinquents by government or voluntary organisations. Delinquency, instead of a panel problem, should be treated as a socio-psycho- logical problem. It requires a change in attitude towards delinquents and delinquency. A change taking place in our country consists in the provision of Children Act, reformatories, approved schools, foster-care programmes and remand homes, on the pattern of other developed countries.

- Regarding the causes underlying crime it can be well inferred that criminals arc always the victims of social maladjustment arising out of the defective environmental conditions and unfavourable circumstances of life. Criminal behaviour is essentially a learned pattern of maladaptive and antisocial behaviour which may be the result of a close interaction of social, psychological and psychiatric factors.
- The preventive measures for criminal behavbiour involve the improvement of social and environmental conditions that are responsible for the germination and perpetuation of the criminal behaviour.
- For the treatment and rehabilitation of criminals the basic requirement demands a change in outlook and attitudes towards criminals and crimes so that criminals may be provided with hospitalization, medical and psychological treatment as curative measures for their serious socio- psychological and psychiatric problems. They should be understood sympathetically, studied individually, treated medically and psychologically, trained and helped educationally as well as vocationally, and finally, rehabilitated to become self-supporting and law-abiding citizens.

## REFERENCES

Udai Shanker (1958), *Problem Children,* Delhi: Atma Ram & Sons

# 17

# ALCOHOLISM AND DRUG ADDICTION

Alcoholism and drug addiction have been a source of serious behavioural problems for thousands of years in the world. Excessive indulgence in them has been considered undesirable or criminal behaviour. From time to time in almost all the countries the law of the land has been given teeth for dealing with this menace but alcoholism and drug addiction are not so much the law and order problems. Recent studies have established that these are more of a psychiatric, psychological and social problem than anything else which ruins the individual and the society emotionally and economically.

## Alcoholism

Alcoholism is usually referred to excessive drinking or dependence on alcoholic beverages, which people drink for many reasons and in many ways, situations and styles. They should not all be considered alcoholics. The World Health Organisation-WHO (1969:228) has defined alcoholics as *"excessive drinkers whose dependence on alcohol has attained such a degree that they show noticeable mental disturbance or an interference with their mental and bodily health, their interpersonal relations and their smooth social and economic functioning, or who show the prodromal (beginning) signs of such developments."*

## The Habit of Alcoholism

The habit of excessive drinking dependence on alcoholic beverages is perpetuated gradually. E.M. Jellinek (1942), an authority on alcoholism has pointed out the following four stages in the development of alcoholism.

1. ***Pre-alcoholic phase***: This initial phase lasts from two months to two years. The beginner who drinks for social reasons or merely on account of curiosity finds that it relieves him of anxiety and tension and as a result learns to use alcohol as a relief measure. Gradually, he begins to experience an increased tolerance for alcohol and needs a large amount to reach the same stage of sedation.

   This phase is characterized by a gradual shift from infrequent or light to frequent or heavy drinking.

2. *Prodromal phase* : At this stage alcohol begins to be used more as a drug and less as a beverage with dependency on it increasing and manifested through the following behavioural phenomena :
   - The individual becomes preoccupied with drinking, worrying where and when he will have his next drink.
   - He feels guilty about drinking and usually avoids references to alcohol in conversations. At the same time he feels a strong urge to drink and thereby often resorts to surreptitious rather than open drinking.
   - There is a sudden onset of 'blackouts' for some of the periods of drinking.
   - There is considerable memory impairment. One may remain conscious at the time of drinking but later unable to recall the events.
3. *The crucial phase*: The third stage is alarming. The dependency on alcohol increases to the extent that there is a danger of an individual losing everything that one values. He may drop friends, lose jobs and leave the members of his family including children and wife but not giving up the habit of drinking. The behaviour compels one to withdraw from the social environment ending in the isolation further making him drink heavily at any time. In this phase drinking is sought to be rationalized as a source of comfort. The need for liquor becomes a constant source of worry, detrimental to diet combined with the harmful effects of alcohol deteriorates his health, lowers his sexual drive and makes him hostile towards the persons and environment completely ruining his harmony and peace.
4. *The chronic phase*: This is the most crucial stage where the individual lives only to drink. His bodily systems become so conditioned that these must be supplied with alcohol or he suffers withdrawal reactions. In case alcohol is not available, he is ready to consume any of the liquid containing alcohol like shaving lotion, hair tonic, spirit or a medical preparation. He loses control upon his behaviour and prolonged bouts of intoxication often lead to marked ethical deterioration (character disorders), complete neglect of personal appearance and concern for others, impairment of mental processes and even alcoholic psychoses in some cases. In comparison with the crucial phase, the chronic phase, results in the loss of tolerance for alcohol usually when even a small amount leads to intoxication. At a more advanced stage, the alcoholic admits defeat and unless he receives treatment is unlikely to give up drinking.

## The Effects of Alcoholism

Alcoholism may result in severe disturbances of physiological, psychological and social functions as given below:

1. *Physiological damage:* Almost every tissue and organ of the body is adversely affected by alcohol. Since an alcoholic largely depends upon alcohol as a major source of food, he neglects his diet. Consequently, he suffers from vitamin and nutritional deficiencies. A drastic reduction in the intake of protein causes cirrhosis of the liver. Prolonged consumption of alcohol can damage the endocrine glands

or cause heart failure, hypertension, shrinking and inflammation of the lining of the stomach, and capillary haemorrhage. It can also lead to the lowering of overall resistance to disease as a result of which the life expectancy of an alcoholic is considerably reduced. The incidence of death in the case of alcoholics may occur on account of depression leading to suicide; inter-current infection, especially from respiratory injections: liver or cardiac failure; and inhalation of vomitus.

2. *Psycho-physiological damage:* This damage may result in a number of neurological and psychotic disorders (brain syndromes) such as pathological intoxication, delirium tremens, alcoholic hallucinosis, alcoholic deterioration and Korsa Koff's syndrome.
3. *Behavioural damage:* Alcoholism may result in one or the other kinds of behavioural damage in the manner like below:

- It can cause severe deterioration in the thought processes and damage intellectual functioning. Sufficient intoxication may lead an individual to 'black out' causing inability to remember what he said or did. Motor behaviour is adversely affected on account of the deterioration in motor coordination, balance, speech and the power of sensation and perception.
- It may cause severe personality or character disorders. There is likely to be a deterioration of personal habits, a lack of regard for one's appearance, self image and self respect. Following release of inhibitions, impairment of judgement, loss of emotional and motor control, disturbance in self evaluation and indifference to self caused by intoxication, alcoholics easily drift towards irresponsible behaviour and anti-social acts.
- Intoxication adversely affects the sex behaviour of an individual who is likely to lose interest in the family. Sexual incapacity caused by alcoholism may further deteriorate the situation. Frustration, lack of inhibitions and defective intellectual and moral judgement may result in sexual deviations and crimes.

Thus alcoholism causes psychological and physiological damage to an individual resulting in incalculable personal and social loss. For alcoholics dire social, occupational and family consequences are inevitable. They are likely to be ruined in terms of physical or mental health, emotional and social relationships and economic loss and moral degradation. It leads one to misery and frustration, and alienates him from the family and society.

## The Causes of Alcoholism

Since no person is born alcoholic, the causes of alcoholism are therefore to be found within the environment of an individual. The beginning of the drinking habit and later its continuation is a learned pattern of maladaptive behaviour. Drinking is learned and acquired like other personality traits and later maintained for its physiological and psychological dependence.

One learns many things from the environment. The behaviour patterns of the elder members of the family and the society work as a model for the younger ones. Therefore the first drink may be taken in a social gathering with other members or secretly without the knowledge of the elders. The child or a youth may be tempted to taste alcohol merely on account of the curiosity or for imitating the elders. The literature in the form of stories, fiction and plays, the movies and the observed behaviour of the parents and elders makes him start drinking as a learned response to develop sociability; to alleviate the feelings of isolation and loneliness; to seek a readily available source of pleasure; to boost one's ego, remove hesitation and become courageous by acquiring feelings of adequacy; to seek relief from tension and worries; to remove ethical restraints to engage in undesirable, immoral or antisocial behaviour without feeling guilty; and to increase sexual interest, stimulation and for acquiring a feeling of sexual adequacy.

People learn to drink excessively as a result of its rewarding effect. As a sedative alcohol is a very quick and effective method of reducing tension, removing hesitations and inhibitions. It leads to a pleasurable feeling of adequacy, relief from worries and sociability. Such rewarding effects reinforce the drinking behaviour. One learns to depend upon drinking as the preferred solution to problems. The psychological dependence further aggravates the situation when the individual consumes more and more alcohol for seeking pleasure and getting relief from the unpleasant reality. Gradually, it leads to prolonged and excessive drinking resulting in physiological, psychological, psychiatric and social problems.

Once an individual becomes physiologically addicted to alcohol, drinking becomes a compulsion for his physical well-being. He experiences withdrawal symptoms like craving for alcohol, tremors, perspiration, weakness, nausea, vomiting, fever, blackouts and hallucinations when he tries to give up the habit. Consequently, he dare not stop drinking and this physiological dependence compels him to drink still more.

## Treatment of Alcoholism

There is no single effective way to deal with the problem of alcoholism. In some cases individuals may stop drinking apparently because of the fear of being arrested and imprisoned. But alcoholism is in fact a medical and psychological problem rather than a law and order problem. Attempts should therefore be made to tackle it on medical, social and psychological levels.

While resorting to treatment one should have a clear knowledge of the early symptoms of alcoholism. These may include continuous and heavy drinking or uncontrolled episodic bursts of drinking; morning drinking; blackouts; gaining no pleasure in drinking; and undesirable, uncontrolled extreme behaviour. It is then time to take corrective measures given below:

1. *Institutionalization and hospitalization*: It is better to arrange institutionalization and hospitalization for the treatment of acute alcoholic intoxication. In many cases, compulsory hospitalization is not needed, but it is important to keep the alcoholics away from aversive life situations and keep their behaviour under control.
2. *Clinical investigation:* It should include investigations like full blood count, chest and skull radiography, liver function tests and as a result proper medical treatment should be provided for the deficiency and damage.

3. *De-intoxication:* The first step in treating alcoholics is de-intoxication, that is, removal of alcoholic substances from the body and treatment of withdrawal symptoms. At this stage much care should be taken to compensate the alcoholic's dietary deficiencies.

4. *Deterrent measures:* After de-intoxication the following deterrent measures in the form of aversion therapy are commonly used for restraining the patient from drinking. The patient may be given drugs like disulfiram (Antabuse) or citrated calcium carbamide (Abstem) for helping him resolve not to drink. These drugs cause episode of intense illness if the individual drinks alcohol and thereby act as strong deterrents in preventing drinking.

   In making the patient develop a hatred for alcohol a substance which produces nausea and vomiting when taken with an alcoholic drink is given. With repetition, it results in a conditioned aversion to alcoholic drinks.

   Shock therapy may also be used as an effective measure to cause aversion for liquor. Sometimes the shocks received from the adverse life situations may prove valuable in treating alcoholics.

5. *Psychotherapy*: When the patient has stopped drinking, he may be given group or individual psychotherapy for helping him gain insight into his behaviour and develop more effective adjustment techniques other than alcohol or drug addiction. However, its use is not recommended with alcoholics who are basically sociopathic.

   A therapist has to work hard with alcoholics. The chronic alcoholics are usually liars and unable *to* keep their promises *of* never drinking again. Fruitful results can be achieved by making the patient realise or learn that a life without alcohol can be more satisfying than a life completely submerged in it. In every case the basic personality must be evaluated with the reactive events leading up to the drinking and the pattern of alcoholic behaviour. The amount of support from families and whether the employment or work is still open to them require investigation.

6. *Sociotherapy:* This treatment involves the modification of environmental situations, change in attitude, and the provision of healthy social gatherings and groups. It is directed towards counselling the patient's wife or family and helping him make a readjustment in the family and community setting. To heal their social contacts in the form of a religious gathering, social clubs emphasizing inspirational and spiritual elements may also prove useful in the treatment of alcoholics. The staging of plays, cultural programmes, showing of movies emphasizing the ill effects of alcoholism and the tranquillity of life may also prove valuable.

   Religious gatherings purify the path of an individual. He may be helped by the Almighty or religious ideas, certainly a power greater than himself, for admitting his mistakes, controlling his drinking with the provision of emotional support. The participation in the social groups like Alcoholic Anonymous (a group composed of people who have given up drinking) may also prove useful for alcoholics to enjoy social fellowships to gain insight into their behaviour and overcome their addiction.

7. *Duration of treatment and follow-up:* The duration of treatment in the case of alcoholics depends largely on the severity of the case. If they remain away from alcohol for five years, they can usually be regarded as cured. But there are many chances and incidences for relapse which is frequent in the first two years. Great care should thus be taken in follow up when treatment is over.

## Drug Addiction

Drug addiction, like alcoholism, is also detrimental to the individual, and the society. It concerns with an abnormal use of certain drugs like hashish, charas, marijuana, cocaine, LSD, mandrax, valium, Dexedrine and mephedrone. The excessive use of these intoxicating drugs leads to increased tolerance and physiological or psychological dependence. With prolonged use, the body system habituates to the particular drug so that larger doses are necessary to maintain similar intoxicating effects. Consequently, the individual develops an increasing physiological and psychological dependence on them to the extent that he feels miserable whenever a particular drug is not administered. He begins to show withdrawal symptoms like lack of appetite, loss of weight, constipation, restlessness, nervousness, nausea, vomiting, diarrhoea, disinterest in sexual and social relationships and even epileptic seizures or acute brain syndromes in some cases. Besides, there is an intense craving for a particular drug which he tries to gratify regardless of consequences. When this happens, the individual is said to be addicted to a particular drug.

This drug addiction is a state of acute intoxication, detrimental to the individual and to society, produced by the prolonged and excessive use of a drug, natural or synthetic, and characterized by (a) an intense craving or compulsion to obtain or consume it regardless of consequences; (b) a tendency to increase the dosage with time; (c) physiological and psychological dependence on the effects of the drug; and (d) manifestation of particular withdrawal symptoms on abrupt discontinuation of the drug.

## Drugs—Types and Effects

Depending upon the nature of their effects, drugs may be classified as stimulant, sedative and deliriant (mind blowing).

1. *Stimulant drugs*: These drugs stimulate the brain and sympathetic nervous system resulting in alertness and increase in response and motor activity. The major drugs of this category are nicotine, cocaine, caffeine, and amphetamines like benzedine, dexedrine and methedrine. The addiction to stimulant drugs makes an individual dependent, physiologically and psychologically, on its ever increasing doses for the continuous stimulation of sense organs. In the long run it results in severe loss of appetite and weight, constipation, increased anxiety and irritability, sleep deprivation, gradual impairment of intellectual functioning and periodic episodes of delirium.
2. *Sedative drugs*: These drugs slow down the activities of an organism and diminish the responses of the brain and nervous system. As a result they are used as pain

relievers and sleep inducers and may be classified as narcotics and hypnotics. The major narcotic drugs are opium, morphine, heroin, codeine, demerol and methadone and hypnotic drugs include barbiturates like amytal, nembutal, seconal, and non-barbiturates like bromides, and paraldehyde chloral hydrate.

The prolonged use of sedative drugs leads to increasing tolerance and physiological as well as psychological craving for them. The immediate effects are pleasant and there is relief from pain and lessening of voluntary movements followed by euphoria. But these effects are short-lived and are followed by a negative phase of craving for more of the drug and the consequent ill effects.

The addiction to narcotics results in loss of appetite and weight, constipation, lack of sexual desire and social interests. Unlike narcotics, the addiction to barbiturates and other hypnotics primarily affects the brain resulting in intellectual impairment and disturbance of the motor functions dependent on the cerebellum.

The sudden withdrawal of sedative drugs results in dangerous withdrawal symptoms like restlessness, nervousness, excessive perspiration, nausea, vomiting, diarrhoea, severe headache, marked tremors, cardio-vascular collapse and painful muscular cramps. In the case of hypnotics the withdrawal reactions may lead to epileptic seizures and delirium. If not treated in time, the seizures can cause death. Tranquillizers like meprobamate also result in addiction and have the same results as with most of the sedatives.

3. *Deliriant or mind-blowing drugs:* These drugs produce transient states resembling psychoses resulting in marked confusion, distortion in thought processes, delirium, illusions and hallucinations. Marijuana produces a euphoric state involving increased self confidence and a pleasant feeling of relaxation characterized by floating imagination. There is a considerable distortion of the sense of time and space. In some cases the individual becomes irritable. There is a marked impairment in the motor and intellectual functioning but the users usually thinks that their efficiency has increased. This false sense of adequacy gives rise to incidents of reckless driving and other antisocial episodes. In many individuals the intoxication of marijuana may produce acute psychotic reactions as found with hallucinogenic drugs.

   The most popular mind blowing or hallucinogenic drug is LSD – 25 or lysergic acid diethylamide. Other hard drugs of this category are mescaline (an alkaloid and the active ingredient of peyote), psilocybin (a crystalline powder from the mushroom) and bufotenine. The outward symptoms of LSD and other hallucinogenic drugs addiction bear a strong resemblance to the behaviour of schizophrenic patients. There, is marked confusion, muddling in one's thinking and development of visual and auditory hallucinations. There is a false sense of well-being and the patient gradually develops a high tolerance and dependence.

   Another drug of this category which is most abused is meth-amphetamine (speed) taken in the form of intravenous injection. Prolonged use of this drug results in malnutrition, brain damage, disturbance of the heart rhythm, and a dangerous impulsive, paranoid unpredictable behaviour.

## Causes of Drug Addiction

Drug addiction is caused in a similar way as alcohol addiction. The actual pattern of tolerance and physiological as well as psychological dependence on a particular drug is the result of the learning process. No one is born a drug dependent but actually becomes so in emulating the behaviour of parents, friends and other members of the society. The first dose may be taken in the form of prescribed medicine or out of curiosity, pursuit of fun and pleasure, looking for new thrills, new kicks and possibility of a mystic experience. Some resort to drugs for the sake of company and others may seek escape from boredom. The behaviour is reinforced and rewarded on account of the false impression of adequacy and well-being, temporary relief from anxiety, pleasant reverie, and short-lived pleasing effects or state of euphoria created by the drug. Gradually, larger and larger doses are needed for same results and one becomes dependent, physiologically as well as psychologically, on a particular drug. Thus what begins as an innocuous experiment ends in disaster.

According to experts, stress is a great factor in turning in individual into a drug addict. The highly competitive, success oriented style of living today creates many odds for a large number of young people. There is crisis of character and deterioration in values. While the aims of life and values of the elders are meaningless, the job opportunities for the youth are rare. The education serves no purpose and there arc inhibitions and taboos. All this leads one to stress situations. One tries to seek instant relief from frustration, tension, anxieties and depression by resorting to drugs. Others use drugs to free themselves from their inhibitions, and some turn to drugs because of guilt, shame, anxiety or disappointment in life.

## Prevention and Treatment of Addiction

Drug addiction is not a law and order problem as is imagined in certain circles. It is predominantly a social and psychological problem. Addicts should be distinguished from criminals who supply them with drugs and live off their misery. The irony of addicts is that they depend on drugs to the extent of pathological craving so powerful that they try and manage to get the drug regardless of legal or other obstacles. The following measures prove fruitful in the treatment of drug addicts.

1. *Compulsory hospitalization:* Compulsory institutionalization and hospitalization is a major step in the treatment of drug addicts. If the doctor waits until the patient voluntarily seeks effective treatment, he may well wait until the patient dies. Drug addicts do not want treatment, they want drugs and in their surroundings and environment they can't be deprived of drugs. The admission in hospitals may be able to cover the following major risks:
   (i) Rejection by family and society that can neither understand nor manage the patient, makes the patient depressed. This situation worsens when drugs are not available during the withdrawal phase.
   (ii) The tendency to go on to harder drugs or mixed drugs to get the desired effect may lead to disaster.
   (iii) There is a risk of killing himself by the patient on account of an accidental overdose or committing suicide when profoundly depressed or a misadventure under the intoxicating effects of drug.

(iv) There is a danger of infection or other complications when the drug is injected in the body by the individual.

2. *De-intoxicating or drying-out the patient: Attempts should **be*** made to de-intoxicate or dry out the patient. It may be achieved through (i) the 'cold turkey' procedure, that is, sudden total discontinuation of drugs; (ii) giving the patient progressively diminishing doses of drug leading towards complete cessation; and (iii) substituting a less addictive drug and later seeking gradual reduction of intake.

3. *Medical measures:* With some patients, especially psychotic addicts, ECT or tranquillizing drugs may prove quite helpful. Adequate care is to be taken for the provision of antibiotics as there is an inherent danger of possible infection. The withdrawal reactions should also be controlled as they lead to physical or mental disaster. Adequate dietary measures in the form of glucose and vitamins are to be ascertained for compensating the drug deficiency and also adequate feeding and fluids should be ensured.

4. *Psychological treatment:* Psychological treatment of drug addicts needs patience and time. Long range psychotherapy and socio-therapy is essential if the patient is to learn to face his problems and seek adjustment in the society without the use of the drug.

5. *Long-term therapy and rehabilitation: The long-term* therapy is also essential. It may be achieved as follows:

   (i) Re-personalization: The drug addicts should be helped to form a proper relationship with therapists, doctors and nurses before they can re-establish any personal identity.

   (ii) Specific therapy: Withdrawal reactions and complications should be well guarded against with the help of specific drugs. For example, epileptics may need anti-convulsant or schizophrenics may need phenothiazines.

   (iii) Re-socialization: The drug addicts must learn to socialize and adjust without the aid of drugs.

   (iv) Re-occupation: Once cured, the drug addicts should be helped in seeking employment and occupational adjustment. They need to be trained in the job skill and in persistence so that they may be accepted by their employers.

   (v) Re-housing: They should be helped in getting adequate family adjustment and re-establish themselves by learning to accommodate and fend for themselves.

   The duration and extent of long-term therapy depends upon the patient's potential, and the original level of maturity which the patient has reached. If adequately cared through therapy and rehabilitation, the patient should be able to lead a full life and to develop his potential abilities.

***Prevention:*** The primary task in the prevention involves educating the public about the causes and consequences of drug addiction. There is a need of restructuring unhealthy environment and reduction in the problems leading to frustrations, tensions and anxieties among the youth. Job opportunities have to be increased and the education system reshaped to include job-oriented and employment-based courses. The energies of students and youth should be channelized into constructive and creative projects like rural reconstruction, welfare of the society and nation, and helping the needy and the poor. This will give them a sense of purpose, an opportunity for adventure and new experiences which they seek by taking drugs. In outlining measures to prevent and control drug addiction the report of a committee headed by Dr C. Gopalan, Director-General, Indian Council of Medical Research, has enunciated the following five basic points for this purpose:

(i) Society can never be free of drugs, the reason being that drugs have specific individual and social purposes and as long as they are not met by other healthier means, drug use or abuse will continue to exist.

(ii) Efforts should be made to reduce the drug evil to the minimum by attacking it at various points, all along the line instead of concentrating the significant efforts at one point.

(iii) Drug abuse, which is a term of deviance, cannot be treated in isolation from other forms of deviance and an attempt at creating any special machinery for the control of the abuse will be counter-productive.

(iv) One should not lose one's perspective and create gigantic and costly structures to deal with the drug problems whose significance is limited in comparison with several other problems facing the country.

(v) All the drugs form a continuum and any overzealous effort to control one drug may lead to an increase in the use of another drug.

At present there are several central ministries in India each dealing with a particular aspect of drug- addiction. For controlling lack of Co-ordination and bringing efficiency the committee has given the following suggestions:

- There should be an integrated machinery like national advisory board with the health minister as its chairman, and comprising representatives of all other ministries and professional organisations concerned with the problem. It will help in the formulation of a comprehensive and balanced policy to prevent and control drug abuse.
- The committee suggested legislation and a single central law instead of many laws dealing with the problem resulting from the dependence-producing drugs. The severity of control and regulation should depend upon the extent to which the drug finds use in medical practice, its potential for abuse, and the gravity of the consequences. On this basis it has been suggested that hallucinogens like LSD, heroin, hashish and charas should be prohibited since these are harmful and have no medicinal value.
- The committee wants deterrent penal provisions against the smuggling of and trade in drugs on the lines of other leading countries like Japan, U.S.A. and Singapore. Whereas addicts should be regarded with sympathy as sick persons and should be permitted, under certain conditions, to possess specified drugs in specific quantities, the traffickers should be dealt with firmly.

## Summary

- *Alcoholism:* The term alcoholism refers to excessive drinking or dependence on alcoholic beverages to the extent of disrupting life and malfunctioning of the behaviour causing severe physiological, psychological and social damage.
- *Phases of alcoholism:* The initial pre-alcoholic phase lasts from two months up to two years and is characterized by a gradual shift from infrequent or light to frequent or heavy drinking. In the second prodromal phase, alcohol is used more as a drug and less as a beverage. In the third crucial phase the dependency on alcohol increases to the extent that there is a danger of losing everything that one values. In the last 'chronic phase' the individual lives only to drink.
- *Effect:* An alcoholic is likely to be ruined in terms of his physical or mental health, emotional and social relationships, and economic and moral assets.
- *Causes:* No person is born alcoholic and therefore the causes of alcoholism are purely environmental. Drinking is learned and acquired like many personality traits and later maintained on account of its physiological and psychological dependence that it provides.
- *Treatment:* Alcoholism is a medical and psychological problem rather than a law and order problem. For treatment, beginning is made with the diagnosis of the early warning signals of alcoholism and then followed with (i) keeping away alcoholics from any aversive life situation and controlling their behaviour; (ii) providing for essential clinical investigations; (iii) de-intoxicating; (iv) using deterrent measures in the form of aversion therapy; (v) providing group or individual psycho-therapy for gaining insight into behaviour and adequate adjustment; and (vi) providing socio-therapy involving modification of environmental situation and improvement of social adjustment.
- *Drug addiction:* It is a state of acute intoxication, detrimental to the individual and to society, produced by the prolonged excessive use of a drug. Drugs may be classified as stimulant, sedative and deliriant depending upon the nature of their effects. There are the stimulants like nicotine, cocaine, caffeine and amphetamines; sedatives like opium, morphine, heroin and methadone; and hypnotics like barbiturates, and non-barbiturates, deliriants like marijuana, LSD and methamphetamine.
- *Causes of drug addiction*: These are purely environmental and drug addiction is a matter of learned behaviour, and an inadequate adjustment to the stresses of life and style of living.
- *Prevention and control:* It involves measures like (i) education of the public to understand causes and consequences of drug addiction; (ii) re-structuring unhealthy environmental and reduction in the problems leading to frustration, tension and anxieties among the citizens; (iii) prohibition of low medicinal value and harmful drugs; (iv) deterrent panel provisions against the smuggling of and trade in drugs.
- *Treatment*: It involves (i) compulsory hospitalization; (ii) de-intoxicating; (iii) adoption of medical measures; (iv) introduction of psychological treatment; and (v) arranging for long-term therapy and rehabilitation.

## REFERENCES

Jellinek, E.M. (Ed.), (1942), *Alcohol Addiction and Chronic Alcoholism,* New Haven: Yale University Press.

World Health Organization (1969), Quoted by Shanmugam, T.E., ***Abnormal Psychology***, New Delhi: Tata McGraw Hill, 1981.

# 18

# SEXUAL DEVIATIONS AND DISORDERS

Deviation is a term used for explaining significant difference from the average or norm. A deviant behaviour is apart from or contrary to the established or acceptable behaviour in a given culture or society. Sexual deviation, in this sense, does not conform to the norms of one's culture and society. Besides, what is regarded as sexual deviation or perversion in one society or culture may be regarded as normal or acceptable in another culture or society. For example, kissing in public is an acceptable sexual behaviour in most of the western countries, whereas it is regarded a sexual deviation or even offence in many eastern countries. Similarly, deviant behaviour like homosexuality, exhibitionism, promiscuity, prostitution, may be regarded acceptable and normal in some cultures and societies

Sexual deviation has been defined as follows:

*George W. Kisker:* Sexual behaviour is more likely to be considered abnormal or deviant only when it interferes with personal and social adjustment—when it is self defeating or damaging to others. (1964:168)

*Rosen Fox and Gregory:* A failure of development associated with anxiety and conflict culminating in a persistent or frequently recurring preference for any form of sexual behaviour that is a substitute for, and does not terminate in, genital coitus with an adult of the opposite sex, is a sexual deviation. (1972:273)

*Anthony Storr:* Sexual deviation can only be understood as failure in the quite complicated process of learning how to love— it is the compulsive substitution of something else for heterosexual intercourse in circumstances where the latter is available. (1964:78)

In the light of the above definitions and recent researches in the field of human sexual behaviour the following conclusion may be drawn about the meaning and nature of sexual deviation.

Sex is one of the major instinctual drives and essential needs. Although people live in spite of sexual deprivation, yet they may never live life to the full without its gratification. To enable one to gratify one's sex need may be a natural instinct but to seek its gratification in some socially desirable ways is the matter of one's learning from elders and environment. In addition to being socially acceptable, a normal sexual behaviour should fulfil the following conditions:

- Sexual gratification is to be received from the adult members of the opposite sex.
- Genital coitus is to be preferred to other modes of sexual gratification.
- It should not be engaged in the attitude of shame, disgust, fear, guilt or inferiority,
- It should neither cause harm to the individuals concerned nor to others.
- It should not cause personal or social maladjustment.

This means that sexual deviation may be understood in terms of learned persistent habit patterns of sexual behaviour which compel an individual to seek sexual gratification from unconventional sources and means other than the genital coitus with an adult member of the opposite sex irrespective of the fact that such natural gratification is available.

## Sexual Deviation and Sexual Offence

It is important to distinguish between 'sexual deviation' and 'sexual offence'. Although most deviations are also sexual offences and vice versa, yet it is not always true. The genital intercourse with an adult member of the opposite sex is considered normal behaviour. But sexual intercourse with the adult member of the opposite sex without his or her consent cannot be termed deviance but a sexual offence in the form of rape and sexual assault. In some countries forcible intercourse even with one's spouse is termed a sexual offence. Similarly, extra marital intercourse even with an adult willing member of the opposite sex is a sexual offence, whereas it cannot be called sexual deviation or perversion in the strict sense of the term. A further distinction between these terms may be made on the ground that where there is an unique stress or persistence in habit patterns in the case of sexual deviations, an occasional departure from an accepted normal behaviour of the society or legal code is enough to label it as a sexual offence.

## Sexual Deviation and Sexual Disorder

Sexual deviation refers to persistence habit patterns of compulsive preference for the unconventional objects or means for the sexual gratification other than genital intercourse with an adult member of the opposite sex. One engages in such behaviour of his own will and purpose and seeks satisfaction of the strong sex urge or compulsion. Sexual deviation in this way, is a psychological phenomenon.

On the other hand, sexual disorders like impotence or frigidity involve the physiological systems too. There is lack of coordination between the sympathetic and parasympathetic systems in impotence and frigidity. They may also be the result of psychological factors like anxiety or guilt. The individual is unable to derive gratification on account of the feeling of inadequacy or a state of incapacity caused by physiological or psychological factors. Such disorders cannot be termed sexual deviation as the individual does not deviate from the norms of the sexual behaviour. Moreover, sexual deviations cannot be termed sexual offences and are not punishable by law as they are not social or legal offences.

## Forms of Sexual Deviations

Sexual deviations may take various forms. In some cases a person of the same sex, or a child or a very close relative or a corpse is used as an object for the sexual act. In others, although the partner may be adult and of the opposite sex, genital intercourse is avoided and some other act substituted for it. Likewise, in some others, no second person is directly involved, but sexual gratification is obtained from objects other than people or from observing the sexual activities of others or exhibiting one's genital organs. In still others, the person himself acts as an object for deviation as found in autoerotic masturbation, transvestism and transsexualism.

The following are some of the major sexual deviations:

1. *Paedophilia*: In this type of deviation, the adult deviant takes a child, girl or boy, for any sexual activity – masturbatory, oral, and or genital. The deviant is usually male and may be of passive or aggressive nature. The passive type desires the child as a love object and often persuades the child for willing partnership. An aggressive type inflicts sexual abuse on the child while sadistically hurting or punishing the child. Paedophilia is dangerous as it leads to physical violence and psychological damage to the victim.

2. *Homosexuality:* In this type of deviation, sexual pleasure is derived from members of the same sex. This deviation may occur among both sexes-males and females. The words 'lesbian' and 'Sapphic' are sometimes used to describe erotic love between women. Overt homosexuality may take the form of mutual masturbation, oral-genital activity (the opposition of mouth to the genitals), and sodomy (intercourse per anus usually performed in male homosexuality). It is quite frequent to play masculine or feminine roles. Thus homosexual behaviour for one or the other partner in the oral or anal sexual behaviour of a male homosexual may be active or passive depending upon his masculine or feminine role. In attempting intercourse, the active male homosexuals use the anus of their passive homosexual partner as a substitute for the vagina.

   One may ask whether the erotic love between the two partners of the same sex may be termed sexual deviation. The accidental or occasional homosexuality occurring under circumstances where the individual has no access to the opposite sex (as found in military service, prisons and boarding schools) cannot be termed sexual deviation in the strictest sense. Similarly, homosexual partnership for women who, for whatever reasons, have no access to male partners should not be taken as deviant behaviour. It becomes deviation only when homosexual partnership is preferred even when the heterosexual partnership is available.

3. *Heterosexual oralism and analism*: In this type of deviation the individual, in spite of having an adult member of the opposite sex as sex partner, does not perform genital intercourse but tries to seek sexual gratification with the exclusive reliance on the anus instead of the vagina for penile insertion. Such behaviour is termed sexual analism. When the deviant depends exclusively on oral genital contacts for gratifying his or her sex needs, such behaviour is referred to as sexual oralism and may take the following forms:

   - Masturbation
   - Cunnilingus, the opposition of mouth to the female genitals.
   - Fellation, the opposition of mouth to the male genitals.

- Exclusive reliance on fore play at the cost of displeasing the partner.

4. *Sadism and masochism* : The term 'sadism' is used to describe the sexual deviation in which erotic excitement or pleasure is derived from the infliction of pain upon the partner. The pain may be inflicted physically by such means as biting, pinching, whipping, mutilating and even committing murder or psychologically by means of abusing or criticism. The term 'masochism', on the other hand, refers to the deviation in which sexual gratification is achieved in being punished or experiencing pain.

   The pain and punishment in these deviations becomes the source of erotic excitement and pleasure. Actually, to engage in minor sadistic or masochistic behaviour or rituals cannot be termed deviation. It is only when such behaviour is extreme or divorced from sexual intercourse, that it can be termed a deviation. A true sadist or masochist obtains sexual gratification from the sadistic or masochistic practice irrespective of the consequences. Sadistic behaviour is often more dangerous than masochism. The sadist wants to hurt while the victim is unwilling and the offender violent.

5. *Fetishism* : The term fetishism is applied to a sexual deviation in which magic appears to reside, not in a whole person but in a part of the person, or an object connected with the person. The fetishist feels a compulsive and irrational sexual attraction towards an inanimate object such as undergarment, shoe, fur, or glove, or is fascinated by some parts of the body other than the genitals such as the buttocks, thighs, feet, breasts or hair. In extreme forms of fetishism such body parts or inanimate objects become most preferred source of sexual attraction and gratification. A fetishist has no desire and gets no pleasure from genital intercourse or other forms of love making with a partner of the same or opposite sex.

6. *Zoophilia or bestiality:* In this type of deviation, animals are used for the achievement of sexual excitation and gratification. The actual sexual pattern may involve masturbation by rubbing against the body of the animal, oral genital contacts, masturbation or actual sexual intercourse. The dependence on animals as an object for sexual gratification becomes pathological where the individual prefers such mode of sex gratification to heterosexual relationship.

7. *Necrophilia:* In this deviation, sexual excitation and gratification is sought through viewing or actually having sexual relations with a dead body. This is a comparatively rare deviation observed in psychopathological males.

8. *Incest* : This deviation is sexual activity between close blood relation, prohibited in a given culture or society such as between a brother and a sister, father and daughter, mother and son, man and his grand-daughter or wife of his son, woman and her grand-son or husband of her daughter, etc. Such incest taboos are essential to prevent a disruption of community and family life.

9. *Exhibitionism:* Exhibitionism is a sexual deviation in which gratification is obtained by exposing the genitals publicly usually to members of the opposite sex or to children who are involuntary observers or completely strangers. It is more

exclusively a male deviation; for although females may expose the genitals or may appear nude or semi-nude in an advertisement, film or other public shows, this is done at the behest of and for the pleasure of others and is never resorted to by females as a means of obtaining sexual gratification.

The urge to expose is overwhelming and virtually uncontrollable and occurs again and again usually in the same place and at the same time of the day in spite of penalties and treatment. Although a male exhibitionist hurts his victim, yet his behaviour is not as threatening and aggressive as in the case of sadism or sexual assault, molestation or rape. His gratification comes from observing her reaction, which is a mixture of surprise, fear, disgust and resentment. The deviation becomes a serious problem when it is a compulsive exclusive mode of seeking sexual gratification.

10. *Voyeurism or scopophilia:* In this deviation sexual gratification is obtained through clandestine peeping and observation of the genitals or sexual behaviour of others. The curiosity to see the genital organs of the opposite sex and watch other people or animals engaged in sexual activity is so widespread that it seems difficult to label voyeurism as a sexual deviation. It may be regarded as a deviation, when it is substituted for other conventional methods of gratification, preferred even to coitus or indulged in at serious risk.

11 *Frotteurism:* In this deviation, sexual satisfaction is obtained by rubbing or pressing against a member of the opposite sex. Mostly in a crowded or lonely place the males try to seek sex gratification by rubbing or pressing the buttocks, hips, breasts or genitals of the females or rubbing their own genitals against the body of the female without engaging in sexual intercourse. Such advances, though distasteful to women, are not always repelled. There can be few men who have not experienced something of frotteurism urge in crowded fairs, religious gatherings, buses or other places where they are liable to be pressed against women. However, this natural urge becomes deviation when it is strongly compulsive and is substituted for other conventional methods of sexual satisfaction.

12. *Transvetism and transsexualism:* The term transvetism is applied to sexual arousal or gratification by wearing clothes appropriate to the opposite sex while regarding himself or herself as a member of his or her own sex. They may also enjoy appearing socially as a member of the opposite sex.

    In case when an individual dresses himself or herself as a member of the opposite sex by believing that nature has been very cruel by giving him or her wrong body, he or she is called transsexual. Transsexuals are unable to achieve sexual gratification as members of their own sex and often take the drastic steps of undergoing ***sex-change surgery.***

## Causes of Sexual Deviation

It is often thought that sexual deviations result on account of defective biological make up—chromosomal abnormalities or abnormalities of endocrine functions—but it has not been proved true as no consistent abnormalities have been observed in any group of sexual deviates. So far the most reasonable and satisfactory causes of sexual deviations are provided by the interaction of several psychological factors. The dynamics of these factors may involve the following patterns.

1. *Pathogenic family environment:* All learning begins at home. The pathogenic family environment is the primary source of causing abnormalities in sex behaviour. The child may copy the abnormal sex behaviour of his parents or elders in the family. He may be shocked at the disharmony, frequent quarrelling between parents, or may develop a distaste or unconscious fear for natural sex behaviour on account of the uncongenial home environment and unpleasant relationships. His natural behaviour may deviate on account of parental rejection or isolation from other children. The needs related with psychological or biological satisfaction may lead him to be trapped in sexual deviation as and when he finds opportunities to do so.

2. *Earlier traumatic sex experiences*: Many times, earlier sexual experiences and episodes start the process of deviation. Homosexuality, for example, may he primarily the result of an experiment of a child or an adolescent with someone of the same age or education by an older homosexual. Similarly, sexual assault of a minor girl by an adult may prove damaging to her normal sex behaviour and thus lead her towards sexual deviations.

3. *Generalized inhibitions and sexual ignorance*: Sex is regarded taboo in most of the societies. There is a natural craving for seeking information on account of the sex-related curiosities among children and youth. This craving coupled with adventurism leads them to unusual experimentation, wrong notions and practices about sex. Sex ignorance may be responsible for many sexual complications, fears and complexes ultimately resulting in abnormal sex behaviour,

4. *Deprivation of outlet for normal sex behaviour*: Sex is a powerful basic urge. It begins to dominate one's behaviour especially after attaining puberty. The denial of satisfaction of this basic need through normal ways may force an individual to seek gratification in unconventional objects or methods. A lonely father deprived of sexual relationship may lean towards his charming preadolescent daughter for his gratification. Under similar conditions or deprivation, an adult may be persuaded to adopt exhibitionism, voyeurism, paedophilia, homosexuality, bestiality or even necrophilia as a substitute for conventional sex behaviour. The individual involved in abnormal behaviour on account of the deprivation never likes to abandon the deviation at a later stage.

5. *Fear and complexes associated with opposite sex and normal sex behaviour:* Many times abnormal sex behaviour is caused by the fear and complexes associated with the members of the opposite sex and establishment of normal sex behaviour with them. Whenever an individual is ridiculed, rebuffed and humiliated in his efforts to approach members of the opposite sex or suffers failures and frustrations in his sex advances, and sex act, he may turn towards other safer sources of affection and sexual outlet. A traumatic experience with natural sexual outlet may develop a number of complexes and feelings of inferiority about one's sexual adequacy and may lead the individual to avoid the conventional

outlet for gratification. Heterosexual frustrations also lead to fear and develop excessive anxiety concerning sex behaviour with the members of the opposite sex or partner. These fears, anxieties and complexes end in a unique distaste for normal sex behaviour.

6. *Conditioning to suitable abnormal pattern of sex behaviour*: Prolonged deprivation of natural sexual outlet or the feelings of hostility, apathy and fear towards conventional sex objects and practices may lead an individual to seek a convenient and safer abnormal pattern of sex behaviour. In case such opportunities are available or he is helped by the older deviants or incidental situations, he may find himself engaging in his first abnormal behaviour. The perpetuation of the sexual deviation now depends upon the result of this first experience. If he gets reward in terms of sexual gratification his behaviour is reinforced. Gradually, he learns to use similar objects or methods for the satisfaction of the sex needs.

7. *Fixation of abnormal sex behaviour:* Encouraged by or satisfied with adopted abnormal pattern of sex behaviour, one is habituated to use it for sex gratification. This behaviour gets fixed on account of the following reasons:
   - One may think it as a convenient means of meeting sex needs.
   - One may resort to it for avoiding possible sex failures and frustrations.
   - One may consider it as safer means of hiding sexual inadequacies and incompetencies
   - One may find it as the most pleasurable act.

The repeated acts of abnormal sex behaviour condition an individual to depend completely on one or more abnormal patterns of sex behaviour for the gratification of sex needs. The individual is no more inclined towards the conventional sex-objects or methods and if provided opportunities, is compelled to prefer unconventional ones to conventional. When that happens, we may label the individual as sexually deviated or perverted.

## Treatment of Sexual Deviations

The treatment of sexual deviations is no different from the treatment of other types of abnormal behaviour. This behaviour, caused by fears, anxieties and complexes related with sex, is the result of the learning of maladaptive responses through early conditioning and fixation at the later stage. The causes are more psychological than anything else and therefore the treatment measures have to be psychological. Various psychotherapies, designed to help the patient gain insight into his motivations, change his basic attitudes and work out more acceptable patterns of sex behaviour are used. Individual and group psychotherapies yield encouraging results for correcting sexual deviates.

In most cases, behaviour therapy proves effective in alleviating the fear, anxiety and complexes related with the opposite sex and normal sex patterns. An appropriate counselling providing adequate sex -information and proper sex techniques proves beneficial for the majority of sexual deviates. As a result, the inhibited deviate may be helped to be less prudish. One may be persuaded to shift from an undesirable object or method to a desirable one.

It is important to note that sexual deviation or perversion cannot be treated through punitive measures. It is a behavioural problem and therefore attempts should be made for effective psychological treatment with adequate follow-up programme of proper rehabilitation.

## Sexual Disorders

Sexual disorders refer to those psycho-physiological disturbances that interfere with the fully enjoyment of conventional sexual relations. As a result genital intercourse, the most lovable and enjoyable sex act, is turned into an unhappy, un-enjoyable ritual for one or both the partners. Impotence and frigidity are the two main sexual disorders of such nature.

### Impotence

Impotence refers to that psycho-physiological disturbance in the sexual behaviour of a man which causes an impairment in his desire for sexual gratification or an inability to achieve' it. This sexual disorder or inadequacy is of the following forms:

1. *Primary impotence*: It refers to the case where the male has never been able to achieve an erection sufficient for successful intercourse, either heterosexual or homosexual.
2. *Situational secondary impotence:* If refers to the case where a male finds himself unable to achieve an erection sufficient for successful intercourse, either heterosexual or homosexual but has been able to do so in the past.
3. *Incidental permanent impotence :* It refers to the case where a person being previously able to get an erection and maintain sexual relations, incidentally develops a permanent impairment in his sexual potency on account of some chronic illness, drug addiction, injuries to the genitalia or disease of the nervous system.
4. *Ejaculatory impotence*: In this type of impotence or sexual inadequacy, the man is unable to inhibit ejaculation long enough for his female partner to have orgasm or sexual satisfaction. In some cases, he ejaculates even without an erection or intromission and in other during penetration or just after intromission. In some rare disorders, he is unable to ejaculate intra-vaginally although erections and intromissions are normal.

### Frigidity

Frigidity is the most common sex-disorder found in females. It is the counterpart of male impotence. Frigid women show considerable lack of interest in desire for sexual gratification or find it difficult to achieve it in their sexual behaviour. This sexual disorder may have some of the following forms.

1. *Primary frigidity*: This refers to the case where a woman has never had an orgasm (ability to get sexual gratification as experienced by a normal sexually adequate female) from either masturbation or intercourse. In a more severe case she experiences no desire for sexual gratification.
2. *Situational secondary frigidity*: This refers to the case where a woman is unable to have orgasms or responds negatively to erotic responses in a specific situation.

## Causes of Impotence and Frigidity

Impotence and frigidity are often accompanied with lack of desire for sexual gratification but it is not always true. Sometimes, despite one's desire to seek sexual gratification, one fails to achieve it on account of his own failure or failure on the part of his or her partner. The possible causes of these disorders may be listed below:

*Physiological factors*: Impotence and frigidity may be attributed to some physical damage to the sex organs or nervous system on account of disease, physical injuries and physiological malfunctioning. In many cases drugs are held responsible for impotence and frigidity. These are phenothiazines (especially Melleril), Similarly, monoamine oxidase inhibitors with tricyclic antidepressants decrease libido. Contraceptive pills also decrease sexual activity. Many illnesses, especially serious infections, diabetes, chronic tuberculosis, cancer growth and malignancy may lead to serious sexual inadequacies on account of the damage to sexual organs or nervous system. Aortic disease may affect the presacral nerves and therefore cause failure of erection. Similarly, clitoral, vaginal or penile infection, biological deformities of the sex organs, malfunctioning of the sex glands may cause sexual apathy and inadequacy.

*Psychological factors*: The cases of impotence and frigidity on account of physiological factors are quite rare. They are more often caused on account of psychological causes resulting from the interaction of one's; self with the circumstances and situations in one's environment. The major psychological factors may be grouped as below:

- Sex guilt
- Fear and complexes surrounding sex.
- Depressions
- Lack of emotional closeness or affection between the sex- partners.
- Sex frustrations.
- Latent or overt homosexuality.
- Sexual perversion or deviation.
- Bed-room mistakes and faulty techniques.

The psychological reasons leading to a feeling of inadequacy in males or females is a learned response. It may be the result of faulty earlier training or experiences for a female who comes to know about the sexual relations as dirty, bad, lustful, evil and harmful. For a male, the fear and anxiety related with inadequacy may work as a potent factor for causing impotency. The lack of emotional closeness to the sex-partner always results in sexual failure causing disappointment, anxiety and self devaluation to one or both the partners. In some cases the feelings of hostility give rise to lack of sexual desire and non-cooperation in the sex act leading to frigidity or impotence. A failure and dissatisfaction in a single act of erotic love and intercourse may either lead to unnecessary hostility and resentment towards the other partner or it may develop fear, anxiety related to one's inadequacy. A vicious circle thus starts the fears and doubts about one's inadequacy and feeling or hostility or frustration may make one less adequate and more hostile or apathetic towards other.

*Prevention of sexual disorders:* It is difficult to control sexual disorders caused by physiological factors like physical injuries to the sex organs, damaging of the nervous system, or severe disturbances of the body chemistry. The preventive measures may prove useful in such cases but not always. The permanent damage done on account of the physical factors is incurable and therefore much attention has to be paid to the sexual disorders caused by psychological factors. The following measures prove fruitful in the prevention of psychological impotence and frigidity:

- Proper sex-education of parents and other members of the society.
- Proper sex-education of the youngsters, adult members before marriage.
- Proper sex-education of the married couple for maintaining ideal sexual relationship emphasizing the knowledge and skill of love-play and sex-techniques.

*Treatment*: The only effective means of treatment of impotence and frigidity consists in the establishment of a stable, intimate, affectionate relationship involving confidence, security and love. A number of psychological therapies like analytical psychotherapy, behaviour therapy, client centred therapy, family and couple therapy gestalt therapy, and group psychotherapy may be attempted for this purpose.

In attempting the treatment, a therapist must take it for granted that leaving aside a few exceptions there are no impotent men or frigid women. They are the victims of situations and events. Their behaviour is a consequence of unhappy sex-experiences and inadequate sex knowledge. Therefore, it is a matter of sexual re-education, de-conditioning of unhappy experiences, removing of unnecessary fear complexes and feelings of inadequacies and eliminating the mental block responsible for the lack of adequate sex response which is to be aimed in any therapeutic measure suitable in a particular case of impotence or frigidity.

## Summary

*Sexual deviations*: These are learned persistent habit patterns of sexual behaviour which compel an individual to seek sexual gratification from unconventional sources and means other than the genital coitus with an adult member of the opposite sex irrespective of the fact that such natural gratification is available.

*Major sexual deviations:*

- Paedophilia involves the deviant behaviour in which an adult picks up a child, girl or boy for sexual activity.
- Homosexuality refers to the deviation in which one prefers to obtain sexual pleasure from the members of the same sex.
- Oralism is the dependence on oral genital contacts for gratifying sex needs.
- Analism refers to exclusive reliance on the anus instead of the vagina for penile insertion.
- Sadism is sexual gratification from the infliction of pain upon the sexual partner.
- Masochism is sexual gratification from being punished or experiencing pain.
- Fetishism is a compulsive and irrational sexual attraction and obtaining sexual gratification from inanimate objects or part of the body other than the genitals.
- Bestiality means using animals for the achievement of sexual excitation and gratification.

- Necrophilia is obtaining sexual gratification through viewing or actually having sexual relations with a dead body.
- Incest is sexual activity between close blood relations.
- Exhibitionism is sexual gratification obtained by exposing the genitals publicly usually to member of the opposite sex or to children who are involuntary observers or complete strangers.
- Voyeurism is sexual gratification obtained through peeping, observation of the genitals or sexual behaviour of others.
- Frotteurism is sexual gratification obtained by rubbing or pressing against a member of the opposite sex.
- Transvestism is sexual gratification obtained by wearing clothes appropriate to the opposite sex.
- Transsexualism is behaving and believing firmly in the change of his or her sex.

*Causes of sexual deviations*: Sexual deviations are, to a great extent, produced by the interaction of several psychological factors. The dynamics of these factors involves the patterns like (i) pathogenic family environment, (ii) earlier traumatic sex-experiences, (iii) generalized inhibitions, and sexual ignorance, (iv) deprivations of outlet for normal sex behaviour, (v) fear and complexes associated with opposite sex and normal sex-behaviour; and (vi) conditioning and fixation of suitable abnormal pattern of sex behaviour.

*Treatment*: Treatment measures are psychological. Psychotherapies like behaviour therapy, analytical therapy and group therapy prove effective in dealing with the sexual deviates. These psychological treatments should be followed by an adequate follow-up programme of proper rehabilitation.

*Sexual disorders:* These are psycho-physiological disturbances that interfere with the full enjoyment of the conventional sexual relations. Impotence and frigidity arc the two main disorders of such nature. Impotence causes impairment in desire for sexual gratification in a man or an inability to achieve it. Frigidity, the counterpart of impotence, is found in females. It creates in them a lack of interest and desire for sexual gratification or difficulty in achieving it.

*Causes:* In some cases, impotence and frigidity may be attributed to physical damage to sex organs or nervous system. But more often they are caused on account of psychological effects, resulting from the interaction of one's environment. These disorders involving the feeling of inadequacies are the learned responses involving factors like sex guilt, fear, complexes, depressions, conflicts, frustrations, sexual perversion and bed-room mistakes.

*Prevention:* Preventive measures should be adopted for the avoidance of physical injury to the sex organs and nervous system. In psychological measures of prevention, proper sex education of parents and adult members (before and after the marriage) may prove fruitful.

*Treatment*: The treatment often consists in establishing a stable, intimate, affectionate relationship involving confidence, security and love. A number of psychological therapies like behaviour, analytical, family and couple therapy may be successfully attempted for this purpose. In some cases of impotence and frigidity medical measures may also prove effective.

## REFERENCES

Kisker, George W. (1964), ***The Disorganised Personality***, (3rd International Students Edition), New York: McGraw-Hill.

Rosen, E., Fox and Gregory (1972), ***Abnormal Psychology***, (2nd, International Student Edition), Philadelphia: Saunders

Storr, Anthony (1964), Sexual Deviation, London: Penguin Books

# 19

# ATTENTION-DEFICIT/ HYPERACTIVITY DISORDER (ADHD) AND AUTISM

In the latest classification of mental disorders, DSM-5 provided by American Psychiatric Association in 2013, the disorders designated as Attention-Deficit or Hyperactivity Disorder (ADHD), and Autism (discussed in the name of *Autism Spectrum Disorder*) fall in the category of Neurodevelopmental disorders. In this sense both of these mental disorders represent the specific disabilities in the functioning of the brain that emerges at birth or very early childhood and affect the individual's behaviour, memory, concentration, and /or ability to learn. These disorders often have significant impact throughout the person's life. In this very chapter we would be concentrating on the discussion of these two disorders. Let us first begin with ADHD.

**What is Attention-Deficit Hyperactivity-Disorder (ADHD)?**

In its simple meaning as suggested through its naming Attention-Deficit Hyperactivity Disorder or briefly referred as ADHD stands for a type of behavioural disorder characterized by the significant deficit and deficiencies in one's attention behaviour devoid of necessary self-restraint. Various authors and researchers have provided their own conception and definitions for the term ADHD. We can take considerable help from their point of view for understanding what ADHD does really mean.

*Barkley*: ADHD is a development disorder of self-control. It consists of problem with attention span, impulse control, and activity level. .... It is not just a temporary state that will be outgrown, a trying but normal phase of childhood. It is not caused by parental failure to discipline or control the child, ant it is not a sign of some sort of inherent "badness" in the child. ADHD is real – a real disorder, a real problem, and often a real obstacle. It can be heartbreaking and nerve-wracking. **(2000:9)**

*Cooper and Bilton:* Attention Deficit/Hyperactivity Disorder (AD/HD) is a medical diagnosis that is applied to children and adults who are experiencing significant behavioural and cognitive difficulties in important aspects of their lives (e.g. in their familial and personal relationships; at school or work). These difficulties can be attributed to problems of impulse control, hyperactivity and inattention. It is believed that these problems are caused primarily by dysfunctions in the frontal lobes of the brain. **(2002:9)**

*Nichcy* : Attention Deficit/Hyperactive Disorder (AD/HD) is a condition that can make it hard for a person to sit still, control behaviour, and pay attention. These difficulties usually begin before the person in 7 years old. However, these behaviours may not be noticed until the child is older. Doctors do not know just what causes ADHD. However, researchers who study the brain are coming closer to understanding what may cause ADHD. They believe that some people with ADHD do not have enough of certain chemicals (called neurotransmitters) in their brain. These chemicals help the brain control behaviour." **(2004)** (Fact Sheet, 19)

*Goldstein*: ADHD is characterized by a constellation of problems with inattention, hyperactivity and impulsivity. These problems are developmentally inappropriate and cause difficulty in daily life. **(1999)**

The definitions and views cited above may help us to draw the following conclusions about the meaning and nature of the Attention-Deficit Hyperactivity Disorder (ADHD).

- It is a quite chronic behaviour or psychological disorder of childhood (usually beginning in the early school years) that may follow them to their adult years, if not diagnosed and treated properly earlier.
- It may cause them to experience significant behavioural and cognitive difficulties in their day-to-day life, schooling and work situations at the different stages of their life.
- Parents and teachers cannot be blamed for the upsurge of this disorder in the children. It is not caused by parental or school failure to discipline or control the child.
- Although what causes ADHD exactly is not known, yet the researchers believe that it is resulted through some deficiencies or dysfunctions of the brain (caused through genetic inheritance or injury to the brain).
- Deficiencies like deficits in certain chemicals called neurotransmitters and dysfunctions of certain lobes of the brain bring impairment in the controlling functions of the brain. It is responsible for making the affected child disabled in terms of self-control.
- Inability in exercising self-control may give birth to three major problems particularly related to inattention, hyperactivity (exhibiting too much acting out behaviours) and impulsivity (acting without thinking), the very hallmarks or symptoms of the ADHD.
- The symptoms of ADHD provide red signals for taking its cognition at the earliest possible. Its presence in the children provides a big challenge to the parents and teachers in terms of its control and treatment. If not cared properly, it may cause unimaginable damage not only to the affected child but also may prove a source of danger to the well being of the society.

  Known in this way, we can draw the following summarized conclusion of ADHD about the nature and concept of ADHD.

*Attention Deficit Hyperactivity disorder (ADHD) refers to a type of behavioural or psychological disorder of childhood often visible in the early years of schooling. It has been found to be caused by the biological reasons mainly associated with deficiencies and dysfunctions of brain generating a lack of ability in exercising self control for making one the victim of three major problems namely inattention, hyperactivity and impulsivity chronic enough for causing serious difficulties in one or more major life areas, home, school, work or social relationships.*

An example of an ADHD child 'Danny' given below may reveal you exactly what the ADHD is.

> Danny, a handsome 9-year-old boy, was referred to us because of his difficulties at school and at a home. Danny had a great deal of energy and loved playing most sports, especially baseball. Academically, his work was adequate, although his teacher reported that his performance was diminishing and she believed he would do better if he paid more attention in class. Danny rarely spent more than a few minutes on a task without some interruption: He would go up out of his seat, riffle through his desk, or constantly ask questions. His peers were frustrated with him because he was equally impulsive during their interactions: He never finished a game, and in sports he tried to play all positions simultaneously.
>
> At home, Danny was considered a handful. His room was in a constant mess because he became engaged in a game or activity only to drop it and initiate something else. Danny's parents reported that they often scolded him for not carrying out some task, although the reason seemed to be that he forgot what he was doing rather than that he deliberately tried to defy them. They also said that, out of their own frustration, they sometimes grabbed him by the shoulders and yelled "Slow down!" because his hyperactivity drove them crazy.

*Source:* Durand and Barlow (2013:486)

The behaviour demonstrated by the child in the above example, may be helpful in lime lighting the important symptoms and characteristics about the children suffering from ADHD such as below:

- Having great difficulty attending to tasks, or behave over-actively and impulsively, or both. ADHD often appears very early in life, before the child starts school.
- The symptoms of ADHD often feed into one another. Children who have trouble focusing attention may keep turning from task to task until they end up trying to run in several directions at once. Similarly, children who move constantly may find it hard to attend to tasks or show good judgment.
- In many cases, one of these symptoms stands out much more than the other. About half of the children with ADHD also have learning or communication problems; many perform poorly in school; a number have difficulty interacting with other children, and about 80 percent misbehave, often quite seriously.
- It is also common for these children to have anxiety or mood problems. (Comer, 2015:583)

## Diagnosis of ADHD

Diagnosis of ADHD among the children is not a simple task. The children affected with ADHD do not differ significantly from the non-affected normal children in terms of physical appearance and other characteristics quite contrary to what happens in the case of identifying other disabilities like deafness, blindness, cerebral palsy etc. As regarding its symptom based observation/identification, ADHD is supposed to be identified on the basis of its three predominantly symptoms/behavioural characteristics namely inattention, hyperactivity and impulsivity. However, these three characteristics are visible at times in different situations to some extent in the behaviour of all children. In fact these are the age-linked characteristics of most of the small children. The difference between those affected with ADHD and not affected is of relativity, i.e. a matter of degree. With ADHD these behaviours occur more vigorously and frequently - far above the expectations of their developmental age - causing difficulties in their day to day life activities at home, school or other social situations. The parents, members of the family, family friends and relatives, teachers all should try to share their opinions about the excess demonstrated and limits crossed by the children in their day to day behaviours e.g. excessive activity and restlessness, impulsiveness, (lack of ability to control impulses). In this way, reports about the typical behaviour of a child suspected as ADHD, may spring from the observations of his behaviour in number of social situations. Now, the diagnosis, whether his behaviour is ADHD or not requires somewhat an objective and widely accepted criteria. Luckily such criterions are readily available now-a-days. The most popular one is the diagnostic criteria prescribed by the American Psychiatric Association (APA). The other one is from the World Health Organization. We are hereby presenting them one by one.

## Criteria Prescribed by American Psychiatric Association (APA)

American Psychiatric Association is credited with stopping all the previous controversies regarding the nomenclature and diagnosis of ADHD. It has provided a largely accepted criteria for the diagnosis of ADHD through its publication "Diagnostic and Statistical Manual of Mental Disorders" (DSM)". In its latest version brought out in 2013 in the name of DSM-5 it has mentioned a criterion for the diagnosis of ADHD in the following way (see **Table 19.1**).

**Table 19.1: Diagnostic Criteria for ADHD**

1. Individual presents one or both of the following patterns:
   (a) For 6 months or more, individual frequently displays at least six of the following symptoms of inattention, to a degree that is maladaptive and beyond that shown by most similarly aged persons:
   - Unable to properly attend to details, or frequently makes careless errors.
   - Finds it hard to maintain attention
   - Fails to listen when spoken to by others
   - Fails to carry out instructions and finish work
   - Disorganized
   - Dislikes or avoids mentally effortful work
   - Loses items that are needed for successful work
   - Easily distracted by irrelevant stimuli
   - Forgets to do many everyday activities

   (b) For 6 months or more, individual frequently displays at least six of the following symptoms of hyperactivity and impulsivity, to a degree that is maladaptive and beyond that shown by most similar aged persons :

- Fidgets, taps hands or feet, or squirms
- Inappropriately wanders from seat
- Inappropriately runs or climbs
- Unable to play quietly
- In constant motion
- Talks excessively
- Interrupts questioners during discussion
- Unable to wait for turn
- Barges in on others' activities or conversations.

2. Individual displayed some of the symptoms before 12 years of age
   1. Individual shows symptoms in more than one setting
   2. Individual experiences impaired functioning.

*Source*: American Psychotic Association (2013), *Diagnostic and Statistical Manual of Mental Disorders (5th ed.)*, American Psychiatric Association: Washington DC.

## Criteria Prescribed by World Health Organization (W.H.O.)

World Health Organization (WHO) has provided a criterion for the diagnosis of Hyper kinetic Syndrome (its own nomenclature for ADHD) through its International classification of Diseases. It is produced here in the **Table 19.2.**

**Table 19.2: Diagnostic Criteria for Hyper kinetic Syndrome**

**A.** Demonstrate abnormality of attention and activity at home, for the age and developmental level of the child, as evidenced by at least three of the following attention problems.

1. Short duration to spontaneous activities.
2. Often leaving play activities unfinished.
3. Over frequent changes between activities.
4. Undue lack of persistence at tasks set by adults.
5. Unduly high distractibility during study (e.g. homework or reading assignment); and by at least two of the following.
6. Continuous motor restlessness (running jumping etc).
7. Markedly excessive fidgeting or wriggling during spontaneous activities.
8. Markedly excessive activity in situations expecting relative stillness (e.g. meal times, travel, visiting church).
9. Difficulty in remaining seated when required.

**B.** Demonstrate abnormality of attention and activity at school or nursery (if applicable) for the age and development level of the child, as evidenced by at least two of the following attention problems.

1. Undue lack of persistence at tasks.
2. Unduly high distractibility i.e. often orienting towards extrinsic stimuli.
3. Over frequent changes between activities when choice is allowed.
4. Excessively short duration of play activities, and by at least two of the following activity problems.

5. Continuous and excessive motor restlessness (running, jumping etc.) in school.
6. Markedly excessive fidgeting and wriggling in structured situations.
7. Excessive levels of off-task activity during tasks.
8. Unduly often out of seat when required to be sitting.

**C.** Directly observed abnormality of attention activity. This must be excessive for the child's age and developmental level. The evidence may be any of the following.

1. Direct observation of the criteria in A or B above, i.e. not solely the report of parent and/or teacher.
2. Observation of abnormal levels of motor activity, or off-task behaviour, or lack of persistence in activities, in a setting outside home or school (e.g. clinic or laboratory).
3. Significant impairment of performance on psychometric test of attention.

**D.** Does not meet criteria for pervasive developmental disorder, mania, depressive or anxiety disorder.

**E.** Onset before the age of 6 years.

**F.** Duration of at least 6 months.

**G.** IQ above 50

The research diagram of Hyper kinetic disorder requires the definite presence of abnormal levels of inattention and restlessness that are pervasive across situations and persistent overtime, that can be demonstrated by direct observation and that are not caused by other disorders such as autism or affective disorders.

Eventually, assessment instruments should develop to the point where it is possible to take a quantitative cut-off score on reliable, valid and standardized measures of hyperactive behaviour in the home and classroom, corresponding to the 95th percentile on both measures. Such criteria would then replace A and B above.

***Source:*** World Health Organization (1990), *The International classification of Diseases (10th edition)*, Geneva: World Health Organization.

ADHD is a difficult disorder to assess properly. There exist some disorders or difficulties (e.g. pervasive Developmental Disorders, Psychotic Personality Disorders, Stressful life events etc.) that can be characterized to produce more or less the same symptoms as visible in the children with ADHD. Hence, the presence of these disorders or difficulties may pose a great difficulty in the diagnosis of a real ADHD. It is therefore quite essential to have a fair diagnosis of ADHD, by getting it separated from these disorders or difficulties. For this purpose, it is essential to observe the child's behaviour cautiously in several situations of multiple environmental settings (school, home, with friends) for ascertaining a continual presence of the main ADHD symptoms in his or her behaviour. Moreover, since children with ADHD often give poor description of their symptoms, it is important to obtain reports of the child's symptoms from the parents and teachers. And finally, for ensuring the presence of ADHD in the child due help may be taken from the diagnostic interviews, ratings scales, and psychological tests available for the assessment of ADHD.

## Causes of ADHD

ADHD is usually attributed to one or the other results arrived through the interactions going on among the three types of mentionable factors named as (i) Neurological or Biological Factors, (ii) Genetic or Hereditary Influences and (iii) Environmental or Sociocultural factors.

For the neurological or biological factors responsible for causing ADHD, the researchers quite often name (i) the abnormality or dysfunction of the brain (particularly prefrontal and frontal lobes of the cerebrum, basal ganglia and cerebellum) and (ii) the impairments in neurological functioning (particularly related to the impairment in the functioning of the two transmitters named, Dopamine and Norepinephrine).

Regarding, the role of genetic or heredity influences in causing ADHD, Barkely (1988) on the basis of research evidences has claimed that heredity accounts about 80 percent of children with ADHD.

Besides, the genetic and neurological factors causing ADHD, the environmental factors-the negative and damaging happenings in the one's physical and sociocultural environment-may be seen to work as germinators as well nourishing or inflaming agents of developing ADHD among the children.

## Treatment of ADHD

The more commonly used approaches adopted currently for treating ADHD consist of the use of Medical or Drug therapy, Behavioural therapy and /or a combination of both

*Medical or Drug Therapy*: The medications that seem to be most effective in the treatment of ADHD sufferers are a class of drugs known as stimulants (stimulating or activating neurological functioning). The most common type of stimulants used for ADHD is *methylphenidate* (trade name Ritalin). The other useful stimulants used are Addrerall, Concerta, Dexedrine, Dextrostat, Metadate, Cylert and Focalin.

In addition to the above mentioned stimulant medications, non-stimulation medications can also be used for normalizing the executive functions of the brain. A widely used medication is named as Strattera, or atomoxetine. Administered once per day, this medication is proving quite helpful in controlling the levels of norepinephrine (a type of neurotransmitters other than Dopamine, believed to play a role in ADHD). The combination of the stimulants (primarily working on dopamine) and non-stimulant (mainly working on norepinephrine thus may be a better formula often prescribed by the physicians for some children. However, the medication as the treatment of ADHD should not be used at the first sign of a behavioural problem and if needed (after proper recommendation of a physician/neurologist) these should be always used in combination with other behavioural management techniques.

*Behaviour Therapy:* The techniques involving behaviour therapy are aimed to decrease or reduce the occurrence of inappropriate behaviour with an equal emphasis on increasing the probability of the child's appropriate or desirable behaviour. For this purpose a number of behaviour management strategies like following may be followed.

1. In one of such strategy (known as token money or point receiving strategy) the desired behaviours that a child needs to be exhibited on his part are brought into his notice by getting them noted in his diary or through putting them on a chart. He is to get points (say five) or a token (say a card) for each of his good/ desired behaviour but also has the risk of losing the same (the five points or token) if he behaves otherwise. After a fixed interval or say a day or week the points or token left with the child may be exchanged for rewards (things which have value to the child).
2. In another strategy the phenomenon of "shaping of behaviour" (a technique of behaviour modification through operant conditioning) may be utilized for producing appropriate behaviours and reducing or eliminating the un-appropriate ones. In this technique one behaviour or its component is chosen as target behaviour. The child is here clearly told that what type of behaviour or behavioural elements are expected from him (as an acceptable or desirable behaviour). Whenever the child demonstrates the desired behaviour or provides a clue for stepping up to the desired behaviour, a suitable reinforcement in terms of earning points or any reward (valuable for him) is given and the process (emitting good behaviour and responding it through reinforcement/reward) is continued till the desired behaviour in toto is learned by the child. In between, the undesirable responses are being ignored (for dying their own death) and only those responses are reinforced or rewarded which are similar or near to the expected behaviour. In doing so the principle "Don't mind the small errors but don't ignore the right step no matter how insignificant it looks" should always be followed.

As a third approach for treating ADHD a combination of behavioural and drug therapies is also desirable because, according to research, children who receive both treatments require lower levels of medication, meaning, of course, that they are less subject to the medication's undesired effects.

## Autism

### *Meaning and Definitions of the term 'Autism'*

It is quite natural and normal most of our children to follow a normal course of their development in terms of their speaking, language acquisition and interacting with their peer and family members. As social creature, we may usually find them smiling, cuddling, laughing, interacting and responding eagerly to games like "peek-a-boo or hind-and-seek". However, in some cases we have a different story to tell. The children, instead of needing and desiring contact with others, isolate themselves in a world of their own, a place characterized by repetitive routines, odd and peculiar behaviour, problems in communication and total lack of social and emotional awareness and bonds with others. The children characterized with such defective and improper outcomes in their normal development are often referred as the children suffering with a specific developmental disorder named as autism. Let us try to know more about the meaning and nature of this disorder from some of its available definitions.

*Cohen, Donnellan & Paul:* Autism, a poorly understood condition, is now considered a pervasive developmental disorder because children who are autistic are challenged by a range of impairments in the normal development of communication, social and cognitive capacities. (**1987** p. xvi).

*Autism Society of America:* The essential features of the condition (named as autism) typically appear prior to 30 months of age and consist of disturbances of (i) developmental rates and/or sequences, (ii) responses to sensory stimuli, (iii) speech, language and cognitive capacities, and (iv)capacities to relate to people, events and objects *(Sturmey & Sevin, 1994)*

*Advani & Chadha:* Autism is a brain disorder that typically affects a child's ability to communicate, form relationships with others and respond appropriately to the environment. Some children with autism are relatively high functioning, with speech and intelligence intact. Others are mentally retarded mute, or have serious language delays. For some, autism makes them seem closed off and shut down there are others who seem locked into repetitive behaviours and rigid pattern of thinking. *(2003 p. 211).*

*Individuals with Disabilities Education Act, (IDEA) USA:* Autism is a "developmental disability, affecting verbal and non-verbal communication and social interaction generally evident before age 3, that affects a child's performance. Other characteristics often associated with autism are engagement in repetitive activities and stereotyped movements, resistance to environmental change or change in daily routines, and unusual responses to sensory experiences." *(1994) 34 CFR, part 300, 300.7(b)(1)].*

The definitions cited above may lead us to derive some specific conclusions about the meaning and nature of the term autism like below.

(i) Autism, as indicated in the first definition, is a pervasive development disorder. That is why in the diagnostic manual used to classify disabilities, the DSM-IV (American Psychiatric Association, 1994), "autistic disorder" is listed as a category under the heading of "Pervasive Developmental Disorders." and in the DSM-5 it has been accepted as one of the category in the list of Neurodevelopmental disorders and has been a given a new name "Autism spectrum disorder".

(ii) The children affected with autism display limitations and defects in terms of their communication, social and cognitive behaviours and performances as early as 30 months or 3 years of their age.

(iii) In addition to their developmental deficiencies or performance deficits in three major areas, communication, social and cognitive behaviours, the children with autism may also be seen to demonstrate the following types of abnormalities in their behaviour.

- Engagement in repetitive activities and stereotyped movements.
- Resistance to environmental change or change in daily routine.
- Unusual responses to sensory- experiences.

(iv) Autism, defined as a neurological or brain disorder by Advani & Chadha, is mainly caused by the impairments in one's neurological functioning or brain damage.

(v) A child with autism is adversely affected in terms of the educational performance and day to day adjustment in his life.

Understood in this way, the term autism may be functionally defined here below:

*Usually evident before age three and mainly caused through the brain dysfunction, autism refers to a pervasive developmental disorder that may bring serious impairments and disabilities in the communication, social, emotional and cognitive behaviours of the affected children demonstrated often in terms of social aloofness and bizarre activities like repetitive and unusual responses to sensory experiences and affecting adversely their educational performance and adjustment in life.*

### *How do the Autistic behave in their environment?*

For knowing exactly how a particular autistic child may behave in his environment, we are hereby producing a few examples of the autistic children:

**Example-1: A parental description of autistic behaviour**

We start with an image - a tiny, golden child on hands and knees, circling round and round a spot on the floor in mysterious, self-absorbed delight. She does not look up, though she is smiling and laughing, she does not call our attention to the mysterious object of her pleasure. She does not see us at all. She and the spot are all there is, and though she is eighteen months old, an age for touching, tasting, pointing, pushing, exploring, she is doing none of these things. She does not walk, or crawl upstairs, or pull herself to her feet to reach the objects. She does not want any objects, instead she circles her spot, or she sits, a long chain in her hand, snaking it up and down, watching it coil and uncoil for twenty minutes, half an hour, longer.

*Source* - **Park, 1998 p. 30 quoted in Hunt Nancy and Marshall Kathleen (2002),** *Exceptional Children and Youth: An Introduction to special education,* **(third edition, Boston: Houghton Mifflin Company).**

**Example -2: A Mother's perspective**

Autism is when your two year old looks straight through you to the wall behind - through you, her father, her sister, his brother, or anybody else. You are a pane of glass, or you are her own personal extension, your hand a tool she uses to get the Cookie she will not reach for herself. Autism is when your eight year old fills a carton with three-quarter-inch squares of cut up paper to sift between her fingers for twenty minutes, half an hour, longer. Autism is when your eleven year old fills sheet after sheet with division - division by three, by seven, eleven, thirteen, seventeen, nineteen.... But that's enough, there are many books about autism now, anyone can read, the symptoms. I read the image for what the symptoms can't convey: this child was happy. It is not happiness to want nothing but what you have? Craving, the Budha taught, was the source of all misery, detachment, the road to the serene equilibrium of nirvana. But nirvana at eighteen months? That's too soon.

*Source* - **Claria Claiborne Park** *"Existing Nirvana"*, **The American Scholar, 67: 2 (1998), 30.**

**Example -3: Bizzare behaviour of an autistic child:**

Consider the case of George, an eight year old. He is difficult to understand because he makes up and uses his own words. He often sits in the backyard holding a branch in his hand, rocking back and forth and talking gibberish to it. He drags a moth - eaten stuffed animal - he calls it "Toe Bunny" - around the house, and will not go to bed without it. Yet he scored about the retarded range on intelligence tests that did not require verbal responses.

*Source* - **Kirk, Samuel A, Gallagher, James, J. and Anastasiow, Nicholas, J. (1993),** *Educating Exceptional Children,* **Boston : Houghton Mifflin Company, p. 468.**

**Example-4: Autistic child Amy roaming in her own world**

Amy, 3 years old, spends much of her day picking up pieces of lint. She drops the lint in the air and then watches intently as it falls to the floor. She also licks the back of her hands and stares at the saliva. She hasn't spoken yet and can't feed or dress herself. Several times a day she screams so loudly that the neighbours at first thought she was being abused. She doesn't seem to be interested in her mother's love and affection but will take her mother's hand to lead her to the refrigerator: Amy likes to eat butter-whole pats of it, several at a time. Her mother uses the pats of butter that you get at some restaurants to help Amy learn and to keep her well-behaved. If Amy helps with dressing herself, or if she sits quietly for several minutes, her mother gives her some butter. Amy's mother knows that the butter isn't good for her, but it is the only thing that seems to get through to the child. The family's paediatrician has been concerned about Amy's developmental delays for some time and has recently suggested that she be evaluated by specialists. The paediatrician thinks Amy may have autism and the child and her family will probably need extensive support.

*Source:* **Durand and Barlow (2013:496)**

## Diagnosis and Identification of Autism

Autism is usually identified by the time a child is 30 months old and always by three years of age. The primary source of such identification is the family members, parents and caregivers of the child. By observing the developmental behaviour of their child (in context with the age specific needs and behaviour of other children of the same age and culture) they may become quite concerned that their child is hard of hearing or deaf, is not yet began to talk, resists cuddling, and avoids interaction with others. Such concerning and complaining behaviour of the parents, then may raise the necessity of having some screening measure for the early detection of the presence or absence of autism in the child.

The primary screening measure, in general, for the diagnosis of autism in their children may be available to them by going through some literature about the autism describing behavioural characteristics of the autistic children. A few of such behavioural characteristics of the children suffering from autism have been pointed out by Comer (2015:588) are given below:

- The individual's lack of responsiveness and social reciprocity (extreme aloofness, lack of interest in other people, low empathy, and inability to share attention with others) should be taken as a central theme of autism.
- Communication problems take various forms in autism spectrum disorder. The non-verbal behaviours of these individuals are often at odds with their efforts at verbal communication. They may not, for example, use a proper tone when talking. It is also common for autistic persons to show a few or no facial expression or body gestures. In addition a number are unable to maintain a proper eye contact during interactions. Usually, also the autistic people have great difficulty understanding speech or using language for conversational purposes. They actually fail in developing essential language skills for communication and conversation. Those who do talk may have rigid and repetitious speech patterns such as *echolalia* (the exact echoing of phrases spoken by others) and *pronominal reversal* or confusion of pronouns (the use of 'You' in place of 'I'). When hungry, an autistic child might say "Do you want dinner"?
- Autistic people also display a wide range of highly rigid and repetitive behaviours, interests and activities that extends beyond speech patterns. Typically they become very upset at minor changes in objects, persons, or routines and resist any efforts to change their own repetitive behaviours.
- People with autism may display motor movements that are unusual, rigid, and repetitive. They may jump, flap their arms, twist their heads and fingers, rock, walk on their toes, spin and make faces. These acts are called self-stimulatory behaviours. Some may perform self-injurious behaviours, such as repeatedly lunging into or banging their head against a wall, pulling their hairs, or biting one's self.
- The symptoms of autism spectrum disorder suggest a very disturbed and contradictory pattern of reactions to stimuli. Sometimes they seem over stimulated by sights& sounds and appear to be trying to block them out, while at other times they seem underestimated and appear to be performing self-stimulatory actions. They may for example, be non-reactive to loud noises yet turn around when they hear soda being poured, or they may fail to recognize that they have reached the edge of a dangerous high place yet immediately spot a small object that is out of position in their room.

The list of the symptoms available for diagnosing ADHD helping otherwise, may sometimes prove quite confusing to derive conclusions particularly to the parents to get their child accepted as an autistic child. At this stage, there arises a need for the existence of some objective and valid criteria or widely accepted measures for the proper diagnosis, identification and screening of the child for labelling them as autistic. Two of such criterion measures are produced below for serving the cause.

## Psychological Diagnostic Criteria for Autism

The satisfactory and reliable psychological diagnostic criteria have been given by the agencies such as American Psychiatric Association (APA) from time to time in its published documents- DSM's (Diagnostic and Statistical Manuals of Mental Disorders). We are hereby producing the extracts for providing diagnosis of autism from the two current manuals of DSM-IV-TR and DSM-5 for the required purpose.

## Criterion 1. (Provided in DSM-IV-TR)

This criterion has been provided by the American Psychiatric Association through its 2000 revision of the Diagnostic and Statistical Manual of Mental Disorders (Fourth edition). It seems as below.

**Table 19.3 DSM IV-TR Criterion for Autism Diagnosis**

**A.** A total of six (or more) items from (1), (2) and (3) with at least two from (1) and one each from (2) and (3).

1. Qualitative impairment in social interaction, as manifested by at least two of the following:
   a) marked impairment in the use of multiple nonverbal behaviours such as eye-to-eye gaze, facial expression, body postures, and gestures to regulate social interaction
   b) failure to develop peer relationships appropriate to development level
   c) a lack of spontaneous seeking to share enjoyment, interest, or achievements with other people (e.g., by a lack of showing, bringing, or pointing out objects of interest)
   d) lack of social or emotional reciprocity.
2. Qualitative impairments in communication as manifested by at least one of the following:
   a) delay in, or total lack of, the development of spoken language (not accompanied by an attempt to compensate through alternative modes of communication such as gesture or mime)
   b) in individuals with adequate speech, marked impairment in the ability to initiate or sustain a conversation with others.
   c) Stereotyped and repetitive use of language or idiosyncratic language
   d) Lack of varied, spontaneous make-believe play or social imitative play appropriate to developmental level.
3. Restricted, repetitive and stereotyped patterns of behaviour, interests and activities, as manifested by at least one of the following:
   a) encompassing preoccupation with one or more stereotyped and restricted patterns of interest that is abnormal either in intensity or focus
   b) apparently inflexible adherence to specific, nonfunctional routines or rituals
   c) stereotypes and repetitive motor mannerisms (e.g. hand or finger flapping or twisting or complex whole-body movements)
   d) persistent preoccupation with parts of objects.

B. Delays or abnormal functioning in at least one of the following areas, with onset prior to age 3 years : (1) social interaction, (2) language as used in social communication, or (3) symbolic or imaginative play.

C. The disturbance is not better accounted for by Rett's Disorder or Childhood Disintegrative Disorder.

**Source** : *Diagnostic and Statistical Manual of Mental Disorders,* (Fourth Edition), Text Revision (DSM)-IV-TR, Washington DC :American Psychiatric Association, 2000).

## Criterion 2. (Provided in DSM-5)

This criterion has been provided by the American Psychiatric Association through its 2013 revision of the Diagnostic and Statistical Manual of Mental Disorders (Fifth edition). It seems as below.

**Table19.4: APA criterion for the diagnosis of Autism (Autism Spectrum) Disorder**

**Autism Spectrum Disorder (APA, 2013)**

1. Individual displays continual deficiencies in various areas of communication and social interaction, including the following:
   (i) Social -emotional reciprocity,(ii) Non-verbal communication (iii) Development and maintenance of relationships.
2. Individual displays significant restriction and repetition in behaviors, interests or activities including two or more of the following:
   (i) Exaggerated and repeated speech patterns, movements, or object use, (ii) Inflexible demands for same routines, statements, and behaviors (iii) Highly restricted, fixated, and overly intense interests, (iv) Over - or under actions to sensory input from the environment.
3. Individual develops symptoms by early childhood
4. Individual experiences significant impairment.

## Causes of Autism

What causes autism, has been a subject of wide research and controversy over a long period of time. At one time autism was considered as an emotional or psychological disorder specially caused by the socio-cultural factors in the shape of uncongenial environment at home and other unfavourable stress related factors present in one's sociocultural environment. However, the recent work in the psychological and biological spheres has persuaded clinical theorists that cognitive limitations and brain abnormalities are the primary causes of this disorder. It is why autism (in the name of Autism spectrum disorder) has been placed in the category of Neurodevelopmental disorder in the latest classification of mental disorders DSM-5, provided by American Psychiatric Association.

It is a known fact that what we do, think and feel is almost decided and executed through our brain and neurological apparatus. If one's brain is not found to function in a normal way and there is some sort of brain dysfunction or neurological impairment, then it is natural for the affected individuals to experience the disturbances and abnormalities in their communication, social and emotional behaviour- the known hallmarks of an autism disorder. It is what actually happens with the autistic.

It has been established through contemporary researchers that a brain of an autistic child shows marked deficits and deficiencies in terms of its structure and functioning in comparison to his non-disabled peers. Let us cite a few examples.

(i) A portion of the brain called Amygdala (responsible for directing our emotional responses) has been found impaired in most of the severely affected autistic children.

(ii) The parietal areas of the brain (responsible for the control of hearing, speech and language) and corpus callosum (a portion of the brain responsible for passing information from one side of the brain to the other) of the autistic children have been found less active than the normal disabled peers.

(iii) The frontal lobes of the cerebrum (a portion of the brain responsible for problem solving, planning ahead, restraining out impulses and understanding the behaviour of others) of the autistic children have been found quite less active and energized than the peers without autism.

In this way, at present, we may claim to have mentionable research evidences in favour of declaring brain dysfunction or neurological impairments as a strong causative factor for autism disorder.

The question may now arise what is behind these brain dysfunction or neurological impairment? All the elements and factors like transmission of defective genes, and the improper happenings with the child in the womb of the mother during pregnancy, at the time of delivery and accidents as well maladjustment suffered by them after birth in the sociocultural environment may be the potential causative factors for germinating as well as perpetuating the dysfunction or impairment in the brain.

On the basis of such findings it is proper to conclude that autism may have multiple neurodevelopmental or biological causes (genetic, prenatal, birth, and postnatal). Each of them in its own and combinations may lead the growing children to a common problem in the brain-a *final common pathway* such as neurotransmitter abnormalities or dysfunction in the brain resulting into the distinguishable features of autism.

## Treatment Measures for the Autism

Treatment measures for any ailment, disturbance or disorder are very much based on the findings of what causes that ailment or disorder. Since autism, as discussed above, may be caused by a host of factors lying in one's heredity and environment. It is why no single method or measure can be termed as a sure shot for the cure and treatment of autism. It has given birth to a number of treatment measures mentioned as below:

1. *Use of Medication and Biochemical treatment:* Some sort of medication and biochemical measures such as below have been found to be useful in the treatment of autism

   (i) Eliminating or decreasing those foods in the diets of the children in which these children show most sensitivity or food allergy.

(ii) Administering the doses of vitamins B6, B12 and magnesium or giving an injection of gamma globulin for decreasing negative behaviour associated with autism.

(iii) Providing drug therapy to the much disturbed and agitated autistic children.

2. *Use of Sensory integration Treatment:* In providing sensory integration therapy to the autistic children they are provided with structured experiences and activities that may challenge their ability to respond properly to sensory stimulation and in this way it may help them in getting rid of their improper behaviour regarding sensory stimulation and its integration.

3. *Providing Communication treatment or training:* This treatment measure is meant for bringing improvement in the deficits and disorders of the autistic children in their communication skills. In providing therapy we may have the services of a person, called facilitator, for providing physical assistance to the autistic child in spelling words using a key board of a typewriter, computer, communication board or other letter display. The facilitator plays the role of an active assistant and offers physical support to the disabled child. The support provided by him may range from hand-over-hand support to a simple touch on the shoulder.

4. *Treatment involving Applied Behaviour Analysis:* The technique of applied behaviour analysis, as a behaviour therapy rests on the basic principles of classical and operant conditioning, schedules of proper reinforcement and shaping of the appropriate behaviour. It adopts a systematic approach in its application as below:

   (i) The first step in the treatment is the analysis of the behaviour of the affected child in context of his environmental set up. It is aimed to determine the role or function of his inappropriate behaviour in his environment.

   (ii) The second step consists in identifying some alternative behaviours that can serve the same function, that is being served by the present inappropriate behaviour of the child.

   (iii) The third step now consists in arranging the environment and providing consequences for increasing the desired new alternative behaviours and decreasing the inappropriate.

To adopt applied behaviour analysis as a technique of behaviour modification several methods and approaches have been invented for the treatment of the autism. One of the most popular and widely used methods for this purpose, has been invented by the psychologist Ivan Lovaas and his colleagues at the University of California at Los Angeles. Known as Lovaas method it can be understood and applied as below:

> ***Lovass method*** *consists of an intensive intervention programme originally designed for pre school-aged children with autism. It begins when the child is 2 to 3 years of age and involves intensive training of teachers or parents. It makes use of behaviour modification techniques – moulding and rewarding desired behaviour, and ignoring or discouraging undesirable ones – to achieve its goals. The trained interventionists – parents or teachers, then provide intensive, discrete trial training to the affected children on a one-to-one basis in the child's home and natural*

*settings of child's behaviour. As an intensive and persistent efforts approach, this therapy usually consists of 4 to 6 hours per day involving 5 to 7 days a week. In this way, it generally aims to provide essential training to the affected child on one to one basis (in the areas like basic communication skills) at least up to 30 to 40 hours week continued for a minimum of 3 years. (Lovass,1994)*

## Summary

- Attention-Deficit Hyperactivity Disorder or ADHD refers to a neuro-behavioural disorder of the childhood often visible before the age of 6 or 7 through the symptoms of excessive inattentiveness, hyperactivity and impulsivity (often also accompanied with the problems of deficient and aggressive behaviour). The children, themselves are not responsible for learning or developing these symptoms in their behaviour. The disorder is almost caused through some dysfunction in their brain and neurological functioning. In turn, it makes them to lose control over their ability for inhibition or self regulation resulting into ADHD behavioural problems chronic enough for causing major difficulties in one's life areas like home, school, work or social situations.
- The diagnostic criteria prescribed by American Psychiatric Association, USA through its publication DSM-5 and ICD-10 brought out by WHO may prove quite useful in the proper diagnosis of the ADHD disorder. For being quite sure about the presence of ADHD a comprehensive evaluation and assessment of the suspected ADHD, may be carried out by seeking information through proper observation of his/her behaviour in a variety of environmental situations, medical examination, use of interview, and a variety of psychological tests. It helps in the diagnosis and identification of true ADHD with or without the presence of certain other behavioural disorders or coexisting conditions.
- ADHD is attributed to the types of multiplicity of factors classified as neurological, genetic and environmental. However, most substantial causes of ADHD fall in the neurobiological realm indicating some or the other impairments in the structure and functioning of the brain contributed through genetic inheritance and environmental factors like brain injuries, brain diseases and fatal exposures to alcohol, smoking drug abuse and high levels of lead both at the pre and post natal stages. Besides causing dysfunctions and impairments in the brain, environmental factors also work as a nourisher or extinguisher of the problems related to ADHD among the children.
- Treatment of ADHD involves a combination of approach including medication (using stimulant as well as non stimulant drugs), as well as use of behaviour modification or management techniques.
- Usually evident before age three and mainly caused through the brain dysfunction, autism refers to a pervasive developmental disorder that may bring serious impairments and disabilities in the communication, social, emotional and cognitive behaviours of the affected children. It is usually demonstrated by them in terms of their social aloofness and bizarre activities like repetitive and unusual responses to sensory experiences and affects adversely their educational performance and adjustment in life.

- Autistic children are found to exhibit quite typical characteristics in their overall behaviour and personality. In terms of their cognitive behaviour they may suffer adversely in learning skills such as reading, writing and computation and sensory deficits like over or under responsiveness to light noise, touch or pain. The most distinguishable characteristics or symptoms of autism are related with the deficits and disorders concerning communication skills, social skills, emotional behaviour and adaptive skills. Many of these children are also seen to exhibit marked peculiarities and disturbances in their behaviour like rigidity or resistance to change, temper tantrums, repetitive stereotyped and self- injurious behaviours.
- Autistic is usually diagnosed and identified by the age of three generally through the initiatives taken by the parents. For the diagnosis and identification of autism in their children parents may go through some useful literature describing general characteristics and symptoms of the autistic children. However, it is always better to take help of some proper diagnostic criteria or guidelines like Diagnostic Criteria for autism provided by American Psychiatric Association through its 2000 as well as 2013 revisions of the Diagnostic and Statistical Manual of Mental Disorders (Fourth and Fifth edition).
- The contemporary researchers are of the opinion that autism is the outcome of the dysfunction or impairment of the brain and neurological transmission. These abnormalities of the brain and neurological functioning are caused by a single or in combination of a number of factors such as transmission of defective genes, and the improper happenings with the children in the womb of the mother during pregnancy, at the time of delivery and accidents as well maladjustment suffered by them after birth in the sociocultural environment.
- The treatment applied to the cases of autism may consist of a number of measures in the shape of (i) Medication and biochemical treatment (involving drug, and vitamin therapy).(ii) Sensory integration treatment(aimed to rectify the deficiencies related to sensory integration ability), and (iii) Communication training or treatment (concentrating on improving the communication skills) and (iv) Treatment involving applied behaviour analysis or behaviour therapy

## REFERENCES


Advani, Lal and Chadha Anupriya, (2003), *You and your special child*, New Delhi: UBS Publishers, Distributors Pvt. Ltd.

American Psychiatric Association (1994)), *Diagnostic and Statistical Manual of Mental Disorders*, Fourth edition (DSM-IV), Washington, DC: American Psychiatric Association.

American Psychiatric Association (2000), *Diagnostic and Statistical Manual of Mental Disorders*, Fourth edition - Text Revision (DSM-IV-TR), Washington, DC: American Psychiatric Association.

American Psychiatric Association (2013), *Diagnostic and Statistical Manual of Mental Disorders*, Fifth edition (DSM-5), Washington, DC: American Psychiatric Association.

Autism Society of America quoted by Sturmey P. & Servin J.A. (1994), Defining and assessing autism In J.L. Matson (Ed.) Autism in Children and Adults : Etiology, assessment and intervention (pp. 33-36), Pacific Grove C.A. : Brooks/Cole.

Barkley, Russell, A. (2000), *Taking Charge of ADHD : The Complete Authoritative Guide for Parents*, New York : The Guilford Press.

Cohen,D.J., Donnellian, A.M. & Paul, R. (Eds), (1987), *Handbook On Autism and Pervasive Developmental Disorders*, Silvers Springs, MD : V.H. Winston & Sons.

Comer, Ronald J. (2015), *Abnormal Psychology* (Ninth Edition), New York: Worth Publishers (A Macmillan Education Imprint)

Cooper, Paul and Bilton, Katherine, M. (2002), *Attention Deficit/Hyperactivity Disorder : A Practical Guide for Teachers* (2nd ed.) London : David, Fulton Publishers.

Durand, V. and Barlow, D. (2013), *Essentials of Abnormal Psychology* (6th ed.), Wadsworth: Cengage Learning.

Goldstein, S. (1999), *The Facts About ADHD: An overview of Attention Deficit Hyperactivity Disorder*, htpp//www.samgoldste4in.com/articles/ 9907.html.

Individuals with Disabilities Education Act, (IDEP) USA (1994), Department of Education, Washington DC.

Kirk Samuel A, Gallagher, James, J. and Anastasiow, Nicholas J (1993), *Educating Exceptional Children* (Seventh Edition), Boston : Houghton Mifflin Company.

Lovass Ivar (1994), Quoted in Heward, William L. (2000), *Exceptional Children : An Introduction to Special Education* (Sixth Edition), Upper Saddle River, New Jersey : Merrill.

Park, Claria Claiborne, (1998), "Existing Nirvana", *The American Scholar*, 67:2

Park, (1998:30), quoted in Hunt Nancy, and Marshall Kathleen, Exceptional Children and Youth (2002), *An Introduction to Special Education*, Boston : Houghton Mifflin Company.

NICHCY (January, 2004), *ADHD Disorder Fact-sheet 19* (FS 19), htpp//www.Nichcy.org.pubs/factshe/ htm. Retrieved on 25/6/2006).

World Health Organization (1990), The International Classification of Diseases (10th ed.), Geneva : WHO.

# 20

# ELIMINATION AND EATING DISORDERS

As we have seen in the chapter 10 of this text, the classification of mental disorders DSM-IV-TR (2000) provided by American Psychiatric Association, has included and described Elimination and Eating Disorders in the category of "Disorders usually first diagnosed during infancy, childhood, or adolescence". In its latest revision,DSM-5 in the year 2013, both of these developmental disorders have been classified at their own in two separate classification categories (i) Elimination Disorders and (ii) Feeding and Eating Disorders. Let us know some essentials about both of these disorders associated with the development and life of the children and adolescents.

## Elimination Disorders

### What are Elimination Disorders?

The nature has made the proper provision of providing outlets to the elimination of the waste products such as urine and faeces in a regular way from our body. The newborns from their very birth onwards may be seen to urinate and pass faces from the provided outlets in a quite natural ways found convenient to them. In their earlier age therefore, it is common to witness for the children to urinate or pass faeces in their clothes, in bed, in the lapses or cloths of others, or on the floor. After reaching a certain age the babies are provided toilet training for urinating and passing faeces in a socially desirable ways in a proper way at the proper places. Moreover, as they grow in age and develop, they are able to exercise needed control over their bladders and bowl. However, the practice of urinating and passing faeces does not go so smoothly with some children even after reaching an age at which they are expected to exercise needed control over their eliminating organs. Contrarily, they may be found, to urinate or pass faeces involuntarily in the ways and means as well as at the places they find to do so. Moreover, it does not at all related with any physical illness suffered by them or happens to them accidently and occasionally. It is repeatedly performed any time during the day but more often at night during sleep and causes a great amount of distress to them and others. The children experiencing this sort of unwelcome behaviour regarding the elimination of urine and faeces from their body are termed as the children suffering from elimination disorders.

## Types of Elimination Disorders

There are two types of elimination disorders, Enuresis and Encopresis, described as below.

## Enuresis

The word enuresis is derived from a Greek word (*enourein*) that means "to void urine". Accordingly the term enuresis stands in the clinical and psychological world for a type of elimination disorder related to the passing of urine on the part of individuals. In defining this disorder, we may say that *"Enuresis is a type of elimination disorder that relates to an abnormal behaviour (involuntary or purposeful) of the toilet trained developing children (more than 4 years old) or adults in which they are found to urinate repeatedly in their clothes and beds"*. It typically occurs to them at night during sleep but may also occur during the day.

The emotional impact of enuresis on a child and family can be considerable damaging. Children with enuresis are commonly punished and are at risk for emotional and physical abuse. Research evidences have demonstrated a number of damaging effect experienced on the part of children suffering from enuresis such as embarrassment and anxiety, loss of self-esteem, and effects on self-perception, interpersonal relationships, quality of life, and school performance.

## Identification and Diagnosis of Enuresis

As far as its identification and diagnosis is concerned, the children suffering from enuresis or bed wetting are no different than the other normal children in appearance or other observable symptoms. The problem with them in its single description lies in the inability to exercise control over the bladder making them urinate in their clothes or bed. Therefore, their wet clothes or bed only are there to tell about their urination related disorder.

For helping in the diagnosis and identification of Enuresis, American Psychiatric Association has laid down the distinctive criteria in its latest version DSM-5 (2013) as below.

**Table 20.1: DSM -5 Criterion for the diagnosis of Enuresis**

1. Repeated voiding of urine into bed or clothes, whether involuntary or intentional
2. The behaviour either (a) occurs at least twice a week for at least 3 consecutive months or (b) results in clinically significant distress or social, functional, or academic impairment
3. The behaviour occurs in a child who is at least 5 years old (or has reached the equivalent developmental level)
4. The behaviour cannot be attributed to the physiologic effects of a substance or other medical condition

Enuresis can be further divided into the following three subtypes on the basis of the time of occurrence

- Nocturnal (i.e. during sleep)
- Diurnal (i.e. during waking hours)
- Nocturnal and diurnal

*Source:* American Psychiatric Association (2013), Diagnostic and Statistical Manual of Mental Disorders, Fifth Edition, (DSM-5), Washington, DC: APA.

## Causes Behind the Development of Enuresis

What causes enuresis among the developing children is not very much specified to the clinicians and researchers. A number of possible factors like below in their various combinations are considered causing such elimination disorder among children.

1. *Genetic Factor-* Enuresis is said to be linked with genetic inheritance. Those with enuresis typically have a close relative (parent, sibling) who has had or will have the same disorder.
2. *Biological Factor:* In view of the physiologists and biologists, the children become victims of the enuresis because (i) they have a small bladder capacity or weak bladder muscles for holding the amount of urine produced.
3. *Developmental Factor:* According to the developmental psychologist, on account of the delay in acquiring necessary maturity, some children do not acquire the needed level of maturity to make them feel that (i) their bladder is full and they should go to the toilet as well as (ii) to arouse them from sleep for the same.
4. *Psychodynamic Factor:* According to psychodynamics theorists, the repressed wishes and underlying conflicts as well as the anxiety and level generated through the happenings with them may be a potent cause for generating enuresis.
5. *Behavioural and Sociocultural Factor:* Psychologists mainly behaviourists and social psychologists view enuresis as an outcome of the disturbed family interactions, faulty upbringing, and improper, unrealistic, or coercive toilet training.

Whatever reason may be there for the germination of the problem related to enuresis out of the factors pointed out above, one thing is certain that the problem gets precipitated by stressful events, uncongenial home and school environment, maltreatment particularly the physical or psychological abuse experienced by the children at one or the other occasions.

## Treatment of Enuresis

Children usually "grow out" of their elimination disorders by the time they reach their teens. If treatment is necessary, the most effective choice for enuresis is behaviour modification, which involves a special pad that the child sleeps on at night. If the pad gets wet, an alarm goes off and the child is directed to go to the bathroom.

Since the prevalence of enuresis decreases with age, most of the younger children suffering from enuresis usually correct themselves even without treatment by the time they grow as adolescents. However, for speeding up the process or dealing with some complicated cases, the treatment method or therapy known as behaviour modification or behaviour therapy is considered most workable and effective. In its applied form it can be used in the ways specified below (Comer, 2015).

1. In one of its form adopting classical conditioning approach for dealing with the problem of enuresis, behaviour therapy may be found to make use of a specific technique termed as "The bell-and -battery technique". In this technique a bell and battery is wired to a pad consisting of two metallic foil sheets, and the entire

apparatus is placed under the child at bed time. Whenever, the child urinates during his or her night sleep, a single drop of urine sets off the bell, awakening the child as soon as he or she starts to wet. Thus the bell (unconditioned stimulus) paired with the sensation of a full bladder (conditioned stimulus) produces the response of waking. Conditioned in this way, eventually, a full bladder alone is able to awaken the child for going to toilet for the purpose.

2. Another effective behavioural treatment method is dry-bed training. Here the children suffering from enuresis are provided necessary training in cleanliness and retention control. The training schedule adopted for this purpose include (i) awakening of the child periodically during the night, (ii) making him or her going to the bathroom for passing urine, and (iii) reinforcing his or such proper behaviour through suitable rewards.

## Encopresis

The word Encopresis has its root in Greek signifying involuntary defecation. In this sense as a mental disorder, "*Encopresis stands for a type of abnormal behaviour (involuntary or purposeful) demonstrated by the toilet trained developing children (more than 4 years old) or adults in which they are found passing of faeces repeatedly into places other than the toilets such as in their clothing or bed, or anywhere on the floor at their convenience.*"

## Symptoms of Encopresis

In addition to defecating in improper places, the children suffering from encopresis may be found to demonstrate a number of physiological, physical and psychological symptoms like below:

1. There are disturbances and problems in their digestive system such as complain of (i) abdominal pain, (ii) loss of appetite, (iii) constipation and/or hard stools, (iv)inability to retain faeces (bowel incontinence), (v) loose, watery stools (bowel movement), and (vi) need of scratching or rubbing the anal area due to irritation from watery pools.
2. They may show a strange behaviour characterizing (i) decreased interest in physical activity, (ii) (iii) remaining aloof by withdrawing from friends and family, (iv) avoiding socially interactive situations such as going on picnic, camping, or even attending functions and classes in the school (v)secretive behaviour associated with the act of having a bowel movement, (vi) nervousness and anxiety for their bowel difficulty, and (vii) haunted with the feelings of shame and embarrassment on account of their wet and spoiled clothes.

## Identification and Diagnosis of Encopresis

In addition to take help from the information derived through the observation or reporting of the presence of the symptoms (outlined above) associated with encopresis, the identification and diagnosis of the children suffering from encopresis may be further assured with the use of the diagnostic criteria available in the DSM-5 brought out by American Psychiatric Association in 2013.

**Table 20.2: DSM -5 Criteria for the Diagnosis of Encopresis**

| | |
|---|---|
| 1. | Patient's chronological age must be at least 4 years; |
| 2. | A repeated passage of faeces into inappropriate places, e.g., clothing or floor. This can be either intentional or involuntary; |
| 3. | At least one such event must occur every month for at least 3 months; |
| 4. | The behaviour is not attributable to the effects of a substance, e.g., laxative, or another medical condition, with the exception of a mechanism involving constipation. |

*Source:* American Psychiatric Association (2013), Diagnostic and Statistical Manual of Mental Disorders, Fifth Edition, (DSM-5), Washington, DC: APA.

In order to get further surety in the diagnosis of encopresis among the suspected children, a complete medical examination including the evaluation of medical history is needed on the part of trained physicians and clinicians. They may make use of certain tests for ruling out other possible causes in the form of physical disorders for the constipation and digestive problems. If no physical disorder or somatic cause is found then they become definite to associate the problem with the mental disorder known as Encopresis.

## Causes Behind the Development of Encopresis

A number of factors-biological, physiological, physical and psychological may be found to work in one or the other combinations for causing Encopresis in the manner outlined below.

1. **Physiological and Physical factors:** The most common cause of encopresis is chronic (long-term) constipation, the inability to release stools from the bowel. It may happen on account of the factors such as (i) unhealthy food habits specially, a diet low in fibre, (ii) lack of sufficient amounts of water,(iii) lack of exercise, (iv) pain caused by a sore in or near the anus, (v) inconsistent bathroom routines (vi) fear or reluctance to use unfamiliar bathrooms, (vii) not taking the time to use the bathroom and (viii) a physical problem related to the intestine's ability to move stool.
2. **Psychological factors :** Apart from the physiological factors, encopresis is also caused and intensified on account of the level of anxiety, stress, or frustrations suffered by the child in his or her sociocultural environment on account of (i) improper and hard ways of toilet training,(ii) stressful events in child's life such as quarrelling and disputes between parents, family illness, maltreatment with the child or even the arrival of a new sibling

## Treatment of Encopresis

Encopresis is found to affect a lesser number of children than the enuresis and is more common in boys than in girls. Like enuresis, it also gets better as the child gets older, although the problem can come and go for years. In order to have better treatment, we need the use of a number of therapies or treatment measures capable of addressing, all the physiological, physical, behavioural and emotional issues associated with this disorder. In general, it remains advantageous to concentrate on the measures like below for this purpose.

1. **Physiological and Medical treatment:** Since constipation and irregular bowel functioning are the major issues with the children suffering from encopresis, sincere efforts should be made to help the children in coming out of these issues by resorting to the means like
   - Clearing any faeces that has become impacted in the large intestine by some suitable means such as enema administration.
   - Providing fibre rich diet.
   - Using stools softeners such as mineral oil, laxatives, and lubricants for stimulating regular bowel functioning.
   - Introducing physical activities and exercise in the daily schedule of the child.
   - Taking help of suitable medication, if necessary, for dealing with the issues of constipation , irregular bowel , digestion and intestine functioning related problems.
   - Providing biofeedback training to help the children for being conscious of passing faeces when needed and bringing improvement in the habit of making scheduled trips to bathroom.
2. **Behavioural and psychological treatment:** Since, encopresis is very much associated with the psychological and emotional factors, its treatment also requires to fight the battle on this front. In this concern, it should be well remembered that punishment in any way is not typically effective, and usually increases, rather than decreases the problems related to this disorder. As a result, it remains beneficial to make use of the treatment measures involving behavioural and psychological therapies like below:
   - Use of behaviour modification techniques involving classical and operant conditioning, schedule of reinforcement and shaping of the behaviour
   - Use of psychotherapy (a type of counselling) for helping the child cope with the shame, guilt, or loss of self esteem associated with the disorder.
   - Planning and providing suitable psychological interventions to the affected children and their families for dealing with the problems related to the disorder.
   - Making use of parental training and family therapy for dealing with the issues related to disorder.
   - Making use of cognitive behavioural therapy and psychotherapy for dealing with the symptoms of anxiety, depression and frustrations associated with the disorder.

## Eating Disorders

### What are Eating Disorders?

*Eating disorders are illnesses in which the people experience severe disturbances in their eating behaviours and related thoughts and emotions. People with eating disorders typically become pre-occupied with food and their body weight* (APA, 2013).

Such consciousness and pre-occupation with food and body weight for looking good and attractive has been a great craving on the part of youngsters – adolescents and youths as a distinguished feature of their age and youthfulness. However, it has gained a great momentum during the modern age of fashion and glamour. The excessive inclination for becoming more and more thin (especially on the part of young girls and women) has led to intensify a number of serious health related problems and behavioural disorders designated as eating disorders.

### Types of Eating Disorders

Eating disorders affect several million people at any given time, most often women between the ages of 12 and 35. There are three main types of eating disorders: anorexia nervosa, bulimia nervosa and binge eating disorder (APA, 2013).

Let us know essentials about these three types of eating disorders in detail.

## Anorexia Nervosa

Anorexia Nervosa is a most pronounced, difficult and dangerous disorder among all the three major eating disorders found in the individuals. The peak age of its onset has been found between 14 and 20 years. Females are more affected with this disorder than their male counterparts as about 90 to 95 percent of all cases of anorexia nervosa are reported in females. The desire of becoming thin by losing weight through dieting makes the whole story of the commencement of this disorder and gradually it may drive the individual to the point of starving and even to the extent of completely ruining his or her health and life to the extent of suicidal death. How does it happen, and what goes in Anorexia nervosa, may be better revealed through the information derived from the case histories like below.

**Julie: The thinner, the better**

Julie was 17 years old when she first came for help. She looked emaciated and unwell. Eighteen months earlier she had been overweight, weighing 140 pounds at 5 feet and 1inch. Her mother, a well- meaning but overbearing and demanding-woman, nagged Julie incessantly about her appearance. Her friends were kinder but no less relentless. Julie, who had never had a date, was told by a friend she was cute and would have no trouble getting dates if she lost some weight. So she did! After many previous unsuccessful attempts, she was determined to succeed this time.

After several weeks on a strict diet, Julie noticed she was losing weight. She felt a control and mastery that she had never known before. It wasn't long before she received positive comments, not only from her friends, but also from her mother, Julie began to feel good about herself. The difficulty was that she was losing weight too fast. She stopped menstruating. But now nothing could stop her from dieting. By the time she reached our clinic, she weighed 75 pounds. Her parents had just begun to worry about her. Julie did not initially seek treatment for her eating behaviour. Rather, she had developed numbness in her left lower leg and a left foot drop-an inability to lift up the front part of the foot-that a neurologist determined was caused by peritoneal nerve paralysis believed to be related to inadequate nutrition. The neurologist referred her to our clinic.

Like most people with anorexia, Julie said she probably should put on a little weight, but she didn't mean it. She thought she looked fine, but she had" lost all taste for food" a report that may not have been true because most people with anorexia crave food at least some of the time but control their cravings. Nevertheless, she was participating in most of her usual activities and continued to do extremely well in school and her extra-curricular pursuits. Her parents were happy to by her most of the workout videotapes available, and she began doing one every day-and then two. When her parents suggested she was exercising enough, and perhaps too much she worked out when no one was around. After every meal, she exercised with a workout tape until, in her mind, she burned up all the calories she had just taken in.

*Source:* **Durand &Barlow, (2013:289)**

On the basis of the things revealed from the case histories like above and the conclusions arrived from research findings, the individuals affected with Anorexia Nervosa have been found to be characterized as below:

1. Becoming thinner and thinner by losing weight is a key goal for individuals with anorexia nervosa.
2. Typically, the disorder begins with a desire of becoming thin on the part of individuals especially on the part of young and adolescent girls slightly overweight or of normal weight (intending to look more attractive and acceptable by others).
3. They resort to dieting (observing fasting and putting severe restrictions on their food intake) for reducing weight and becoming thin. However, the desire of reducing weight and becoming thin is soon converted into an obsession for becoming thinner and thinner besides getting haunted with a morbid fear of gaining weight and losing control over eating.
4. In the process of going through their obsession of weight reduction, they may be found to pick up a variety of means other than fasting or severe food restrictions such as
   - Heavy exercising and physical activities.
   - Trying to throw out their food intake by vomiting or take large doses of laxatives (the drugs or medicines tending to stimulate or facilitate evacuation of the bowels)
5. Strangely enough with their desire as well as attempts for remaining away from the food intake, people with anorexia are preoccupied with food demonstrable through their behaviours such as
   - Spending considerable time thinking and even reading about food and planning their limited meals.
   - Cooking elaborate meals for others while eating nothing themselves
   - Reporting that they feel fed while seeing the food items or eating them by other's in real encounters or even in the pictures or videos.
6. Persons with anorexia nervosa have a such low opinion of their body shape, that they are never satisfied with the results obtained through the measures taken

on their part in this concern. The perception of a girl suffering from Anorexia Nervosa reveals this fact in the manner given below:

*I look in a full- length mirror at least four or five times daily and I really cannot see myself as too thin. Sometimes after several days of strict dieting, I feel that my shape is tolerable, but most of the time, odd as it may seem, I look in the mirror and believe that I am too fat. (Bruch, 1973), Comer, 2015:35.*

7. On account of their too much craving for becoming thin, and dissatisfaction with the results in this concern as well as possession of a quite distorted perception on their part about their body image, it is quite usual for the persons with anorexia nervosa consider themselves always fatty (still needing to lose some weight from some parts of the body) when others are viewing them as emaciated, sickly, and a structure of skins and bones in the state of semi-starvation.
8. People with anorexia nervosa may also be found to be affected from a number of psychological, social, and behavioural problems and typical behaving patterns like below.
   (i) They usually suffer from depression, anxiety, low self-esteem, and insomnia or other sleep disturbances.
   (ii) Many of them may be grappled with substance abuse.
   (iii) They may display typical obsessive-compulsive behaviour patterns such as setting rigid rules for food preparation and or even cutting food into specific shapes, prioritizing exercise over most other activities in their lives etc.
   (iv) Behaving as a perfectionist, a characteristic that typically precedes the onset of the disorder.
9. The people with anorexia nervosa, eventually, suffer from a number of medical problems on account of their persistent obsession of becoming thinner and thinner such as below:
   - Suffering from a quite mentionable problems on account of poor nutrition such as losing hair from the scalp, and getting rough, dry and cracked skin, brittle nails and blue feet etc.
   - Having lowered body temperature, low blood pressure, body swelling, reduced bone mineral density, and slow heart rate.
   - Development of amenorrhoea, the absence of menstrual cycles on the part of women
   - Suffering from the problems related to Metabolic and electrolyte imbalances causing death by heart failure or circulatory collapse

## Identification and Diagnosis of Anorexia Nervosa

The observation and reporting of the symptoms and characteristics of the individuals suffering from Anorexia Nervosa provide a lot of evidences and clues regarding the presence of such eating disorder. For getting ensured a further help may be taken from the Criteria of diagnosing them provided in DSM-5 by American psychiatric Association (2013).

**Table 20.3: DSM-5 Criteria for the diagnosis of Anoxia Nervosa**

| |
|---|
| 1. Individual purposely takes in too little nourishment, resulting in a body weight that is very low and below that of other people of similar age and gender |
| 2. Individual is very fearful of gaining weight, or repeatedly seeks to prevent weight gain despite low body weight |
| 3. Individual has a distorted body perception, place inappropriate emphasis on weight or shape in judgments of herself or himself, or fails to appreciate the serious implications of her or his low weight. |

*Source:* American Psychiatric Association (2013), Diagnostic and Statistical Manual of Mental Disorders, Fifth Edition, (DSM-5), Washington DC: American Psychiatric Association.

## Bulimia Nervosa

A less difficult but somewhat quite dangerous and harmful eating disorder in the name of Bulimia nervosa is often visible among the individuals. Like Anorexia nervosa it also occurs in females, again in 90 to 95 percent of the case. It also begins in adolescence or early adulthood and often lasts for years, with periodic letup. In a perfect similarity with Anorexia nervosa, it is also dominated with a morbid fear of gaining weight and extremely consciousness and craving for appearing thin and slim. However, for becoming thin where the people suffering from anorexia nervosa resort to fasting until the point of starving, the people with bulimia nervosa while avoiding regular meals on one hand before others go on frequent eating binges quite often secretly and then force themselves to vomit or take other extreme steps to keep from gaining weight. On account of its distinguished feature, eating binges and then purging afterward, the bulimia eating disorder is also known as binge-purge syndrome. In all its functioning and outcomes, the bulimia nervosa and individuals suffering with bulimia nervosa are found to be characterized as below:

1. The hallmark of bulimia nervosa is to get engaged in the repeated, out of control, episodes of binges, i.e. eating a large amount of food typically, more junk food (usually sweet, high-calories foods with a soft texture, such as ice cream, cookies, doughnuts, and sand witches) at a time quite rapidly with minimal chewing. Here the person eats much more food than most people would eat during a similar time span.
2. Another distinguished feature of Bulimia nervosa is that the people with this disorder repeatedly perform attempts to compensate for such eating and potential gain by forcing themselves to vomit; misusing laxatives, diuretics or enemas; fasting; or exercising excessively.
3. The third important diagnostic characteristic of bulimia nervosa is the excessive preoccupation with body shape and weight. Accordingly, they feel that their continuing popularity and self-esteem would largely be determined by the weight and shape of their body. They are weight conscious and like people with anorexia nervosa they also remain haunted with the fear of weight gain. But unlike them, who get success in losing weight, the weight of people with bulimia nervosa usually stays within a normal range or fluctuating markedly within that range even after going through a lot of purging and other compensatory measures.
4. As with anorexia nervosa, a bulimic pattern typically begins during or after a period of intense dieting, often one that has been successful and earned praise from family members and friends.

5. The behaviour related to falling prey to the binge episodes is usually preceded by feelings of great tension. However, as a tension reliever and pleasurable act in itself, it is soon developed into an obsessive as well as compulsive act performed by the individual as a secret mission.
6. Failure to achieve the mission of losing weight results in (i) inducing the feelings of extreme self -blame, shame, guilt, and depression, and (ii) intensifying the fears related to the gaining of weight and disclosure of the secret mission of binge episodes.
7. Although people with either disorder -anorexia and bulimia worry about the opinions of others, yet, those with bulimia nervosa tend to be more concerned about pleasing others, being attractive to others, and having intimate relationships.
8. The individuals suffering from Chronic bulimia nervosa besides suffering from a host of psychological problems particularly related to anxiety, depression, obsession-compulsion and mood disorders are also found to suffer from a number of medical consequences such as below (Durand and Barlow (2013:288).
   - Women with bulimia nervosa also may suffer from a quite irregular menstrual periods problem such as suffered by those suffering from anorexia nervosa however in a lesser number than them.
   - Bathing of teeth and gums in hydrochloric acid in the process of repeated vomiting may result into serious dental problems such as eroding of the dental enamel on the inner surface and tearing of the oesophagus of the front teeth. and even loss of teeth.
   - The act of frequent purging may also result into (i) Enlargement of salivary gland and (ii)Upsetting of the chemical balance of bodily fluids, including sodium and potassium levels leading to serious medical complications such as disrupted heart- beat, seizures, and kidney failure.
   - Binge eating and laxative abuse may result into a number of indigestion and intestine problems such as severe constipation, or permanent colon damage.

## Identification and Diagnosis of Bulimia Nervosa

The observation and reporting of the symptoms and characteristics of the individuals suffering from Bulimia Nervosa provide a lot of evidences and clues regarding the presence of such eating disorder. For getting ensured a further help may be taken from the Criteria of diagnosing them provided in DSM-5 by American psychiatric Association (2013).

**Table 20.4: DSM-5 Criteria for the diagnosis of Bulimia Nervosa**

| | |
|---|---|
| 1. | Repeated binge eating episodes. |
| 2. | Repeated performance ill-advised compensatory behaviors (e.g. forced vomiting) to prevent weight gain. |
| 3. | Symptoms take place at least weekly for a period of 3 months. |
| 4. | Inappropriate influence of weight and shape on appraisal of self. |

*Source:* American Psychiatric Association (2013), Diagnostic and Statistical Manual of Mental Disorders, Fifth Edition, (DSM-5), Washington DC: American Psychiatric Association.

## Binge Eating Disorder

Binge eating disorder is the latest addition in the list of eating disorders. It is less common, cumbersome and problematic than its both the counterparts -anorexia and bulimia nervosa eating disorders. Only 2-7 percent of the total population are estimated to be affected with Binge eating disorder. It is also to be seen that while the disorders anorexia nervosa and bulimia nervosa usually occur in the females, binge-eating disorder is evenly distributed among both the sexes. The main distinguished features and symptoms related to the Binge eating disorder may be outlined as below:

1. The chief characteristic of this disorder is an overwhelming, all-encompassing drive to be thin, much similar as experienced in the other two nervosas - bulimia and anorexia.
2. Moreover, like people with bulimia nervosa or anorexia nervosa, those with binge-eating disorder typically are preoccupied with food, weight, and appearance; base their evaluation of themselves largely on their weight and shape; misperceive their body size and are extremely dissatisfied with their body; struggle with feelings of depression, anxiety and perfectionism; may abuse substances; and typically first develop the disorder in adolescence or young adulthood (Comer, 2015:358).
3. For their binge eating behaviour it may be said properly that much like those with bulimia nervosa, people with binge-eating disorder engage in repeated eating binges during which they feel no control over their eating.
4. However, in contrast to the other eating disorders, anorexia nervosa and bulimia nervosa, Binge eating disorder, has been found to be characterized with special features and symptoms like:
   - The individuals with binge eating disorder do not demonstration inappropriate compensatory behaviour like purging, excessive exercising, and resorting to misuse of drugs and laxatives after eating binge.
   - The binge-eating disorder does not necessarily begin with efforts at extreme dieting.
   - Although aspiring to limit their eating, people with binge-eating disorder are not as driven to thinness as those with anorexia nervosa and bulimia nervosa.
   - The people suffering from binge eating disorder are more social and sexually active than those with anorexia nervosa and bulimia nervosa.
5. It has also been found that where most overweight people do not have binge-eating disorder, two thirds of those with binge-eating disorder become overweight or even obese.
6. It has also been found that about half of the individuals with Binge eating disorder try dieting before bingeing, and half start with bingeing and then attempt to diet. Those who began bingeing first become more severally affected by Binge eating disorder and are more likely to have additional disorders (Durand and Barlow, 2013:291)

## Identification and Diagnosis of Binge eating disorder

The observation and reporting of the symptoms and characteristics of the individuals suffering from Binge eating disorder provide a lot of evidences and clues regarding the presence of such eating disorder. For getting ensured a further help may be taken from the Diagnostic Criteria provided by American Psychiatric Association (2013) in its DSM-5.

**Table 20.5: DSM-5 Criteria for the Diagnosis of Binge Eating Disorder**

| **Binge Eating Disorder** (APA, 2013) |
|---|
| 1. Recurrent binge-eating episodes |
| 2. Binge-eating episodes include at least three of the following features<br>(i) Unusual fast eating, (ii) Absence of hunger, (iii) Uncomfortable fullness,<br>(iv) Secret eating due to a sense of shame, (v) Subsequent feelings of self-disgust, depression, or severe guilt. |
| 3. Significant distress |
| 4. Binge-eating episodes take place at least weekly over the course of 3 months |
| 5. Absence of excessive compensatory behaviours. |

*Source:* American Psychiatric Association (2013), Diagnostic and Statistical Manual of Mental Disorders, Fifth Edition, (DSM-5), Washington DC: American Psychiatric Association

In the description carried out in the above pages about all the three types of eating disorders, all essentials about their meaning, nature, functioning and outcomes have been highlighted. How do these three main disorders differ with one another? Drawing a summarized conclusion in this concern Comer (2015:350) writes as below:

> *In the former two eating disorders (anorexia nervosa and bulimia nervosa) there lies a morbid fear of gaining weight and extremely consciousness and craving for appearing thin and slim. Here the sufferers of anorexia nervosa are very much convinced that they need to be extremely thin, and they lose so much weight that they may starve themselves to death. People with bulimia nervosa go on frequent eating binges, during which they uncontrollably consume large quantities of food, and then force themselves to vomit or take other extreme steps to keep from gaining weight. A third eating disorder, binge-eating disorder, in which people frequently go on eating binges but do not force themselves to vomit or engage in other such behaviours, appears to be on the rise. People with binge eating disorder do not fear weight gain to the same degree as those with anorexia nervosa and bulimia nervosa, but they do have many of the other features found in those disorders.*

## What Causes Eating Disorders?

Eating disorders of one or the other kind are said to be the function of a multiplicity of causes governed by biological, psychological, and sociocultural factors. Let us know about their impacts in generating and perpetuating these disorders.

## Biological Factors

Biological and genetic theorists talk about the role of biological and genetic factors in causing eating disorders among the people and in their support put forward the following research evidences and arguments

- Like most psychological disorders, eating disorders are found running in families and thus seem to have a genetic component. Family history studies conducted in this concern reveals that relatives of people with eating disorders are found six times more likely than other people the chances of developing the disorders themselves.
- It has been also found that in case one identical twin has one or the other eating disorder, the other twin also develops the disorder in as many as more than 50 percent of the cases. However, in contrast, the rate for fraternal twins, (who are generally less similar in comparison to identical twins), for showing such similarity is quite less than the identical twins.
- There has been found a link between eating disorders and the genes responsible for the production of one of the neurotransmitters, known as serotonin, the lower level of which in an individual has been seen responsible for contributing towards eating disorders- for example, building a lot of depression and obsessive-compulsive disorders associated with eating disorders and also by causing the body to crave and binge on high carbohydrate foods.
- Apart from such genetically based evidences, biological processes are also quite active in the regulation of eating and thus of eating disorders, and substantial evidence points to the hypothalamus as playing an important role in the development of eating disorders.

However, what ever evidences like above may exist for substantiating the role of genetic and biological components in generating eating disorders, they remain quite hollow and weightless as researchers and biologists have not been able to point out a single pair of any defective genes, or inherited biological apparatus responsible for transmitting or causing eating disorder or abnormalities to the next generation. Moreover, eating disorders, like all other mental or psychological disorders and behaviour abnormalities, are the results of ongoing maladjustment faced on account of what has happened in the past or happening at present to him or her in the available sociocultural environment. Let us therefore look for the related psychological and sociocultural factors for the explanation of eating disorders.

## Psychological Factors

The clinical observations and research evidences have been able to suggest a number of psychological factors working behind generating and perpetuating eating disorders among the children and adolescents. These may be named as (i) Low self- esteem, (ii) Diminished sense of personal control and confidence in their own abilities accompanied by a distorted self -perception of body image and (iv) An increased level of anxiety and depression

The children and adolescents who lack in self confidence and self-reliance are more prone to be victimized with the abnormalities of the eating disorders. Such children and adolescents are easily influenced by the opinion of others about their body appearance and then are driven towards dieting or other food restrictions for their ego defence. Their own distorted perception of body image, accompanied with their increased level of anxiety for becoming thin then pushes them to pick up a strange obsession and compulsion for looking thin in the eyes of others and the self in the shape and form of one or the other eating disorders. To throw light on the strange situation faced by the growing children and adolescents in this concern Bruch (1978:128) writes:

> *There is a peculiar contradiction- everybody thinks you're doing so well and everybody thinks you're great, but your real problem is that you think that you are not good enough. You are afraid of not living up to what you think you are expected to do. You have one great fear, namely that of being ordinary, or average, or common-just not good enough. This peculiar dieting begins with such anxiety. You want to prove that you have control, that you can do it. The peculiar part of it is that it makes you feel good about yourself, makes you feel "I can accomplish some- thing". It makes you feel "I can do something nobody else can do"*

As a major psychological factor increased level of anxiety converted into a mood and depressive disorder may also prove a quite potent factor in causing one or the other types of eating disorders. The claim that depressive disorder sets the stage for eating disorders may be supported by four kinds of evidences put forward by Comer (2015:362) as below:

> *First, many more people with an eating disorder qualify for a clinical diagnosis of major depressive disorders than do people in the general population. Second, the close relatives of people with eating disorders seem to have a higher rate of depressive disorders than do close relatives of people without such disorders. Third, many people with eating disorders, particularly bulimia nervosa, have low activity of the neurotransmitter serotonin similar to the serotonin abnormalities found in depression. And finally, people with eating disorders are often helped by some of the same depressants drugs that reduce depression.*

## Sociocultural Factors

These are the sociocultural factors and things inherent in one's sociocultural environment that works really as a birth place and originator as well developer of one or the other abnormalities and problems related to the eating disorders. Even what we know as psychological factors such as ego deficiency, lack of confidence, low self- esteem , distorted self- perception of body image, aroused level of anxiety and depression are itself may be said the by- product of the maladjustment and negativity experienced by the individuals in their sociocultural environment available at home, family, school, community and other social and cultural settings. Let us try to look into the role of sociocultural factors in the development of eating disorders.

1. Hilde Bruch, a pioneer in the study and treatment of eating disorder, has claimed that disturbed mother-child interactions lead to serious *ego deficiencies* in the child

(including a poor sense of independence and control) and to severe *perceptual disturbances* that jointly help produce disordered eating. (Bruch, 2001)

2. Defective style of parenting may not be able to develop genuine self-reliance and self confidence among the growing children capable of having faith in their abilities, and acceptance of their self (including their body shape) in its present form. It may also make them unable to exercise proper control over their needs and impulses reflecting in their uncontrollable binge eating and compensatory behaviour demonstrable in the eating disorders.
3. The uncongenial and improper environment available at the home and in the families may play a quite damaging role in germinating as well as perpetuating eating disorders. Besides, pushing the child in imbibing with anxiety, and depression symptoms, it can provide incentives as well as role models for learning and practicing the behaviour associated with one or the other eating disorders. The description provided here below by a 16 year- old girl may reveal how the behaviour of a mother may drive a child into getting imbibed with an eating disorder.

When I was a kid, say 6 or 7, my Mom and I would go to the drug store all the time. She was heavy and bought all kinds of books and magazine on how to lose weight. Whenever we talked, like after I got home from school, it was almost always about dieting and how to lose weight...I(went) on diets with my Mom, to keep her company. I just got better at it than she did. My eating disorder is my mother's therapy... It's also the way we have time together-working on the diets and exercise and all of that. We've stopped talking about diets since I got anorexia, and now I don't know what we can talk about.

***Source:*** Zerbe, K.J. (2008:20-21), Integrated treatment of eating disorders beyond the body betrayed, New York: W.W. Norton

4. The sociocultural trend available in todays' society in the form of remaining thin for looking good is found to play a substantial role of putting societal pressure in pushing the individuals especially the adolescents and young women towards eating disorders. In learning an eating disorder related behaviour, the beginning for becoming thin, thus, directly results in intense dieting, the first dangerous step down the slippery slope to anorexia and bulimia nervosa (Durand & Barlow, 2013:294). The trend of looking attractive by becoming thin is so universal that it is not uncommon to find a number of performers, models, cine stars, and even athletes around the globe to get trapped in the race of getting thinner and thinner and thus getting victimized as the patients of eating disorders.

## How are Eating Disorders Treated?

Treatment of eating disorders is quite difficult task in its actual operation. In its varying capacity and uniqueness, it stands for the use of a number of therapies and treatment procedures involving hospitalization, medical and drug therapy, supportive psychotherapy, behavioural therapy, group therapy and family therapy. However, no royal road or uniform procedure can be followed in the treatment of all types of eating disorders. Treatment differs for each of the disorders classified as Anorexia nervosa, Bulimia nervosa and Binge eating disorder. Let us therefore discuss the procedure and methods adopted for the treatment of them one by one.

## Treatments for Anorexia Nervosa

Anorexia nervosa is the most dangerous in its consequences among all the three eating disorders There is a considerable weight loss and in case it is quite severe for an individual (say 40% or more below expected normal weight), dehydration, serve chemical imbalances, and possibly organ damage may result. We have the need to provide them medical treatment as early as possible. The difficulty here may arise on account of the unwillingness of the affected individuals. The people with anorexia nervosa neither asks nor agrees for their treatment as they consider themselves O.K. in all aspects. Actually, after hearing comments or concern about their thinness their disorder related behaviour is reinforced and they go further in their slimming efforts. In such a situation, a single alternative lies in getting them compulsory hospitalized or provide them needed medical therapy before reaching the dangerous point. For providing such treatment one has to proceed in the manner as below:

1. In dealing with severe and life- threatening cases of anoxia nervosa, clinicians may need to force tube and intravenous feedings on a patient who refuses to eat.
2. At the next stage, attempts should be made in the form of helping patients with anorexia nervosa gain weight quickly and return to health within weeks. It needs to make use of a good technique helpful in realizing its aim by taking into confidence the patient for this purpose. The popular weight restoration technique named as *nutritional rehabilitation program* may be effectively used for treating the patients. Here the services of a trained nurse are employed for this purpose. She is supposed to (i) gradually increase a patent's diet over the course of several weeks, and (ii) educate patients about the program, track their progress, provide encouragement, and help them recognize that their weight gain is under control and will not lead to obesity.

Restoring weight is thus the main and only aim of the treatment performed through medical measures. However, initial weight gain is a poor predictor of long-term outcome in anorexia nervosa. Without attention to the patent's underlying dysfunctional attitudes about body shape and interpersonal disruptions in his/ her life, the patent will almost always relapse (Durand & Barlow, 2013: 302). After providing necessary medical treatment, therefore, focus of attention should be shift to helping him or her through other treatment measures such as the use of cognitive behavioural therapy and family therapy.

*Use of Cognitive-Behavioural Therapy*: Cognitive-behavioural therapy represents a treatment measure involving a perfect combination or synthesis of two types of interventions-cognitive and behavioural. While providing cognitive intervention, the use of this therapy is meant for bringing the needed change in their mind set by making them able to (1)identify their "core pathology"(the deep- seated belief that they should in fact be judged by their shape and weight and by their ability to control these physical characteristics,(ii) learn alternative ways of coping with stress and solving problems, (iii) recognize their need for becoming independent and learn more appropriate ways to exercise control, and (iv) identify their internal sensations and feelings in a better way along with developing trust in them.

On the other side, in providing behavioural intervention in this therapy patients are made to behave in a more appropriate ways by (i) learning monitoring of their feelings, hunger levels, and food intake in a better way along with a proper understanding about their mutual relationship, (ii) bringing needed changes in their attitudes about eating and weight, (iii) removing their maladaptive assumptions and fears associated with anorexia nervosa such as " our weight and shape determine our worth and value in the society" , or " For being perfect, I should lose weight and appear lean and thin",

In this way, as a whole, total emphasis on the cognitive -behavioural therapy through cognitive and behavioural interventions is laid over bringing changes in the mind set and maladaptive and abnormal eating behaviour of the patients.

Although cognitive -behavioural techniques are often of great help, yet it is better to supplement it with other approaches to bring better results such as family therapy.

*Use of Family Therapy:* What is done by the clinicians and therapists in the form of providing medical or cognitive- behavioural treatment to the patients of anorexia nervosa need to be supplemented and followed by the help received through other approaches or therapies such as family therapy.

In the approach related to the use of Family therapy, a therapist, behavioural psychologist or professional has to work with family members in the actual existing family set up for educating them about the rehabilitation of the anorexia nervosa patient. The attempts made by him in this direction mainly focus on bringing attitudinal and functional changes in the behaviour of the family towards child / adolescent along with his or her distinctive eating disorder issues. For realizing his goal, he may proceed as under:

- He meets the family as a whole in its natural functioning situations and tries to find out what is going on the family related to the disorder of the affected child. He then acquaints the family members with the troublesome family patterns responsible for creating difficulty to the affected child, and help the members and family as a whole to bring needed modification in the environment and behaviour of the family members.
- In addition, every effort is made by him to include the family to accomplish two goals. First, the negative and dysfunctional communication in the family regarding food and eating must be eliminated and meals must be made more structured and reinforcing. Second, attitudes towards body shape and image distortion are discussed at some length in family sessions. Unless the therapists attend to these attitudes, individuals with anorexia nervosa are likely to face a lifetime preoccupation with weight and body shape, struggle to maintain marginal weight and social adjustment, and be subject to repeated hospitalization. Family therapy directed at the goals mentioned here seems to be effective, particularly with young girls (Durand & Barlow, 2013: 302).

## Treatments for Bulimia Nervosa

Treatment programs for Bulimia nervosa much like Anorexia nervosa also involve the practices like medical, cognitive-behavioural, and family therapy for the treatment of the people suffering from bulimia nervosa. However, the treatments carried out with these methods may differ in some ways in their application and outcomes in the ways as discussed ahead.

*Medical treatment or Therapy:* The people with bulimia nervosa seldom requires emergency services of getting hospitalized like the anorexia nervosa sufferers. Still then, it remains always safe and useful to utilize the services of eating disorder clinics and professional for helping the sufferers for coming out from their troubles and difficulties. The treatment programs carried out in these clinics are aimed to serve two types of objectives- immediate and general. In serving immediate goal, here attempts are made for helping clients to eliminate their binge-purge patterns and establishing good eating habits. The serving of the general goal on their part side by side focuses on eliminating the underlying causes of bulimic patterns. Here help may also be taken with the use of drug therapy.

The use of drug therapy which is of limited help to people with anorexia nervosa appears to be quite effective in many cases of bulimia nervosa. For this purpose, clinicians and therapists often prescribe one or the other antidepressant drugs similar to those considered effective for the treatment of mood disorders and anxiety disorders.

However, the clinical treatment and use of drug therapy may be seen to serve their goal of providing immediate and temporary relief to the affected individual. They need to be accompanied and followed by cognitive -behavioural therapy for deriving the long- lasting effect.

*Cognitive-behavioral Therapy:* The use of cognitive-behavioural therapy has been found particularly effective and helpful in treating the individuals suffering from bulimia nervosa- perhaps even more than those suffering from anorexia nervosa. It is particularly aimed to bring needed modifications in the problematic eating behaviour (binge eating and purging) and associated attitudes about the overriding importance and significance to body weight and shape known to be associated with the eating disorder bulimia nervosa.

A general procedure involved in the use of the cognitive- behavioural treatment or therapy may involve the activities like below: (Durand & Barlow, 2013: 302)

- Teaching the patients consequences of binge eating and purging and the ineffectiveness of vomiting and laxative abuse for weight control.
- Educating the patients about the adverse effects of dieting
- Schedule them to eat small, manageable amount of food 5 or 6 times per day aimed to eliminate the alternating periods of overeating and dietary restriction- the hallmarks of bulimia.
- Focusing on altering dysfunctional thoughts and attitudes about body shape, weight and eating.
- Teaching them to make use of coping strategies for resisting the impulse to binge

and purge besides getting them pre-occupied with useful activities for denying them empty time to get engaged in binge eating.

In order to bring desired modification in the behaviour and attitudes of the bulimia nervosa patients, one or the other useful behavioural modification techniques and psychotherapies may also be utilized by the counsellors, and therapists. Talking about such treatment measures, Comer (2015:374) writes:

*Cognitive-behavioural therapists may also use the behavioural techniques of exposure and response prevention to help break the binge-purge cycle. This approach in general involves exposing people to situations that would ordinarily raise anxiety and then preventing them from performing their usual compulsive responses until they learn that the situations are actually harmless and their compulsive acts unnecessary. For bulimia nervosa, the therapists* require *clients to eat particular kinds and amounts of food and then prevent them from vomiting to show that eating can be a harmless and even constructive activity that needs no undoing. Typically, the therapist sits with the client while the client eats the forbidden foods and stays until the urge to purge has passed studies find that this treatment often helps reduce eating –related anxieties, bingeing, and vomiting.*

*The use of Family and Group Therapy:* The techniques and measures related to the use of family therapy for the treatment of the people suffering from bulimia nervosa may be successfully taken well on the lines as done in the case of providing treatment and follow up help to the victims of anorexia nervosa. In addition, here in dealing with the cases of bulimia nervosa, we can also make use of group therapy as an approach to their treatment. Group therapy is delivered in a group set up rather than on individual basis as done in medical, cognitive- behavioural and other psycho- therapies. In one of the approaches adopted in group therapy, the therapist may begin with the formation of self -help groups of the sufferers of bulimia nervosa. In these groups, these victims of bulimia nervosa get valuable opportunities for sharing their concerns and experiences with one another. It helps them to acquire valuable information, self -confidence and self- help lessons for dealing with their eating disorder problems. For example, here they may learn that (i) their disorder is not unique or shameful, (ii) their binge eating behaviour is quite common in their companions and there is no need to maintain secrecy for it, (iii) Their obsessive- compulsive behaviour patterns related to their disorder can be successfully controlled if tried properly on their part etc. In their group all are on the same footing, suffering from the same problems, therefore there is no need for them to hide their weaknesses, or fear about getting exposed and criticized by others. They are free to give and receive support to each other in the form of an honest feedback and insight by sharing their difficulties and measures proved helpful to them in winning over their difficulties

## Treatment for Binge-Eating Disorder

In making difference to the previously known eating disorder Bulimia nervosa, the newly discovered Binge eating disorder is characterized as "bingeing without purge". Here the affected individual although practicing an obsessive- compulsive behaviour of binge eating does not engage in purging. However, except purging, all other behavioural characteristics are significantly alike in both these disorders. Perhaps it is the reason that for the treatment of the patients suffering from the Binge eating disorder we at present are employing the same techniques and methods of treatment or therapies as being followed in the treatment of the Bulimia nervosa discussed above in the form of drug therapy, family therapy, group therapy, and behaviour modification therapies such as cognitive-behavioural therapy, or other forms of psychotherapy. It has been found that the use of such therapies and treatments certainly helps in reducing or eliminating the binge eating patterns besides bringing needed changes in the attitude of the affected individuals particularly related to over concern with weight and shape. It has also been noted that all such treatment measures, therapies and intervention-cognitive or behavioural provide only the short- term help. There are all possibilities for the treated binge eating disorder patients to get victim of a relatively high risk of relapse. Moreover, it is also not uncommon to find treated patients turning overweight and obese, the problem that requires further attention. Thus, in all its dimensions and forms, the treatment as well as follow up programs chalked for the people suffering from binge eating disorder needs further study for doing its job in a satisfactory way.

## Summary

- The developmental disorders such as elimination and eating disorders are found to show their presence among the individuals first during their infancy, childhood or adolescence.
- In general, the children experiencing abnormal and unwelcome behaviour regarding the elimination of urine and faeces from their body are termed as the children suffering from elimination disorders classified as enuresis and encopresis.
- Enuresis is a type of elimination disorder that relates to an abnormal behaviour (involuntary or purposeful) of the toilet trained developing children (more than 4 years old) or adults in which they are found to urinate repeatedly in their clothes and beds. It typically occurs to them at night during sleep but may also occur during the day. The emotional impact of enuresis on a child and family can be considerable damaging. The disorder related to enuresis can be diagnosed and identified on the basis of the children's inability to exercise control over the bladder making them urinate in their clothes or bed.
- The elimination disorder, encopresis may be defined as a type of abnormal behaviour (involuntary or purposeful) demonstrated by the toilet trained developing children (more than 4 years old) or adults in which they are found passing of faeces repeatedly into places other than the toilets such as in their clothing or bed, or anywhere on the floor at their convenience. In the diagnosis and identification of encopresis, first attempts should be made to derive information from the observation of the physiological, physical and psychological symptoms related to this disorder and then same should be get assured through some standard diagnostic criteria such as DSM-5 criteria provided by American Psychiatric Association and the medical report available for this purpose.
- A number of possible factors in their various combinations classified as Genetic,

Biological, Developmental, Psychological, Behavioural and Sociocultural factors may be considered working behind causing and intensifying one or the other types of elimination disorders among children. However, the chronic-long term constipation and the increased level of anxiety and stress on one or the other account is found to play a major role for encopresis.

- Regarding treatment of enuresis it can be seen that most of the younger children suffering from enuresis usually correct themselves even without treatment by the time they grow as adolescents. If needed, then, it remains quite useful to make use of behaviour therapy techniques named as (i) the bell-and -battery technique, and (ii) dry-bed training method. Like enuresis, encopresis also gets better as the child gets older. For seeking its treatment, a number of treatment measures classified as (i) physiological and medical treatment and (ii) Behavioural and psychological treatment may be used for addressing all the physiological, physical, behavioural and emotional issues associated with this disorder.
- Eating disorders may be known as the illnesses or disorders in which the people experience severe disturbances in their eating behaviours and related thoughts and emotions. People with eating disorders typically become pre-occupied with food and their body weight. There are three main types of eating disorders: anorexia nervosa, bulimia nervosa and binge eating disorder.
- Anorexia nervosa is an eating disorder in which people pursue extreme thinness and lose dangerous amounts of weight. The central features of this disorder are a drive for thinness, intense fear of weight gain, and disturbed body perception and other cognitive disturbances. Typically, the disorder begins after a person who is slightly overweight or of normal weight has been on a diet and females are more affected with this disorder than males. In ter ms of its outcomes, people with this disorder are found to develop various medical and health problems such as Skin metabolism and heart related problems and particularly amenorrhoea (the absence of menstrual cycles in women).
- In a perfect similarity with Anorexia nervosa, Bulimia nervosa is also dominated with a morbid fear of gaining weight. However, for becoming thin instead of resorting to rigorous fasting, the people with bulimia nervosa while avoiding regular meals on one hand before others go on frequent eating binges quite often secretly and then force themselves to vomit or take other extreme steps to keep from gaining weight. The binges are often in response to increasing tension and are followed by feelings of guilt and self-blame. In terms of consequences, people with Bulimia nervosa are found to be affected with a number of psychological problems (particularly related to anxiety, depression, obsession-compulsion and mood disorders) and medical problems associated with their teeth and gums, indigestion and intestine disturbances and menstrual periods cycles problem in women.
- Binge-eating disorder is an eating disorder in which people have frequent binge-eating episodes but do not display inappropriate compensatory behaviours. Although most overweight people do not have binge-eating disorder, two thirds of those with binge-eating disorder become overweight. Unlike anorexia

nervosa and bulimia nervosa, this disorder is more evenly distributed among males and females.

- Eating disorders of one or the other kind are said to be the function of a multiplicity of causes governed by biological, psychological, and sociocultural factors. In this concern where, biological and genetic theorists talk about the role of biological and genetic factors in causing eating disorders among the people, psychologists and behaviourists blame the psychological factors such as ego deficiency; lack of self-confidence and self-reliance; and increased level of anxiety, depression and stress for the development of these disorders. The sociocultural perspective in this concern asserts that it is the defective upbringing, uncongenial environment and defective role model available at home, school and community that lead to the development of psychological problems responsible for the germination as well as perpetuation of the eating disorders.
- Treatment of eating disorders involves the use of a number of therapies and treatment procedures such as hospitalization, medical and drug therapy, supportive psychotherapy, cognitive behavioural therapy, group therapy and family therapy. However, treatment in its actual operation differs for each of the disorders. In treating the patients of Anorexia nervosa, the priority lies in getting them hospitalized and take measures for helping them to gain weight and return to normal health. Afterwards, focus of attention should be shift to helping them through other treatment measures such as the use of cognitive-behavioural therapy and family therapy with an objective of bringing changes in the mind set and modifying as well as normalizing the maladaptive and abnormal eating behaviour of the patients. Treatment programs for Bulimia nervosa aim to help the patients in eliminating their binge-purge patterns and establishing good eating habits. For carrying out these objectives a combination of treatment procedure involving the use of medical therapy (including the use of antidepressant drugs and medication), cognitive behavioural and other alternative psychotherapies, family and group therapy, etc. may be employed. For the treatment of the patients suffering from the Binge eating disorder, we at present are employing the same techniques and methods of treatment or therapies as being followed in the treatment of the Bulimia nervosa in the form of drug therapy, family therapy, group therapy, and behaviour modification therapies such as cognitive-behavioural therapy, or other forms of psychotherapy. It has also been noted that all such treatment measures, provide only the short- term help and the possibility of turning their as obese can't also be ruled out.

## REFERENCES

American Psychiatric Association (2013), *Diagnostic and statistical manual of mental disorders (5th ed.),* Arlington, VA: American Psychiatric Publishing.

Bruch, H. (1973) *Eating disorders: obesity; anorexia nervosa and the person within,* New York: Basic Books.

Bruch, H. (1978), The golden age: The enigma of anorexia nervosa, Cambridge MA: Harvard University Press.

Carr, A. 2014. The evidence base for family therapy and systemic interventions for child-focused problems. *Journal of Family Therapy,* DOI: 10.1111/1467-6427.12032

Cohen, D.P. 2011. Encopresis: A medical and family approach. *Pediatric Nursing,* 37, 107-112.

Comer, Ronal J. (2015), *Abnormal Psychology* (Ninth Edition), New York: Worth Publishers (A Macmillan Education Imprint)

Durand, V. and Barlow, D. (2013), *Essentials of Abnormal Psychology* (6th ed.), Wadsworth: Cengage Learning.

Klyko, W.M. & Kay, J. (Ed.), (2012), *Clinical Child Psychiatry.* (3rd Ed.) Oxford, UK. Wiley Blackwell.

Medhekar, D. & Gupta, N. (2010), Use of sertraline in childhood retentive encopresis, *The Annals of Pharmacotherapy,* 44, 395. doi: 10.1345/aph.1M280

What are Eating Disorders? Retrieved on22.04.2019 from https://www.psychiatry.org/patients-families/eating-disorders/what-are-eating-disorders

Zerbe, K.J. (2008), *Integrated treatment of eating disorders beyond the body betrayed,* New York: W.W. Norton

# 21

# SLEEP DISORDERS

## INTRODUCTION

Our sleeping behaviour is a natural behaviour that is closely associated with the satisfaction of one of our essential biological or physiological need named as need to sleep after the long hours of daily chorus. The satisfaction of this need in an appropriate way is quite necessary for keeping us in good health much in the same capacity as consumption of food, drinking of water and inhaling of oxygen in a proper amount help us in our physical wellbeing. Apart from physical, it also affects our psyche and mental health in a variety of ways and it is why, normality maintained in our sleeping behaviour keeps us quite normal in our functioning and overall wellbeing. Any abnormality or irregularity in our sleeping behaviour in terms of sleep disturbances, deprivations and disorders may result into one or the other types of psychophysical, neurotic and psychotic abnormalities and disorders. In what different ways one can fall victim to such disturbances, abnormalities and disorders, let us try to know all about this. But before doing this let us first, try to know what happens with us usually during our night sleep.

## The Types and Stages of Sleep

Normally the people after remaining awake for a quite long hours in the day fall asleep during the night hours ranging from five to eight hours. During this duration of their night sleep, they are found to go through several different stages of sleep involving two types of sleep named REM (Rapid eye movement) sleep and NREM (Non rapid eye movement) sleep. While falling asleep, the people first go through an episode of NREM sleep involving first three stages of their night sleep named as (i) the transitory or lightest stage of sleep, (ii) the stage of light sleep and (iii) the stage of deep sleep. After then they enter the fourth stage of their night sleep characterized by REM type of sleep.

NREM sleep aims to provide complete rest, relaxation and healing to the body and mind specially through the third stage of its deep sleep. REM sleep associated with the fourth stage of one's sleep is characterized with rapid movement of one's eyes in different directions. Being an active type of sleep, it is unable to provide such rest and peace as available in NREM sleep. In comparison to NREM sleep it is more popularized as a dreaming stage of one's sleep as 90% of one's total dreams are experienced in this stage of sleep. Besides this, awakening as well as arousals can occur more easily in this type of sleep. However, the voluntary muscles are generally paralysed during REM sleep, therefore, one's body is unable to act upon the dreams experienced in REM dreams (bad dreams and nightmares) in the way as happens in NREM dreams involving night terror, and sleep walking.

## Sleep Disorders-Concept and Types

Sleep disorders represent the irregularities, disturbances and abnormalities, occurred in one's night sleep. These disorders have been identified and categorized by the researchers and clinicians in the two major categories named as Dyssomnias and Parasomnias.

*Dyssomnias sleep disorders:* In this category, we may include the sleep disorders that are mainly associated with the disturbances occurred in the amount, timing or quality of one's sleep. The people suffering with such sleep disorders are found complaining in the manner that (i) I am unable to have enough sleep, (ii) I feel difficulty in falling asleep when I need or desire so, (iii) My sleep is disturbed with a slight noise or sometimes with no reason, (iv) I don't feel refreshed even after sleeping the whole night, etc. Dyssomnias sleep disorders on account of their varying characteristics may be further categorized as (a) Primary insomnia, (b) Primary hypersomnia, (c) Narcolepsy, (d) Breathing-related sleep disorder, and (e) Circadian rhythm sleep disorder (sleep-wake schedule disorder).

*Parasomnias sleep disorders:* In this category, we may include the sleep disorders that are mainly associated with the disturbances in arousal and sleep stage transition from one stage of sleep to another that intrude into the sleep process. People suffering with such type of sleep disorders are found to demonstrate a quite typical abnormal behaviour in their sleep (both NREM and REM) such as night mare, night terror and sleep walking. In this way, parasomnias sleep disorders are not problems with sleep itself but also involve abnormal events that occur either during sleep or during that twilight time between sleeping and waking. Parasomnias sleep disorders may be further categorized into two distinct types (i) those that occur during REM sleep such as nightmares and (ii) those that occur during NREM sleep such as night terrors and night sleep walking.

The above categorization and sub-categorization of various Sleep disorders suffered by the people during their sleep may be well illustrated through the figure 21.1 given below.

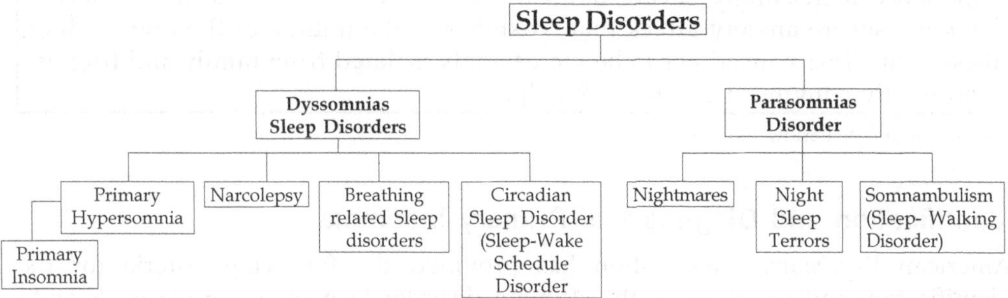


Fig 21.1: The categorization and sub-categorization of sleep disorders.

Let us know the needed essentials about the nature and characteristics of all these sleep disorders classified in the figure given above. For this purpose, let us first discuss the sleep disorders falling in the category of Dyssomnias.

## Primary Insomnia

The term insomnia in its word meaning stands for one's inability to sleep. It may imply that a person suffering from such sleeping disorder may be found awakened all the time. However, the total lack of sleep is not possible in the case of living being since a higher degree of its occurrence may eventually leads to death. In its practical application, the term primary insomnia is found to be associated with some typical problems and difficulties arising in one's night sleep characterized as:

(i) *Difficulty initiating sleep:* The people suffering from primary insomnia may complain that it becomes too difficult for them to fall asleep despite their best efforts in doing so. They have to wait for it continuously for hours.

(ii) *Difficulty in maintaining sleep:* They may complain that they are unable to enjoy sound sleep for a satisfactory duration. They wake up frequently during their night sleep and once awakened, it becomes difficult for them to go back to sleep.

(iii) *Non restorative sleep:* They may complain that their night sleep is not fulfilling the required restorative function as even after spending a reasonable number of hours in their night sleep, they are unable to feel fresh for doing the next day activities.

The above cited typical features found in the people suffering from primary insomnia may be more clearly visualized through the case history given below:

> Sonia was a 23-year-old law student with the history of sleep problems. She reported that she never really slept well, both having trouble falling asleep at night and usually awakening again in the early morning. Since she started law school last year, her sleep problems had grown even worse. She would lie in bed awake until the morning hours thinking about school, getting only 3-4 hours of sleep on atypical night. In the morning, she had a great deal of difficulty getting out of bed and was frequently late for her early-morning class. Sonia's sleep problems and their interference with her schoolwork were causing her to experience increasingly severe depression. In addition, she recently reported having a severe anxiety attack that woke her in the middle of the night. All of these difficulties caused her to be increasingly isolated from family and friends, who finally convinced her to seek help.

***Source:*** Durand & Barlow (2013:311)

### Identification and Diagnosis of Primary Insomnia

American Psychiatric Association has provided the following criteria for the identification and diagnosis of the sleeping disorder Primary insomnia in its DSM IV TR.

**Table 21.1: Diagnostic criteria for Primary Insomnia**

- Difficulty initiating or maintaining sleep, or non-restorative sleep, for at least one month.
- The sleep disturbance (or associated day time fatigue) causes clinically significant distress or impairments in functioning
- The sleep disturbance does not occur exclusively during the course of narcolepsy, a breathing-related sleep disorder, a circadian rhythm sleep disorder, or a parasomnia.
- The disturbance does not occur exclusively during the course of another mental disorder.
- The disturbance is not due to the direct physiological effects of a substance (e.g. a drug of abuse, a medication) or a general medical condition.

*Source:* APA (2000), DSM-IV-TR

## Causes related to Primary Insomnia:

A number of biological, psychological and environmental factors act towards causation of Primary insomnia among the individuals. Durand and Barlow (2013:313) have mentioned about the following as some of the factors responsible for causing interference with one's sleeping:

1. Drug use and a variety of environmental influences such as changes in light, noise, or temperature.
2. Various Psychological stresses
3. Unrealistic expectations about how much sleep they need
4. As a learned behaviour, it may be acquired by associating the bedroom and bed with the frustration and anxiety that go with insomnia.
5. Biological vulnerability interacting with sleep stress may result in sleep disorder

## Primary Hypersomnia

Hypersomnia sleeping disorder run quite contrary to the insomnia sleeping disorder both in its nature as well as functioning. The difference among these disorders are self- revealing through the prefixes "hyper" and "in" appearing in their word composition. In their usual meanings where 'hyper' stands for greater amount or abnormal excess of a thing or phenomenon, the prefix 'in' stands for lacking or without. Accordingly, while people suffering from primary insomnia are not getting enough sleep, the people suffering from hypersomnia, on the other hand, are grappled with the problem of sleeping too much. Besides sleeping in a greater amount and duration in the night, these people are also found to fall asleep several times the next day.

Clinically speaking, the causation of primary hypersomnia is linked with some or the other dysfunction of one's central nervous system. In its symptomology, it is revealed through major sleep episode and excessive sleepiness consisting of prolonged (one or two hour) episodes of non-rapid eye movement sleep. It has a similar presentation to narcolepsy, but is not generally associated with cataplexy or sleep-onset rapid eye movement. In its outcomes, it is known as one of the serious sleep disorders often disrupting the work, family life and interpersonal ties of the sufferers. The characterized feature of this sleeping disorder may be properly revealed through a case history provided below:

A 32-year-old Caucasian woman came to us with complaints of excessive daytime sleepiness (EDS). She had no problems with her sleep or general health until two years before, when she began to experience excessive daytime fatigue. Her condition progressed and at the time of presentation she was able to sleep for extended periods of time (up to two to three days at a stretch) and still be hyper somnolent in the day. On questioning, she denied cataplexy, hypnagogic hallucinations or sleep paralysis. There was no prior history of closed head injury, meningitis or any focal cerebrovascular symptoms. During her initial diagnostic work-up for fatigue, she was found to have a mildly elevated TSH level. She was started on thyroxine, but her symptoms persisted (in spite of TSH value subsequently returning to normal). She had been working in an office setting, but quit her job a month before on account of her EDS and difficulty in concentrating. She stopped driving because she had found herself in the wrong lane on occasion and not sure how she got there. She is married with two children and there is no family history of excessive daytime sleepiness.

*Source:* John.DJ. Manoharan A, Varghese R., A case of primary hypersomnia, Ann Indian Acad, Neurol, 2007, 10: 58-60.

## Identification and Diagnosis of Primary Hypersomnia

American Psychiatric Association has provided the following criteria for the identification and diagnosis of the sleeping disorder Primary Hypersomnia in its DSM IV TR.

**Table 21.2: Diagnostic criteria for Primary Hypersomnia**

- Excessive sleepiness for at least 1 month (or less if recurrent) as evidenced by either prolonged sleep episodes or daytime sleep episodes that occur almost daily
- The excessive sleepiness causes clinically significant distress or impairment in functioning
- The excessive sleepiness is not better accounted for by insomnia, does not occur exclusively during the course of some other sleep disorder, and cannot be accounted for by an inadequate amount of sleep
- The disturbance does not occur exclusively during the course of another mental disorder.
- The disturbance is not due to the direct physiological effects of a substance or a general medical condition.

*Source:* APA (2000), DSM-IV-TR

## Narcolepsy

In the category of Dyssomnias sleep disorders, Narcolepsy is considered a quite serious and chronic sleep disorder usually characterized by the features like (i) excessive daytime sleepiness, (ii) sleep attacks and (iii) the rapid eye movement (REM) sleep abnormalities such as cataplexy, sleep paralysis and hypnagogic hallucination.

On account of their appearance in the abnormal behaviour of other disorders, the symptoms of narcolepsy cited above may be often mistaken for branding the people suffering from those disorders, for example,

- The excessive daytime sleepiness of narcolepsy patients may be mistaken for identifying them as suffering from primary hypersomnia or with the fatigue of atypical depression,
- The cataplexy exhibited in the functioning of the narcolepsy patients may be mistaken for considering them as suffering from epilepsy, and
- The vivid hypnagogic hallucinations exhibited in the behaviour of the narcolepsy patients may be mistaken for getting them affected with the true hallucinations of a psychotic disorder.

However, Narcolepsy differs from the other so mentioned disorders in its possession of a unique characteristic signifying the presence of all the three REM sleep abnormalities- cataplexy, sleep paralysis and hypnagogic hallucination besides being loaded with the symptom of excessive sleepiness and sleep attacks. Let us know about the nature and characteristics of all these three REM sleep abnormalities visible in the Narcolepsy patients.

By the term cataplexy, we here mean a sudden loss of muscle tone at the time of their REM sleep on the part of narcolepsy patients for the duration ranging from several seconds to several minutes. It is usually preceded by strong emotion such as anger or happiness. As example of the negative outcomes of cataplexy (sudden loss of muscle tone) experienced on the part of narcolepsy patients we may quote the instances such as suddenly falling asleep (for a brief duration) while cheering your favourite team, or collapsing to the floor in a sound sleep while having heated verbal duel with someone. In seeking reasons for such behaviour Durand & Barlow (2013:315)) write:

*Cataplexy appears to result from a sudden onset of REM sleep. Instead of falling asleep normally and going through the four non-rapid eye movement (NREM) stages that typically precede REM sleep, people with narcolepsy periodically progress right to the dream-sleep stage almost directly from the state of being awake. One outcome of REM sleep is the inhibition of input to the muscles, and this seems to be the process that leads to cataplexy.*

The second REM sleep related characteristic or terrifying experience demonstrated by the narcolepsy patients in their abnormal behaviour is known by the term sleep paralysis. Here they are subjected to a paralysis like attack in their REM sleep i.e. inability to move or speak for a brief immediately after their awakening.

The last third REM sleep related characteristic visible in the narcolepsy patients is passing through a quite terrifying experiences in the shape of hypnagogic hallucinations such as experiencing vivid illusion of being caught in a fire or flying through the air.

The characterized features of the Narcolepsy may be properly revealed through a case history provided below:

| A 22-year-old woman consulted with our department because of her excessive daytime sleepiness and sleep attacks. Her daytime sleepiness began when she was around thirteen years old and it had been getting worse. When she was in high school, she couldn't stay wake during her classes or exams. When she worked at a department store as a saleswoman after graduating from high school, she frequently dozed off standing up, and for this she was dismissed. She also got into a collision while driving due to a sudden sleep attack. Cataplexy developed as her daytime sleepiness got worse, and after the age of nineteen, it would occur almost every day. Cataplexy occurred when she laughed, got angry or exchanged jokes. It even occurred when she was excited, surprised and embarrassed, and when she reminisced about happy moments. Her knees would suddenly buckle and her jaws sagged. She also complained of seeing ghosts or animals and hearing her name called when she was lying down at night. She experienced realistic and often scary dreams throughout the night; when she awoke, she was unable to move. There was no history of trauma to the head or any psychiatric illnesses. However, her father did suffer from constant sleepiness and fatigue, and also occasionally sudden muscle weakness of both knees when laughing. Although he consulted various hospitals, they told him nothing was out of the ordinary, but they recommended that he see a psychiatrist. The psychiatrist prescribed him 37.5 mg of venlafaxine and 0.75 mg of alprazolam for depression. However, he was still sleepy and languid in spite of those medications. |
|---|

*Source:* Yoon-Kyung Shin .et al, (2007), Case Study of a Narcoleptic Patient with a Family History of Narcolepsy, Department of Neuropsychiatry, St. Vincent's Hospital, Korea.

## Identification and Diagnosis of Narcolepsy

American Psychiatric Association has provided the following criteria for the identification and diagnosis of the sleeping disorder Narcolepsy in its DSM IV TR.

**Table 21.3: Diagnostic criteria for Narcolepsy**

- Irresistible attack of refreshing sleep that occur daily over at least 3 months
- The presence of one or both of the following:
  - (i) Cataplexy (i.e. brief episodes of sudden bilateral loss of muscle tone, most often in association with intense emotion)
  - (ii) Recurrent intrusions of elements of rapid eye movement (REM) sleep into the transition between sleep and wakefulness, as manifested by either hypnopompic or hypnagogic hallucinations or sleep paralysis at the beginning or end of sleep episodes

The disturbance is not due to the direct physiological effects of a substance or another general medical condition.

*Source:* APA (2000), DSM-IV-TR

## Breathing-Related Sleep Disorders

The term breathing-related sleep disorders is used for the type of sleep disorders in which there lie some physical origin-namely problems with the breathing of the people while asleep causing them to experience widely disrupted sleep at night and excessive sleepiness (insomnia) during the whole day. Their breath related problems are quite unique, harmful and damaging in their nature and consequences. Let us peep through the origin and nature of these problems.

It is quite natural for our muscles in the upper airway relax during sleep. Such relaxation of the muscles causes the constriction of airway passage and it then leads to create some difficulty and hurdles in our breathing. However, in the case of some individuals known to be grappled with breathing related disorders, the constriction of these muscles, during their sleep, is in such a great amount that it may stop their breathing altogether for a shorter period of 10 to 30 seconds. This phenomenon is named as sleep apnea in the world of medicines and abnormal psychology.

There are three types of sleep apnea (named as obstructive, central and mixed sleep apnea) each causing a distinctive type of breath related sleep disorder among the affected individuals. Let us see how.

*Obstructive sleep apnea:* In this type of sleep apnea, there occurs a short- term stoppage of breathing despite the normal functioning of one's respiratory system. It happens due to some obstruction caused to one's breathing on account of much narrowness of the airway or the interference caused to the ongoing efforts of breathing by some abnormality or damage to breathing organs. The sleep disorder caused by such sleep apnea is well distinguished in the form of one' loud and frightening snoring at night. The affected person remains quite unaware of his or her snoring problem in spite of troubling others present in the vicinity. Obstruction sleep apnea, however, may create a lot of obstruction and difficulties in the continuity of their sound sleep and they may be found to wake up frequently during their night sleep. In addition to snoring and frightening episodes of interrupted breathing and disrupted sleep, the other noticeable symptoms found in the behaviour of the persons suffering from obstructive sleep apnea are (i)partial or complete cessation of breathing during sleep, (ii) reduction in blood oxygen levels ,(iii) heavy sweating during the night, (iv) morning headaches, and (v) excessive day time sleepiness or insomnia.

The people belonging to all ages, including children may be found to be affected with obstructive sleep apnea. However, as a whole the overweight adults (particularly the men rather than women) are found to be affected with such disorder in a greater proportion who snore heavily and show all other visible symptoms of obstructive sleep apnea.

*Central sleep apnea:* In this type of sleep apnea, there occurs the total cessation of respiratory activity for brief periods. It is alleged to be caused with the disorders or diseases related to one's central nervous system such as cerebral vascular disease, head trauma, and degenerative disorders (Durand & Barlow,2013:315). Like obtrusive sleep apnea, the people suffering from central sleep apnea are also found to experience obstruction and interruption in their sound sleep. They may wake up frequently during the night. However, in its consequences this sleep disorder differs a lot from the obtrusion related sleep apnea in the sense that (i) the people suffering from this disorder do not report excessive daytime sleepiness or insomnia,(ii) it does not exhibit the major breathing problem symptoms such as abnormal snoring, (iii) it does not causes much difficulty or problem to the sufferers in their day business and as a result they seldom come forward for seeking treatment to this disorder.

*Mixed sleep apnea:* True to its naming, this type of sleep apnea is a combination of both obstructive and central sleep apneas. The persons suffering from this type of sleep disorder thus may be found to exhibit a combination of symptoms and face difficulties as faced by the obstructive and central apneas patients. As a whole thus they may be found to experience breathing difficulties of the nature interrupting their sleep and result in symptoms similar to those of insomnia.

### Identification and Diagnosis of Breathing-Related sleep disorders

American Psychiatric Association has provided the following criteria for the identification and diagnosis of the Breathing -related sleep disorders in its DSM IV TR.

**Table 21.4: Diagnostic criteria for Breathing-related sleep disorders**

- Sleep disruption, leading to excessive sleepiness or insomnia, that is judged to be due to sleep-related breathing condition (e.g. obstructive or central sleep apnea syndrome, central alveolar hypoventilation syndrome)
- The disruption is not better accounted for by another mental disorder and is not due to the direct physiological effects of a substance or another general medical condition.

*Source:* APA (2000), DSM-IV-TR

## Circadian Rhythm Sleep Disorders

The term Circadian Rhythm Sleep Disorders is used for the type of sleep disorders in which the affected individuals are found to experience disturbances and interruptions in their night sleep on account of some or the other types of shift in their sleep-wake schedule. With a close association to the shift in the sleep-wake schedules of the affected individuals these disorders are also named as sleep-wake schedule disorders. American Psychiatric Association (2000) in its DSM IV -TR manual has named them as a product of the mismatch between the sleep-wake schedule required by a person's environment and his or her circadian sleep-wake cycle. Let us look into one or the other possibilities of witnessing such mismatch or shift in the sleep-wake schedule of the affected people.

1. One of such possibility may arise in experiencing jet-lag related situation in one's day to day living. When we happen to visit a county or tourist place having a different clock timing such as USA, we may clearly experience the sleep related problems in a quite distinctive form. In USA as you know it is the day when there are night timings in our country and vice versa. As a result, we may find ourselves falling asleep during the day time and getting awakened during the night timings of that country in the usual follow up of our sleep -wake schedule. Such type of difficulty and disturbances experienced in our sleep is named as jet lag type of circadian rhythm sleep disorder.

2. The other possibility of getting victim of circadian rhythm sleep disorder may arise in the situation where the type of work done or duties performed in an occupation requires from the individuals to remain awakening at the sleeping hours of the night and have sleep in day hours in a quite contradiction to their habitual sleep-wake pattern. The situation gets more worsened or complicated when they have to work sometimes in the night or other times in the day shifts as per demand of their work environment. Such type of alterations and fluctuations in one's work schedule makes the people to fall prey to the unwanted outcomes of atypical type of sleep disorder known as shift work type sleep disorder.
3. In addition to these two well- known types of circadian rhythm sleep disorders, Durand and Barlow have mentioned about the presence of a third type of circadian rhythm sleep disorders existing among the affected persons described as below:

*In contrast with jet lag and shift work sleep-related problems, which have external causes such as long-distance travel and job selection, several circadian rhythm sleep disorders seem to arise from within the person experiencing the problems. Extreme night owls, people who stay up late and sleep late, may have a problem known as delayed sleep phase type. Sleep is delayed or later than the normal bedtime. At the other extreme, people with an advanced sleep phase type of circadian rhythm disorder are "early to bed and early to rise" Here sleep is advanced or earlier than normal bed-time (2013:316).*

The characterized features of a circadian rhythm sleep disorder may be properly revealed through a case history provided below:

A 24-year-old male patient reports difficulty falling asleep, followed by daytime sleepiness, a pattern that has persisted for about 5 years since his days as a student. His excessive sleepiness has become more severe during the past year due to the 8 AM starting time for his work shift. He recently needed to take 2 personal days off from work due to inability to report on time. Once asleep, he does not have difficulty staying asleep. His bedtime ranges from 11:30 PM to 1:00 AM, with time required to fall asleep averaging 2 hours. His wake time is scheduled for 6:45 AM on workdays. Weekday mornings are particularly difficult. The patient feels "out of it" until about noon. He has fallen asleep while driving to work and has had several near-miss traffic accidents the past month. His blood pressure is stable at 130/80 mm Hg, and he has a body mass index (BMI) of 26. His mother and brother both suffer from similar types of insomnia symptoms.

*Source:* Zee, Phyllis C. (2011), Case Histories in Circadian Rhythm Sleep Disorders, Med Scope

## Identification and Diagnosis of Circadian Rhythm Sleep Disorders

American Psychiatric Association has provided the following criteria for the identification and diagnosis of the circadian sleep disorders in its DSM IV TR.

**Table 21.5: Diagnostic criteria for circadian sleep disorders**

- A persistent or recurrent pattern of sleep disruption leading to excessive sleepiness or insomnia that is due to a mismatch between the sleep-wake schedule required by a person's environment and his or her circadian sleep-wake pattern

- The sleep disturbances clinically significant distress or impairment in functioning
- The disturbance does not occur exclusively during the course of another sleep disorder or other mental disorder
- The disturbance is not due to the direct physiological effects of a substance or a general medical condition

*Source:* APA (2000), DSM-IV-TR

## Treatment of Dyssomnias Type Sleep Disorders

In the list of Dyssomnias type sleep disorders we have here included the sleep disorders named as primary insomnia, hyper insomnia, narcolepsy, breathing related disorders and circadian-rhythm sleep disorders. The treatment measures applied to all these dyssomnias type disorders may be classified as medical measures, environmental measures and psychological measures. Let us try to discuss the use of these measures in the treatment of such type of sleep disorders.

### *Medical Measures*

The use of medicine or medical treatment is one of a widely used practices for seeking remedy to any disturbance-physical or mental in the human body. In this sequence, clinicians and physicians may be found to prescribe a number of suitable medicines shown in the table below for the treatment of various dyssomnias type sleep disorders.

**Table 21.6: Medication used for the treatment of various Dyssomnias**

| The Dyssomnias type sleep disorder | The prescribed medicine or medical measure for treatment |
|---|---|
| Primary Insomnia | One of several benzodiazepine including (i)short acting drugs such as triazolam (Halcion), zaleplon (Sonata), and zolpidem (Ambein) and (ii) long - acting drugs like flurazepam (Dalmane). |
| Primary Hypersomnia | Stimulants such as methylphenidate (Ritalin) or modafinil. |
| Narcolepsy | Antidepressant drugs to deal with the cataplexy (loss of muscle tone) attacks. |
| Breathing -related sleep disorders | (i) Recommending weight loss to the obese patients<br>(ii) Using a mechanical device-called the continuous positive air pressure (CPAP) machine for improving breathing in the people suffering from obstructive sleep apnea.<br>(iii) Recommending surgery to help remove blockage in parts of the airways. |
| Circadian rhythm sleep disorders | There is no usual practice to recommend medications for the treatment of these sleep disorders. |

Practically speaking, the use of medication, especially the prescription of drugs is generally made to seeking treatment to insomnia (excessive sleepiness). However, the use of drugs is severally criticized on account of the drawbacks or ill consequences like below resulted through their use.

- The use of drugs may intensify the problem by causing excessive sleepiness.
- It can make people too much dependent on them.
- People may be found to make their misuse deliberately or non-deliberately.
- These medications have a limitation to work for the short-term treatment (not longer than 4 weeks) of insomnia. They can't work well for the treatment of long-term chronic sleep problems. Moreover, in their longer use there lies an inherent danger of promoting dependence and rebounding insomnia.
- According to the latest researches, the use of some medications prescribed for the treatment of insomnia have a possibility of increasing the likelihood of sleep walking-related problems such as sleep-related eating disorders.

### Environmental Measures

For the treatment of Dyssomnias type sleep disorders, a certain type of special measures involving environment modifications or changes in the prevalent circumstances are also used by the practitioners and professionals on a number of occasions. The use of such measures can help much in seeking treatment for the cases affected with circadian rhythm sleep disorders.

In making environmental setting adjustment for dealing with circadian rhythm sleep disorder problems one may be advised to follow certain good measures like:

1. It remains always better to move bedtime later than moving bedtime earlier. In case you feel sleepy in the day time while staying in USA, it will be better for you to delay your sleeping until the scheduled hours of night bedtime. In this way People can best readjust their sleep patterns by going to bed several hours later each night until bedtime is at the desired hour. Similarly scheduling shift changes in a clockwise direction (going from day to evening schedule) seems to help workers adjust better to their sleep awake cycle.
2. The use of phototherapy (bright light) is also found also help much in dealing with circadian rhythm related problems. While making use of this therapy the affected people are typically asked to sit in front of a bank of fluorescent lamps that generate light greater than an amount significantly different from normal indoor. Several hours of exposure to this bright light have successfully reset the circadian rhythms of many individuals (Durand &Barlow,2013:319).

### Psychological Measures

The abnormality of behavioural functioning lies well in the roots of dyssomnias type sleep disorders and that's why their appropriate remedy lies in the making use of one or the other psychological treatments chiefly based on the behaviour modification techniques or therapies.

We can name the important ones as

(i) Cognitive behavioural therapy, (ii) Guided imagery therapy, (iii) Meditation therapy, (iv) Progressive relaxation therapy, and (v) Stimulus control therapy.

*Cognitive behavioural therapy (CBT):* Treatment carried out in this behavioural approach aims to bring changes in the defective cognitive functioning of the affected people particularly related to their dysfunctional beliefs and unrealistic expectations about their sleep lying in the roots of their chronic insomnia such as (i) having over concern about the total sleep duration i.e. "I must have 8 hours of sleep each night" and in case if I get less than 8 hours of sleep, it will make me ill" (ii) "excessive sleepiness or insomnia is dangerous, it may lead to insanity" etc. CBT aims to replace these views with more adaptive substitutes. For this purpose the therapist try to bring alterations in the unrealistic beliefs and attitudes of the patients about sleeping by having discussion on the topics such as normal amounts of sleep, our ability to compensate for lost sleep, providing correct information about the sleeping behaviour in terms of normal amounts of sleep needed, the ability to compensate for lost sleep and removal of misperceptions if any in this concern.

*Guided Imagery Therapy-* An imagery stands for the process of creating an experience/image in the mind of an individual in the absence of any external stimuli. In the treatment of the insomnia, the therapists try to make use of suitable and appropriate imageries putting the affected individuals to experience the act of sleeping in their mind. The experiencing of such imagery on their part helps in providing them relaxation and relief from their sleep related anxiety associated with their difficulty sleeping.

*Meditation therapy-* The anxiety and stress related situations and the unfavourable attitude developed in the individuals about their sleep may work as a strong factor in creating hurdles and having difficulty sleeping on their part in their routine sleep. The mediation technique practiced by the affected people may play wonder in getting relief and remedy in this situation. The practice of meditation such as transcendental meditation proves a quite helping hand in providing the needed relaxation and thought control device for seeking remedy to the anxiety and stress ridden difficulty sleep of the affected people.

*Progressive relaxation therapy-* The technique of progressive relaxation may be successfully used in the treatment of anxiety and stress ridden sleep problems. In its practical application, progressive relaxation begins with the affected person lying on his back with arms extended to the side. One by one, major muscle groups of the body are first tensed and then slowly relaxed. It is aimed to assist in the identification of the various muscle systems within the body and to help the affected individual to learn how to discriminate between tensed and relaxed muscle conditions. The step by step relaxation of the tensed muscles then helps the affected individual to seek remedy to his or her difficulty sleep.

*Stimulus control therapy:* This type of behavioural therapy is based on the assumption that stimuli present in one' sleeping environment play a key role in the quantity and quality of one's sleep. Therefore, due care should be taken for exercising needed control over these stimuli for ensuring trouble fee sleep. Thus, the main focus in this therapy lies in helping the patients to learn the way of exercising needed control over the environmental stimuli affecting their sleep. For this purpose, due attention in this therapy is given in helping the patients learn the art of (i) re-associating their bedtime and the sleep environment with their sleeping and (ii) seeking correction of the learned maladaptive behaviour that disrupt their sleep. A therapist while making use of this therapy may be found to work for instructing and advising the concerned patients to adapt to the following schedule and practices in their sleeping behaviour.

- They should avoid to make use of their bed and bed room for anything extra than sleeping such as reading, eating, laying idle on the bed or watching TV etc.
- It should be made in to their habit to go to bed only when sleepy.
- In case, they are unable to fall asleep in a reasonable duration say 20 or 30 minutes, then they should not unnecessary struggle for it. It remains better for them to get up and go to another room. Stay up as long as they wish and then return to the bedroom to sleep.
- They should be made to follow a set schedule of sleep-awake for helping their body acquire a consistent sleep rhythm. For this purpose, they should be advised to set the alarm and get up at the same time every morning regardless of how much sleep they had received during the night.
- They should be advised to avoid napping during the day for enjoying uninterrupted scheduled sleep in the night.
- It should also be made into their habit to avoid any recovery sleep in the day to compensate for the loss of sleep during the previous bad night.

## Parasomnias Sleep Disorders

Let us now know about all the three parasomnias sleep disorders-nightmares, night sleep terrors and night sleep walking falling one by one.

## Nightmares

As told earlier, nightmares in the form of bad dreams occur during one's REM or dream sleep. These may be experienced in the form of a peculiar type of bad dreams by all persons of all ages but are more common with the children and tend to decrease with age. These are distinguished from the bad dreams in the sense that where nightmares are defined as disturbing dreams that awaken the sleeper; bad dreams are those that do not awaken the person experiencing them. Moreover, to qualify as a nightmare disorder, these bad dream experiences must be so distressful and terrifying that they impair a person's ability to carry on normal activities i.e. making a person too anxious to try to sleep at night (Durand &Barlow, 2013:320). Other distinguished features of the nightmares are known in the form of (i) not making people move around as happens to them in the NREM sleep related disorders- night terror and sleep walking, and (ii) Vividly remembered on the part of the dreamers immediately upon waking.

The above cited characterized features of the nightmare sleep disorder may be properly revealed through a case history provided below:

> David was a 70-year-old retired lorry driver. He consulted on the insistence of his adult daughter after she witnessed what she thought was her father having a seizure one night. David admitted to a seven-year history of disturbed sleep. Every two to three weeks he experienced a night where his dreams were vivid and violent involving being chased by animals or attacked by strangers.
>
> The dreams manifested themselves in physical actions such as David punching the wall or flinging himself out of bed. These actions were carried out while still asleep but would jerk him awake. Sleep-walking was never a feature. He did not feel unduly tired after one of these disturbed nights but had suffered some minor bruising. On other nights he would get approximately eight hours unbroken sleep. David prided himself on keeping fit, undertaking some kind of activity every day. He had no past medical history and was taking no regular medications.

*Source:* Topp, Julia,(2009),Case study-Disturbed sleep and Vivid Nightmares.

## Identification and Diagnosis of Nightmares

American Psychiatric Association has provided the following criteria for the identification and diagnosis of the sleeping disorder Nightmares in its DSM IV TR.

**Table 21.7: Diagnostic criteria for Nightmares**

- Repeated awakening from the major sleep period or naps with detailed recall of extended and extremely frightening dreams, generally during the second half of the sleep period.
- On awakening from the frightening dreams, the person rapidly becomes oriented and alert
- The dream experience, or the sleep disturbance resulting from the awakening, causes significant distress or impairment in functioning
- Nightmares do not occur exclusively during the course of another mental disorder and are not due to the direct physiological effects of a substance or a general medical condition.

*Source:* APA (2000), DSM-IV-TR

## Night sleep terrors

*Night sleep terrors* are also termed as the bad dreams and may resemble nightmares in some ways such as the child cries and appears frightened much like in nightmares. However, unlike nightmares, they have a distinction of (i) representing a state of panic (e.g. unable to move, breathe) experienced by the dreamers in their sound sleep, (ii) occurring during one's NREM deep sleep, (iii) making dreamers act up on their dreaming experience in the form of sitting up, screaming, running around the sleeping room, defending the self from the unseen attacker, etc. while remaining under the state of their sound sleep, (iv) providing no chance to awake and comfort the terrified child as possible during a nightmare, and (v) no remembering on the part of children what happened to them during a night-terror episode.

The characteristics features of sleep terrors visible among the affected children may be more clearly understood by a glimpse on the case history of a sleep terror affected child given below:

We report a case of sleep terror in a 4-year-old boy. The parents observed that for the past month, after the child going bed to sleep, he happened to being wake up in the middle of the night. This behaviour occurs once or twice a week. On these occasions, the child is found standing somewhere in the house, crying and seemingly disoriented with rapid breathing and profuse sweating. When the parents attempt to comfort him or return him to his room, he becomes quite upset, striking out at them and screaming loudly. He continues to scream and fight for several minutes, followed by spontaneous cessation. Once the child is calmed, the parents can put him back in his bed, and he sleeps through the rest of the night without incident. In the morning, he wakes up in usual happy mood and does not remember what occurred the previous evening. The parents are worried that he might be having seizures or developing a severe behavioural problem. Lab blood work-up is solicited, including an electroencephalogram (EEG). All returned normal results.

*Source:* Guzman, Carlos Simon and Wang, Yuan Pang, "Sleep terror disorder: a case report", Brazilian Journal of Psychiatry, Vol.30, No.2 Sao Paula, June 2008.

## Identification and Diagnosis of Sleep terrors

American Psychiatric Association has provided the following criteria for the identification and diagnosis of the sleep terror disorders in its DSM IV TR.

**Table 21.8: Diagnostic criteria for Sleep terror disorders**

- Recurrent episodes of abrupt awakening from sleep, usually occurring during the first third of the major sleep episode and beginning with a panicky scream.
- Intense fear and signs of automatic arousal such as tachycardia, rapid breathing, and sweating, during each episode
- Relative unresponsiveness to efforts of others to comfort the person during the episode
- No detailed dream is recalled, and there is amnesia for the episode
- The episode causes clinically significant distress or impairment in functioning
- The disturbance is not due to the direct physiological effects of a substance or a general medical condition.

*Source:* APA (2000), DSM-IV-TR

## Sleep Walking or Somnambulism

Sleep walking as the name signifies represents the state of a person in which he or she is seen to walk or engage in one or the other type of activities at his or her will. Like sleep terrors, the sleep walking phenomenon occurs during one's NREM sleep. Occurrence of this phenomenon during one's NREM sleep naturally implies that when people walk and engage in the activities in their sleep, they are probably not acting out a dream. Moreover, since it occurs during the deepest stages of NREM sleep, waking someone during the sleep walking episode is difficult; if the person is somehow awakened, he or she typically will not remember what has happened. Besides, sleep walking and engaging in some or the other routine and day to day activities, some of the somnambulism patients are found to commit serious offences and engage in undesirable social behaviour and violence including homicide and suicide. There are instances where the people suffering from sleep walking disorders, travelled a long journey in their deep sleep and have committed offences like murder, stealing, and dacoity and then got acquitted with the charges on account of their innocence of doing these acts under the influence of uncontrollable sleep disorder.

In this way, somnambulism, the sleep walking disorder is characterized with atypical distinguished features making it as a unique act full sleep disorder visible among some people. The nature and outcomes of this disorder may be made clearer to you by going through some case histories like below:

A male child aged 8 years, 10 months, a student of the fourth grade, hailing from a Hindu nuclear family of middle socio-economic status and an urban background presented to our centre with the complaint that he had been walking in his sleep for the past five months. After going to bed at about 11 pm, he would get out of bed between 12 midnight and 3 am and perform a variety of activities—go to the toilet and urinate, recite pieces of conversation, act out a scene from a TV serial, etc. During this period, he would never attempt to leave the room and never injured himself. He would walk with his eyes open, but he did not respond to the calling out of his name. Each episode would last for 5-7 minutes and would end with the patient returning to his bed and resuming his sleep. Only one episode would occur in a single night and these would occur once every 1-2 weeks. The patient had no recollection of the episode on waking up. In the month prior to his presentation at the clinic, the episodes had increased to once every alternate night. There was no history suggestive of any daytime interference in the scholastic and interpersonal functioning of the child. Past history was unremarkable and the child had attained normal developmental milestones. There was a family history of a psychotic illness in a cousin and alcohol dependence in a paternal uncle. There was no family history of sleep walking or epilepsy. No stressors could be identified and the mental status examination was unremarkable. Mean intelligence quotient (IQ) at the time of detailed assessment was 116.

*Source:* Bhardwaj Rahul and Suresh Kumar, Somnambulism: Diagnosis and Treatment, Indian Journal of Psychiatry, 2007, April-June, 49 (2): 123-125.

## Identification and Diagnosis of Sleep Walking Disorder

American Psychiatric Association has provided the following criteria for the identification and diagnosis of the sleep walking disorder in its DSM IV TR.

**Table 21.9: Diagnostic criteria for Sleep walking disorder**

- Repeated episodes of rising from bed during sleep and walking about, usually occurring during the first third of the major sleep episode
- While sleepwalking, the person has a blank, staring face; is relatively unresponsiveness to the efforts of others to communicate; and can be awakened only with great difficulty

- On awakening (either from the sleepwalking episode or the next morning), the person has amnesia for the episode
- Within several minutes after wakening from the sleepwalking episode, there is no impairment of mental activity or behaviour (although there may initially be a short period of confusion or disorientation)
- The sleepwalking causes clinically significant distress or impairment in functioning
- The disturbance is not due to the direct physiological effects of a substance or a general medical condition.

*Source:* APA (2000), DSM-IV-TR

## The Underlying Causes of Parasomnias

There has been a little knowledge and understanding about the exact causes lying behind the occurrence of the various Parasomnias-nightmares, night terrors and sleep walking. However, a number of theories or viewpoints have been put forward for this purpose by the researchers and practitioners from time to time depending upon their own theoretical grounds and research findings. As a result, the genetic, psychoanalytic, biological and medical, psychological and environmental maladjustment have thus been blamed in its own way for the causation of these sleep disorders. For example, while emphasizing possibility of genetic component involved in the causation of parasomnias (nightmares, night terrors or sleep walking), hereditarians talk about the higher incidence of their occurrence among the identical twins and within families. The psychoanalyst and socio-psychological scientists, in this concern, blame the unfulfilled wishes, maltreatment and maladjustment received by the children in their sociocultural environment, extreme fatigue, anxieties and stresses, sleep deprivation, or the use of sedative or hypnotic drugs for the causation of these sleep disorders. The biologists and medical professionals on the other hand here name the biological and constitutional defects as well as illnesses and diseases for the outcomes of these sleep disorders i.e. the failure of the brain mechanism (that normally inhibit the voluntary muscles) for doing various undesirable acts under the influence of somnambulism.

## Treatment of Parasomnias

Treatment for parasomnias (nightmares, sleep terrors and sleep walking) usually begins with a recommendation to ignore infrequent episode of such disorder as well as wait and see if they disappear on their own. However, in case these are persistent, lead to the potential for injury, are disruptive to family members, or result in embarrassment, sleep disruption or extreme day time sleepiness to the individual, then well thought attempts should be made for the needed treatment suiting to the nature and seriousness of the faced disorder. In their practical application, these treatment approach usually focuses on promoting safety and eliminating causes or triggers associated with such sleep disorders. We can try to adopt one or the other approaches mentioned as below.

1. *Treating the underlying condition or cause*: In adopting this approach, therapists and professionals first try to find out the underlying conditions or inherent causes lying behind parasomnias (nightmares, sleep terrors and sleep walking). In case, these are associated with an underlying medical or mental health condition or another sleep disorder (such as obstructive sleep apnea or restless legs syndrome) then treatment should be planned to get away with this problem. Similarly, if these are the result of a particular medication, then attempts are made to bring alterations in the dosage or prescription to eliminate this unwanted side effect.
2. *Addressing anxiety, stress and depression:* In the causation of parasomnias related sleep disorders, an increased level of stress, anxiety and depression is many times found to contribute in a big way. It is therefore quite natural for the affected persons to take help from the counsellors and therapist in getting due relief from the anxiety, stress and depression associated with their disorder. The therapists and counsellors may be found to make use of a number of stress, tension and depression relieving strategies involving cognitive behavioural therapy, hypnosis, biofeedback or relaxation therapy including meditation for this purpose.
3. *Scheduled awakening*: This approach involves waking the person who has episodes of Parasomnias (nightmare, sleep terror or sleepwalking) at the scheduled time say 15-20 minutes before atypical episode of these disorders (usually occurring in the same time each night.) and keeping them awake for a suitable duration at least till the usual time of the occurrence of episodes.
4. *Seeking self- help:* In getting rid of a problem, self-help is always considered the best help. Therefore attempts need to be made for making the sufferers to seek prevention and treatment of the parasomnias by learning and practicing the measures of self- help such as (i) keeping a regular wake-sleep schedule, (ii) engaging in regular exercise including yogic asanas, breathing practices and meditation, for alleviating sleep disorders causing anxiety, depression and stress, (iii) practicing good sleep hygiene for preventing the sleep deprivation, (iv) practicing the methods of self-hypnosis, (v) caring about night sleep environment such as making one's bedroom a relaxing place reserved for sleep, and (vi) avoiding the use of alcohol, caffeine, cocaine, and nicotine etc.
5. *Seeking medical treatment and medication:* The help of medical treatments in the form of surgery or other suitable means may be taken for the necessary correction of the physiological and neurological abnormalities and defects responsible for causing parasomnias related problems among the individuals. In addition, in case of need suitable medication or drugs may be prescribed for the treatment of the parasomnias focusing on getting the nightmare, sleep terror or sleep walking problems under control and help the sufferers get a better night's rest. The various types of drugs often prescribed by medical professional for this purpose may be cited as under.
   (i) Antidepressants such as Trazodone or Benzodiazepines
   (ii) Sedative drugs such as Prosom, and
   (iii) Anticonvulsants such as Klonopin.

All of these medications can be helpful in reducing the frequency and severity of nightmare, sleep terror or sleepwalking episodes. However, the decision regarding the suitability of the particular one must be taken by the medical professional caring for the patient. Moreover, the decision regarding the drug related treatment should be taken with a necessary caution as all of these drugs have their own side effects and are not meant for long-term use.

## Summary

- Our night sleep involves two types of sleep named REM (Rapid eye movement) sleep and NREM (Non rapid eye movement) sleep. While falling asleep the people first go through an episode of NREM sleep involving first three stages of their night sleep characterized as lightest, light and deep sleep. After then they enter the fourth stage of their REM type of sleep. NREM sleep aims to provide complete rest, relaxation and healing to the body and mind specially through the third stage of its deep sleep. REM. Awakening as well as arousals can occur more easily in the fourth stage of sleep-REM sleep.
- Sleep disorders represent the irregularities, disturbances and abnormalities, occurred in one's night sleep. These disorders have been categorized into two broad categories named as Dyssomnias (disturbances occurred in the amount, timing or quality of one's sleep) and Parasomnias (disturbances in arousal and sleep stage transition from one stage of sleep to another).
- Dyssomnias are further sub-categorized as Primary insomnia, Primary hypersomnia, Narcolepsy, Breathing-related sleep disorder, and Circadian rhythm or sleep-wake schedule disorder. Parasomnias may also be further sub-categorized into two distinct types (i) those occurring during REM sleep such as nightmares and(ii) those occurring during NREM sleep such as night terrors and night sleep walking.
- The term insomnia in its word meaning stands for one's inability to sleep. In general, the people suffering with the primary insomnia are found to experience some typical problems and difficulties in their night sleep such as difficulty in initiating and maintaining sleep and the unfulfilment of the required restorative function by their night sleep.
- Hypersomnia sleeping disorder run quite contrary to the insomnia sleeping disorder both in its nature as well as functioning. While people suffering from primary insomnia are not getting enough sleep, the people suffering from hypersomnia, on the other hand, are grappled with the problem of sleeping too much. Besides sleeping in a greater amount and duration in the night, these people are also found to fall asleep several times the next day.
- In the category of Dyssomnias sleep disorders, Narcolepsy is considered a quite serious and chronic sleep disorder usually characterized by the features like (i) excessive daytime sleepiness, (ii) sleep attacks and (iii) the rapid eye movement (REM) sleep abnormalities such as cataplexy(a sudden loss of muscle tone resulting into the abnormal behaviour such as falling asleep for a brief duration while cheering a favourite team), sleep paralysis (inability to move or speak

for a brief period immediately after awakening in REM sleep) and hypnagogic hallucination (passing through a quite terrifying experiences such as experiencing vivid illusion of being caught in a fire or flying through the air).

- The term breathing -related sleep disorders is used for the type of sleep disorders in which there lie some physical origin-namely problems with the breathing of the people while asleep causing them to experience widely disrupted sleep at night and excessive sleepiness (insomnia) during the whole day. Their breathing problems are reflected in experiencing a phenomenon of the stoppage of their breathing altogether for a shorter period of 10 to 30 seconds referred to as sleep apnea in the world of medicines and abnormal psychology. There are three types of sleep apnea (named as obstructive, central and mixed sleep apnea) each causing a distinctive type of breath related sleep disorder among the affected individuals.
- The term Circadian Rhythm Sleep Disorders is used for the type of sleep disorders in which the affected individuals are found to go through a persistent or recurrent sleep disruption leading to excessive sleepiness or insomnia on account of a mismatch between the sleep-wake schedule required by their environment and their circadian sleep-wake cycle such as happens in experiencing jet-lag related situation while visiting a county having a different clock timing like USA or providing night shift duty in the work schedule.
- Nightmares in the form experiencing some type of bad dreams occur during one's REM or dream sleep in contrast to two other parasomnias type disorders sleep terror and sleep walking occurring in one's NREM sleep. They differ with the normal bad dreams in terms of proving too distressful and terrifying to impair a person's ability to carry on normal activities i.e. making a person too anxious to try to sleep at night. Other distinguished features of the nightmares are known in the form of (i) not making people move around as happens to them in the NREM sleep related disorders- night terror and sleep walking, and (ii) Vividly remembered on the part of the dreamers immediately upon waking.
- Night sleep terrors while appearing similar to the night mares differ from them in the sense of (i) occurring during one's NREM deep sleep, (ii) representing a state of panic (e.g. unable to move, breathe) experienced by the dreamers, (iii) making dreamers act up on their dreaming experience while remaining under the state of their sound sleep, (iv) providing no chance to awake and comfort the terrified child as possible during a nightmare, and (v) no remembering on the part of children what happened to them during a night-terror episode.
- Sleep walking represents the state of a person in which he or she is seen to walk or engage in one or the other type of activities such as eating in the kitchen and also doing other desirable or undesirable acts such as murder, steeling, suicidal attempts etc. during their sleep walking.
- Regarding the causation of one or the other sleep disorders of the dyssomnias and parasomnias types, while hereditarians talk about the higher incidence of their occurrence among the identical twins and within families, the psychoanalyst and socio-psychological scientists, blame the unfulfilled wishes, maltreatment and maladjustment received by the children in their sociocultural environment,

extreme fatigue, anxieties and stresses, sleep deprivation, or the use of sedative or hypnotic drugs for this purpose. The biologists and medical professionals on the other hand here name the biological and constitutional defects as well as illnesses and diseases for the outcomes of these sleep disorders.

- Regarding the identification and diagnosis of the various dyssomnias and parasomnias type sleep disorders we can make use of the criterion provided in the Diagnostic Statistical Manuals provided by American Psychiatric Association such as DSM-IV-TR (2000).
- The treatment measures applied to all the dyssomnias type disorders may be classified as medical measures, environmental measures and psychological measures. In this sequence where medical measures are found to make use of one or the other suitable drugs, and medication prescribed by the qualified professionals for taking control of one or the other type of dyssomnias, the environmental measures are intended to seek environmental modification for seeking treatment of the affected individuals especially the circadian rhythm sleep disorder patients. The psychological measures used in the form of a number of behavioural therapies such as Cognitive behavioural therapy, Guided imagery therapy, Meditation therapy, Progressive relaxation therapy, and Stimulus control therapy may prove quite effective in controlling and treating the cases affected with one or the other dyssomnias type disorders.
- The treatment measures applied to all the parasomnias type sleep disorders-nightmares, night terrors and sleep walking first follow the policy of wait and watch for their disappearance on their own. In case of their persistence and seriousness, the measures adopted may be named as (i) treating the underlying condition or cause associated with the disorder, (ii) addressing anxiety, stress and depression by making use of cognitive behavioural therapy, hypnosis, biofeedback or relaxation therapy including meditation, (iii) scheduled awakening, say 15-20 minutes before atypical episode of these disorders (iv) seeking their prevention and treatment by learning and practicing the measures of self- help and (v) seeking medical treatment and using medication or drug therapy.

## REFERENCES

American Psychiatric Association (2000), *The Diagnostic and Statistical Manual of Mental Disorders*, Washington D.C.: American Psychiatric Association.

Bhardwaj Rahul and Suresh Kumar, Somnambulism: Diagnosis and Treatment, Indian Journal of Psychiatry, 2007, April-June, 49 (2): 123-125 retrieved from

https://www.ncbi.nlm.nih.gov/pmc/articles/PMC2917078/

Durand, V. Mark and Barlow, David H. (2013), *Essentials of Abnormal Psychology*, (6th ed.), Belmont CA: Wadsworth

Guzman, Carlos Simon and Wang, Yuan Pang, "Sleep terror disorder: a case report", *Brazilian Journal of Psychiatry*, Vol.30. No. 2, Sao Paula, June, 2008. Retrieved from

http://www.scielo.br/scielo.php?script=sci_arttext&pid=S1516-44462008000200016.

John DJ, Manoharan A, Varghese R., A case of primary hypersomnia, Ann Indian Acad. Neurology (serial online), 2007 (cited 2019 May 14), 10:58-60, retrieved from: http: www, annalsofian. Org/text. asp?2007/10/1/58/31489

Topp, Julia,(2009),Case study-Disturbed sleep and Vivid Nightmares. Retrieved from https://www.gponline.com/case-study-disturbed-sleep-vivid-nightmares/neurology/article/965128

Yoon-Kyung Shin .et al,(2007), Case Study of a Narcoleptic Patient with a Family History of Narcolepsy, Department of Neuropsychiatry, St. Vincent's Hospital, Korea, Psychiatry Investigation, 2007;4:121-123 retrieved from http://www.psychiatryinvestigation.org/upload/pdf/0502007022.pdf

Zee, Phyllis C. (2011), Case Histories in Circadian Rhythm Sleep Disorders, Med Scope, retrieved from

https://www.medscape.org/viewarticle/745357

# 22

# OLD AGE OR DEGENERATIVE DISORDERS

## INTRODUCTION

It is natural to have a considerable decrease in the physical and mental strengths and capacities of the individuals with the increase in age during their old age period. As a result, we may find the old aged to fall victims of physical and mental weaknesses giving birth to one or the other physiological and mental disorders and diseases. Besides, becoming patients of certain physical illnesses and diseases, it is quite common for the old aged people to suffer from a number of neurocognitive disorders and diseases demonstrating visible symptoms of one or the other types of abnormal and disruptive behaviour and named as Delirium, Dementia, Alzheimer's disease, Pick's disease, Parkinson's disease, and Huntington's disease.

Let us know about these disorders and diseases in detail.

### Delirium

Etymologically, the word delirium is derived from the Latin words de (meaning 'out of') and lira (meaning 'track'). The term delirium thus may be found to stand for "being off-track or deviating from the usual state or condition of the mind" resulting into a state of utter confusion or clouding of one's consciousness. It is why, delirium is also known as acute state of confusion or clouding of one's consciousness carrying the quite distinguishing features like below.

1. The acute state of confusion representing delirium typically develops over a shorter period of time, usually hours or days.
2. In its developed form it is characterized by some distinguishable symptoms like:
   - Extreme trouble focusing attention making them unable to concentrate and thinking in an organized way, leading to misinterpretations, illusions and on occasion hallucinations.
   - Profound disturbances in the sleep-awake cycle resulting in making them drowsy during the day yet awake and agitated at night opening the way of experiencing vivid dreams, nightmares and sleep terrors in a greater amount on their part.

- Major disturbances in their orientation to environment and perception resulting in to such incidents as making them to believe that it is morning in the middle of the night, that they are home when actually they are in the hospital room and also committing such blunders such as mistaking unfamiliar to familiar, and inability to tell about what day it is and who they are.
- Major disturbances and difficulties felt in speech and communication making them impossible to engage in proper conversation and speak in a clearly understanding ways.
- Memory impairment, especially for recent events, is common among them.
- A lot of incoherence and swings in their activity and mood display resulting into some or the other typical behaviour such as ripping the clothes in one moment and sitting lethargically the next, looking quite alert, happy and enjoying at one time and lost, careless, and sad in the next moment.
- Demonstrating a lot of emotional instability in their behaviour such as switching rapidly from one emotion to another and negativity involving depression, anxiety, anger, euphoria, and irritability etc.
- A common presence of certain physical symptoms such as flushed face, dilated pupils, tremors, rapid heartbeat, elevated blood pressure, and incontinence of urine and faeces. Moreover, they may also be found to become stupors and lethargic if their delirium gets worsened.
- People of any age are subject to detect delirium, but it is more common among children and older adults. Among older adults it is particularly common in nursing homes and hospitals. (Kring, et. al. 2015:461).

Elderly hospitalized patients frequently develop altered mental status as a complication of their illness exemplified in the case history of an older hospitalized woman given below:

**Delirium in an Older, Hospitalized Woman**

An 86-year-old woman, admitted with complaints of shortness of breath and cough, was found to have pneumonia. Her past medical history included cataract surgery, hypertension controlled with medications, and type 2 diabetes controlled by diet. She was ambulatory, lived alone, and at baseline completed all activities of daily living independently. According to her daughter, the patient was never disoriented. At admission, the patient appeared mildly dehydrated on physical examination. Her oxygen saturation was 94% on 2 litres oxygen by nasal cannula, and an arterial blood gas showed a normal pCO2 of 40 mmHg. Her daughter requested to spend the night at the bedside but was told she could not stay.

*Overnight, the patient was noted to be disoriented by the nursing staff. She began pulling at her intravenous lines and attempting to get out of bed. The covering physician was called and ordered that the patient be placed in four-point restraints.*

The following morning, the daughter returned to find her mother in restraints, speaking incoherently and severely short of breath. Upon finding her mother confused, the daughter asked the nurse what had happened and reiterated to the nurse that her mother had never been confused before.

*Source:* Deborah D'Avolio, Case study: Delirium in an Older Hospitalized Woman, NIDUS, Network for Investigation of Delirium: Unifying Scientists,

## Identification and Diagnosis of delirium

American Psychiatric Association (2013) has provided the following criteria for the identification and diagnosis of the old age disorder delirium in its DSM- V

**Table 22.1: Diagnostic criteria for delirium**

| |
|---|
| 1. Over the course of hours or a few days, individual experiences fast-moving and fluctuating disturbances in attention and orientation to the environment. |
| 2. Individuals also display a significant cognitive disturbance. |

*Source:* APA (2013), DSM-V

## Causes of Delirium

Delirium, by its very definition is known as an organically caused decline from a previous baseline level of mental function that develops over a short period of time (APA,2013). It makes us to conclude that delirium is secondary to an underlying medical condition, deterioration in one's physical and mental health, concurrent diseases and illnesses suffered by the individual in the course of his or her life. The things and factors representing to such deterioration and underlying medical conditions may be briefly named and categorized as under:

- Fever, and certain diseases (like shock, heart attacks, hypoxia, anemia, hyperthyroidism, cancer etc.)
- Infections (like pneumonia, urinary tract infections)
- Neurological disorders (like head trauma or seizures),
- Drug addiction and drug-withdrawal reactions
- Medication misuse, whether deliberate or inadvertent
- Intoxication by certain substances, such as side effects of the prescribed drugs or change in drug prescription
- Strokes and stress (including the trauma of surgery)
- Metabolic and nutritional imbalances (as in dehydration, uncontrolled diabetes, thyroid dysfunction, kidney or liver failure, congestive heart failure, or malnutrition)
- Brain damage and dementia

## Treatment of Delirium

As we know, the course of a remedy or treatment very well lies in taking care of the causes lying behind the problem. Therefore, while taking measures for the treatment of delirium, due attention should always be paid over the things responsible for causing delirium. Beginning in this direction, should thus be made to have a thorough examination of the patient for all possible underlying causes of the disorder, such as drug intoxication, fever, infections, diseases, strokes and stresses, metabolic and nutritional imbalances etc. and then suitable treatment should be planned accordingly in view or treating the underlying medical conditions. Besides taking course to such appropriate all-time treatment for the delirium patients, immediate, urgent as well as supporting measures may be employed in the shape of prescription of one or the other suitable drugs for treating delirium symptoms. These may usually include one or the other antipsychotic drugs (to treat agitation and hallucinations and to improve sensory problems) such as (i) Haloperidol, (ii) Risperidone, (iii)Olanzapine and (iv) Quetiapine. However, in case the patient has alcohol or drug withdrawal problem, then it remains useful to prescribe benzodiazepines (such as diazepam, lorazepam, chlordiazepoxide, or oxazepam) for this purpose.

## Dementia

Etymologically, the word dementia is derived from the Latin words de (meaning 'without') and mens (meaning 'mind') which join together to mean "without mind" or "senseless". However, in its practical use in medical and psychological world, the term is used for "an acute deterioration in one's cognitive abilities affecting one's functioning in a variety of ways". It is in this sense that in the DSM-IV-TR and DSM V, the term dementia has been categorized and defined as "a Neurocognitive disorder that results into multiple cognitive deficits including impairment in memory." The WHO's classification ICD-10, however has provided more elaborated explanation by terming dementia as *"a syndrome due to disease of the brain, usually of a chronic or progressive nature, in which there is disturbance of multiple higher cortical functions, including memory, thinking, orientation, comprehension, calculation, learning capacity, language, and judgment. Consciousness is not clouded. The impairments of cognitive functions are commonly accompanied, and occasionally preceded, by deterioration in emotional control, social behaviour or motivation."*

Concludingly, in this way, by the term dementia we may hereby clearly mean a disorder or a disturbed state of one's mind representing the deterioration of one's cognitive abilities to the point that his or her overall functioning gets impaired in a variety of ways including a great memory loss.

The distinguishable characteristics and features of the disorder dementia in the light of the definitions and explanations provided in DSM's and ICD's may be briefed as below:

- A great memory loss demonstrable in terms of one's difficulty remembering things, especially recent events such as (i)leaving the task unfinished on account of forgetting what was to be done,(ii) inability in remembering the names of familiar objects in their environment i.e. the name of a daughter or son and their own day to day belongings, (iii) forgetting about their daily routines such as taking bath or dress properly,(iv) getting lost themselves even in their day to day familiar surroundings etc.
- A great deterioration in one's other cognitive abilities and functioning related to several cognitive domains including, thinking, reasoning and problem solving, making judgments, drawing conclusions and inferences, difficulty comprehending situations and making plans or decisions, learning one or the other things, having computation and calculation of a quite simple nature, etc.

- No clouding of consciousness turning one into a state of acute confusion as happens with the patients of delirium
- Accompanying or preceding of cognitive functioning impairment by deterioration in emotional control, and social behaviour reflected in their otherwise abnormal behaviour such as losing control of their impulse using coarse language in conversation, cutting inappropriate jokes, shoplifting, and making sexual advances to strangers.
- Demonstrating the symptom of depression, delusions, delirium and hallucination related behaviours.
- Defined as mental deterioration of organic or functional origin, dementia is known to be caused on account of one or the other types of strokes and diseases of the brain, usually of a chronic or progressive nature.
- Moreover, the course of dementia may be progressive, static, or remitting, depending on the cause. Many people with progressive dementia eventually become, withdrawn and apathetic. In the terminal phase of illness, personality loses its sparkle and integrity. Relatives and friends say that the person is just not himself or herself anymore. Social involvement with others keeps narrowing. Finally, the person is oblivious to his or her surroundings. (Kring et.al, 2012)

The above cited typical features found in the old aged people suffering from dementia may be more clearly visualized through the case history of a patient suffering from Alzheimer's type dementia provided below:

A 37-year-old male patient visited outpatient clinic, with complaints of gradual cognitive decline which had started 3 years earlier. Working as an industrial researcher, he started to make serious calculation mistakes that made him quit the job and began working as a manager in a company. However, his frequent forgetfulness, along with aggravation in recent memory impairments hampered him from fulfilling his duties, making him change jobs frequently. Apraxia and apathy had started 2 years before his visit to our clinic, and disorientation to time and person was worsened to a degree which it became impossible to commute daily between his workplace and home. At time of his visit to our clinic, not only he was fired from his recent job, but also, he needed frequent reminder from his family to maintain hygiene. His sleep disturbance became prominent, frequently waking up middle of the night self-talking. Before his visit to our clinic, he had visited two hospitals for evaluation and management of his symptoms, but to no avail. For a thorough examination of his symptoms, he was immediately admitted to our psychiatric ward. His laboratory findings did not reveal any abnormalities, and his tests for human immunodeficiency virus, syphilis all turned out to be negative. In his cognitive tests, in contrast to his relatively preserved language function, he displayed serious impairments in free recall, 20-minute delayed recall and recognition.

*Source:* Yoo, Hyun, et.al. (2017), A case report of a 37-year-old male patient of the Dementia of the Alzheimer's type, Psychiatry Investigation

## Identification and Diagnosis of Dementia

American Psychiatric Association has provided the following criteria for the identification and diagnosis of the old age disorder dementia in its DSM IV TR.

**Table 22.2: Diagnostic criteria for dementia**

- Development of multiple cognitive deficits that include memory impairment and at least one of the following cognitive disturbances:
  - (i) aphasia (The loss or impairment of the power to use words as symbols of ideas)
  - (ii) apraxia (The loss or impairment of ability to execute movements without muscular paralysis)
  - (iii) agnosia or a disturbance in executive functioning (The loss of the ability to recognize familiar objects by seeing, hearing, or touching).
- The cognitive deficits must be sufficiently severe to cause impairment in occupational or social functioning and must represent a decline from a previously higher level of functioning

*Source:* APA (2000), DSM-IV-TR

## Distinction Between Delirium and Dementia

Delirium and dementia both falling in the category of neurological disorders in late life have a number of overlapping features and symptoms making the task of differentiation between them a little difficult. Each of them may be misdiagnosed in the presence of other in a patient. However, both have their own uniqueness and speciality sufficient enough to distinguish them from each other. In a simple way we may safely distinguish between the terms delirium and dementia on the basis of being named respectively as 'a deterioration of cognitive abilities' and 'a state of mental confusion'. In this regard, Knight (1996) has offered a useful suggestion for having the required distinction between them in the following words.

*The clinical "feel" of talking with a delirium is rather like talking to someone who is acutely intoxicated or in acute psychotic episode. Whereas the demented patient may not remember the name of the place where she or he is, the delirious patient may believe it is different sort of place altogether, perhaps mistaking a psychiatric ward for a used car lot (pp 96-97).*

In helping the task of distinction between dementia and delirium further in this connection, Kring et.al (2012) have listed a variety of features in making comparison among them in the following way.

**Table 22.3: Comparative Features of Dementia and Delirium**

| Dementia | Delirium |
|---|---|
| Gradual deterioration of abilities | Rapid onset |
| Deficits in memory for recent events | Trouble concentrating and staying with a train of thought |

| Caused by disease processes that are directly influencing the brain | Secondary to another medical condition |
|---|---|
| Usually progressive and nonreversible | Fluctuations over the course of a day |
| Treatment offers only minimal benefit | Usually reversible by treating underlying condition, but potentially fatal if cause- e.g. infection or malnutrition-not treated. |
| Prevalence increases with age | Prevalence is highest in the very young as well as the old. |

*Source:* Kring, et.al. (2012:461)

## Types of Dementia

There are many different types of dementia. These may be divided into following categories on the basis of their etiology (Kring et al, 2012:454).

- Dementia of the Alzheimer's type
- Vascular Dementia
- Dementia due to other general medical conditions
- Substance-induced persisting Dementia
- Dementia due to multiple etiologies
- Dementia not otherwise specified; when cause cannot be determined.

## Causes of Dementia

Dementia is caused by damage to or loss (death) of nerve cells and their connections in the brain. Depending on the area of the brain that is affected by the damage, dementia can affect people differently and cause different symptoms giving birth to one or the other types of dementia. This damage or loss of the nerve cells may be caused either by (i) a head injury, a stroke, or a brain tumour, or by (ii) a neurodegenerative disease (progressive brain cell death that happens over time). Such damage or loss of nerve cells, in turn, puts obstacles in the path of ongoing communication among the brain cells. This lack of communication between the brain cells is responsible for adversely affecting the thinking, feeling, and acting behaviour of the affected persons in their own ways. As we know that the human brain has many distinct regions, each of which is responsible for different functions (for example, memory, judgment and movement). The damage or loss of cells in a particular region results into the failure of that region in carrying out its own functioning giving birth to one or the other types of dementia related problems or diseases such as Vascular dementia, Alzheimer's disease, Pick's disease, Parkinson's disease, and Huntington's disease. Let us know about some essentials about them. However, among all these dementia related neuro-cognitive disorders and diseases, Alzheimer's disease is known to be more pronounced and common among the older age people. Let us therefore try to focus first on its discussion.

## Alzheimer's Disease

Alzheimer's disease was first identified in one of his dementia's patient in 1907 by a German psychiatrist Alois Alzheimer. It is in his honour, that the disease has been named as Alzheimer's disease. Alzheimer's disease is known for giving birth to a particular type of dementia, named as 'Dementia of the Alzheimer's type' symptomizing a great loss of memory on the part of the affected individuals. Let us see what happens in this disease that results in such loss of memory.

As pointed out before dementia (the deterioration in several cognitive domains) is caused by some particular types of damage or loss of brain cells of the different regions of the brain. A particular region of the brain affected by such brain cells damage or loss gives birth to a particular type of cognitive deterioration. In the case of Alzheimer's disease, the region of the brain called the hippocampus (the center of learning and memory) is adversely affected on account of the damage or loss of the brain cells belonging to this region.

In terms of its early onset, Alzheimer's disease may be found to appear among some individuals in their late 50's or early 60's, but in majority of cases it generally appears in the late 60's or early 70's and then gets increased by reaching in their late 70's and early 80's. The time between the onset and death is typically 8 to 10 years among affected individuals. As a progressive disease, the patients suffering with this disease may be found to demonstrate the distinctive symptoms like below in their behaviour:

1. In the first phase or beginning of this disease, the patients are found to exhibit mild problems associated with their memory and environmental orientation such as forgetfulness, lapses of attention and difficulty in language and communication.
2. In the second phase of this disease with the notable increase in the associated symptoms, the patients are found to suffer with more deterioration in their memory resulting in facing difficulties in completing tasks, remembering important appointments and getting confused in their thinking and judgment day by day.
3. In the later phase with a more intensification of the disease associated symptoms, the Alzheimer's patients are found to demonstrate a quite abnormal behaviour characterized with the features like:

- Withdrawal behaviour reflecting in their attitude and actions of remaining aloof and cutting them socially and emotionally from others.
- Confused state of mind reflecting in their attitude and actions demonstrating a considerable lack of time sense, wandering here and there aimlessly, distortion in their perceptual and judgmental ability, and failure of recognizing people (even close relatives and family members) and places (even their homes and the most familiar one's).
- Becoming increasingly uncomfortable at night and taking frequent naps during the day.

4. In the latest phase of their disorder, they are found to become fully dependent on other people needing constant care for their safety and living.

## Identification and Diagnosis of Alzheimer's Disease Disorder

American Psychiatric Association has provided the following criteria for the identification and diagnosis of the Alzheimer's Disease Disorder in its DSM IV TR.

**Table 22.4: Diagnostic criteria for Alzheimer's Disease Disorder**

A. The development of multiple cognitive deficits manifested by both
 (i) memory impairment (impaired ability to learn new information or to recall previously learned information)
 (ii) One (or more) of the following cognitive disturbances:
  (a) Aphasia (language disturbance); (b) apraxia (impaired ability to carry out motor activities despite intact motor function; (c) agnosia (failure to recognize or identify objects despite intact sensory function); (d) disturbance in executive functioning (i.e planning, organizing, sequencing, abstracting)

B. The cognitive deficits in criteria A (i) and A (ii) each cause significant impairment in social or occupational functioning and represent a significant decline from a previous level of functioning.

C. The course is characterized by gradual onset and continuing cognitive decline.

D. The cognitive deficits in Criteria A(i) and A (ii) are not due to any of the following:

- Other central nervous system conditions that cause progressive deficits in memory and cognition (e.g. cerebrovascular disease, Parkinson's disease, Huntington's disease, subdural hematoma, normal pressure hydrocephalus, brain tumor)
- Systematic conditions that are known to cause dementia (e.g. hypothyroidism, vitamin B12 or folic acid deficiency, niacin deficiency, hypercalcemia, neurosyphilis, HIV infection)
- Substance-induced conditions
- E. The deficits do not occur exclusively during the course of a delirium
- F. The disturbance is not better accounted for another Axis I disorder (e.g. Major depressive disorder, Schizophrenia)

*Source:* APA (2000) DSM —IV-TR

## Factors Responsible for Causing Alzheimer's Disease

Alzheimer's disease is caused by a combination of genetic and environmental factors that affect the brain over time. Let us know about this.

## The Role of Genetic Factors

The hereditary transmission in the form of defective genes play a great role in the causation of Alzheimer's disease. However, in playing their roles in this direction, the different types of genes are said to be responsible for giving birth to the early-onset and late-onset types of Alzheimer's disease in the way described as below (Comer,2015:621):

(i) The early-onset type of Alzheimer's disease can be caused by abnormalities in the genes responsible for the production of two proteins-the *beta-amyloid precursor protein* (beta-APP) and the *presenilin* protein. However, in the case of late-onset type of Alzheimer's disease, a gene called the *apolipoprotein* E (ApoE) gene (and particularly its one of the forms, ApoE-4), located on chromosome 19, is normally responsible for the excessive formation of beta-amyloid proteins.

(ii) The production of the type of proteins by the respective genes, in both the cases, results into spurring of the formation of plaques and in turn, the breakdown of the tau protein, the formation of numerous tangles, the death of many neurons, leading to the onset of one or the other types of Alzheimer's disease.

## The Role of Environmental Factors

The heredity or genetic factors alone are not the exclusive factors for causation and development of the Alzheimer's or other likewise neurocognitive degenerative disorders of the old age. The environmental factors of one or the other nature like below may also play their significant role in the causation and precipitation of these disorders.

1. **Past head trauma-** The trauma caused by an accident, stroke, or head injury may play a great part in the damage or loss of brain cells responsible for the causation of Alzheimer's disease.
2. **Acute exposure to and poisoning with heavy metals and pesticides-** Acute exposure and poisoning with heavy metals and pesticides such as the long-term accumulative exposure and accumulation of lead and aluminium has been found responsible for the causation and development of Alzheimer's and other neurodegeneration disorders.
3. **Air pollution-** Exposure to polluted air containing a toxic cocktail of organic and non-organic compounds, metals, and gases may also work towards the causation and development of Alzheimer's disease.
4. **Unhealthy lifestyle-**There may be some or the other negativity lying in one's life style that may be held responsible for the causation and development of Alzheimer's disease and other related neuro-degenerative disorder. These may be named as below:
   - Lack of physical activity and exercise
   - Obesity
   - Poor sleep patterns, such as difficulty falling asleep or staying asleep,
   - Smoking or substance abuse
   - Poor nutrition and unhealthy diet intake.
5. **Poor health and fatal diseases:** The poor health conditions and fatal diseases such as high blood pressure, heart disease, poorly controlled type 2 diabetes, chronic infection and medical conditions including HIV infection, meningitis and advanced syphilis may work as a potent cause for the initiation and perpetuation of the Alzheimer's disease.

6. **Psychological Factors-** A number of psychological factors inducing a high level of anxiety, depression and stress among the individuals particularly among the aged prove quite fatal to their health and wellbeing increasing the probability of getting them affected with Alzheimer's disease and other types of neurocognitive disorders.

## Treatment of Alzheimer's Disease

Treatment of the patients of Alzheimer's disease and other like wise neurocognitive disorders involving dementia may involve a combination of different treatment measures depending up on the onset stage, causation and seriousness of the disorder. In this connection, the treatments in a general way may involve some of important measures and approaches named as medication or drug therapy, cognitive therapy, behavioural therapy, and sociocultural therapy. Let us try to know about them in brief.

## Medication or Drug Therapy

The immediate first care and treatment of the Alzheimer's patients in the early mild stage of the disease generally begins with the introduction of some useful and well tested drugs (meant for helping them in their memory, cognition and communication related difficulties) such as:

(i)tacrine -trade name *cognex*, (ii) donepezil- trade name *aricept*, (iii) rivastigmine- trade name *exelon*, (iv) galantamine- trade name *reminyl*, and (v)memantine- trade name *namenda*.

The clinicians are also seen to prescribe vitamin E tablet or capsule along with one or the other above prescribed drugs to help slow down further cognitive decline among the people suffering from Alzheimer's disease.

### Cognitive Therapy

There is a considerable loss of the brain cells related with the memory, reasoning and judgment of the brain regions in the case of the Alzheimer's patients. The techniques used in cognitive therapy are carried out for dealing with this deficiency. For this purpose, efforts are made to carry on specific cognitive activities, including computer-based cognitive stimulation programs with the Alzheimer's patients aimed to help them in the rehabilitation of those brain parts that are linked to memory, reasoning and judgment.

### Behavioural Therapy

The use of behavioural therapy in the case of treating Alzheimer's patients is found to involve a number of useful behaviour modification and management techniques such as modelling, role playing, operant conditioning and reinforcing the appropriate behaviour of the patients. In its application each of these techniques all alone or in combinations are focused for providing needed behavioural intervention to help improve specific symptoms displayed by Alzheimer's patients such as wandering at night, loss of bladder control, demands for attention, and inadequate personal care. In addition of providing such behavioural interventions to the patients, efforts are also initiated for providing behavioural therapy assistance for the family members and care givers of the Alzheimer's patients for helping them to cope with the distress, fatigue, stress and difficulties resulting on account of their unaccounted attention, time and energy for taking care of the Alzheimer's patients.

### Sociocultural Therapy

Sociocultural environment and facilities available to the Alzheimer's patients play a quite important role in their needed caring, treatment and rehabilitation. Some of the suitable attempts made in this direction can be outlined as below:

- Establishment of suitable day-care facilities with an objective of providing treatments programs and activities for outpatients during the day and returning them to their homes and families at night.
- Establishment of needed facilities in the form of community centers, boarding and lodging houses, and recreative clubs including the presence of the well-trained assistive personnel for helping the Alzheimer's patients enjoy a caring environment, receive assistance in their treatment, and take part in various activities that bring more joy and stimulation to their lives.
- To establish help centres at call in the police station and NGO's offices for locating the patents who may wander off for their security and safe return to their homes. The developed technology may also be utilized for tracking the position of the wandering patients in the form of equipping them with the GPS trackers tied to their wrist or kept in their shoes.

After having necessary discussion about the most pronounced disease or disorder associated with dementia, let us now have a look in brief into the nature and characteristics of some other similar neurocognitive disorders and diseases faced by the older people.

### Vascular Dementia

In terms of its formal definition, Vascular dementia may be considered as a general term describing problems with one's cognitive abilities like reasoning, planning, judgment, memory and other thought processes caused by brain damage from impaired blood flow to one's specific areas of the brain. This impairment of blood flow is concerned with the process of cutting off the flow of the blood to the specific areas of the brain responsible for carrying out the specific cognitive functions including memory and reasoning on account of one or the other conditions like below.

1. *Blockage or damage of brain artery-* A cerebrovascular accident, or stroke may result in blocking or damaging a brain artery responsible for the flow of blood in one or the other specific regions of the brain.
2. *Narrowing or chronically damaging brain blood vessels-* Conditions that narrow or inflict long-term damage on one's brain blood vessels may also lead to vascular dementia. These conditions may be found to be caused through the factors like

natural process of aging, abnormal aging of blood vessels (atherosclerosis), high blood pressure, high cholesterol and smoking, diabetes, and brain haemorrhage.

In its effect and outcome, vascular dementia is widely considered the second most common cause of dementia after Alzheimer's disease, accounting for 5 percent to 10 percent of cases. Like Alzheimer's disease this disorder is also progressive and is often found to coexist with Alzheimer's disease. However, it differs from Alzheimer's disease in the manner like below:

- The symptoms related to vascular dementia begin suddenly rather than gradually.
- The person's cognitive functioning may continue to be normal in areas of the brain that have not been affected by the stroke, in contrast to the broad cognitive deficiencies usually displayed by Alzheimer's patients.

## Pick' Disease

It is a rare neurological condition or disorder that possess uniqueness in affecting the two important parts or lobes of the brain-frontal and temporal at the same time. It is why it is also named as *Fronto-temporal neurocognitive disorder or disease.* In its medical and physical consequences, it resembles much to Alzheimer's disease, but can be distinguished well from it during autopsy. Some of the well- known distinctive features of the Pick's disease can be summarized as below:

(i) It results into a cortical dementia similar to that of Alzheimer's disease.

(ii) In its scope and dimension, it is found to affect about 5% of the overall population of the people suffering from dementia.

(iii) The course of this disease is believed to last from 5 to 10 years.

(iv) Its cause is still unknown despite the collaborated research findings and individual attempts.

(v) Like Huntington's disease, Pick's disease usually occurs relatively early in life-during a person's 40s or 50s-and is therefore considered an example of pre-senile dementia. (Durand & Barlow, 2013:520).

## Parkinson's Disease

It is a slowly progressive degenerative brain disorder or disease that creates a number of motor and behavioural problems to the affected individuals in a quite slow and progressive way characterized as below.

- Symptoms start gradually, sometimes starting with a barely noticeable tremor in just one hand.
- The progression of symptoms is often a bit different from one person to another due to the diversity of the disease. However, in general, the tremors get common and are followed by other motor problems such as stooped posture, slow body movements, tremors, and jerkiness in walking, gate and balance problems, loss of automatic movements and reflex actions, and slowing down of the voice reflecting in one's speaking in a soft monotone and hesitation etc.
- In a long run, the people affected with Parkinson's disease are generally found

to develop sub-cortical dementia. It is estimated that 75% of people who survive more than 10 years with Parkinson's disease develop sub-cortical dementia (Durand & Barlow, 2013:519)

- Parkinson's disease is found to invite a number of complications such as thinking difficulties, depression and emotional changes, swallowing problems, chewing and eating problems, sleep problems and sleep disorders, bladder problems, constipation, blood pressure changes, sexual dysfunction etc.
- Treatment options vary and include medications and surgery. There is no permanent cure of this disease. However, the course of the disease and treatment varies widely, with some individuals functioning well with treatment.

What happens to the Parkinson's patients with regard to their motor problems is said to be the result of the damage to the pathways of a neurotransmitter named dopamine. It can be damaged on account of the adverse impact of the Parkinson's disease on the dopamine producing neurons in a specific area of the brain called substantia nigra. Because dopamine is involved in complex movement, a reduction in this neurotransmitter makes affected individuals increasingly unable to control their muscle movements, which leads to tremors and other difficulties and problems related to their movement.

## Huntington's Disease

Huntington's disease (HD) is a fatal genetic disorder that causes the progressive breakdown of nerve cells (neurons) in the brain. Certain neurons appear to be more vulnerable to damage in HD. In later phases of the disease, other regions of the brain are also affected. Damaging of the brain cells in one or the other areas of brain is responsible for bringing motor, cognitive and psychological problems among the affected individuals. As a progressive disease, these problems get increased gradually over many years until the death of the individual.

In its initial stage, it affects one's motor movements, typically in the form of *chorea*, involuntary limb movements. Later on, the movement problems become too problematic, such as severe twitching and spasms. In the coming years, the cognitive and psychiatric problems may also surface in a considerable amount. Just as with Parkinson's disease, the persons affected with this disease may also display dementia of the sub-cortical type.

In its full bloom, a person affected with Huntington's Disease manifests a quite visible symptoms of a triad of motor, cognitive, and psychiatric disorders mentioned as below.

- *Motor or Movement disorders* associated with both involuntary movement problems and impairments in voluntary movements, such as (i) Involuntary jerking or writhing movements (chorea), (ii)Muscle problems, such as rigidity or muscle contracture (dystonia) ,(iii)Slow or abnormal eye movements, (iv) Impaired gait, posture and balance and (v) Difficulty with the physical production of speech or swallowing
- *Cognitive disorders* involving cognitive impairments or difficulties such as (i)

Difficulty organizing, prioritizing or focusing on tasks,(ii)Lack of flexibility or the tendency to get stuck on a thought, behaviour or action (perseveration), (iii) Lack of impulse control that can result in outbursts, acting without thinking and sexual promiscuity, (iv)Lack of awareness of one's own behaviours and abilities, (v) Slowness in processing thoughts or "finding" words, and (vi)Difficulty in learning new information

- *Psychiatric disorders* involving Depression (visible through the symptoms like feelings of sadness, apathy, irritability, social withdrawal, insomnia, fatigue and loss of energy and frequent thoughts of death, dying or suicide) as a major common disorder accompanied with some or the other psychiatric disorders like Obsessive-compulsive disorder, Mania and Bipolar disorder.
- In addition to the above symptoms, weight loss is common in people with Huntington›s disease, especially as the disease progresses.

Regarding the causation of Huntington's disease, it is said to be caused by an inherited defect in a single exceptional gene belonging to chromosome 4. It has also been well established through the ongoing researches that it is inherited in an autosomal dominant fashion, so that each child of an affected parent has a 50% chance of developing the disease. Symptoms usually appear between the ages of 30 to 50, and worsen over a 10 to 25-year period adversely affecting the individual's ability to reason, walk and speak and developing serious complications for his or her health and living. Eventually, a person with Huntington's disease requires help with all activities of daily living and care. Late in the disease, he or she will likely be confined to a bed and unable to speak.

Medications are available to help manage the symptoms of Huntington's disease. It is said to be incurable in the sense that the provided treatments can't prevent the physical, mental and behavioural decline associated with the condition.

## Summary

- It is quite common for the old aged people to suffer from a number of old age neurocognitive disorders and diseases such as Delirium, Dementia, Alzheimer's disease, Pick's disease, Parkinson's disease, and Huntington's disease.
- Delirium is a disorder in which the affected person feels a major disturbance in his or her attention (such as inability to concentrate and thinking in an organized way), and orientation to the environment accompanied with the clouding of consciousness leading to a state of utter confusion (i.e. memory impairment, misinterpretations, illusions and on occasion hallucinations such as mistaking unfamiliar to familiar, and inability to tell about what day it is and who they are).
- Regarding the causation of delirium, it is said to be caused and progressed through some or the other organic or underlying medical conditions such as deterioration in one's physical and mental health, concurrent diseases and illnesses suffered by the individual in the course of his or her life.
- Suitable treatment for the delirium should be planned in view of treating the underlying medical conditions causing delirium in the patient. Besides this urgent

as well as supporting measures may be employed in the shape of prescription of one or the other suitable drugs for treating delirium symptoms.

- The term dementia stands for a disorder or a disturbed state of one's mind representing the deterioration of one's cognitive abilities to the point that his or her overall functioning gets impaired in a variety of ways including a great memory loss.
- Dementia and delirium both falling in the category of neurological disorders in late life have a number of overlapping features and symptoms. However, where in dementia there is a considerable deterioration of cognitive abilities including a great memory loss, in delirium one experiences clouding of consciousness resulting into a state of utter confusion.
- Dementia is caused by damage to or loss (death) of nerve cells and their connections in the brain. This damage or loss of the nerve cells may be caused either by (i) a head injury, a stroke, or a brain tumour, or by (ii) a neurodegenerative disease such as vascular disease, Alzheimer's disease, Pick's disease, Parkinson's disease, and Huntington's disease.
- Alzheimer's disease is known for giving birth to a particular type of dementia, named as 'Dementia of the Alzheimer's type' symptomizing a great loss of memory on the part of the affected individuals. In the case of Alzheimer's disease, the region of the brain called the hippocampus (the center of learning and memory) is adversely affected on account of the damage or loss of the brain cells belonging to this region resulting into such great loss in memory. It is a progressive degenerative disease that gets developed along the years with more deterioration in the memory and subsequent loss in the overall functioning of the patients. In the latest phase of their disorder patients are found to become fully dependent on other people needing constant care for their safety and living.
- The hereditary transmission in the form of defective genes play a great role in the causation of Alzheimer's disease. However, the heredity or genetic factors alone are not the exclusive factors for causation and development of the Alzheimer's or other likewise neurocognitive degenerative disorders of the old age. The environmental factors of one or the other nature like past head trauma, acute exposure to and poisoning with heavy metals and pesticides, air pollution, unhealthy life style, poor health and fatal diseases and psychological factors like high level of anxiety, depression and stress may also play their significant role in the causation and precipitation of these disorders.
- Treatment of the patients of Alzheimer's disease and other like- wise neurocognitive disorders involving dementia may involve a combination of different treatment measures and approaches named as medication or drug therapy, cognitive therapy, behavioural therapy, and sociocultural therapy.
- Vascular dementia may be considered as a general term describing problems with one's cognitive abilities including memory and other thought processes resulted on account of (i)Blockage or damage of brain artery through a cerebrovascular accident, or stroke or (ii) Narrowing or chronically damaging of the brain blood vessels through aging, high blood pressure, high cholesterol and smoking, diabetes,

and brain haemorrhage. In its effect and outcome, vascular dementia is widely considered the second most common cause of dementia after Alzheimer's disease.

- Pick' Disease also known as *Fronto-temporal neurocognitive disorder or disease* is a rare neurological condition or disorder that possess uniqueness in affecting the two important parts or lobes of the brain-frontal and temporal at the same time. Pick's disease usually occurs relatively early in life-during a person's 40s or 50s-and is therefore considered an example of pre-senile dementia.
- Parkinson's Disease is a slowly progressive degenerative brain disorder or disease that creates a number of motor and behavioural problems to the affected individuals
- Resulting into a lot of difficulties in their motor functioning including their proper speaking. In a long run, the people affected with Parkinson's disease are generally found to develop sub-cortical dementia and a number of complications in their health, and cognitive as well as social functioning. Treatment options vary and include medications and surgery. However, there is no permanent cure of this disease.
- Huntington's disease is a fatal genetic disorder that causes the progressive damaging of the nerve cells resulting into a number of problems associated with motor, cognitive and psychological functioning of the affected individuals. Just as with Parkinson's disease, the persons affected with this disease may also display dementia of the sub-cortical type. Huntington's disease is said to be inherited in an autosomal dominant fashion, so that each child of an affected parent has a 50% chance of developing the disease. Symptoms usually appear between the ages of 30 to 50, and worsen over a 10 to 25-year period to the extent of the total dependence of the patient over others. It is incurable but proper medication and looking after may help in managing the symptoms and problems of the patients.

## REFERENCES

American Psychiatric Association (2000), *The Diagnostic and Statistical Manual of Mental Disorders, DSM-IV-TR,* Washington D.C.: American Psychiatric Association.

American Psychiatric Association (2013), *The Diagnostic and Statistical Manual of Mental Disorders, DSM-IV-TR,* Washington D.C.: American Psychiatric Association

Comer, Ronald J. (2015), *Abnormal Psychology* (Ninth Edition), New York: Worth Publishers (A Macmillan Education Imprint)

Deborah D'Avolio. (2018), *Case study: Delirium in an Older Hospitalized Woman,* NIDUS, Network for Investigation of Delirium: Unifying Scientists, retrieved from

https://deliriumnetwork.org/case-study-delirium-in-an-older-hospitalized-woman/

Durand, V. Mark and Barlow, David H. (2013), *Essentials of Abnormal Psychology,* (6th ed.), Belmont CA: Wadsworth

Knight, B.G. (1996), *Psychology with the older adults,* (2nd ed.), Thousand Oaks, CA: Sage

Kring, A.M., Johnson, S.L., Davison, G.C. and Neale, J.M. (2012), *Abnormal Psychology* (Twelfth Edition), New York: John Wiley & Sons, Inc.

World Health Organization (1992), *International Classification of Diseases,* 10th revision. Geneva: World Health Organization.

Yoo, Hyun, et.al. (2017), *A Case Report of a 37 year old male patient of the dementia of the Alzheimer's type,* Psychiatry Investigation, retrieved from https://www.ncbi.nlm.nih.gov/pmc/articles/PMC5561413/

# 23

# TREATMENT OF ABNORMAL BEHAVIOUR

ABNORMAL behaviour is undesirable and harmful to the individual as well as to the society. Every care therefore needs to be taken to avoid the occurrence of such behaviour through preventive measures. However, the cases of abnormality in behaviour or mental illness are bound to occur and therefore, suitable curative measures are to be taken essentially for helping the maladjusted and sick individuals. Mental illness or abnormality in behaviour is an individual as well as situational problem and it is not possible to lay down a general treatment. Moreover, the illness needs to be treated in terms of superficial symptoms as well as at the root causes. Therefore, the problem of the treatment of mental patients or abnormal should include medical, psychological and sociological procedures. In this way the therapies of abnormal behaviour may be grouped into three broad categories:

A. Medical or Somatic Therapy
B. Psychological or Psychotherapy
C. Sociological or Sociotherapy

## A. Medical or Somatic Therapy

Medical therapy concerns the physiological treatment of abnormal behaviour. Some of the main measures in this category are drug or chemotherapy, shock therapy and brain surgery.

### Drug or Chemotherapy

There has been a widespread use of psycho-therapeutic drugs derived from chemical substances in the treatment of mental illness. These drugs can be grouped into the categories—(i) major tranquillizers, (ii) minor tranquillizers, (iii) anti-depressives, (iv)sedatives, and (v) hallucinogenic.

Let us know about the uses and importance of all such drugs.

- Major tranquillizers are used with psychotic patients but may be found useful in the case of alcoholic and senile patients also. They diminish anxiety, agitation, aggressive behaviour, hallucinations and delusions and thus help to control various psychotic symptoms without impairing intelligence or clarity of consciousness. Chlorpromazine, a drug derived from phenothiazine and reserpine, a crystalline alkaloid extracted from Rauwolfia serpentina, are the two notable tranquillizers which have been found effective.

- Minor tranquillizers like meprobamate and chlordiazepoxide reduce anxiety, apprehension and tension. Usually, they have no elicit on psychotic symptoms but are widely used with neurotic and psychosomatic patients.
- Anti-depressive drugs like phenelzine, isocarboxazid, imipramine, and amitriptyline diminish apathy and lethargy and are therefore widely used in controlling depressive reactions.
- Sedative drugs like phenobarbital, reduce anxiety, over-activity and insomnia. Sedatives carry side effects such as interference with clarity of consciousness, and causing drowsiness and therefore in many cases, the use of tranquillizers is widely recommended in place of sedatives.
- Depressants like lithium carbonate are mainly used in the treatment of agitated depression.
- Anticonvulsant drugs like trimethadione, sodium diphenyl hydantoinate are found to be effective in controlling several types of epilepsy.
- Hallucinogenic drugs such as LSD and mescaline, are useful in the treatment of schizophrenic patients particularly children.
- The use of drugs has been effective in reducing the severity of symptoms and making the management of the patients convenient in the hospital or at home. It has made possible for many patients to function in the community instead of remaining in the hospital. The drugs make many more patients accessible to psychological and sociological treatment.

However, the use of drugs has many limitations and drawbacks. The drugs and the dosage vary for different illness and patients. Therefore matching drug and dosage to meet the needs of a given patient in a particular situation is an uphill task. Moreover, the drugs may also carry side-effects. The advantages are not also enduring as the drugs tend to 'mask' symptoms rather than to come to grips with the actual causes of abnormal behaviour. Hence, drug therapy cannot be taken as a complete treatment for an abnormal behaviour and has to be supplemented with other physical or psychological measures.

## Shock Therapy

It involves an artificial induction of deep comas, convulsions or both by shock inducing drugs or electric current. This therapy is recommended to patients who are difficult to control or do not benefit from drug therapy.

In Insulin Shock Therapy (1ST) or Insulin Coma Therapy (ICT), the patient is given insulin injection intramuscularly early in the morning causing decrease in the blood sugar level. As a result, he passes through the stages of restlessness, unconsciousness, convulsions and eventually goes into a coma in which he does not respond even to a pinprick or other painful stimulation. He remains in this stage of coma for about an hour and then his blood sugar level is raised through his own body chemistry or by giving sugar contents resulting in the end of the insulin shock episode. Although insulin shock therapy was formerly used extensively in the treatment of schizophrenia, it has been largely replaced either by newer drug therapies or electro convulsive therapy.

In Electro Convulsive Therapy (ECT), also referred to as Electro Shock therapy (EST), convulsion is produced by passing electric current through the brain of the patient. For this purpose he is placed on a comfortable bed and electrodes arc placed on each side of his head and an alternating current, usually between 100 and 200 volts, is passed between them for a period of about two seconds. Patients are generally given muscle relaxant before administering ECT. While inducing current, the shoulders and limbs of the patient are held lightly by nurses and attendants and a rubber gag is placed between his teeth to prevent injury during the convulsion. About five to ten ECT's are given two to three times a week depending upon the requirement of the situation. There is confusion and loss of memory during the period immediately before and after treatment, but it gradually returns in a few weeks.

The ECT has been found helpful for depression, involutional melancholia, mania, schizophrenia and other psychotic reactions. It is quite popular for controlling cases of agitated depression and schizophrenia and is found useful for patients who do not respond well to drug therapy.

## Psychosurgery

It involves surgical operation of the patient's brain arid aims to destroy or isolate certain maladaptive cell complexes in the frontal areas of the brain responsible for undesirable emotional responses and mental disorders. This is done in one of the following ways:

- Some of the nerve connections are severed between the frontal lobes and the thalamus. This technique is known; as lobectomy or prefrontal lobectomy (leucotomy).
- Certain parts of the frontal lobes are actually removed. This technique is known as topectomy.
- Certain nerve tracts in the thalamus are severed by the insertion of a surgical electric needle. This technique is known as talectomy.

The removal of maladaptive cell complexes in the frontal lobes or the cutting of nerve pathways between the prefrontal lobes of the brain and the thalamus or hypothalamus by the surgical operations described above results in reducing the emotional torment of disturbing thoughts, apathy, delusions and hallucinations. Consequently, psychosurgery may be found useful with a wide range of mental patients including schizophrenics, involutional melancholic, antisocial personalities, alcoholics, manic depressives and patients suffering from stubborn obsessive and other severe neurotic reactions.

Psychosurgery as a method of treatment of the mental patients involves considerable risk and negative consequences. It may reduce or even impair the patient's intellectual abilities. There may be temporary or permanent organic complications including convulsions, aphasia, increased appetite and rectal or vesical incontinence. In some cases brain surgery may lead to death. Therefore, in all cases psychosurgery should be the last resort and its use restricted to patients with whom everything else has been tried and failed, so that any improvement at all may be considered a great gain.

## B. Psychological or Psychotherapy

The majority of cases of behavioural disorders or mental illness may be adjudged as products of severe maladjustment caused by psychological factors. Physical or medical treatment in such cases does not prove much useful. Such patients need psychological treatment for solving their psychological difficulties and achieving better personality adjustment. This form of psychological treatment is known as psychotherapy.

Psychotherapy is a difficult term to define. However, it may be understood as a method of treatment of psychological problem or disorder of an individual (known as patient) by a trained person (known as therapist) through a behavioural approach in the form of establishing a psychological relationship with the patient for the purpose of solving the patient's emotional difficulties and promoting adequate personality growth and adjustment.

The main objective in psychotherapy is to bring about changes in the patient's perception of himself and of his environment and thus resulting in positive enduring changes in his behaviour for achieving adequate adjustment and regaining better mental health. For the realization of this objective a number of systematic approaches to psychotherapy, differing in goals and procedures, have been evolved. These are psychoanalytic therapy, client centred therapy, behaviour therapy and group therapy.

### *Psychoanalytical Therapy*

The founder of the psychoanalytical therapy was Sigmund Freud who developed the theory and technique of psychoanalysis. Freud believed that earlier conflicts, desires, painful or anxiety arousing experiences, though repressed and unconscious, are responsible for the present abnormal behaviour of an individual. He used the technique of free association and dream analysis for tracing the real causes of the present problem by uncovering the repressed conflicts.

In the technique of free association, the patient is made to lie on a couch, with the analyst (therapist) sitting out of his range of sight. The patient is asked to 'free associate', that is, to speak freely about whatever comes into his mind, no matter what it is and to go on talking about his thoughts and feelings as subsequent associations reveal themselves. He is expected to talk frankly. He must not hold back past or present events, attitudes towards the therapist or fantasies, no matter how unpleasant or embarrassing they may be.

In case the patient remains silent or claims that 'nothing comes to mind' it may be his resistance to treatment. He is told that all thoughts and feelings are important to the treatment process. If he insists that he is really trying, it may be postulated that the resistance is caused by unconscious parts of his mind. Such resistances themselves provide clues to the patient's conflicts.

Dream analysis is another major technique used in psychoanalytical therapy for uncovering unconscious motivation and repressed conflicts. During sleep, the defences of the ego are lowered, allowing repressed material to reach the conscious. For this reason, dreams, to some extent, may be taken as the 'royal road' to the unconscious. Expressing his views in this concern, Freud asserts, that one's dreams, are loaded with repressed material, although in symbolic form. The manifest content of the dream is the actual dream and its events, but the latent content is the hidden, symbolic meaning of those events that would, if correctly interpreted, reveal the unconscious conflicts that were creating the nervous disorder. (Freud, 1900)

Consequently, through the analysis of material produced by means of free association and patient's dreams, the analyst begins to get all the clues about the possible underlying causes of the behavioural disorder of his patient. For the most part, the analyst has to rely for his subject matter on the verbal responses based on the memories of the patient. Later on, some more direct evidences become available. The patient's personality is reflected in the way he behaves during the analytic period. His habitual patterns of behaviour his way of looking at things, his likings and love, his prejudices and bias, may all affect the way in which he deals with his analyst. His total behaviour is to be analysed by the therapist for going deep into his problem.

Many times, on account of the phenomenon of transference the patient's attitudes and behaviour towards his therapist is unrealistic. During the interaction in the process of psychoanalytical therapy, the patient and therapist develop a complex emotionally charged relationship. As a result, the patient usually transfers his deepest emotions to the analyst, the analyst becoming the love object or the hate object depending upon the early experiences of the patient with his parents or other important persons. For example, a female patient may view the analyst as an ideal husband and lover or may exhibit feelings she had as a child towards her father. The mechanism of transference is important in effecting the cure of the patient as *it* allows letting of repressed feelings towards persons resembling husband, lover or father figures. The analyst intelligently establishes rapport and relationships for the uncovering of the unresolved conflicts and repressed feelings and tries to make interpretations based on the emotional attitude and behaviour shown by the patient towards the analyst.

In brief, the psychoanalytical therapy rests on the following assumptions and techniques.

(i) Abnormal behaviour of the patient is the result of the repressed desires or conflicts experienced earlier in one's life.

(ii) Through free association and recalling day to day dreams the patient is given art opportunity to uncover his unconscious desires and repressed conflicts.

(iii) The mechanism of transference helps in the task of uncovering the conflict as it is once again made into an interpersonal one, this time between the patient and the therapist.

(iv) The analysis of free association, dreams, transference and overall behaviour of the patient helps in knowing the abnormal behaviour of the patient.

(v) The therapist tries to show the patient how some early experiences affected his emotional life and finally helps him to achieve new and more adaptive modes of adjustment in order to lead a normal life.

(vi) Finally, the therapist tries to break the bond of interpersonal relationship between himself and his patient in order to make the patient face the realities of life and solve his problems Independently (after developing an impressive insight into his problem) without any emotional support from the therapist.

The prevalent mode of psychoanalytical therapy has been modified in many ways from orthodox psychoanalysis propagated by Freud and his followers in the manners such as below.

- The couch is gone, and the client (the term used now in place of the Freud's term patient for the individual seeking therapy) may sit face to face with the therapist and he or she may also stand or walk about.
- Rather than remaining quiet until the client says something or revealing, the modern psychoanalyst is far more directive, asking questions, suggesting helpful behaviour, and giving opinions and interpretations earlier in the relationship, which helps speed up the therapeutic process.
- The treatment session now may go on two to four times a week for two or more years. These sessions are more likely to be focused on current situations, interpersonal relationships and other sources of conflict. The therapist may also take advantage of such treatment adjuncts as play therapy, art therapy, group therapy and hypnosis instead of being dependent upon free association and dream analysis only.
- Today's psychoanalysts also focus less on the "id" as the motivator of behaviour, instead looking more at the "ego" or sense of "self" as the motivating force behind all actions. Some psychoanalysts also focus on the process of transference more than on other typical aspects of traditional psychoanalysis, leading to the more general method called psychodynamic therapy. Psychodynamic therapy is typically shorter in duration than traditional psychoanalysis.
- Even so, all the psychodynamic techniques require the client to be fairly intelligent and verbally able to express his or her ideas, feelings and thoughts effectively. People who are extremely withdrawn or who suffer from the more psychotic disorders are not good candidates for this form of psychotherapy. People, who have non-psychotic adjustment disorders, such as anxiety, somatoform or dissociative disorders, are more likely to benefit from psychodynamic therapy (Ciccerelli &White, 2012)

### *Client-centered Psychotherapy*

This is also known as non-directive therapy and is the outcome of the philosophy and experiences of an American psychologist Carl Rogers (1902-1987) who had full faith in the worth and competencies of the human individual. His assumption was that people are innately good and effective. They have an innate tendency for self -actualization, that is, to realize their potentials. As the self has an innate tendency towards self- actualization, the most important evaluation should come from the self of a person. In case where a person accepts evaluation from others and if these evaluations are negative or conditionally positive the result is conflict between self-evaluation and the evaluation of others. This type of conflict may give rise to undue anxiety and tension and thus in due course cause abnormalities. For example, a newly married normal girl may develop abnormal behaviour by considering herself worthless after being repeatedly criticized by her mother-in-law or husband.

Consequently, Rogers' therapy demands from the individual to return to his basic nature of evaluating himself positively. It believes that the client (the term used for a patient) is quite competent to resolve his conflict as he has within himself resources for self-actualization and healthy adjustment. He needs only a deep affectionate relationship with the therapist to learn how to use his resources. Rogers' therapy involves very strong conviction about the client's worth and his basic urge for self-actualization. The therapist is there not to direct but merely to help the client direct himself for his healthy adjustment. On account of this non-directive role of the therapist, Rogers' therapy is known as non-directive therapy. It is known as client-centred therapy (and more recently as person-centered therapy) because it revolves totally around the client or the person seeking therapy as may be seen in some of the following steps associated with this therapy.

1. In Rogers therapy, the client himself approaches the therapist for help in order to get rid of some psychological stress. During the first interview, the therapist instead of solving his difficulty him-self assures him of his help in working out the client's own solutions.
2. In the next interview, the client is encouraged to talk about his most deeply felt emotions as freely as possible. In this way, the negative feelings that have been bottled up inside the client come out into the open. Here the therapist does not intervene but creates suitable therapeutic conditions which would facilitate the client to talk in a more honest arid emotional way about himself and his problem.
3. The next move is concerned with helping the client to gain an insight into his emotional conflicts. It involves acceptance, recognition and clarification of the feelings of client by the therapist. Here attention is paid to the emotional aspect rather than to what the client says. The therapist tries to provide environment for removing the emotional conflicts which are blocking self- actualization by selecting and focusing on statements and feelings expressed by the client. It is a sort of help rendered by the therapist to the client for learning suitable ways to evaluate himself and his environment in a true perspective.

As a result, the client gains insight by (i) understanding the causes behind his behaviour, (ii) recognising and accepting his self in its real position, and (iii) working towards his positive self-growth and better adjustment.

1. After gaining insight into his problem, the client is helped in seeking some minor positive actions for the solution of his problem. Here also the therapist is not to direct or lead but to recognize and render clarification about the possible courses of action. The minor positive actions bring satisfaction and develop self-

confidence paving the way for more positive action and thus helping the client in his self-actualization.

2. Finally, there comes a stage when the client, after gaining confidence in his self, feels that he does not need further therapeutic interviews. As such the decision for ending the therapeutic relationship comes from the client. At this stage, he is known to acquire his original drive for self- actualization by learning positive ways of understanding and promoting his self.

Evidently, from beginning to end, Rogers' therapy is centred round the client. He is the main actor who has to play the leading role. The therapist encourages and sets the therapeutic environment for helping him, to discover ways of self- actualization by gaining insight into his problem, removing discrepancy between his real self and his idealized self-image and developing confidence in his self for healthy adjustment. Unlike other psychotherapy Rogers' therapy does not demand any special, intellectual and professional knowledge of human behaviour from the therapist. Rogers asserts that it is only the ability of establishing good interpersonal relationship that counts much in being a good therapist. For this purpose, he emphasizes the following therapeutic traits:

(i) The therapist must be genuinely and not superficially in relationship with his client. He should be what he is. Anything going on in him, which is relevant to the relationship, can be seen by his client. He should be able to bring a direct personal encounter with his client, meeting him on a person to person basis.

(ii) The therapist should have the capacity for empathy. To sense the client's inner world of private meanings as if it were his own, without losing the "as if" quality, is empathy. He should also be able to communicate some of the significant fragments of that understanding. By showing *empathy,* by sensing and reflecting their clients' feelings, therapists can help clients experience a deeper self-understanding and self-acceptance. As Rogers (1980:10) explained:

> *Hearing (active listening) has consequences. When I truly hear a person and the meanings that are important to him at that moment, hearing not simply his words, but him, and when I let him know that I have heard his own private personal meanings, many things happen. There is first of all a grateful look. He feels released. He wants to tell me more about his world. He surges forth in a new sense of freedom. He becomes more open to the process of change. I have often noticed that the more deeply I hear the meanings of the person, the more there is that happens. Almost always, when a person realizes that he has been deeply heard, his eyes moisten. I think in some real sense he is weeping for joy. It is as though he were saying, "Thank God, somebody heard me. Someone knows what it is like to be me."*

(iii) The therapist must experience a warm, positive, acceptance towards what is in the client. He must praise and respect his client as a person and thus pay a positive regard. As far as possible, this positive regard should be unconditional.

The therapist acts in such a way that his client may perceive the genuineness of the acceptance and empathy which the therapist experiences for him. The perception of such a psychological climate in the relationship by the client results in the constructive personality growth and desirable changes in the behaviour of the client. Thus, Rogers' therapy heavily depends upon the attitudes of the therapist.

The acceptance, positive regard and clarification of the feelings of the client by the therapist is properly reciprocated resulting in the removal of the discrepancy between his ideal self and present self and thus paving the way to his healthy adjustment and better self- actualization.

As far as the suitability of the therapy is concerned, Rogerian therapy may not, in fact, be appropriate for a severe psychological disorder. It may, however, work well with mildly disturbed people if handled properly by a therapist in appropriate environment of interpersonal relationship.

### *Behaviour Therapy*

Like psychoanalytically based psychotherapy, the behaviour therapy does not aim to root out the underlying causes of the patient's abnormal behaviour. It merely sets itself to remove individual pieces of behaviour that are disabling. Similarly, behaviour therapy unlike the Rogers client centered are action based rather than insight (understanding of one's motives and actions) based. The basic assumption underlying behaviour therapy is the belief that behaviour in its all forms and shapes is learned. The abnormal behaviour grows out of maladaptive or defective learning. Therapy, in turn, becomes an attempt to provide corrective learning experiences through the use of the same kinds of learning techniques that people (and animals) use to learn any new responses.

As a term thus, behaviour therapy denotes the use of experimentally established principles of learning for the purpose of changing un-adaptive or abnormal behaviour. As far as the origin of the maladaptive or defective learning is concerned, it is traced either in classical conditioning as advocated by Pavlov or in operant conditioning as explained by Skinner. Based on these two approaches, various methods of behaviour therapy (discussed ahead) have come into existence.

1. *Counter-conditioning:* One may learn maladaptive or abnormal behaviour through conditioning. As a result, a person may show fear responses in the presence of certain normally neutral stimulus objects and events. When that happens we say that he has developed some unrealistic fear or phobia. Fear of animals, height, water, darkness, closed or open places, all such phobias may be seen as a result of defective learning or improper conditioning. The treatment of such behaviour lies in its counter-conditioning.

For illustration, let us take the case of a child who has developed a generalized fear of rabbits through conditioned fear responses. In this case, the treatment may be worked out by associating some pleasant or favourable responses with the presence of a rabbit. The child may be given his most liked eatables or allowed to listen to the most enjoyable tune or play the game in the presence of a rabbit. The rabbit may be kept at some distance and then gradually moved closer on successive occasions. The fear responses can thus be gradually eliminated.

The sexual dysfunctions like frigidity, impotence and early ejaculation may also be treated by the process of counter-conditioning. Most often such dysfunctions are the result of anxiety which causes sexual inhibition. Thus the treatment process involves conditioning as below:

- To attempt sex relations only when there is a minimum of anxiety, for example, in situations in which there is a clear desire,
- To attempt sex relations only when desirable support, cooperation or assistance is available from the sex partner.

Gradually the reaction of anxiety to sexual experiences may be eliminated because they will now not be permitted to happen, and adequate sexual responses may in time be strengthened resulting in the treatment of a particular sexual dysfunction.

2. *Desensitization methods:* Conditioned anxiety responses are the root causes for the development of many abnormalities in the behaviour of individuals. The treatment of such abnormalities may involve a variety of techniques designed to increase the individual's capacity to tolerate an anxiety-provoking situation. Two such techniques are described, below:

(i) *Systematic desensitization:* This technique was developed by Joseph Wolpe, an American psychologist. It aims to reduce levels of anxiety related to an anxiety-provoking situation progressively through some well-planned systematic steps like relaxation, outlining hierarchy of individual's anxieties, and desensitization. In this initial stage, attempts are made to develop an anxiety hierarchy. For this purpose, the patient's anxieties are studied and ranked according to the intensity of anxiety to the different stimuli ranging from most to least frightening. Side by side, in the earlier session of therapy, the patient is made to learn the art of relaxation of the muscles of the body.

When the patient has mastered the relaxation technique, the desensitization process begins The patient is made to relax completely in a, comfortable chair or a couch with his eyes closed, and asked to imagine and experience the scene in the hierarchy which is the least anxiety-provoking and progressively reaches the scene which is highest in the hierarchy. The motor relaxation is viewed by Wolpe as antagonistic to anxiety. The patient imagines and experiences the scene with little or no anxiety, and thus his sensitivity to the imagining of such experiences is de-conditioned. Treatment is terminated when the patient reaches a stage of relaxing completely and imagining vividly and without any anxiety the scenes which evoked the greatest anxiety before the commencement of the treatment.

There may be certain variations of the desensitization procedure. Instead of imagining a situation, the patient may be exposed to the real stimuli which evoke anxiety. This is termed as desensitization in vivo. In such a procedure, a patient who has a fear of humiliation at making mistakes may be made to commit minor errors and then progressively more serious ones in the presence of the therapist in each instance until all feelings of anxiety disappear. In another variation, desensitization may be done using a tape-recorder or video film eliciting anxiety-provoking situations.

(ii) *Flooding or implosive therapy:* In this method of desensitization, the patient is exposed immediately to the greatest anxiety- provoking situation. He is not gradually introduced to the anxiety- provoking situations starting from the least to the most as in systematic desensitization but is encouraged to face the frightening or distressing situation and remain there, regardless of how much anxiety *h* generated, until a spontaneous decrease in anxiety takes place. A child who fears rabbits may be confronted with a rabbit through a videotape or by way of real-life situation. It may be seen that his peak anxiety does not last very long and he eventually gets used to it and feels that his fear was irrational.

3. *Aversive conditioning:* Aversive conditioning involves the modification of behaviour patterns through pain or punishment. This treatment has proved effective in overcoming obsessional thinking, compulsive acts, homosexuality and other sexual deviations, alcoholism, over eating, smoking, drug dependence, gambling, etc. The method consists of administering a noxious stimulus {resulting in an unpleasant response) to the patient in an appropriate time relation to the stimulus to which aversive conditioning is desired. The assumption of such treatment is that the patient will gradually learn to avoid abnormal pattern of behaviour and prefer a more desirable and normal one. For example, in treating a man for homosexuality, the aversive conditioning would involve an introduction of a punishment (electric shock or some other punishment) while he is made to look at the picture of an attractive male but would be permitted to look at the picture of a female or some sexually attractive parts of a female figure without being punished.

   Similarly, in the treatment of chronic alcoholism aversion conditioning may be achieved with the help of a drug *Antabuse*. The person who is chronic alcoholic is persuaded to take the drug. A drink of alcoholic beverages, after taking the drug, results in strong unpleasant and uncomfortable physical reactions like increased pulse rate, difficulty in breathing, severe headache and nausea. The repetition of such unpleasant experiences results in the avoidance of alcoholic beverages.

4. *Modelling:* Modelling is a therapy technique in which a patient's behaviour is modified as a result of observing the appropriate and normal behaviour of other people used as models. One may use modelling therapy for eliminating a child's fear of rabbits by making him observe that the other children are playing with the rabbits without fear. Similarly, one's phobia of snakes may also be overcome through modelling therapy. Such patients may be made to observe both real and filmed incidents of people (models) and snakes in which people (models) may be seen approaching the snakes gradually with no signs of anxiety and fear.

   The modelling as a technique may also be used for learning more adaptable and desirable ways of personal and social adjustment. People may also be helped in the treatment of sexual dysfunctions by means of films or live models depicting practical techniques and normal sex behaviour.

5. *Method of positive reinforcement:* In this method, carefully selected rewards and schedules of reinforcement are used to modify a patient's behaviour in the direction of socially desirable well adaptive behaviour. Anorexia nervosa, a condition in which the person affected refuses to eat, has been found to be successfully treated by arranging for eating to be followed by a proper schedule

of positive reinforcement or rewards such as to be allowed to go to a movie, play a favourable game, use of a radio or provision of a good company etc.

A technique known as 'token economy' is also used as a method for treating abnormal behaviour. It is based on the principle of positive reinforcement. In this method, plastic or metal tokens are used as rewards for reinforcing the positive and desirable behaviour shown by the patients. These tokens may, later, be exchanged for special privileges such as television viewing, single room accommodation, to obtain special food, magazines or novels etc. This token economy as a behaviour modification technique has been found most effective in improving and modifying the behaviour of people in institutions or hospitals.

6. *Cognitive-Behavioural Therapy:* This behavioural therapy is aimed to bring needed changes in one's cognitive behaviour-thinking and drawing conclusions for feeling and acting in a desirable way.

   Cognitive behavioural therapy takes a double-barrel approach for dealing with behavioural problems and disorders. Where, on one hand, it aims to bring desirable change in people's way of thinking, side by side, on the other it also works towards altering the way they act.

In this way, this treatment approach helps in deriving two sided benefits of both the cognitive as well as behavioural approaches for treating abnormal behaviour (i) by making people aware of their irrational negative thinking and to replace it with new ways of thinking and (ii) training them to practice the more positive approach and way of living in their life. For the realization of these objectives, the cognitive behavioural therapists may be found to proceed in the manner as laid down below.

1. The beginning in the use of this approach is made to bring needed changes in the irrational negative attitude and thought process of the problem ridden individual. In general, the people suffering from depression, anxiety and mood disorders, for example are found to be grappled with pessimistic and negative thinking, and over generalized self- blaming behaviour such as " I am worthless, I will not be able to face the interview board, the other candidates are far better than me, they are looking so relaxed and confident, I will get surely nervous in answering the questions, so on and so forth" .
2. To change such self -defeating, over blaming, and pessimistic behaviour of the individuals, into a desirable one, therapists now try to teach the affected people to restructure their thinking and behaving positively in stressful situations. The first task in this concern is to replace, negative self- talk with positive, confident and assuring one. He can thus help them in restructuring their thought process. It can then be followed, to train them to act in a desirable way guided through their restructured thinking.

In practice, the use of cognitive-behavioural therapy has been found quite encouraging and helpful for a number of people suffering from anxiety, depression and mood disorders. While going through such treatment, the affected people get valuable opportunity to replace their negative thinking and self- defeating pessimistic behaviour with more realistic appraisals of themselves and practice behaviour that helps them in getting rid of their problems. How cognitive behavioural therapy is practiced and what gains are available with the use of this therapy may be made clear by going through the following description provided by Myers, David G. (2014:556).

> *In one study, people with obsessive-compulsive behaviours learned to re-label their compulsive thoughts. Feeling the urge to wash their hands again and again, they would tell themselves, "I 'm having a compulsive urge". They would explain to themselves that the hand-washing urge was a result of their brain's abnormal activity, which they had previously viewed in PET scans. Then, instead of giving in, they would spend 15 minutes in an enjoyable, alternative behaviours, such as practicing an instrument, taking a walk, or gardening. This helped "unstuck" the brain by shifting attention and engaging other brain areas. For two or three months, the weekly therapy sessions continued, with re-labelling and refocusing practice at home. By the study's end, most participants' symptoms had diminished, and their PET scans revealed normalized brain activity. Many other studies confirm cognitive-behavioural therapy's effectiveness for those with anxiety, depression, or anorexia nervosa.*

All these treatment methods have one-to-one relationship involving one helping person (the therapist) and one person coming for help (the patient). There are other behavioural approaches that involve two or more persons in seeking and providing treatment help. Let us know about them.

7. *Group therapy:* In contrast with such one-to-one relationship group therapy demands the involvement of a group (two or more persons) at a time with a single or several therapists. According to Kisker (1964:388), *"Group therapy is a method of treatment in which a number of people are treated at one time or in which group dynamics are used in the treatment of one person."*

In group therapy, a group usually consists of six to twelve members who meet one or more times a week. This group is somewhat homogeneous with respect to age, sex and type of disorder. Usually the group is led by a therapist. The different therapeutic measures like psychoanalytical therapy, client-centred therapy and behaviour therapy used in individual therapy may also be successfully used in group therapy which may take several forms. There are differences in objectives, approaches and techniques. Some groups are conducted in the format of individual therapy, others are essentially educational, featuring the presentation of certain materials which the members discuss and apply to themselves. A few groups are largely inspirational, others seek to promote insight to release experiences or problems, pent up emotions or unconscious impulses to facilitate self-discovery or to teach social skills.

In modern group therapy a group situation known as 'encounter group' is used for the treatment of maladaptive behaviour. In such a group the patients are encouraged to behave in an unguarded fashion. They get immediate and open feedback from fellow members and the therapist or the group leader. In some encounter groups the members engage in group activities like singing, games, physical exercises, physical intimacy, dance, dramas and other entertainment programmes. The idea behind such group activities is to induce fatigue or pleasure in order to break resistances for the closer group interaction, and proper catharsis or sublimation of their unconscious improper motives.

Group therapy has many advantages over the individual therapy, the foremost being the economy in terms of time, labour and financial resources as the treatment may be given to a number of patients in the group affected with the same disorder. Beyond this, the group therapy provides an environment for the learning of desirable social skills and unlearning of maladaptive behaviour through the use of group dynamics. It also permits persons with common problems to support and help one another.

However, group therapy does not necessarily work well with all types of disorders and patients. For example, some people find it impossible to talk about themselves and their problems in group. In some cases of agitated depression or psychotic disturbances the group encounter may prove dangerous. As a result, there is a need for considerable skill on the part of therapist who deals with a group of patients. It is his competency, art of group dynamics, and understanding between him and his patients which prove helpful in bringing encouraging results of group therapy.

8. *Family therapy:* Family therapy is a variation of group therapy in which two or more members of a family are treated together as a unit. The family group in this therapy may consist of a troubled married couple, or it may be a set of parents and one or more of their children. Sometimes it is the whole family being treated in a clinic or in its natural habitat—the home.

Family therapy has grown out of the realization that each member of a family is influenced by every other member. Usually, unhealthy intrafamilial relationships are responsible for the maladaptive abnormal behaviour of an individual. On the other hand, an abnormal may prove a potent factor in turning the environment of family uncongenial and thus paving the way for making other members maladjusted and abnormal.

A proper treatment procedure must care for the related factors in one's family along with his treatment. In order to bring about a desirable modification in the behaviour of an individual we have to take care of the intrafamilial relationships within his family. If we attempt to change the patient Without changing the others in family, we may find family circumstances conspiring to keep him as he is. That is why, many patients who improve in the hospital or clinic are found to manifest a reappearance of symptoms when they return to their families.

Family therapy is a challenging and promising approach. It helps the family members to discuss their attitudes with each other and acquire insight in the intrafamilial relationship. It brings desirable changes in the whole family interaction, ensuring that changes in one person will not be counteracted by the behaviour of others. This approach brings all or a large portion of the family under study and thus helps in maintaining the family's equilibrium and allows the family to work its adjustment problems as they occur.

The treatment through family therapy often reveals that the patient who first seeks help or is referred for help is not necessarily the most maladjusted. He may the victim of the maladjustment or defective interpersonal relationship of his parents or other members of the family. For example, difficulties in the marital relationship of the parents may cause difficulties in parenting and it may, in turn, cause behavioural abnormalities in the children. In such cases, improvement in marital relationship of the parents through a well planned family therapy always brings desirable improvement in the behaviour of a child patient.

9. *Dramatic therapy:* Dramatic therapy uses the enactment of roles and incidents, when problems are acted out instead of being talked about. Role playing and psychodrama are examples of such therapy.

In role playing, the patient acts out the behaviour of individual in a certain situation. In doing so he either repeats his own previous behaviour or gives indication of his possible behaviour in that situation. In this way, role play gives the patient and therapist an opportunity to gain insight into the patient's behaviour. It also provides an opportunity and stage to achieve catharsis and to practise more adaptive ways of one's behaviour. Psychodrama involves a more elaborate procedure than role play for acting out behaviour. It generally involves five elements on the pattern of a dramatic setting: a stage, the therapist in the role of director, the patient as a hero, helping characters (other persons or therapists) and the audience. The patient is made to act out his problems. All concerned persons are made to participate in the spontaneous acting out of problem situations related to the patient's life.

## C. Sociotherapy

This treatment involving sociological measures may also be termed situational or milieu therapy. According to Coleman (1970:603), *"Sociotherapy refers primarily to some modification of the environment in order to provide a life situation in which the patient has a reasonable chance of making a successful adjustment."*

Thus while medical therapy and psychotherapy focus on the patient, sociotherapy shifts the focus to physical and social milieu (environment). Here attempts are made (to bring about desirable changes in the situations—physical and social settings—concerned with a patient.

Sociotherapy is usually carried out by the psychiatric social worker with the help of voluntary and non-voluntary social welfare agencies. The treatment in this approach usually works on the assumption that one's environment—physical and social—has a considerable bearing on one's happiness and well-being. An unhealthy and defective social environment causes maladjustment and develops maladaptive behaviour pattern. Therefore, if we want to modify or bring changes in one's maladaptive behaviour, we must direct our attempts towards modifying the defective environment or providing a new and more favourable one. This may involve attempts at improving or restructuring the defective marital relationship between the parents in order to treat a child with behaviour problems. In some cases it may demand the placement of the child in a foster home or boarding house on account of the destructive nature of the child's family environment. In other cases, it may involve the modification or alteration of the situations concerning one's neighbourhood, social and college environment or work environment. Let us try to understand the use of sociotherapy in relation to a number of environmental surroundings needed to be modified or restructured for the benefit of the clients.

(i) *Home and family environment*: Here the therapist analyses interpersonal relationships existing among the members of the family. The parents may be provided valuable guidance and assistance concerning child rearing, marital and other life problems. Sometimes the defective family environment needs a change in the whole family environment so that there may be a desirable improvement in the behaviour of the family members. In case it is a broken family or if there is no family, the individual is provided with a new environment which may be a foster family, boarding institution or other residential setting, serving as a semi-family

(ii) *Neighbourhood surroundings* : Many times, the abnormal behaviour of an individual is caused on account of his unavoidable maladjustment to his immediate milieu, that is, the neighbourhood. In such cases it is essential to remove the individual fioin this neighbourhood or to modify it.

(iii) *School and college environment*: An educational institution has its own distinctive atmosphere composed of things and people in complex interaction. A defective physical, social and educational environment of an institution may result in maladjustment and maladaptive behaviour. Social therapy, in such a situation, demands desirable improvement in the physical surroundings, interpersonal relationships, curricular and co-curricular programs of the institution. In some cases it recommends the placing of the student in another school or college which provides opportunities for better adjustment.

(iv) *Work environment*: Professional and occupational maladjustment caused by improper interpersonal relationships and defective physical or social structures of the work-setting results in severe impairment of the physical and mental health of the employees. In such circumstances, social therapy aims at desirable improvement in the physical as well as social surroundings of the world of work. For this purpose it may attempt for better physical facilities and cheerful surroundings, healthy interpersonal relationships, better working conditions, involvement of the employees in administration, and enhancement of power, prestige and status of the employees.

(v) *Hospital environment:* Sociotherapy, to a large extent, aims at desirable modification (suiting the patients) in the physical and social environment (including its therapeutic program) of a mental hospital. In order to achieve the goal of sociotherapy, the whole set-up of the hospital may work as a therapeutic community in which the inmates are placed in minimum security settings. They are urged to join recreational and occupational groups and to share responsibility for the daily programs of the hospital. Attempts are made to design liberal and elaborate probationary and parole programs for keeping the patient in close contact with the community or return him to it as soon as possible. The opportunities for desirable interaction between him and the community are also provided within the set-up of the hospital environment. The interaction with the community on account of socio-therapeutic attempts may result in the following positive achievements:

- Members of the community, at large, develop more positive attitudes towards mental patients and mental hospitals.
- There is an increase in the proportion of voluntary admissions. Treatment of

mental illness is regarded essential and convenient as for physical ailments.

Thus socio-therapeutic measures help a patient in his overall adjustment by bringing desirable changes in his physical, social, educational, professional, and therapeutic environment. Moreover, these measures prove effective in the development of program for the systematic care of patients after their | discharge from the hospitals.

The socio-therapist renders valuable guidance to the family members about what to expect of the patient and how to react to him. With his periodic visits he is able to help many patients to adjust satisfactorily in the community and thus minimise the chances of their relapse and dependence on hospitalization. Besides, by seeking cooperation from the community, government or some voluntary agencies, he may also help the patient to find employment. In cases, where patient returns to his previous job, he may help him in his occupational adjustment by advising the employer to understand the patient's illness and recovery.

## Summary

- The treatment of abnormal behaviour may be classified into three broad categories namely, somatic therapy, psychological therapy and sociological therapy.
- *Somatic or medical therapy* concerns the physiological treatment of abnormal behaviour. Some of the main measures belonging to this category are drug or chemotherapy, shock therapy and brain surgery. (i)Various drugs prove effective in reducing the severity of symptoms and make the management of the patient convenient in the hospital or at home. But the drugs also carry severe side-effects and the treatment docs not remove the actual causes of abnormal behaviour. Drug therapy has therefore to be supplemented by other physical or psychological measures. (ii)Shock therapy involves an artificial induction of deep comas, convulsions or electric current. Insulin shock therapy has now been completely replaced by BCT which has been found useful for agitated depression, schizophrenia and other psychotic reactions. (iii)Psychosurgery involves surgical operation of the patient's brain for reducing the emotional torment of disturbing thoughts, apathy, delusions and hallucinations. However, it involves considerable risk and negative consequence and should be taken as a method of last resort.
- Psychotherapy is a method of treatment of psychological problem or disorder of an individual (known as patient) by a trained person (known as therapist) through a behavioural approach in the form of establishing a psychological relationship for the purpose of solving the patient's emotional difficulties, achieving adequate adjustment, and gaining better mental health. Psychoanalytic, client centred, behaviour and group therapy constitute the major psycho- therapies. (i) Psychoanalytical therapy assumes that repressed desires or conflicts experienced earlier in one's life are the real source of the causation of abnormal behaviour. The analysis of material produced by means of free association, dreams and other measures helps in getting clues for the underlying causes of behaviour disorder. The therapist then tries to acquaint the patient with the effect of his early experiences and helps him to achieve new and more adaptive modes, of adjustment, (ii) Client-centred psychotherapy is centred around the client. It

creates proper therapeutic environment ***for*** helping him to discover ways of self actualization by ***gaining insight*** into his problem, removing discrepancy between his real self and his idealized ***self- image*** and developing confidence in his self for ***his*** healthy adjustment, (iii) *Behaviour therapy* denotes ***the*** use of experimentally established principles of learning for the purpose of changing unadaptive or abnormal behaviour. ***Based*** on the classical conditioning or operant conditioning, it involves important methods like counter ***condition***ing, desensitization, flooding, aversive conditioning, modelling and ***method*** of positive reinforcement., (iv) *Cognitive behavioural therapy* helps in deriving two sided benefits of both the cognitive as well as behavioural approaches for treating abnormal behaviour by (a) making people aware of their irrational negative thinking and to replace it with new ways of thinking and (b) training them to practice the more positive approach and way of living in their life. (v)*Group therapy* is a method of treatment in which a number of people are treated simultaneously or in which group dynamics are used in the treatment of one person. In modern group therapy a group situation—encounter group—has proved effective in treating behavioural disorders, (vi) *Family therapy* is variation of group therapy in which two or more members of a family are treated as a unit and (vii) *Dramatic therapy* makes use of the enactment of roles and incidents. Here the problems are acted out instead of merely talking about them. Role playing and psychodrama are examples of such therapy.

- *Sociotherapy* refers primarily to modification of the environment in order to provide a life situation in which the patient has a reasonable chance of making a successful adjustment. Various socio-therapeutic measures carried out by the psychiatric social worker with the help of voluntary and non-voluntary social welfare agencies help a patient in his overall adjustment by bringing desirable changes in his physical, social, educational, professional and therapeutic environment. Moreover, these measures prove effective in providing systematic care of the patients after their discharge from the hospital in terms of follow-up treatment and proper rehabilitation.

## REFERENCES

Ciccarelli, Saundra K. and White, J Noland (2012), *Psychology*, New York: Pearson Prentice Hall

Coleman, James C. (1970), *Abnormal Psychology and Modern Life*, Bombay: D.B. Taraporewala & Sons.

Freud, S., (1935), *A General Introduction to Psychoanalysis*, New York: Liveright,

Freud, S. (1900). *The interpretation of dreams*, In Strachey, J. Trans. & Ed., The standard edition of the complete psychological works of Sigmund Freud (Vols. 4-5, pp. 1-628). Hogarth Press/Institute of Psychoanalysis London, UK. (Original work published 1886-1939).

Kisker, George W. (1964), ***The Disorganized Personality***, (3rd International Students Edition), New York: McGraw-Hill.

Myers, David G. (2014), *Exploring Psychology*, New York: Wordsworth

Rogers, C.R. (1961), *On becoming a person: A therapist's view of psychotherapy*, Boston: Houghton/ Mifflin.

Rogers, C.R. (1980), *A way of being*, Boston: Houghton Mifflin.

# BIBLIOGRAPHY


Adams, Henry E. (1972), *Psychology of Adjustment,* New York: Ronald Press Company.

Adler, A. (1928), *Understanding Human Nature,* London: Allen & Unwin

Advani, Lal and Chadha Anupriya, (2003), *You and your special child,* New Delhi: UBS Publishers, Distributors Pvt. Ltd.

Alloy, Lauren B., Riskind, John. H., & Manos, Margaret J. (2004), *Abnormal Psychology: Current Perspectives* (9th Ed.) New York: McGraw Hill

American Psychiatric Association (1952), ***Diagnostic and Statistical Manual of Mental Disorders,*** Washington D.C.: American Psychiatric Association.

American Psychiatric Association, (1968), *Diagnostic and Statistical Manual of Mental Disorders* (2nd ed.), DSM-II, Washington D.C.: American Psychiatric Association.

American Psychiatric Association, (1980), ***Diagnostic and Statistical Manual of Mental Disorders*** (3rd ed.), DSM-III Washington D.C.: American Psychiatric Association.

American Psychiatric Association (1994)), *Diagnostic and Statistical Manual of Mental Disorders,* Fourth edition (DSM-IV), Washington, DC: American Psychiatric Association.

American Psychiatric Association (2000), *The Diagnostic and Statistical Manual of Mental Disorders,* Washington D.C.: American Psychiatric Association.

American Psychiatric Association (2013), *Diagnostic and Statistical Manual of Mental Disorders* (5th ed.), Washington, DC: American Psychiatric Association.

Arkolf, Abe,(1968), Adjustment and Mental Health, New York: McGraw- Hill.

Autism Society of America quoted by Sturmey P. & Servin J.A. (1994), "Defining and assessing autism" In J.L. Matson (Ed.), *Autism in Children and Adults: Etiology, assessment and intervention* (pp. 33-36), Pacific Grove C.A.: Brooks/Cole.

Bandura, Albert, (1977), Quoted by Shanmugam, T.E., *Abnormal Psycology,* (1981:244-45), New Delhi: Tata McGraw Hill, 1981.

Barlow, David (2012). *Abnormal Psychology: An Integrative Approach.* Belmont, CA, USA: Wadsworth Cengage Learning.

Barkley, Russell, A. (2000), *Taking Charge of ADHD: The Complete Authoritative Guide for Parents,* New York: The Guilford Press.

Bhardwaj Rahul and Suresh Kumar,(2007), "Somnambulism: Diagnosis and Treatment", *Indian Journal of Psychiatry,* April-June, 49 (2): 123-125 retrieved from https://www.ncbi.nlm.nih.gov/pmc/articles/PMC2917078/

Bonney, M.E. (1960), *Mental Health in Education,* Boston; Allyn & Bacon, Inc.

Boring, Longfield & Weld, (1961), *Foundations of Psychology,* New York: John Wiley & Sons.

Broen, W.E.(1969), *Schizophrenia: Research and Theory,* New York: Academic Press, 1969.

Brown, J.F.(1969), *The Psychodynamics of Abnormal Behaviour,* New Delhi: Asia Publishing House (Indian reprint).

Bruch, H. (1973) *Eating disorders: obesity; anorexia nervosa and the person within*, New York: Basic Books.

Bruch, H. (1978), *The golden age: The enigma of anorexia nervosa*, Cambridge MA: Harvard University Press.

Burt, C., (1938), *The Young Delinquent* (Third ed.), London: University of London Press

Burt, C., (1955), *The Subnormal Mind*, London: Oxford University Press, (Third ed.).

Calhoun, J.F; Acocella, J.R. & Goodstein, L.D.(1977), *Abnormal Psychology – Current Perspectives* (Second ed.), New York: CRM/Random House.

Carr, A. (2014), "The evidence base for family therapy and systemic interventions for child-focused problems", *Journal of Family Therapy*, DOI: 10.1111/1467-6427.12032

Carroll, Herbert A. (1969), *Mental Hygiene – The Dynamics of Adjustment*, New Jersey: Prentice-Hall.

Ciccarelli, Saundra K. and White, J Noland (2012), *Psychology*, New York: Pearson Prentice Hall

Clekly, H.91964), *The Mask of Sanity* (Fourth ed.), St Louis: Mosby.

Cohen, D.P. (2011), "Encopresis: A medical and family approach", *Pediatric Nursing*, 37, 107-112.

Cohen,D.J., Donnellian, A.M. & Paul, R. (Eds), (1987), *Handbook On Autism and Pervasive Developmental Disorders*, Silvers Springs, MD : V.H. Winston & Sons.

***Coleman, James C. (1970);*** *Abnormal Psychology and Modern Life* (Third ed.), *Bombay:* B. Taraporewala & Sons,

Combs, A.W. and Snygg, D., (1959), *Individual Behaviour* (Revised edition), New York: Harper &Row Publishers.

Comer, Ronald J. (2015), *Abnormal Psychology* (Ninth Edition), New York: Worth Publishers (A Macmillan Education Imprint)

Cooper, Paul and Bilton, Katherine, M. (2002), *Attention Deficit/Hyperactivity Disorder: A Practical Guide for Teachers* (2nd ed.) London: David, Fulton Publishers

Davison, Gerald C. & Neale, John M. (1978), Abnormal Psychology, (second edition), New York: John Wiley & Sons.

Deborah D'Avolio. (2018), *Case study: Delirium in an Older Hospitalized Woman*, NIDUS, Network for Investigation of Delirium: Unifying Scientists, retrieved from

https://deliriumnetwork.org/case-study-delirium-in-an-older-hospitalized-woman/

Durand, V. Mark and Barlow, David H. (2013), *Essentials of Abnormal Psychology*, (6th ed.), Belmont CA: Wadsworth

Douglas O.B. & Holland, B.F.(1947), *Fundamentals of Educational Psychology*, New York: The Macmillan Co.

Ellis, Albert and Prancale, Ralph.(1956), *The Psychology of Sex Offenders*, Illinois: C.C. Thomas.

Eysenck, H. J. Behaviour, (1960), *Therapy and the Neurosis*, Oxford: Pergamon Press.

Fisher, V.E., *An introduction to abnormal Psychology*, cited by Labh Singh & G.P. Tiwari, *Essentials of Abnormal Psychology*, Agra: Vinod Pustak Mandir, 1971.

Foucault, M. (1967), *Madness and Civilization: A History of Insanity*, London: Tavistock.

Freud, S. (1900). *The interpretation of dreams*, In Strachey, J. Trans. & Ed., The standard edition of the complete psychological works of Sigmund Freud (Vols. 4-5, pp. 1-628). Hogarth Press/ Institute of Psychoanalysis London, UK. (Original work published 1886-1939).

Freud, S; (1933), *New Introductory Lectures on Psychoanalysis New York: W.W. Norton.*

Freud, S., (1935), *A General Introduction to Psychoanalysis*, New York: Liveright.

Freud, S., (1949) *An Outline of Psychoanalysis*, New York: W.W. Norton & Company, Inc.

Gates. A.S. & Jersild, A.T(1973), *Educational Psychology,* New York: Macmillan Sc Vo.

Gilmer, B. Vonhaller (1970), *Psychology,* Harper, International edition,1970.

Goldstein, S. (1999), *The Facts About ADHD: An overview of Attention Deficit Hyperactivity Disorder,* htpp//www.samgoldste4in.com/articles/ 9907.html.

Good, Carter V.(1945), *Dictionary of Education,* New York:McGraw-Hill.

Guttmacher, Manfred S. (1951), *Sex Offences,* New York: W.W. Norton.

Guzman, Carlos Simon and Wang, Yuan Pang,(2008), "Sleep terror disorder: a case report", *Brazilian Journal of Psychiatry,* Vol.30. No. 2, Sao Paula, June, 2008. Retrieved from http://www.scielo.br/scielo.php?script=sci_arttext&pid=S1516-44462008000200016.

Hansell, James and Lisa Damour (2005).Abnormal Psychology. New Jersey: John Wiley and Sons.

Individuals with Disabilities Education Act, (IDEP) USA (1994), Department of Education, Washington DC.

James F.C.(1977), *Abnormal Psychology – Current Perspectives (Second ed.),* London: CRM/ Random House.

Jellinek, E.M. (Ed.), (1942), *Alcohol Addiction and Chronic Alcoholism,* New Haven: Yale University Press

John DJ, Manoharan A, Varghese R. (2007), *A case of primary hypersomnia, Ann Indian Acad. Neurology* (serial online), 2007 (cited 2019 May 14), 10:58-60, retrieved from: http: www, annalsofian. Org/text.asp?2007/10/1/58/31489

John, G.(1975), *World History of Psychiatry,* Howells Bruner (ed.), New York: Mazeli.

KalpJan, Bert (ed.)(1964), *The Inner World of Mental Illness,* New York: Harper & Row Publishers.

Katkovsky, Walter & Gorlow, Leon (ed.) (1976), *The Psychology of Adjustment,* McGraw-Hill.

Katz, Barney & Lehner, G.F. (1953), *Mental Hygiene in Modern Living,* New York: The Ronald Press Company.

Kinsey, A.C. et al. (1948), *Sexual Behaviour in the Human Male,* Philadelphia: W.B. Saunders & Co.

Kinsey, A.C. et. Al. (1953), *Sexual Behaviour in the Human Female* Philadelphia: W.B. Saunders *Sc* Co.

Kirk Samuel A, Gallagher, James, J. and Anastasiow, Nicholas J (1993), *Educating Exceptional Children* (Seventh Edition), Boston: Houghton Mifflin Company.

Kisker, George W, (1964); *The Disorganised Personality,* International Student Edition III , New York: McGraw-Hill,

Klyko, W.M. & Kay, J. (Ed.), (2012), *Clinical Child Psychiatry.* (3rd Ed.) Oxford, UK. Wiley Blackwell.

Knight, B.G. (1996), *Psychology with the older adults,* (2nd ed.), Thousand Oaks, CA: Sage

Kolb, L.C. (1977), *Modern Clinical Psychiatry,* Philadelphia: W.B. Saunders & Co.

Kring, A.M, Johnson, S.L., Davison, G.C., and Neale, J.M., (2012), Abnormal Psychology (12th edition), New York: John Wiley & Sons.

Lazarus, Richard S. (1976), *Patterns of Adjustment,* McGraw-Hill Kogakusha Ltd., International Student Edition.

Lehner, George & Ela Kubo(1964), *The Dynamics of Personal Adjustment,* New York: Prentice Hall Inc.

Lovass Ivar (1994), Quoted in Heward, William L. (2000), *Exceptional Children: An Introduction to Special Education* (Sixth Edition), Upper Saddle River, New Jersey: Merrill

Mahoney, Michael J. (1980), *Abnormal Psychology,* San Francisco: Harper & Row.

***Maier,*** N.R.F.(1949), *Frustration,* New York: McGraw-Hill Book Company.

Mangal, S.K.(1983), *Educational Psychology,* Ludhiana: Prakash Brothers, Fourth Edition.

Marks, I.M. (1987) Fears, Phobias and Rituals: Panic, Anxiety, and Their Disorders. Oxford University Press, Oxford.

Marks, M.(1969), *Fears and Phobias,* ***New*** York: Academic Press.

Martin, B.(1973); *Abnormal Psychology,* Illinois: Scott. Foresman & Co.

Maslow, A.H., (1954), *Motivation and Personality,* New York: Harper & Row Publishers.

McDougall, William, (1952), *An Outline of Abnormal Psychology,* London: Methuen, 1952.

McSullach. M.J.(1971), *Homo Sexual Behaviour – Therapy and Assessment,* Oxford: Pergamon Press.

Medhekar, D. & Gupta, N. (2010), Use of sertraline in childhood retentive encopresis, *The Annals of Pharmacotherapy,* 44, 395. doi: 10.1345/aph.1M280

Millon, T. & Millon R. (1974), *Abnormal Behaviour and Personality,* London: W.B. Saunders & Company.

Mitehcll, A.R.K. (1971); *Psychological Medicine in Family Practice,* London: Bailliere Tindall.

Morgon, C.T. (1961), *Introduction to Psychology,* New York: McGraw-Hill.

Myers, David G. (2014), *Exploring Psychology,* New York: Wordsworth

Nayer, B.R. (1975), *Violence and Crime in India,* New Delhi: The Macmillan Company of India.

NICHCY(January,2004),ADHDDisorderFact-sheet19(FS 9),htpp//www.Nichcy.org.pubs/factshe/htm. Retrieved on 25/6/2006).

Nolen-Hoeksema, Susan (2013). *Abnormal Psychology* (6th ed.). Boston: McGraw-Hill.

Page, James D. (1976), *Abnormal Psychology,* New Delhi: Tata McGraw-Hill.

Park, Claria Claiborne, (1998), "Existing Nirvana", *The American Scholar,* 67:2

Park, (1998:30), quoted in Hunt Nancy, and Marshall Kathleen, *Exceptional Children and Youth* (2002), *An Introduction to Special Education,* Boston: Houghton Mifflin Company.

Perry, London and David Hosenhaf (ed) (1968), *Foundations of Abnormal Psychology,* New York: Holt Rine & Winston, Inc.

Price, John Harding (1972), *Psychiatric Investigations,* London: Butterworths, 1972.

Priest Robert G & Steinert. J. (1977), *Insanity,* Estover: Macdonald & Evans Ltd.

Reiss, S. and Peterson, R.A. et al, (1977), *Abnormality – Experimental Clinical Approach,* New York: Holt, Rinehart and Winston.

Rogers, C.R. (1951), *Client- centered Therapy,* Boston: Houghton Mifflin.

Rogers, C.R.,(1970), *Carl Rogers on Encounter Groups,* New York: Harper & Row.

Rogers, C.R. (1961), *On becoming a person: A therapist's view of psychotherapy,* Boston: Houghton Mifflin.

Rogers, C.R. (1980), *A way of being,* Boston: Houghton Mifflin.

Rosen E. Fox Ronald & Gregory Evan (1972), *Abnormal Psychology,* Saunders International Student Edition III.

Rosenhan, D. L., & Seligman, M. E. P. (1989), *Abnormal Psychology (Second Edition),* New York: W.W. Norton.

Ruch F.L.(1970), *Psychology and Life,* Bombay: D.P. Taraporewala Sons & co.

Selye. H.(1956), *The Stress of Life,* New York: McGraw-Hill.

Shanker, Udai, (1958), *Problem Children,* Delhi: Atma Ram & Sons.

Shanmugam, T.E.(1981), Abnormal Psychology, New Delhi: Tata McGraw- Hill.

Shorter, E. (1997), *A History of Psychiatry from the Era of the Asylum to the Age of Prozac,* New York: Wiley.

Singh, Labh & Tiwari G.P, (1971), *Essentials of Abnormal Psychology,* Agra: Vinod Pustak Mandir.

Singh, U.P.(1973), Personality of Criminals, Agra: Shri Ram Mehra & Company.

Stengel, E. and Cook, N.G.(1958), *Attempted Suicide,* London: Oxford University Press.

Sternbach R.A.; *Principles of Psychophysiology,* New York: Academic
Press, 1966.

Still, A. (2010) *A History of Psychology,* London: Sage.

Storr, Anthony; *Sexual Deviation,* London: Penguin Books, 1964.

*S'tmz,* T.S.; *The Myth of Mental Illness,* New York: Norton, 1961.

Thorpe, Louis P & Katz, Barney (1948), *The Psychology of Abnormal Behaviour,* New York: The Ronald Press Company.

Toch, H. (1969), *Violent Men,* Chicago: Aldine.

Toffler, A.(1970), *Future Shock,* New York Random House..

Topp, Julia,(2009),*Case study-Disturbed sleep and Vivid Nightmares.* Retrieved from https://www.gponline.com/case-study-disturbed-sleep-vivid-nightmares/neurology/article/965128

Verma, Paripurnand (1979), *Sex Offences in India and Abroad,* New Delhi: B.R. Publishing House.

Wallace, E.R. IV and Gach, J. (eds) (2008) *History of Psychiatry and Medical Psychology,* New York: Springer.

West, D.J.(1960), *Homosexuality,* Harmondsworth: Penguin Books.

White, R.W.(1964), *The Abnormal Personality,* New York: Ronald Press Co.

WHO (1965), International Classification of Diseases, 8th Revision, (ICD-8), Geneva: World Health Organization.

WHO (1977), International Classification of Diseases, 9th revision, (ICD-9), Geneva: World Health Organization.

WHO (1992), International Statistical Classification of Diseases and Related Health Problems, 10th revision (ICD-10), Geneva: World Health Organization.

World Health Organization (2010), *The ICD-10 Classification of Mental and Behavioural Disorders: Clinical Descriptions and Diagnostic Guidelines,* 10th ed. Geneva: World Health Organization.

Wiseman Jacqueline P.(1976), *The Social Psychology of Sex,* New York: Harper & Row, Publishers.

What are Eating Disorders? Retrieved on22.04.2019 from https://www.psychiatry.org/patients-families/eating-disorders/what-are-eating-disorders

Wolpe, J. (1974), *The Practice of Behaviour Therapy,* (Second ed.), New York: Pergamon.

Wolman, B.B. (ed.) (1965), *Hand Book of Clinical Psychology, New* York: McGraw-Hill.

Yoo, Hyun, et.al. (2017), *A Case Report of a 37 year old male patient of the dementia of the Alzheimer's type,* Psychiatry Investigation, retrieved from https://www.ncbi.nlm.nih.gov/pmc/articles/PMC5561413/

Yoon-Kyung Shin .et al,(2007), *Case Study of a Narcoleptic Patient with a Family History of Narcolepsy,* Department of Neuropsychiatry, St. Vincent's Hospital, Korea, Psychiatry Investigation, 2007;4:121-123 retrieved from http://www.psychiatryinvestigation.org/upload/pdf/0502007022.pdf

Zee, Phyllis C. (2011), *Case Histories in Circadian Rhythm Sleep Disorders,* Med Scope, retrieved from https://www.medscape.org/viewarticle/745357

Zerbe, K.J. (2008), *Integrated treatment of eating disorders beyond the body betrayed,* New York: W.W. Norton

# GLOSSARY

| | |
|---|---|
| Acrophobia: | Fear of heights. |
| Acute disorder: | Disorder with sudden onset and of short duration. |
| Adaptability: | Flexibility in meeting changed circumstances or demands. |
| Adaptation: | In general, adjustment to environmental conditions. |
| Addiction: | Physiological or psychological dependence on alcohol and drugs. |
| Adjustment: | A person's interaction with his environment. |
| Adrenal glands: | Endocrine glands located at the upper end of the kidneys. |
| Adrenalin: | Hormone secreted by adrenal glands. |
| Affect: | Emotional feeling, tone or mood. |
| Affective disorder: | Personality disorder marked by extremes in mood. |
| Agitation: | Marked restlessness and psychomotor excitement. |
| Agnosia: | Inability to recognize persons or objects. |
| Agoraphobia: | Morbid fear of open places, |
| Agraphia: | Loss of ability to put language in writing. |
| Alcoholic hallucinosis: | Brain syndrome due to alcoholism. |
| Alcoholism: | Addiction to alcoholic beverages to the extent of hampering one's life adjustment. |
| Alexia: | Inability to understand written language. |
| Algophobia: | Morbid fear of pain. |
| Allergy: | Hypersensitivity of body tissue to some external substances like dust, smoke or chemical agent. |
| Alzheimer's disease: | A presenile brain disorder. |
| Amnesia: | Loss of memory. |
| Androgens: | Male sex harmones, |
| Anorexia nervosa: | An eating disorder in which people pursue extreme thinness and lose dangerous amounts of weight. The central features of this disorder are a drive for thinness, intense fear of weight gain, and disturbed body perception and other cognitive disturbances. |
| Anorexia nervosa: | Loss of appetite due to psychological reasons. |
| Anoxaemia: | Insufficient supply of oxygen in the blood and tissues. |
| Antabuse: | Drug used in the treatment of alcoholism. |

| | |
|---|---|
| Anti-depressant drugs: | Drugs used to treat depression. |
| Anxiety: | A feeling of painful or apprehensive uneasiness accompanied by various forms of physiological arousal. |
| Aphasia: | Impaired ability to understand or use language meaningfully. |
| Approach- Approach-conflict: | Simultaneous attraction to several incompatible courses of action. |
| Approach-avoidance conflict: | Simultaneous attraction to and repulsion for a course of action. |
| Arteriosclerosis: | A physiological disorder marked by hardening of the arteries. |
| Asthma: | A respiratory physiological disorder. |
| Ataxia: | Impairment of muscular coordination of the arms and legs. |
| Attention-Deficit Hyperactivity Disorder (ADHD): | A disorder of the childhood caused through some dysfunction in the brain and neurological functioning in which children are found to exhibit the symptoms of excessive inattentiveness, hyperactivity and impulsivity. |
| Autism: | A disorder of the childhood caused through the brain dysfunction in which children are found to exhibit serious abnormality in their behaviour demonstrable in terms of their social aloofness and bizarre activities like repetitive and unusual responses to sensory experiences. |
| Autonomic nervous-system: | A part of the nervous system that is not subject to voluntary control and regulates internal bodily charges during emotion or stress. It includes sympathetic and parasympathetic system. |
| Autosome: | Chromosome that does not affect the sex of an individual. |
| Aversion therapy: | A form of therapy in which punishment or some other aversive stimulation is used to eliminate undesired responses. |
| Aversive stimulus: | A stimulus that evoks physical or psychological pain or discomfort. |
| Avoidance-Avoidance conflict: | Simultaneous repulsion for several courses of action, but to escape one, another must be carried out action, but to escape one, another must be carried out. |
| Barbiturates: | Commonly used sedative drugs. |
| Behaviourism: | The school of psychology which considers overt behaviour as its field of study. |
| Bestiality: | A sexual deviation involving sexual relations with animals. |
| Binge -eating disorder: | An eating disorder in which people have frequent binge-eating episodes but do not display inappropriate compensatory behaviour like forced vomiting. |
| Biofeedback: | Providing a person with information about bodily functions under the control of the autonomic nervous system, like heart rate blood pressure etc. |
| Birth trauma: | Shock of birth. |
| Bisexual: | An individual sexually attracted to both males and females. |

Blocking: Involuntary interference in the chain of thought or speech due to emotional factors.

Body dysmorphic disorder: An obsessive-compulsive disorder in which people become preoccupied with a type of imagined or greatly exaggerated belief that they have certain defects or flaws in their physical appearance.

Brain pathology: Diseased or disturbed conditions of the brain.

Breathing sleep disorders: The type of sleep disorders in which there lie some physical origin-namely problems with the breathing of the people while asleep causing them to experience widely disrupted sleep at night and excessive sleepiness during the whole day.

Bronchi: Blood vessels in the lungs helping the passage of air.

Bulimia nervosa: A eating disorder in which the people while avoiding regular meals are found to go on frequent eating binges quite often secretly and then force themselves to vomit or take other extreme steps to keep from gaining weight.

Cardiovascular: Pertaining to the circulatory system of the body.

Cataplexy: A REM sleep abnormality representing a sudden loss of muscle tone resulting into the abnormal behaviour such as falling asleep for a brief duration while cheering a favourite team.

Catatonia: A type of schizophrenia marked by decreased motor activity, mutism and periods of waxy flexibility.

Catharsis: The therapeutic event involving the reexperiencing and purging of recalled emotional experience during psychoanalysis.

Central nervous system: The brain and the spinal cord.

Central sleep apnea: The type of sleep apnea representing a state of the total cessation of respiratory activity for brief periods.

Cerebral arteriosclerosis: Hardening of the arteries in the brain.

Chemotherapy: Use of drugs or chemicals in the treatment of mental disorders.

Chloral hydrate: Sedative drug.

Chlordiazepoxide: Minor tranquillizer.

Chlorpromazine: A commonly used tranquillizing drug.

Chorea: A disturbance of the central nervous system causing involuntary spasmodic movements of the head and extremities.

Chromosomes: Minute rod like structures that carry the genes. Human cells normally carry twenty three pairs of chromosomes.

Chronic: A relatively permanent maladaptive pattern.

Circadian Rhythm Sleep Disorders: The type of sleep disorders in which the affected individuals are found to go through a persistent or recurrent sleep disruption as witnessed in jet-lag related situation while visiting a county having a different clock timing or providing night shift duty in the work schedule.

| | |
|---|---|
| Classical conditioning: | Basic form of learning associated with Pavlov in which a previously ineffective stimulus (the conditioned stimulus) comes to elicit a response after having been paired with on unconditioned stimulus that innately elicits the response. |
| Claustrophobia: | Irrational fear of closed places. |
| Client-centred psychotherapy: | A form of psychotherapy designed by Rogers in which the client—rather than the therapist's interpretation of the client's feelings and actions—is the focus of attention. |
| Cocaine: | Drug obtained from the leaves of the coca plant that has stimulating and pain reducing results. |
| Cognitive behavioural therapy: | A therapy helpful in dealing with abnormal behaviour by providing two sided benefits- bringing desirable change in people's way of thinking and side by side working towards altering the way they act. |
| Coitus: | Sexual intercourse. |
| Coma: | A serious condition of unconsciousness (stupor). |
| Compensation: | A defence mechanism used to overcome inferiority. |
| Compulsion: | Unwelcome repetitive action. |
| Confabulation: | Distortion of memory in which the person fills in memory gaps with false and often irrelevant details. |
| Conflict resolution: | The method of seeking a balanced compromise in one way or the other between the conflicting desires. |
| Conflict: | Competition among several patterns of behaviour. |
| Congenital: | Existing since birth. |
| Conscience: | A person's ideas of right and wrong which influence his behaviour. |
| Constitution: | Total biological make up of an individual. |
| Conversion reaction: | Neurotic state in which anxiety is converted unconsciously and symbolically into physical symptoms. |
| Convulsion: | Pathological muscular extraction. |
| Coping with stress: | The process carried out for reducing or eliminating the effect of stress. |
| Cortin: | A collective name for the several hormones secreted by the adrenal cortex. |
| Counterconditioning: | The teaching of new behaviour using a particular stimulus to establish a more adaptive response. |
| Covert: | Concealed or disguised. |
| Cretinism: | A form of mental retardation resulting from thyroid insufficiency during foetal life or early infancy. |
| Criterion: | A measure or event that serves as a standard for judging other measures or events. |
| Cunnilingus: | Opposition of mouth to the female genitals. |

| | |
|---|---|
| Defence mechanism: | Technique used by an individual to defend or protect himself from the unpleasant, threatening or anxiety provoking situations. |
| Delinquency: | Criminal behaviour of a minor (person below 18 years of age). |
| Delirium | Confused and excited state of organic origin marked by incoherence, illusions, hallucinations and disorientation. |
| Delirium: | A disorder in which the affected person feels a major disturbance in his or her attention and orientation to the environment accompanied with the clouding of consciousness leading to a state of utter confusion. |
| Delusion: | Firm but false belief contrary to reality and held in spite of evidence and common sense. |
| Dementia: | A disorder or a disturbed state of one's mind representing the deterioration of one's cognitive abilities to the point that his or her overall functioning gets impaired in a variety of ways including a great memory loss. |
| Dementia: | A severe mental disorder involving impairment of mental functioning. |
| Demonology: | Belief that mental illness is caused by possession by the evil spirits. |
| Depersonalization: | Loss of sense of reality or identity in which an individual may feel his body rotten or dead or someone else's. |
| Depression: | A psychological state marked by lowered activity, gloomy thoughts, anxiety, feelings of worthlessness, and an inability to deal effectively with life. |
| Desensitization: | Therapeutic technique of reducing intensity of traumatic experiences by repeatedly exposing the individual to them in a mild form. |
| Detoxification: | Treatment directed towards ridding the body of alcohol or other drugs. |
| Directive therapy: | Therapy in which therapist provides direct solutions to problems and takes up the res- possibilities of directing the course of action. |
| Disintegration: | Loss of organisation in any organised system. |
| Disorientation: | Mental confusion about time, place and person. |
| Displacement: | The defence mechanism by which emotions are transferred from original source into a more acceptable substitute. |
| Dissociative reaction: | Neurotic reaction involving splitting of consciousness into two or more semi-independent parts (multiple personality; amnesia or somnambulism). |
| Dizygotic twins: | Twins that develop from two separate ova (fraternal twins). |
| Down's syndrome: | A type of mental retardation associated with chromosomal anomalies. |
| Dramatic therapy: | Psychotherapy involving use of the enactment of roles and incidents. |

| | |
|---|---|
| Dysfunction: | Abnormal functioning. |
| Dyslexia: | Impairment of the ability to read. |
| Dyssomnias: | A group of sleep disorders representing the disturbances and abnormalities in one's sleep with regard to its amount, timing or quality. |
| Ego involvement: | Perception of a situation in terms of its importance to the individual. |
| Ego-centric: | Self-centred, having little interest and concern for others. |
| Electroconvulsive therapy (ECT) | Treatment involving passage of an electric current through the brain. |
| Electroencephalography (EEC): | Graphic recording and interpretation of brain wave patterns. |
| Empathy: | Sensing and understanding the feelings and thoughts of another. |
| Empirical: | Pertaining to observable and tangible events. |
| Encephalitis: | Inflammation of the brain. |
| Encopresis: | A type of elimination disorder in which the toilet trained developing children (more than 4 years old) or adults are found passing of faeces repeatedly into places other than the toilets such as in their clothing or bed, or anywhere on the floor at their convenience. |
| Encounter group: | A therapeutic group technique in which personal and interpersonal problems are worked out through direct expression of feelings among participating members. |
| Endocrine glands: | Ductless glands that secrete harmones into the blood. |
| Enuresis: | A type of elimination disorder in which the toilet trained developing children (more than 4 years) or adult are found to exhibit their inability to exercise control over the bladder making them urinate in their clothes or bed in their night sleep or day time. |
| Enuresis: | Involuntary discharge of urine. |
| Epilepsy: | A group of disorder characterized by convulsive seizures, disturbances of consciousness, or both. |
| Erotic: | Pertaining to sexual stimulation and gratification. |
| Essential hypertension: | High blood pressure chiefly of a psychological origin. |
| Estrogen: | Female sex hormone. |
| Etiology: | A systematic study of the causes or origins of a disease or disorder. |
| Euphoria: | An exaggerated feeling of well-being. |
| Excoriation disorder: | An obsessive-compulsive disorder in which people repeatedly pick at their skin resulting in significant sores or wounds. |
| Exhibitionism: | Sexual deviation for obtaining gratification by exposing the genitals, publicly. |

| | |
|---|---|
| Extinction: | Decrease in behaviour resulting from lack of reinforcement. |
| Familial: | Pertaining to the family, hereditary. |
| Family therapy: | Group psychotherapy involving two or more members of a family rather than any single member. |
| Fantasy: | A defence mechanism for finding satisfaction in imaginary constructions such as make- believe play, reveries and daydreams. |
| Fetishism: | A sexual deviation for obtaining gratification from inanimate objects or parts of the body other than the genitals. |
| Fixation: | A defence mechanism denoting the arrest of normal development and persistence of an individual's behaviour at an immature level. |
| Flight of ideas: | Rapid succession of ideas without logical association or continuity. |
| Flooding: | Behaviour modification technique involving direct exposure to stress situations leading to a high level of anxiety. |
| Focal lesion: | A defect that is localised to a specific area |
| Foetus: | Human embryo after the sixth week following conception. |
| Frigidity: | Inability of the female to enjoy sexual intercourse. |
| Frustration tolerance: | Level of one's ability to accept frustration. |
| Fugue: | Dissociative reaction in which amnesia and physical flight occur. |
| Functional disorders: | Disorders of the behaviour without clearly defined physical cause or structural changes in the brain. |
| General paresis: | Inherited influence or disposition. |
| Genitals: | A term used for the sexual organs of reproduction. |
| Gonads: | The sex glands. |
| Grand mal: | Major convulsive seizure. |
| Hallucination: | Perception without an appropriate external stimulus, that is, hearing of voices in a completely silent room. |
| Hallucinogen: | A drug or chemical substance capable of producing hallucinations. |
| Hebephrenia: | A sub-type of schizophrenia marked by delusions, bizarre behaviour, and inappropriate emotional responses. |
| Heroin: | Narcotic drug derived from morphine. |
| Heterosexuality: | Sexual interest or behaviour directed towards a person of the opposite sex. |
| Hoarding Disorder: | An obsessive-compulsive disorder in which people are compelled to save items and become very distressed if they try to discard them, resulting in an excessive accumulation of items. |
| Homeostasis: | Maintenance of a balance or equilibrium in physiological processes. |

| | |
|---|---|
| Homosexuality: | Sexual interest or behaviour directed towards a person of the same sex. |
| Humanism: | A doctrine or approach giving supremacy to the human interests values and dignity. |
| Huntington's Chorea: | An incurable organic brain syndrome presumably of hereditary origin. |
| Hydrocephaly: | A condition characterized by unusually enlarged head due to excess of cerebrospinal fluid in the cranium resulting in mental subnormality. |
| Hypersomnia: | The type of sleeping disorder in which people are grappled with the problem of sleeping too much in the night and also falling asleep several times the next day. |
| Hypertension: | High blood pressure. |
| Hyperthroidism: | Over activity of the thyroid glands. |
| Hyperventilation: | Rapid and deep breathing associated with intense anxiety. |
| Hypnagogic hallucination: | A REM sleep abnormality in which people are found to go through a quite terrifying experiences such as experiencing vivid illusion of being caught in a fire or flying through the air. |
| Hypnosis: | Sleep-like highly suggestible state induced by an artificial process called hypnotism. |
| Hypnotism: | A term coined by Braid to replace the term 'Mesmerism'. |
| Hypochondria: | Persistent and exaggerated concern about health and illness. |
| Hypomania: | Earliest stage in the development of the manic reaction. |
| Hypothyroidism: | Under activity or thyroid gland. |
| Hysteria: | A neurotic syndrome associated with conversion or dissociation reactions. |
| Id: | One-of the three major divisions of personality proposed by Freud representing the most inaccessible, primitive and pleasure seeking portion of one's personality. |
| Identical twins: | Twins developed from a single fertilized egg. |
| Identification: | A defence mechanism in which a person derives satisfaction from the successes and achievements of another person by identifying or associating himself with him. |
| Idiopathic epilepsy: | Convulsive disorder of unknown causation presumed to be inherent in the individual's constitutional make-up. |
| Illusion: | Misinterpretation or false perception of a real sensory experience. |
| Implosive therapy: | Behaviour therapy in which desensitization is achieved by flooding the individual's life with such events or situations which cause specific disorder in the individual. |
| Impotence: | Inability of the male to perform sexual intercourse. |
| Incest: | Sexual relations between close relatives of opposite sexes like brother and sister. |

Incoherence: Disconnected and unrelated thoughts.

Insanity: Legal term for mental illness implying individual's inability to be responsible for his act.

Insomnia: The type of sleeping disorder in which people are found to experience some typical problems in their night sleep such as difficulty in initiating and maintaining sleep and not getting the benefit of restorative functions through their sleep.

Insomnia: Difficulty in sleeping.

Involutional melancholia: Depressive psychotic reaction of the late middle age.

Jacksonian epilepsy: An epileptic seizure localised in arm, leg or face.

Kleptomania: Compulsive urge to steal.

Korsakoff's syndrome: An organic psychosis associated with alcoholism.

Lesbian: A female homosexual.

Lesion: Injury or wound.

Lethargy: Morbid drowsiness; inaction and apathy.

Lobectomy: Form of psycho-surgery which involves the cutting of nerve fibres that connect the frontal lobes to the thalamus.

LSD-25: Lysergic acid diethylamide; a widely used hallucinogen.

Macrocephaly: A form of mental subnormality characterized by large headedness resulting from excessive growth of supportive cells in the brain.

Maladjustment: The state of a person having problems in adjusting to his or her environment and the self.

Malinger: To pretend to be ill.

Mania: A state of great excitement, activity, and violence.

Marihuana: A drug obtained from the hemp plant.

Masochism: Sexual deviation in which sexual pleasure is obtained by inflicting pain upon one's self.

Masturbation: Sexual pleasure obtained by manual or mechanical stimulation of the genitals.

Melancholia: Severe depression.

Meningitis: A virus infection of the membranes covering the brain and the spinal cord.

Menopause: Natural end of the menstrual cycle.

Metrazol: A drug used in convulsive therapy.

Microcephaly: A form of mental subnormality characterized by small headedness and retarded development of the brain.

Migraine: Severe form of familial headache.

Milieu therapy: Social therapy involving modification of the patient's life circumstances or immediate environment.

Modeling: Technique for behaviour modification involving the imitation of a model behaviour.

Mongolism: A form of mental subnormality in which the patient has the facial characteristics of a member of the Mongolian race.

Morbid: Unhealthy, pathological.

Morphine: Narcotic drug derived from opium.

Multiple personality: Dissociative reaction in which an individual takes two or more personality systems independent of one another.

Mutism: Inability or refusal to speak.

Narcissism: Excessive self-love.

Narcolepsy: A quite serious and chronic sleep disorder characterized with abnormalities such as excessive daytime sleepiness, sleep attacks and the REM sleep abnormalities

Narcotic: Sedative drug producing sleep.

Necrophilia: A sexual deviation in which one gets sexual pleasure from the dead bodies.

Negativism: A form of aggressive withdrawal which involves refusal to obey or doing the opposite of what has been asked.

Nervous breakdown: A term loosely applied to various conditions in which the person is acutely incapacitated by his anxieties, frustrations and conflicts.

Neurasthenia: Neurotic disorder with complaints of general fatigue and weakness.

Neurosis: Psychological disorder characterized by excessive use of avoidance behaviour and defence mechanism for controlling anxiety.

Neurosyphilis: Syphilis of the nervous system.

Night sleep terrors: Particular type of bad dreams occurring in people's NREM deep sleep making them experience a state of panic such as unable to move or breathe in their dream.

Nightmares: Particular type of bad dreams occurring in one's REM or dream sleep proving too distressful and terrifying to impair a person's ability to carry on normal activities i.e. making a person too anxious to try to sleep at night.

Non-directive therapy: Rogers' technique of psychotherapy in which the therapist refrains from advice or direction of the therapy.

NREM sleep: Known as Non rapid eye movement sleep involves the first three stages of night sleep lightest, light and deep sleep aimed to provide complete rest, relaxation and healing to the body and mind.

Nymphomania: Insatiable impulse for sexual gratification in women.

Obsession: Persistent recurrence of an unwanted idea, thought or impulse.

Obsessive compulsive neurosis: A neurotic disorder marked by persistent obsessional thoughts, compulsions or both.

| | |
|---|---|
| Obstructive sleep apnea: | The type of sleep apnea representing a state of a short- term stoppage of breathing despite the normal functioning of one's respiratory system due to some obstruction caused to one's breathing distinguished well in the form of one' loud and frightening snoring at night. |
| Organic brain syndrome: | Mental disorders associated with brain pathology. |
| Orgasm: | Peak sexual tension followed by relaxation. |
| Overt behaviour: | Behaviour or activities which can be observed by an outsider. |
| Oxycephaly: | Distortion of the skull giving the head a steeple- shaped appearance. |
| Paedophilia: | Sexual deviation in which an adult takes a child for sexual activity. |
| Paranoid disorders: | Psychotic disorders involving highly systematized and stable delusions of persecution and grandeur. However there is no splitting of mind as in the case of paranoid schizophrenia. They may be sub-divided as paranoia and paranoid state depending upon the severity of the disorder. |
| Parasomnias: | A group of sleep disorders representing the disturbances and abnormalities in one's sleep in terms of frequent arousal and difficulty faced in the transition from one stage to another stage of sleep. |
| Parasympathetic system: | Segment of the autonomic nervous system. |
| Paresis: | Syphilis infection of the brain. |
| Parkinson's disease: | A chronic progressive disease of the central nervous system characterized by severe and continual muscular tremors and mask-like expressionless face. |
| Pathogenic: | Factors conducive to abnormal condition or disorder. |
| Pathology: | Any manifestation of disease or abnormality. |
| Petitmal: | A type of epileptic seizure in which the patient loses consciousness for a few seconds but does not suffer convulsion. |
| Phenobarbital: | A widely used sedative drug. |
| Phenylketonuria (PKU): | Disorder of protein metabolism usually associated with mental retardation. |
| Phobia: | An irrational obsessive fear. |
| Pick's disease: | A presenile brain disorder caused by progressive degeneration of the central nervous system, mainly involving frontal and temporal lobe atrophy. |
| Pituitary: | Endocrine gland located at the base of the brain. |
| Play therapy: | Treatment of children involving play material. |
| Posturing: | Maintaining unusual postures for long periods. |
| Precipitating cause: | The particular event or stress occurring immediately or shortly before its effects (producing a disorder). |
| Predisposing cause: | A cause that occurs quite early but paves the way for the appearance of a disorder. |

Prenatal: Senile brain deterioration occurring at premature age.

Prodromal: Pertaining to an early indication or warning sign of a disease or disorder.

Prognosis: Prediction of the course and outcome of a disorder.

Projection: A defence mechanism, involving attribution of one's own negative qualities to other.

Psychiatry: Branch of medicine specially dealing with the diagnosis and treatment of mental disorders.

Psychoanalysis: A term invented by Freud to refer to his theory of personality and his method of psychotherapy.

Psychodrama: Psychological treatment in which a patient is made to act out deliberately his feelings, emotions and conflicts.

Psychogenic: Pertaining to psychological origin.

Psychomotor: Motor behaviour associated with psychological processes.

Psychopath: The old term used for sociopath or antisocial personality.

Psychophysiologic or psychosomatic disorders: Disorders of the behaviour involving both the organic and psychological factors.

Psychosis: Severe mental disorder involving loss of contact with reality, delusion, hallucinations etc.

Psychosurgery: Brain surgery for treating mental disorder.

Psychotherapy: Treatment of mental disorders and behavioural problems by psychological methods.

Puberty: Period during early adolescence when secondary sex characteristics appear.

Pyromania: Compulsive urge to set fire.

Rapport: A feeling of reciprocal emotional acceptance between two people such as therapist and patient.

Rationalization: Defence mechanism in which a person tries to justify his otherwise unjustified behaviour by giving socially acceptable reasons for it.

Reaction-formation: Defence mechanism in which one strives to behave in ways that are sharply in contrast with the ways in which he tends to behave.

Regression: Defence mechanism of behaving in a manner more appropriate to the earlier, happier periods of life.

Rehabilitation: Providing re-education and suitable environment in dealing with criminals and delinquents.

Reinforcement: The strengthening of a response.

Rejection: Lack of acceptance, or failing to provide necessary attention and care.

REM sleep: Known as Rapid eye movement sleep, is one of the stages in one's night sleep characterized with easily awakening and arousal.

| | |
|---|---|
| Remission: | Period of improvement in the course of mental disorder. |
| Repression: | Defence mechanism in which the threatening or anxiety producing experiences and unfulfilled wishes are pushed down into the layer of un- conscious mind. |
| Resistance: | Tendency to maintain symptoms and resist treatment by not cooperating with the therapist. |
| Retardation: | Slowing down of thinking and overt activity. |
| Role-playing: | Dramatic therapy in which the person acts out the behaviour of a certain individual in a particular situation. |
| Sadism: | Sexual deviation in which sexual gratification is obtained by inflicting pain on others. |
| Sadomasochism: | The term used for the coexistence of both sadism and masochism (sex deviations) in an individual. |
| Schizophrenia: | A group of psychotic reactions in which there are fundamental disturbances in reality relationships and in emotional and intellectual processes. |
| Secondary gain: | Secondary or indirect advantages like excessive care, sympathy derived from a neurotic symptom. |
| Sedative: | Drugs used to induce relaxation and reduce tension. |
| Self image: | One's conception of his own worth in terms of his traits. |
| Self-actualization: | Fulfilment of one's potentialities to the maximum level. |
| Self-devaluation: | Lowering one's self-esteem and feelings of worth. |
| Senile dementia: | A form of psychoses caused by progressive degeneration of the old age. |
| Senile: | Pertaining to old age. |
| Sexual deviation: | Unconventional sex behaviour. |
| Sexual inadequacy: | Inability or incompetency to give or share sexual gratification. |
| Sheltered Workshops: | Workshops where mentally subnormal or other handicapped persons can engage in community work. |
| Shock therapy: | Use of shock in treating mental disorders. |
| Sibling rivalry: | Rivalry between the children of the same parents. |
| Sibling: | Children of the same parents. |
| Sleep apnea: | The state of the individuals suffering from breathing sleep disorders in which they are found to experience the stoppage of their breathing altogether for a shorter period of 10 to 30 seconds. |
| Sleep paralysis: | A sleep abnormality representing one's inability to move or speak for a brief period immediately after awakening in REM sleep. |
| Sociogenic: | Of sociological in origin. |
| Sociopath: | Term used for the antisocial behaviour of individuals who are basically unsocialized and whose behaviour pattern brings them repeatedly into conflict with society. |

Sodotherapy: Treatment of the mental disorder by improving social relationships and modification of the environment.

Somatic: Pertaining to the body.

Somnambulism: Popularly known as sleep walking disorder represents the state of a person in which one is found to walk or engage in one or the other type of activities in his or her NREM deep sleep.

Somnambulism: Walking in a sleeplike state.

Stereotype mannerism: Conscious grimace, gesture or movement of the whole body.

Stress tolerance: A term used for indicating the amount of stress one can tolerate before breaking down under the pressure of stress.

Stress: Any condition that puts strain on the coping Capacities of an individual.

Stressors: Events or conditions causing stress.

Stupor: State of lethargy and immobility with partial or complete consciousness.

Sublimation: Gratification of primitive impulses in a socially approved manner or as a defence expression of a frustrated motive in socially sanctioned ways.

Substitution: Acceptance of substitute goals or gratification in place of those originally aimed or desired.

Suicide: Taking one's own life.

Superego: In psycho analysis, the perfection seeking, ethical moral arm of one's personality. personality

Supportive therapy: Psychological treatment designed to remove symptoms by reinforcing existing defences.

Suppression: Deliberate inhibition of threatening stimuli.

Symptom: An observable manifestation, sign or indication of some sickness.

Symptomatic: Pertaining to a specific symptom.

Syndrome: Term used for representing a fairly well organised group or cluster of symptoms that may be found in a particular disorder.

Systematic desensitization: Behaviour therapy technique aimed to reduce levels of anxiety related to an anxiety provoking situation progressively through some well planned systematic steps.

Tay-Sach's disease: Hereditary disorder of fat metabolism.

Therapeutic community: Term for a modern mental hospital that employs, group and milieu therapy and gives patients, considerable responsibility.

Therapy: Treatment.

Thyroid: Endocrine glands located in the neck.

Thyroxine; Hormone secreted by the thyroid glands.

Tic: Involuntary jerking of a small muscle group.

| | |
|---|---|
| Token economy: | A technique of behaviour modification in winch people are rewarded for appropriate behaviour with tokens that can he exchanged for desired items or privileges. |
| Tonic phase: | First phase of the Grand mal convulsion, muscular rigidity. |
| Toxic: | Poisonous. |
| Trails: | Lasting and consistent characteristic of an individual which can be observed or measured. |
| Tranquilliser: | A drug used to calm and relax a person and make him less anxious, agitated, excited or aggressive. |
| Transference: | Process in psychotherapy in which the clients project attitudes and emotions applicable to another significant person on to the therapist. |
| Trans-sexualism: | Behaving and believing firmly in the change of one's sex. |
| Transvestism: | Sexual-deviation of obtaining sexual gratification by wearing clothes appropriate to the Opposite sex. |
| Trauma: | Shock or injury. |
| Tremor: | Rhythmic and involuntary muscle movements. |
| Trichotillomania: | An obsessive-compulsive disorder in which people repeatedly pull out hair from their scalp, eyebrows, eyelashes, or other parts of the body. |
| Unconscious: | Without awareness. |
| Visceral: | Pertaining to the internal organs! |
| Voyeurism: | Sexual deviation in which sexual gratification is obtained through peeping, that is, observation of the genitals of sexual behaviour of others. |
| Waxy flexibility: | Condition in which a person will maintain the position in which his limbs are placed for an unusually long period of time. |
| Withdrawal symptoms: | Physical and psychological symptoms associated with the attempt to stop the use of alcohol or other drugs. |
| Word salad: | Jumbled and incoherent use of words by psychotics or disorganised persons. |
| Worry: | Persistent concern about past behaviour or anticipated dangers. |
| Zoophilia bestiality: | Sexual relations with an animal. |
| Zygote: | Fertilized ovum. |

# INDEX

●●●